# STUDIES IN IMPERIALISM

general editor John M. MacKenzie

Established in the belief that imperialism as a cultural
phenomenon had as significant an effect on the dominant
as on the subordinate societies, Studies in Imperialism
seeks to develop the new socio-cultural approach which
has emerged through cross-disciplinary work on popular
culture, media studies, art history, the study of education
and religion, sports history and children's literature.
The cultural emphasis embraces studies of migration and
race, while the older political and constitutional,
economic and military concerns will never be far away.
It incorporates comparative work on European and
American empire-building, with the chronological focus
primarily, though not exclusively, on the nineteenth and
twentieth centuries, when these cultural exchanges were
most powerfully at work.

## *Britain in China*

MANCHESTER
UNIVERSITY PRESS

# Britain in China

## COMMUNITY, CULTURE AND COLONIALISM 1900–1949

## Robert Bickers

MANCHESTER
UNIVERSITY PRESS
Manchester and New York

distributed exclusively in the USA by
ST. MARTIN'S PRESS

Published by MANCHESTER UNIVERSITY PRESS
OXFORD ROAD, MANCHESTER M13 9NR, UK
and ROOM 400, 175 FIFTH AVENUE, NEW YORK, NY 10010, USA
http://www.man.ac.uk/mup

Distributed exclusively in the USA by
ST. MARTIN'S PRESS, INC.
175 FIFTH AVENUE, NEW YORK, NY 10010, USA

Distributed exclusively in Canada by
UBC PRESS, UNIVERSITY OF BRITISH COLUMBIA,
6344 MEMORIAL ROAD, VANCOUVER, BC, CANADA V6T 1Z2

British Library Cataloguing-in-Publication Data
A catalogue record for this book is available from the British Library

Library of Congress Cataloging-in-Publication Data applied for


ISBN 0 7190 4697 1 hardback
     0 7190 5697 7 paperback

First published 1999

06 05 04 03 02 01 00 99        10 9 8 7 6 5 4 3 2 1

Typeset in Trump Medieval
by Northern Phototypesetting Co Ltd, Bolton
Printed in Great Britain
by Biddles Ltd, Guildford and King's Lynn

For Joan and Bob Bickers
and for Carol Murphy

# CONTENTS

# LIST OF TABLES

# LIST OF ILLUSTRATIONS

# GENERAL INTRODUCTION

The British empire was not only extensive; it was also exceptionally complex and diverse. Just how complex and diverse is very well revealed in this book. The author demonstrates the manner in which the treaty ports and international settlements in China in the late nineteenth and early twentieth centuries operated as 'semi-colonies', imperial enclaves acting as the drivers of the system of informal empire in the Far East. These enclaves have seldom been incorporated into the work of imperial historians, while their position in the historiography of China has been ideologically formalised or stereotyped. In fact their history has a good deal to offer studies of both the imperial and the Chinese past.

The treaty ports represent an aspect of the imperial project which was in many respects repudiated by the imperialists themselves. They rested uneasily within both colonial and diplomatic structures, and they often seemed to offer more problems than they solved. Yet in retrospect their economic, social and cultural history provides many insights into the myth that trading relations within unequal networks of power and uneasy racial and cultural relationships required such systems of foreign settlement and extraterritoriality. They acted as a distorting prism through which the West viewed China and China viewed the West. It was a prism which was frequently shaken and twisted into producing strangely refracted versions of cultures grappling with each other. But in many ways their history also reflects the development and transformation of East–West relations in the course of the twentieth centuries.

Robert Bickers offers the most comprehensive account yet of the cultural and social, political and economic history of these foreign settlements. He has much to say about the strategies of expatriate companies and missionary societies, municipal councils and the military and policing guardians of empire. In the spirit of the new globalised imperial history, this book should be read by all with an interest in imperial and Far Eastern history as well as by those concerned with representations and fragmentary enclavism. Much remains to be written about the treaty ports and international settlements, not least about the ways in which they brought together multiple minorities in strangely overheated political and cultural contexts, but this book will remain a vital starting point for all such work.

John M. MacKenzie

# ACKNOWLEDGEMENTS

Many institutions funded or supported the research on which this book is based: the British Academy; the ESRC and British Academy's China exchange programme; the British Council, which helped out on one trip to Beijing in 1993; the Warden and fellows of Nuffield College, Oxford, with a Prize Research Fellowship and support for various research trips east and west; the CNRS, which supported a stint as *chercheur associé* at the Institut d'Asie Orientale, Lyon; the IAO's director, Christian Henriot, for arranging the visit; the Universities' China Committee, for funding a research trip in 1993, and for a Fellowship in Modern Chinese Studies held at the Faculty of Oriental Studies, Cambridge, to whom thanks are also due; the President and fellows of Wolfson College, Cambridge, with a Senior Research Fellowship. My thanks to them all. For their encouragement and engagement I also thank Chiara Betta, Peter Hibbard, Tess Johnston and Peter Robins. For his assistance I must thank Edwin Green, Group Archivist, and HSBC Holdings PLC. I owe many thanks to Mrs J. E. Baldry at Manchester City Library's Local Studies Unit, and debts of particular gratitude to Charlotte Havilland for her help at the archives of John Swire & Sons and to Rosemary Seton, archivist at the School of Oriental and African Studies, and her staff. Material in chapter 1 has been drawn from my 'Shanghailanders: The Formation and Identity of the British Settler Community in Shanghai, 1843–1937', *Past and Present*, 159 (1998), with the permission of the Past and Present Society. Material in chapter 6 has been drawn from my 'Hong Kong's Transitions: The Colony's Shifting Position in the British Informal Empire in China', in Judith M. Brown and Rosemary Foot, eds, *Hong Kong's Transitions, 1842–1997* (1997), with the permission of Macmillan Press Ltd. My thanks to Olivier Barge for the map.

This volume owes its intellectual genesis to Timothy Barrett and Gary Tiedemann, and its progress along the way to the conversation, time, readings and encouragement of Adam Brookes, Mike Bullen, Charles d'Urban Jane Duckett, Lisa Clothier, John Darwin, Christian Henriot, Susan Lawrence, Meira Levinson, Rana Mitter, Kirsty Reid, SinhaRaja Tammita-Delgoda, Andy N. Thompson, Jeffrey N. Wasserstrom and Susan Whitfield. In particular the book owes a great deal to a great many arguments with Heather Bell. None of the above is at all responsible for the text you have in your hands. Most of all, thanks to Kate.

R.B.

# LIST OF ABBREVIATIONS

| | |
|---|---|
| APC | Asiatic Petroleum Company |
| BAT | British American Tobacco Company |
| BMS | Baptist Mission Society |
| BRA | British Residents' Association |
| BWA | British Women's Association |
| CIM | China Inland Mission |
| CMC | Chinese Maritime Customs |
| CPF | China Printing and Finishing Company |
| ICI | Imperial Chemical Industries |
| KMA | Kailan Mining Administration |
| LMS | London Missionary Society |
| *NCDN* | *North China Daily News* |
| *NCH* | *North China Herald* |
| SMC | Shanghai Municipal Council |
| SMP | Shanghai Municipal Police |
| SVC | Shanghai Volunteer Corps |
| WMMS | Wesleyan Methodist Missionary Society |

# CHAPTER ONE

# Introduction

At a couple of seconds to midnight on 20 June 1997 the union jack was hauled down at a sober, spartan ceremony held inside the hurriedly constructed Hong Kong International Convention Centre, and shortly afterwards the flag of the People's Republic of China was raised in its stead. The territory once known as the Crown colony of Hong Kong reverted to rule by the Chinese state as a Special Administrative Region. The ceremony marked the end of 157 years of British rule over the island of Hong Kong, and ninety-nine years of control of the leased area known as the New Territories. It also marked the end of a seventy-year process during which the British presence throughout China was dismantled piecemeal. This book examines the nature of that presence, particularly the semi-autonomous status of the settler communities on the China coast, and identifies the processes by which Sino-British relations were brought under the control of the British state by 1943.

It was more than a diplomatic or political process. The British community in China was rooted in the diverse cultures of imperial Britain. It was part of a world opened up through empire, both formal and informal, offering opportunities for migration, for personal advancement, for employment and even escape in the new communities forged outside the British Isles. New identities were constructed by Britons overseas, and new British identities formed within the British Isles as a result.[1] Dismantling the British presence in China before 1943 meant rooting out one set of such new communities, constructed over the previous century and a half. Such weeds clung fast. This book offers an analysis of the creation and maintenance of the new identities acquired by Britons in China. Here the culture of the coloniser stretched from London's Limehouse by the side of the Thames, through Hong Kong to Hankou's Bund on the middle Yangzi, and incorporated metaphorically, as it existed literally, both these locations. The empire of the mind has been much dissected in the last two decades, but in the process it has become divorced from the empire of place, and of contingent individual experience. This book reunites them.

With the hand-over of Hong Kong, the government of the People's Republic of China (PRC) belatedly concluded a process that began under its predecessor, the Guomindang's National government (1927–49), of terminating concessions extracted in the decades after 1842 of what is glibly constructed in China as 'National Humiliation' (guochi).[2] When the PRC was established in October 1949 this process of decolonisation had in fact mostly been completed. The foreign presence had already been divested of its colonial trappings and pretensions. Decolonisation under the Guomindang had meant that a network of up to thirty-four small, but economically and politically significant, foreign enclaves – covering some nineteen cities – which had been surrendered to foreign administration had been retroceded by 1949. The larger slices of the Chinese melon had been reclaimed: Weihaiwei (Britain, 1898–1930), Guangzhouwan (France, 1898–1945), Jiaozhouwan (Germany/Japan, 1898–1922), Luda[3] (Russia, Japan, 1898–1945), Manchuria (Japan, 1931–45) and Taiwan (Japan, 1895–1945). Extraterritoriality, which underpinned these networks, had been abolished in treaties with individual states, beginning with Belgium (1928), and China's tariff autonomy had been restored (1928). Stemming from the populist 'educational rights' recovery movement', laws had been enacted in effect nationalising foreign-run educational institutions, while the patchwork of treaty-based or precedent-based privileges enjoyed by foreign residents had been abolished. By the end of Nationalist rule on the mainland, most aspects of foreign activity in China had been brought under the jurisdiction of Chinese law.[4]

The Sino-British and Sino-American friendship treaties of February 1943 were the culmination of this process, with the finer details of dismantling the surviving foreign-administered zones being worked out at the close of the Pacific War. In the British case the treaty was also the culmination of a different process: the effective 'nationalisation' of British–Chinese relations, that is, the assertion of British state control over its subjects in China. Far from marking any 'retreat from China', the improvised response of British diplomats to Chinese nationalism in the 1930s was to strengthen the position of a much more narrowly defined set of 'national interests' than had previously been accepted and protected. What had previously been accepted and protected by British diplomats is labelled in this book 'Britain in China'. This neologism is used to differentiate the British presence from any conventional expatriate trading presence. The British state had previously preferred to distance itself from the quotidian activities of British nationals (and protected subjects) in China. It was responsible, certainly, for the opening up of China to British trade as a result of the Opium Wars (1839–42, 1857–60). It also enjoyed jurisdiction over British nationals in China under the system of extraterritoriality first outlined in the 1842 Treaty of Nanjing. The Chefoo Convention (1875, ratified 1885), and the Boxer protocol (1901) both significantly extended the scope of British activity in China. Advantages secured by other nations' treaties also benefited Britons as a result of most-favoured-nation clauses. But the British state largely contented itself with the protection of treaty rights and its nationals' interests; in no way did it try to order or direct Britons in China. It did not want another India, and it did not seek territorial acquisitions. If there ever was a 'fit of absence of mind' in the history of the British empire, it lay in the benign neglect by British diplomats of Britain in China, which enabled it to grow and to acquire the concrete presence, identity and ambitions outlined in this book.

Britain in China's particularities and problems have been lost in wider accounts of the progress of Sino-British relations. These have examined the processes of diplomatic innovation and adaptation which became necessary in the face of the 1911 revolution (which overthrew the Qing monarchy); the Versailles peace conference; the Washington conference (1922); and the successive triumphs of the nationalist Guomindang in 1926–27, Japanese militarism in Manchuria in 1931 and in China proper after 1937, and finally the Chinese Communist Party (CCP) in 1949.[5] The metropolitan-based interest group politics of the China Association or the China Committee have dominated most works on this painful diplomatic process. Britain in China gets short shrift, even in studies which have explicitly adopted theories of imperialism for their analytical framework.[6] This book argues that the problems faced by the British state in China stemmed from this pseudo-colonial presence. Britons who dominated the affairs of Britain in China, moulded its identity, and represented their own particular interests as British interests, were settlers, not sojourners or expatriates. Through the intractable fact of their very presence these settlers distorted British China policy; through their actions they could destabilise Sino-British relations; through their stubborness they could hamper policy reform.

One event in particular starkly dramatises the key role of Britain in China in Sino-British relations. Although the need for revision of the Qing era treaties had long been recognised by foreign diplomats, starting with the Washington conference, it was precipitated most bluntly for the British government by the calamitous May Thirtieth incident of 1925. On that day Sikh police of the Shanghai International Settle-

**Figure 1**   Scene in front of the Louza police station shortly after the 30 May 1925 shooting in Shanghai

ment police force, led by an inspector, Welshman E. W. Everson, opened fire on Chinese demonstrators, killing eleven. This incident, and the anti-British May Thirtieth Movement which succeeded it, almost completely undid the British position in China. In the turmoil that followed there were separate shooting incidents involving British troops or volunteer militia in Hankou (eight dead) and Canton (the 'Shaji massacre', at least fifty two dead). A sixteen-month-long strike and boycott crippled Hong Kong's trade. The May Thirtieth incident was rooted in the complacency and inefficiency of the British-dominated Shanghai Municipal Council (SMC), which administered the International Settlement and exercised what its chairman succinctly described in 1893 as its 'pretty free hand'. The *status quo* allowed Britons not under diplomatic control to commit such sanguine blunders, and then to compound them, as the SMC did, by its defiantly bellicose handling of subsequent events in the city, and of the investigation into the shootings. Reining-in Britain in China became a matter of some urgency for the British Foreign Office; May Thirtieth had changed everything.[7]

By way of response to these developments, and to the Guomindang's revolutionary Northern Expedition (1926–28), which set out to conquer central and northern China, the Foreign Office issued the so-called 'December memorandum' to the other Washington powers of

1926. This suggested renouncing any idea 'that the economic and political development of China can only be secured under foreign tutelage' and furthermore that:

> the Powers should yet recognise both the essential justice of the Chinese claim for treaty revision and the difficulty under present conditions of negotiating new treaties in place of the old, and they should therefore modify their traditional attitude of rigid insistence on the strict letter of treaty rights.[8]

These intentions announced a new set of criteria for policy in China and specifically for policy towards the Guomindang. The memorandum was the touchstone of future British policy announcements and was followed up on 27 January 1927 with a 'January Offer', which unilaterally offered a package of concessions, most notably an offer to discuss the status of the British concessions. Other compromises dealt with the recognition of the competence of modern Chinese law courts, the extraterritorial status of missionary institutions, the status of Chinese Christian converts and mission ownership of land.[9] In the four years after the high tide of the Nationalist revolution, many of these issues were the subject of negotiation and retrocession (see chapter 4 below). The Sino-Japanese undeclared war (which began in 1937) dealt a further and severe blow to the morale, numbers and assets of the various foreign communities, and it was a much reduced and culturally altered foreign presence which faced the transition to rule under the Chinese Communist Party. Britain moved smoothly and swiftly to recognise the new regime in 1950, secure in the knowledge that the process of decolonisation in China itself had already taken place. Hong Kong was another matter, and remained another matter for both powers for thirty more years.[10]

If the history of Hong Kong became, belatedly, well known and widely reported in Great Britain in late June 1997, the same cannot be said for the history of the broader British presence, which has largely been forgotten. Yet after 1842 the Sino-British relationship was intimately physical rather than abstractly diplomatic. British relations with China took place mostly within China itself: in the privately administered or dominated British concessions and settlements; in mission stations; through British businesses; and also through arms of the British state (consulates, the Legation and the British military presence). On three occasions the British state fought limited wars against China on Chinese soil (1839–42, 1857–60, 1900). The acquisition of a secure depot for the China trade – a British Macao – had been an aspiration as early as the first British embassy to China, that of Lord Macartney and his entourage in 1792–94. In the years after the 1842

Treaty of Nanjing, which delivered that depot – Hong Kong – and first opened China to British residence and trade, a British presence developed in China which was neither formally colonial nor merely definable as 'informal influence'. Hong Kong nominally became an orthodox colony. Administrative forms and practices were recognisable within the context of the wider British empire and the policies and practices of the Colonial Office, which administered the territory.[11] What evolved in the parts of the rest of China in the interstices of the system of treaties fashioned between the Qing state and the foreign powers was quite singular, and owed no direct loyalties, or dues of obedience, to the British state. This was largely private enterprise imperialism: as such it was also international in character, even when it was nominally British.

## Imperialism and modern Chinese history

Imperialism is no new subject for scholars of modern Chinese history. However, although it dominated studies in the West before the 1970s, it has been out of fashion for some years now. The working paradigms of Chinese studies identified by Paul Cohen in his 1984 study *Discovering History in China*, which stemmed from this domination, have since been superseded by the 'China-centred' work Cohen himself called for. This work built on the methodological triumphs of the Fairbankian Harvard school to reconstruct modern China's history from within rather than focus on Western 'impacts'.[12] There can be absolutely no doubt of the need for this shift, nor of the richness of the work that has appeared as a result. Nevertheless, there is no doubting, either, the absurdity of writing modern Chinese history as if there was no Western presence, or with a caricatured foreign presence, which has often been the net effect. Aspects of Shanghai's history, for example, have dominated much recent Western research into republican era Chinese history. But the foreign presence, and foreign political, economic and military power in that city, so crucial to its development, are underexamined, or clichéd.[13] Cohen called for more regional studies to look at the impact of 'exogenous factors on each region, and within a given region, on core and peripheral areas'.[14] However, China-centred history, and an uncomfortableness about working on non-Chinese actors in modern China have reinforced one another, with the result that historians of the 'Shanghai school' have reconstructed a city history in which, Japan apart, the 'exogenous' factors – the foreigner and foreign power – have been all but written out.

Cohen himself called upon historians to deal with imperialism, which he considered a force 'of critical explanatory importance', arguing that the task was to 'define with precision ... the specific situations with regard to which imperialism was relevant and then to show how it was relevant'.[15] In fact, with a few important exceptions, the historiography of modern China outside the PRC has become notably silent on the question of imperialism.[16] In the face of regional disparities, the absence of formal colonialism, and the acknowledged intertwining of Chinese and foreign capital in the Chinese economy, historians of China have not bothered themselves much about the ambitions, pretensions and practices of foreign power in China. Exceptions have emerged in the work of Jürgen Osterhammel, who sought a working definition of 'informal empire' from the China case, or among some scholars of the Japanese presence in China, seeking to locate Japanese activities in the wider context of colonial expansion.[17]

Meanwhile, the fundamental orthodox interpretation of modern Chinese history in the PRC with regard to the foreign presence has developed little since the early years of the regime. Echoing W. H. Auden, 'Imperialism's face/And the international wrong' stand pilloried in a historiography grounded in Marxist orthodoxies.[18] Classic accounts are Hu Sheng's *Imperialism and Chinese Politics* (1955) and Ding Mingnan *et al.*'s. *Diguozhuyi qinhua shi* (History of Imperialist Aggression against China) (1958 – reprinted as recently as 1992). Both were broad-brush attacks on an external scapegoat that is rarely well defined. British imperialism is a rhetorical villain in Sa Benren and Pan Xingming's *Ershi shiji de ZhongYing guanxi* (Sino-British Relations in the Twentieth Century) (1996), but it is barely analysed.[19] However, in the 1980s and 1990s the disjuncture between what Chinese historians will say in private conversation and what they can print broadened greatly, and a more sober analysis developed. Nevertheless, for younger scholars who have implicitly questioned in print the accuracy of the caricatures used about the past, such heterodoxy can still call forth sharp and rapid denunciation.[20] One new departure has been the profusion of recent studies on the treaty ports (the cities opened to foreign trade and residence under the various treaties). These efforts are located partly in the requirement of recent Five Year Plans for social scientists to study urban history to provide historical input and lessons for the running of Special Economic Zones.[21] They also grow out of the local history preferences of historians in China today – and the acceptance, for example, that the history of Shanghai must also include the history of the International Settlement.[22] However, what is still missing, even in China, is a history which combines broader issues of Sino-British relations with the history of those relations where they were mostly conducted: in the treaty ports. Even though foreign activities are in a certain measure being discreetly reintroduced into modern history in a neutral fashion – some foreign biographies now grace the pages of the new standard local histories of Shanghai[23] – the Hong Kong hand-over was preceded in the PRC with a self-abasing orgy of rhetoric about foreign imperialist aggression and National Humiliation. The past still serves the present. The lesson in 1997 was that China must be 'strong': Chinese weakness had led to the earlier success of aggressive external encroachment.[24]

In the West there has been one influential exception to the pattern of non-engagement with the problem of imperialism in China and of non-incorporation of China into broader colonial trends. Rhoads Murphey included the treaty ports in what he wildly identified as Britain's 'grand colonial design' for China. But in fact much of what came to characterise the establishment of those whom he labelled the 'outsiders' in China evolved haphazardly in the interstices of a British China policy that was hardly grand, was certainly not colonial and was arguably not at all designed.[25] Cohen pointed out that 'the failure to scrutinise with care the distinctive colonial environment that prevailed in China has been a major limitation on the productiveness of the entire imperialism controversy' in Chinese studies. Imperialism in China, he argued, was multiple and layered: China was in one sense, after all, a Manchu colony, and only a 'semi-colony' of the European powers. While this argument was mostly targeted at the crude polemics of Frances Moulder's *Japan, China and the Modern World Economy* (1977), Cohen's words have a continued and wider resonance.[26] Mainstream China historians are still ignoring the distinctiveness of the foreign engagement with China.

For their part, although some recent scholars of imperial history have incorporated China selectively into their work – notably P. J. Cain and A. G. Hopkins in their two-volume *British Imperialism* (1993) – imperial historians still mostly exclude the country from their field of view. China was subject to multiple imperialisms, which competed and co-operated. It was never subject to power relations and domination on the mainstream colonial pattern. It has remained a region whose details are somewhat unfathomed by imperial historians, but certainly not by the history of imperialism.[27] The exceptions, to an extent, are the theorists of imperial expansion, and its limits, and of 'informal empire'.[28] China, in its survival as a non-partitioned sovereign state, has continued to puzzle commentators. Relations between Chinese society, economy and polity often demonstrated all the themes discernible in the processes of incorporation of African and Asian states into the European empires. Most strikingly, the compradore, the most prominent of the Chinese partners, has almost been the ideal type of non-European collaborator. However, the interpenetration of Sino-Western capital and interests in the treaty port world, particularly in the case of the compradore, makes China an awkward topic for imperial historians. One key reason for this awkwardness is the continued misrepresentation of Britain in China. The compradore may indeed have been the collaborator of theory, but the British in China themselves also acted as collaborators: they were in fact the 'ideal prefabricated collaborator[s]' identified by Ronald Robinson in his influential essay 'Non-European Foundations of European Imperialism' (1972). In their orderly concessions and settlements British settlers provided safe and secure bridgeheads for British and imperial trade in China. For that reason their little local pretensions were tolerated by the British state. When their activities proved too potentially destabilising for British interests, the diplomats chose new collaborators – expatriate interests – whose development of new relations with Chinese elites and markets they actively encouraged.[29]

This study is therefore also located firmly in the recent profusion of studies of the culture of colonialism and the society of the settler, which have greatly enriched our understanding of the processes of colonial expansion, consolidation, retrenchment and, in particular, the resistance of settler – or, at the very least, settled – interests to decolonisation. Missionaries have long been known to have had a different agenda, and to have clashed with colonial thinking; but now beginning to be strongly delineated are the conflicts and competitions between and among other groups in colonial societies. Studies of the settler have also turned to look at the gulf between settler dreams and settler realities, and the disappointments of colonialism.[30] C. A. Bayly's call for Britain, and British social and intellectual history, to be put back into studies of South Asia identifies some of the further insights, firmly rooted in British studies, to be gained from an examination of the coloniser. Domestic class, nationality and gender tensions were exported with settlers, administrators and missionaries; and these tensions found new modes of expression, especially as they interacted with issues of race, as they underpinned the improvised communities of empire.[31] Studies of British popular imperialism have also shown the interpenetration of empire and metropole, and China has been shown to have been fully integrated into the narratives and visions of empire that the British evolved in the nineteenth and early twentieth centuries. This body of work has also argued strongly for locating empire and diaspora in British society and culture, and has examined closely such processes as socialisation into colonial societies and into colonial administrative services.[32] This book is concerned with identifying both the singularity of Britain in China and at the same time the incorporation of 'China' into Britain-abroad.

It is important, then, for historians of China, of empire, and of Sino-British relations, to understand properly the nature of this problematic British presence and the opportunities it offered to those functioning under the British flag and British law. As William C. Kirby noted, 'Nothing mattered more' in republican China than issues of foreign relations – 'at home and abroad'.[33] We need to understand the varieties of the foreign presences in China if we are to understand the intractability of the problems they presented. The British presence was of paramount importance among the foreign powers active in China before the advent of Japan in the 1930s. Although later eclipsed by this imperial rival (and also by its nominally anti-imperial rival, the United States) the British presence in China still demands attention.

## Britain in China

Under the protection and jurisdiction of the union jack in China at the start of 1927 might be found the following: a Crown colony, two leased territories, two British-dominated international settlements, six concessions and a settled presence in cities and towns stretching from Manchuria to the borders with Burma. British interests penetrated deep into the interior of the country through shipping lines and railways and through commercial and missionary networks. Britain in China extended beyond the treaty ports, and beyond any strict legal definition of what constituted the treaty port world. Treaty port *mores*, patterns and expectations were to be found wherever in China Britons lived, worked or travelled. Where there were British subjects, there was Britain in China. The confidence of this world and its concrete achievements can be gauged nicely through the pages and illustrations of a volume published in London in 1908. *Twentieth Century Impressions of Hong Kong, Shanghai and other Treaty Ports of China*, an 850 page survey of the history and present of the treaty port world, emerged in a series of works on 'Britains over the seas': the dominions, colonies and British establishments in South America and China. Here the achievements, personalities, 'potentialities' – and paradoxes – of Britain in China were recorded and celebrated, and incorporated into the Greater British imperial enterprise.[34]

Whatever the confidence of this world, its place among the Britains over the seas cannot be properly understood without reference to figures for investment and trade. Hou Chi-ming's estimates of British investment in China, and the proportion it formed of total foreign investment, give some idea of the value of the British bet on the myth and reality of the China market (Table 1, p. 12). Hou further breaks down the figures for 1931 into loans to the Chinese government and

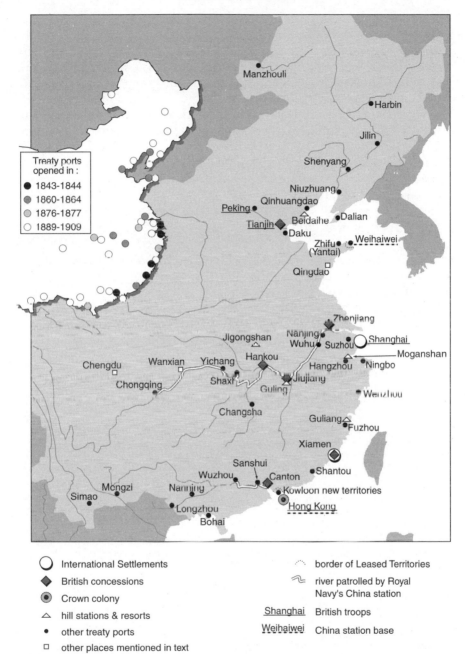

**Figure 2** Britain in China, 1 January 1927

direct investment. The latter comprised: trade (50 per cent), real estate (21 per cent), utilities (5 per cent), manufacturing (18 per cent) and mining (2 per cent). The figures in Table 1 have to be kept in proportion. China's share of UK trade remained small, falling from 2.15 per cent in 1920 to 1.31 per cent in 1930.[35] From the British perspective China was merely a modest part of a bigger picture. From the Chinese perspective the British presence in China was highly visible. Although the modern sector of China's economy only accounted for an estimated 13 per cent of GDP in 1933, prominent sectors of it were dominated by foreign finance, or firms. British interests were especially prominent in coastal and Yangzi shipping, in foreign trade and in real estate, manufacturing and utilities in Shanghai.[36] Chinese nationalist politics and British business pressure groups were both interested in talking up the importance of this presence, but revisionist economic history has sharply downgraded the impact of the foreign economic presence generally. Nevertheless, the British presence in the China market was the most important strand in the Sino-British relationship before 1941, and this study is rooted in that fact.

Deciding what was British and what was masked as British is not easy, however, and Hou's figures are no guide here. The union jack certainly served as a flag of convenience in wartime, but it did so in peace-

**Table 1** British investment in China, 1902–36

| Year | British investment, $US millions | As % of total foreign investment in China |
|------|------|------|
| 1902 | 260.3 | 33.0 |
| 1914 | 607.5 | 37.7 |
| 1931 | 1,189.2 | 36.7 |
| 1936 | 1,220.8 | 35.0 |

Source Hou Chi-ming, *Foreign Investment and Economic Development in China, 1840–1937* (Cambridge MA, 1965), 17. Hou's figures were laregely taken from C. F. Remer's *Foreign Investments in China* (New York, 1933).

**Table 2** Breakdown of British investment in China, 1902–36

| Type | 1902 | 1914 | 1930 | 1936 |
|------|------|------|------|------|
| Direct investment | 57.6 | 65.8 | 81.0 | 86.8 |
| Loans to Chinese Government | 42.4 | 34.2 | 19.0 | 13.2 |

Source Hou, *Foreign Investment*, 225.

time too. To take one example, an estimated one-third of 'British' real estate in Shanghai was actually Chinese-owned in 1926.[37] Ownership of shares in companies such as the nominally 'British' Hongkong & Shanghai Bank, or the Shanghai Land Investment Company, was also Chinese and international.[38] Some 90 per cent of the shareholders (and 80 per cent of the capital) of Jardine's Ewo Cotton Spinning & Weaving Company in 1921 were Chinese.[39] And, as B. R. Tomlinson has argued of British firms in India, 'British' is not necessarily a clearly meaningful analytical category for firms of various types operating in very different sectors.[40] 'British' investment also included investment by the 'other Westerners', namely British-protected subjects: Baghdadi Jews, Indian Parsis, Straits Settlement and Hong Kong Chinese, and Eurasians with British protection. These groups were certainly in a minority in the twentieth century, although in the 1833 Parsis had outnumbered Britons, and in 1844 they made up a fifth of the foreign trading presence.[41] As Table 3 indicates, the size of the British presence grew steadily after 1900 – although it was dwarfed by the increases in the number of Russian refugees after 1917, and of Japanese residents. There were also, in 1931 for example, a further 6,800 Britons in Hong Kong, excluding servicemen.[42]

Unlike Britain's relationship with its colonial or dominion peoples, this extensive presence was established within a separate sovereign

Table 3 Number of British companies and residents in China (excluding Hong Kong), 1910–30

| Year | British companies[a] | Total Foreign companies | British residents | Total foreign residents |
|------|---------------------|------------------------|-------------------|------------------------|
| 1910 | 601 | 3,239 | 10,140 | 141,868 |
| 1915 | 599 | 4,735 | 8,641 | 182,404 |
| 1920 | 679 | 7,375 | 11,082 | 326,069 |
| 1925 | 718 | 7,743 | 15,247 | 336,841 |
| 1930 | 1,027 | 8,279 | 13,015 | 255,686 |

Source Chinese Maritime Customs, *Foreign Trade of China* (Shanghai: Chinese Maritime Customs), 1915, 1920, 1925, 1930; *China Year Book*, 1912, 413.

Note

a These numbers are a little awkward, mainly because different branches of the same company were counted as separate units. However, as this method gives us a closer picture of the number of different British enterprise units actually active in China, it is rather to be welcomed. The Customs stopped reporting these figures after 1931, and it is difficult to find replacements. Enumeration in the later 1930s was also hindered by increasing registration of British companies in Hong Kong to evade Chinese commercial legislation, real or threatened.

state, whose sovereignty Britain always formally recognised, although it nonetheless dominated the Chinese Maritime Customs service (CMC) and the Salt Gabelle, important revenue-generating organs of the Chinese state. Much of this presence was not controlled, or even effectively influenced, by agents or organs of the British state: it was mostly developed under private impetus, and made manifest through private organisations such as missionary societies and trading firms. But private Britons' residence was made possible by the web of state treaties, the consular service which guarded those treaties, and by the formal establishment of British diplomats, sailors and soldiers, notably the Royal Navy's China station and its Yangzi and West River gunboat flotillas.

Providing military protection meant more than just flying the flag, and armed force was resorted to on a large scale to protect what were perceived as British interests during the Opium and Boxer Wars. More important, the military presence was quotidian, and the use of force on a small scale was routine, especially in the 1920s.[43] Military protection on the cheap was aided by the formation of Volunteer corps by the British communities themselves. These dealt with little local difficulties until the arrival of regular military reinforcements, though the destabilising effects of Volunteer shootings – for example, at Hankou in 1925 – came to far outweigh the advantages of the system.

Britons in China were divided, roughly, into four often overlapping camps: settlers, expatriates, officials and missionaries. Domestic class differentiation often transcended these boundaries, while notions of race often fractured them, since Britain in China technically also included the 'other Westerners'. These latter groups aside, the British in China possessed multiple identities: they were British, and imperial but their local 'imagined' identity, so easily and readily dismissed by contemporaries and by historians, was of crucial importance to them, and to the Sino-British imbroglio. At different times their British, imperial or local identity was more prominent than the others, but all three identities were everpresent. Missionaries and officials require little definition, but the distinction between expatriates and settlers needs explaining. My use of the term 'settler' is deliberate, and I argue in this book that comparisons can and should be made between British settlers in China, and settlers in the British empire. Size is not an issue here: we can understand Britain in China only if we acknowledge that it was comprised chiefly of settlers, even if only a few thousands and that its social practices served settler purposes.

The settler communities of Shanghai, Tianjin and Hankou in particular bedevilled Sino-British relations as the British state attempted to renegotiate its informal presence in the face of the Nationalist revolution. The most problematic group resided in Shanghai, and called themselves Shanghailanders. Others lived in smaller concentrations at Hankou and Tianjin, and in the much smaller 'outports'. These were the small treaty port people, whose fortunes were inextricably tied up with the existence of the British concessions and extraterritorial privileges. They worked in treaty port service occupations (administration, service sector, police), or worked for, or ran, utility companies, land investment and real estate firms. Regardless of their social class or economic clout, their livelihoods were largely non-transferable, unlike those of the 'expatriates': British businessmen who worked for the largest China companies (Jardine Matheson, Butterfield & Swire), or for the multinationals (British American Tobacco (BAT), Imperial Chemical Industries (ICI), Asiatic Petroleum Corporation (APC)), and whose interests and activities form the subject of most accounts of Sino-British relations.[44]

Settlers built large residential, commercial and industrial suburbs in the Chinese cities open to them, constructed racecourses, jetties, roads, harbours, parks (probably in that order), established public utilities, municipal administrations, *faux* hill stations on the Indian model, styles of architecture – such as Tientsin Gothic – newspapers, bodies of literature, publishers, schools, churches, Masonic lodges, hospitals, prisons and all the other social institutions and infrastructure that might be expected. The largest settler communities were self-governing; even the smallest were still self-replicating. As chapters 2 3 show, they developed histories, and they developed 'birthrights' and futures. There was little self-doubt even at the worst of times, and certainly none at the onset of the 1920s, a decade in which settler pretensions and ambitions seemed to have firmly entrenched themselves both in China and in Sino-British relations.

## Nationalising Sino-British relations

This book focuses on the structure and workings of this establishment in the decades before the Pacific War. In this period, that singular presence reached its fullest form and presented its gravest dangers to the British state's relations with China. Specifically, this survey, rooted first in an examination of China in Britain and in the British imagination, examines the processes by which Britain in China evolved, how it replicated itself and represented itself (and China). It also looks at how it attempted to reform itself in the face of the militant state and mass nationalism it met in China in the mid-1920s and after, and in the face of the efforts of the British state to regain control over it and to decolonise the British presence. The beginnings of the road to Hong Kong 1997 lay in Hankou 1927, when on 4 January Chinese demonstrators, guided and led by Guomindang Left activists, occupied the British concession in the city. Royal Marines held the line over two days of intense pressure, then disarmed the bellicose British Volunteer corps and evacuated British residents, turning the concession over to the protection of Wuhan's Guomindang authorities. This *fait accompli* was formally recognised in an agreement signed on 19 February 1927 which surrendered the Hankou concession, and a smaller one at Jiujiang. That action by agents of the British state marked not just the first step in the dismantling of the British presence but one of the first active steps in that process's necessary corollary: the establishment of control over Britain in China by the British government.[45]

This was no easy process, and it is the task of this book to explain why it was that British diplomats and politicians found it difficult to bring Britain in China back under their control – indeed, how it was that they had little direct control over it in the first place – and also how it came about that British residents of Hankou had to be disarmed by British troops, and persuaded of the error of their thinking. Two years later Douglas Yates, formerly Assistant Secretary of the British Municipal Administration in the city, formally noted in a (rebuffed) claim for compensation to the Foreign Office that 'Had His Majesty's Government not surrendered the British Concession at Hankow, I should certainly be holding that position still, with reasonable prospect of eventually returning [to Britain] with sufficient to provide for the remainder of my life'.[46] This book is, however, more than just the story of the British China coast communities: it is also an examination of the formation of British settler societies and British settler mentalities. As such, it has to be located both in China and in Britain.

This book is divisible into two parts. The first examines the nature of Britain in China and its members. Underpinning the physical presence was a cultural relationship – no less physical and real – that forms the subject of the first chapter. The sources here, fictions, guidebooks and treaty port polemics, are examined in the wider context of British relations with Chinese – in London's Limehouse, for example – in the early twentieth century. As much as it was a product of individuals' socialisation into the British China communities, the treaty port mind was also located in Britain. Metropolitan society and culture taught Britons that Chinese were a subject people, even if China always remained an independent state. The next chapter provides an examination of the nature of British society in the Chinese treaty ports, its structures, and its replication. The creation of treaty port Britons, and the protection of that identity, form the twin themes of the second chapter. This examines memoirs, private papers, and institutional and commercial archives to look at the peculiarities of treaty port society.

What comes through most strongly is the hegemonic role of settler values and requirements, which dominated other sectors of treaty port society and were intended to protect settler identity.

The second part of the book deepens this study of treaty port society by examining its three broad constituents: concession administrations, businesses, and missions. It does so by looking at attempts both by individuals and by bodies within these sectors, and by British diplomats and officials outside them, to reform the British presence, and to 'decolonise' – or plainly disabuse – the treaty port mind after 1927. This was a matter of the personal behaviour of individuals and of the institutions and practices that the British had hitherto accepted as suitable for China. As British diplomats renegotiated the framework of treaties that Britain in China was based on, they also worked to take control of Britain in China, partly by forming alliances with what were perceived as progressive and realistic elements in that presence. The aim was to stave off further May Thirtieths, and in the longer term to smooth the path towards treaty reform. British relations with the 'other Britons', and with other Westerners were also areas of sensitivity.

The political crisis in Sino-British relations was accompanied by other crises which reinforced the need for change in the nature and character of British activities in China. Reforms in missions, businesses and concession administrations were also necessitated by socio-economic change in China, and in each particular case by specific new situations and problems thereby engendered. Notable changes included the rise of an urban Chinese bourgeoisie in Shanghai and Tianjin, and the growth in the modern sector of Chinese competitors – as well as a developing (though problematic) relationship between those groups and the new Nationalist regime. The projection of the power of the Chinese state into new fields – through commercial and educational legislation – also forced changes on the foreign presence, and was sometimes deliberately designed to reclaim Chinese sovereignty. As a result, foreign firms, foreign administrations, foreign educational, social and religious institutions had to attempt to integrate themselves much more closely into Chinese markets. Using Chinese personnel, language, methods and knowledge became the key to survival, as well as prosperity – they had to make themselves Chinese.

Thomas Rawski has argued that extraterritoriality provided no tangible benefits for foreign firms in China; profitability was a matter of market sensitivity. The point has been emphasised by other scholars, and is well made. It needs qualifying, however, in a way that makes the assertion applicable not just to businesses but to other bodies which had business in China – for example, missions or educationalists. While extraterritoriality gave no clear advantage, it certainly served to cosset those privileged by it from the realities of change in China, particularly in the years after World War I. The decade of warlord factionalism, and of what were caricatured as comic opera governments in Beijing, was a period in which treaty port life became comfortably complacent. Somerset Maugham's acid vignettes in his *On a Chinese Screen* (1922) are perhaps the best record we have of this phase of the British treaty port mentality and its certainties. The world of Maugham's desiccated Taipan, intolerant missionary, quirky consuls and life-beaten Yangzi skippers has a stale feel to it. Such certainties were terminated, as Arthur Waldron and Hans van de Ven pointed out, by civil wars on a scale which knocked the humour out of the comic opera caricatures – the Zhejiang–Jiangsu fighting in 1924–25, the revolt of the Northern Coalition in 1930 – and by foreign aggression on an unprecedented scale: the Japanese assault on China. May Thirtieth, followed shortly by the Northern Expedition of the Guomindang's National Revolutionary Army, which began in July 1926, forced Britons to examine closely how unresponsive they had become to the realities of life and business in China.[47]

The journey along the road from Hankou to Hong Kong has taken longer than almost any other act of decolonisation. War and revolution served to hasten the process, and then leave it in a hiatus after 1949. This is not a history of the whole seventy-year-long process of British decolonisation in China. It is, instead, an examination of its most significant decades: the renegotiation of the British presence in the aftermath of the victory of Chinese revolutionary nationalism in the mid–1920s. This was an act of decolonisation, on the periphery of empire, led by agents of the British state but also by many of the private individuals who had staffed Britain in China. It was a process in which the grey areas of multiple semi-colonialisms, hitherto benignly neglected in China, were found to be wanting by the British state, and were surrendered in return for the black and white of colony and non-colony. The boundaries between the British empire and China were not simply redrawn but formally drawn for the first time since 1842, and the informal imperium was abandoned. Assumptions about the relationship between the British state and British interests in China therefore need to be rethought: the most marked period of the state's involvement with its wards in China lay in those years when it set about reordering and regulating Sino-British commercial relations.

This process of renegotiation was starkly terminated in the months before the Pacific War, when Shanghai was decreed not to be an imperial interest, and consequently was not included within the boundaries that the British empire was prepared to defend against Japan. Only Hong Kong remained, and it remained – having been reoccupied after the Pacific War – as a wholly British possession until 1997 under the benevolently despotic rule of the Colonial Office and its successor departments. The mental and literal withdrawal from China was certainly one of the last acts of British decolonisation in the twentieth century, but it was also one of the first.

## Notes

1 P. J. Marshall, 'Imperial Britain', *Journal of Imperial and Commonwealth History*, 23 (1995), 379–94.
2 W. C. Kirby, 'The Internationalization of China: Foreign Relations at Home and Abroad in the Republican Era', *China Quarterly*, 150 (1997), 433–58.
3 Port Arthur, now Dalian.
4 The best account of this process is Kirby, 'The Internationalization of China'.
5 For example: Akira Iriye, *After Imperialism: The Search for a New Order in the Far East, 1921–1931* (Cambridge MA, 1965); W. Roger Louis, *British Strategy in the Far East, 1919–1939* (Oxford, 1971); Christopher Thorne, *The Limits of Foreign Policy: The West, the League, and the Far Eastern Crisis of 1931–1933* (London, 1972); B. A. Lee, *Britain and the Sino-Japanese War, 1937–1939: A Study in the Dilemmas of British Decline* (Stanford CA, 1973); Nicholas R. Clifford, *Retreat from China: British Policy in the Far East, 1937–1941* (London, 1967); Chung-p'ing Fung, *The British Government's China Policy, 1945–1950* (Keele, 1994); J. T. H. Tang, *Britain's Encounter with Revolutionary China, 1949–1954* (New York, 1992). Unless dealing specifically with imperialism or Hong Kong, Chinese histories of Sino-British relations have a similar basic focus: for example, Sa Benren and Pan Xingming, *Ershi shiji de ZhongYing guanxi* (Sino-British Relations in the Twentieth Century) (Shanghai, 1996).
6 E. S. K. Fung, *The Diplomacy of Imperial Retreat: Britain's South China Policy, 1924–31* (Hong Kong, 1991), 1–12.
7 *Annual Report of the Hankow Municipal Council, 1926*; SMC, *Annual Report, 1893*, 262; R. W. Rigby, *The May 30 Movement: Events and Themes* (Canberra, 1980).
8 The full text of the memorandum, and other relevant documents, can be found in Sir Frederick Whyte, *China and Foreign Powers: An Historical Review of their Relations* (London, second and revised edition, 1928), Appendix V. On the Washington Treaty powers see Fung, *Diplomacy of Imperial Retreat*, 16–19.
9 For the text of the offer see Whyte, *China and Foreign Powers*, 64–8. The best account of this process is Fung, *Diplomacy of Imperial Retreat*.
10 On the policies of the PRC toward the foreign presence see Beverley Hooper, *China Stands Up: Ending the Western Presence, 1948–50* (Sydney, 1986). For discussions of Hong Kong as a separate matter see Judith M. Brown and Rosemary Foot, eds, *Hong Kong's Transitions, 1842–1997* (London, 1997), and Wm. Roger Louis, 'Hong Kong: The Critical Phase, 1945–49', *American Historical Review*, 102 (1997), 1052–84.
11 The picture is qualified in Christopher C. Munn, 'Anglo-China: Chinese People and British Rule in Hong Kong, 1841–1870' (University of Toronto Ph.D. thesis, 1998).
12 On Fairbank see Paul M. Evans, *John Fairbank and the American Understanding of Modern China* (Oxford, 1988), and Paul A. Cohen and Merle Goldman, *Fairbank Remembered* (Cambridge MA, 1992).
13 For an introductory bibliography to this research on Shanghai see Christian Henriot, 'Cities and Urban Society in China in the Nineteenth and Twentieth Centuries: A Review Essay in Western Literature', in *Jindai Zhongguo shi yanjiu tongxun* (Newsletter of Modern Chinese History), 21 (1996), 151–75. The singular exception in the Shanghai case is Nicholas R. Clifford, *Spoilt Children of Empire: Westerners in Shanghai and the Chinese Revolution of the 1920s* (Hanover NH, 1991).
14 Paul A. Cohen, *Discovering History in China: American Historical Writing on the*

*Recent Chinese Past* (New York, 1984), 143.
15  *Ibid.*, 147.
16  Exceptions include Joseph W. Esherick, *The Origins of the Boxer Uprising* (Berkeley CA, 1987); Paul A. Cohen, *History in Three Keys: The Boxers as Event, Experience, and Myth* (New York, 1997); James L. Hevia, *Cherishing Men from Afar: Qing Guest Ritual and the Macartney Embassy of 1793* (Durham NC, 1995); Tani E. Barlow, ed., *Formations of Colonial Modernity in East Asia* (Durham NC, 1997); J. Y. Wong, *Deadly Dreams: Opium, Imperialism, and the Arrow War (1856–1860) in China* (Cambridge, 1998). More specific studies include Munn, 'Anglo-China', and John M. Carroll, 'Colonialism and Collaboration: Chinese Subjects and the Making of British Hong Kong', *China Information*, 12 (1997), 12-35.
17  Jürgen Osterhammel, 'Semi-colonialism and Informal Empire in Twentieth Century China: Towards a Framework of Analysis', in W. J. Mommsen and Jürgen Osterhammel, eds, *Imperialism and After: Continuities and Discontinuities* (London, 1986); Peter Duus, Ramon H. Myers and Mark R. Peattie, eds, *The Japanese Informal Empire in China, 1895–1937* (Princeton NJ, 1989); Louise Young, *Japan's Total Empire: Manchuria and the Culture of Wartime Imperialism* (Berkeley CA, 1998).
18  'September 1, 1939', in Edward Mendelson, ed., *The English Auden: Poems, Essays and Dramatic Writings* (London, 1977), 245.
19  For an early analysis of this orthodoxy see Albert Feuerwerker, 'China's History in Marxian Dress', in Feuerwerker, ed., *History in Communist China* (Cambridge MA, 1968), 24–7.
20  Robert Bickers and Jeffrey N. Wasserstrom, 'Shanghai's "Chinese and Dogs Not Admitted" Sign: History, Legend and Contemporary Symbol', *China Quarterly*, 142 (1995), 447–8.
21  See, e.g., Zhang Zhongli, ed., *Dongnan yanhai chengshi yu Zhongguo jindaihua* (The History of the South-east Coastal Cities and China's Modernisation) (Shanghai, 1996).
22  A good example among many is Fei Chengkang, *Zhongguo zujie shi* (History of Concessions in China) (Shanghai, 1991).
23  Businessmen, consuls, and missionaries can be found in Shanghai's Huangpu district gazetteer, Shanghai shi Huangpu quzhi bianji weiyuanhui, (ed.), *Huangpu quzhi* (Shanghai, 1996).
24  David Buck, 'Appraising the Revival of Historical Studies in China', *China Quarterly*, 105 (1986), 141; Tim Wright, '"The Spiritual Heritage of Chinese Capitalism": Recent Trends in the Historiography of Chinese Enterprise Management', in Jonathan Unger, ed., *Using the Past to serve the Present: Historiography and Politics in Contemporary China* (Armonk NY, 1993), 214.
25  Rhoads Murphey, *The Outsiders: The Western Experience in India and China* (Ann Arbor MI, 1977), 12–35.
26  Cohen, *Discovering History in China*, 144.
27  Surveys of the literature can be found in Cohen, *Discovering History in China*, 97–147, and Osterhammel, 'Semi-colonialism and Informal Empire in Twentieth Century China'.
28  John Darwin, 'Imperialism and the Victorians: The Dynamics of Territorial Expansion', *English Historical Review*, 112 (1997), 614–42. Further, stimulating, exceptions were published too late for discussion in this book: Jürgen Osterhammel. 'Britain and China, 1842–1914', in Andrew Porter, ed., *The Oxford History of the British Empire*, III, *The Nineteenth Century* (Oxford, 1999), 146–69, and Jürgen Osterhammel, 'China', in Judith M. Brown and Wm. Roger Louis, eds, *The Oxford History of the British Empire*, IV, *The Twentieth Century* (Oxford, 1999), 643–66. My thanks go to the author for kindly allowing me to see these chapters in proof.
29  Ronald Robinson, 'Non-European Foundations of European Imperialism: Sketch for a Theory of Collaboration', in R. Owen and B. Sutcliffe, eds, *Studies in the Theory of Imperialism* (Harlow, 1972), 124.
30  See, for example, John G. Butcher, *The British in Malaya, 1880–1941: The Social History of a European Community in Colonial South-east Asia* (Kuala Lumpur,

1979); Helen Callaway, *Gender, Culture and Empire: European Women in Colonial Nigeria* (Basingstoke, 1987); Frederic Cooper and Ann Laura Stoler (eds), *Tensions of Empire: Colonial Cultures in a Bourgeois World* (Berkeley CA, 1997); Dane Kennedy, *Islands of White: Settler Society and Culture in Kenya and Southern Rhodesia, 1890–1939* (Durham NC, 1987); Dane Kennedy, *The Magic Mountains: Hill Stations and the British Raj* (Berkeley CA, 1996); Ann Stoler, 'Rethinking Colonial Categories: European Communities in Sumatra and the Boundaries of Rule', *Comparative Studies in Society and History*, 31 (1989), 134–61; Nicholas Thomas, *Colonialism's Culture: Anthropology, Travel and Government* (Oxford, 1994).

31  C. A. Bayly, 'Returning the British to South Asian History: The Limits of Colonial Hegemony', *South Asia*, 17 (1994), 1–25.

32  On this topic see, for example, John M. Mackenzie, ed., *Imperialism and Popular Culture* (Manchester, 1985); J. A. Mangan, *The Games Ethic and Imperialism: Aspects of the Diffusion of an Ideal* (Harmondsworth, 1986); J. A. Mangan, ed., *Making Imperial Mentalities: Socialisation and British Imperialism* (Manchester, 1990).

33  Kirby, 'The Internationalization of China', 433.

34  Arnold Wright, ed., *Twentieth Century Impressions of Hong Kong, Shanghai and other Treaty Ports of China* (London, 1908), preface.

35  Department of Overseas Trade, *Trade and Economic Conditions in China, 1931–33* (London, 1933), 15.

36  Thomas Rawski, *Economic Growth in Prewar China* (Berkeley CA, 1989), 9.

37  Remer, *Foreign Investments in China*, 394.

38  Rawski, *Economic Growth*, 8; R. T. P. Davenport Hines and Geoffrey Jones, 'British Business in Asia since 1860', in Davenport-Hines and Jones, eds, *British Business in Asia since 1860* (Cambridge, 1989), 14–15.

39  Kang Chao, *The Development of Cotton Textile Production in China* (Cambridge MA, 1977), 135.

40  B. R. Tomlison, 'British Business in India, 1860-1970', in Davenport-Hines and Jones, eds, *British Business in Asia*, 113.

41  Claude Markovits, 'Indian Communities in China, c. 1842–1949', paper presented to the conference on 'Foreign Communities in East Asia in the Nineteenth and Twentieth Centuries', Lyon, March 1997, 10.

42  *China Year Book*, 1930, 2; *China Year Book*, 1933, 2; *Hong Kong Administrative Reports for the Year 1932* (Hong Kong, 1933), 'Medical and Sanitary Report for the Year 1932', M30.

43  C. J. Bowie, 'Great Britain and the Use of Force in China, 1919 to 1931' (University of Oxford D.Phil. thesis, 1983).

44  Roberta Dayer, *Bankers and Diplomats in China, 1917 to 1925: The Anglo-American Relationship* (London, 1981); S. L. Endicott, *Diplomacy and Enterprise: British China Policy, 1933–37* (Manchester, 1975); Fung, *Diplomacy of Imperial Retreat*; Jürgen Osterhammel, 'British Business in China, 1860s–1950s', in Davenport-Hines and Jones, eds, *British Business in Asia*, 212–14; Jürgen Osterhammel, 'Imperialism in Transition: British Business and the Chinese Authorities, 1931–37', *China Quarterly*, 98 (1984), 260–86; Nathan A. Pelcovits, *Old China Hands and the Foreign Office* (New York, 1948); Pauline Y. N. Thomas, 'The Foreign Office and the Business Lobby: British Official and Commercial Attitudes to Treaty Revision in China, 1925-30' (London School of Economics Ph.D. thesis, 1981); L. K. Young, *British Policy in China, 1895–1902* (Oxford, 1970).

45  H. Owen Chapman, *The Chinese Revolution, 1926–27: A Record of the Period under Communist Control as seen from the Nationalist Capital, Hankow* (London, 1928), 32–5; Fung, *Diplomacy of Imperial Retreat*, 113–28.

46  Public Record Office, London (hereafter PRO), FO 228/4230/1 40d, D. Yates to Foreign Office, 9 November 1929.

47  Arthur Waldron, *From War to Nationalism: China's Turning Point, 1924–1925* (Cambridge, 1995); Hans van de Ven, 'The Military in the Republic', *China Quarterly*, 150 (1997), 352–74.

# CHAPTER TWO

# China in Britain,
# and in the British imagination

A man (usually a man) getting off the boat from home on arrival in China in the early inter-war period would have been carrying baggage, mental as well as literal. No less than in the nineteenth-century treaties, and in accumulated precedents and practices, Britain in China was rooted in the mind. To understand how Britons in China saw their world, or learned how to act in it and structure their relations with Chinese, we must first understand how China and the Chinese were represented to them. China's place in the British imagination dictated its place in the minds of newcomers. Moreover, Britain in China replicated itself through the socialisation of these recruits, making Shanghailanders and Tientsiners out of Lancastrians, Ulstermen, Scots and others, by fashioning new identities out of existing ones (British, imperial, dominion). These recruits came already equipped, or set out to equip themselves through reading, through classes or through conversation. None of them came to the real China untouched by the imaginary China examined in this chapter.

As a recruit to Britain in China our traveller might have been directed before he arrived by his superiors, or friends with China connections, to read up on the country, or on the history of its foreign presence, or else might have read up out of curiosity, choosing a book from the ship's library on the long voyage east. There was no shortage of literature, written by missionaries, academics or sinophiles, but the dominant voices, and the ones most likely to be recommended to him, were those of writers with a vested interest in telling *The Truth about the Chinese Republic* (as diehard treaty port newspaper editor H. G. W. Woodhead's 1925 volume put it). Although few in number, such authors dominated writing on China available in Britain until the 1930s. They were British or American residents of the treaty ports, journalists and editors like Woodhead, hacks and activists.[1] Not only did they write the contemporary commentaries, but they also dominated news reporting from China by serving as China correspondents of domestic newspapers. These men were propagandists for a cause, and their cause was Britain in China, a settler bridgehead in a foreign sovereign state. In their works they described it, gave it a history and, implicitly, demanded a future for it. Their version of 'The truth about the Chinese Republic', or about the Chinese character, politics or socio-economic affairs, was designed to bolster Britain in China. It was also designed to protect their own jobs against Chinese competition.

Still, our new recruit – not necessarily of the highest quality if bound for China – may not have read anything in particular, although it is unlikely that he would be completely unfamiliar with China as news. The Boxers, the anti-Manchu revolution in 1911, the warlord disintegration of the 1920s, and the Nationalist revolution of 1923–28, were all firmly fixed in the British popular imagination. Even if these exciting events had passed him by, British popular culture was steeped in China and the Chinese. In thrillers, on the stage, in romances and in film, in both children's and adults' literature, China and the Chinese – and the Chinese in Britain too – were represented to such an extent that those pleading for improvements in relations between Chinese and Britons routinely joked about the fact. Missionary administrator Harold Hodgkin wrote in 1925 of the son of a friend who 'knew all about Chinamen; they were cruel, wicked people; he had seen lots of them at the pictures' [2] Knowing all about Chinese cruelty and wickedness meant that Britons of every age knew what to expect in their encounters with Chinese, and how to act in response.

These were the building blocks of Britain in China. Popular culture and treaty port propaganda overlapped in two ways. First, treaty port propagandists wrote novels and thrillers; they cashed in on China's newsworthiness and their self-ascribed expertise, but they also wrote with propagandist intent. They reviewed fiction, and recommended novels for the light they might shed on events. They joked about Yellow Peril thrillers, but they also wrote them. Second, treaty port propagandists and popular culture were highly prescriptive in terms of the way Britons ought to behave in China, and with Chinese. Factual reporting and popular culture's fictions identified difference, taught distance and encouraged distrust. China and the Chinese were denigrated, their politics and society ridiculed. Moreover, these mediums supplied the vocabulary through which treaty port recruits made sense of their world, and they shaped the behaviour of treaty port Britons.

This discourse on China took place within a strong-rooted and well developed general discourse on the 'Oriental' and the 'Orient', one that was monopolised neither by Britain nor by Europe alone.[3] China was arguably less important as a subject than India or the Near East, in a

hierarchy which favoured proximity to Europe and political importance within the British empire, and this has been reflected in the literature on orientalism.[4] For their part, fictions on China can in many
ways be little distinguished from other fictions with imperial themes,
except for the striking intersection of the metropolitan and the imperial in the Yellow Peril thriller and the Limehouse tale. Fictions on
China, and on Britons in the East, were fed by fictions on the East in
Britain.

Using a selection of works and writers likely to have been recommended to the traveller to China, this chapter examines what may
have been encountered by those in Britain searching for information
about China, or by those merely searching for relaxation. The publications include a work of anthropology by Arthur H. Smith, a siege
memoir by Putnam Weale (pseudonym of Bertram Lenox Simpson), a
history of modern China by J. O. P. Bland and Edmund Backhouse, a
survey of contemporary China (1926) by Rodney Gilbert, and a repre-
sentatively alternative attack on Britain in China by *Manchester
Guardian* journalist Arthur Ransome. A treaty port history (F. L.
Hawks Pott) and a guidebook (C. E. Darwent) might also be consulted
as reference works, and these are also included. The chapter then looks
at the fictional works of Sax Rohmer, Louise Jordan Miln and W. Somerset Maugham, but also points to the context in which they were read,
which involved understanding and quite probably visiting China in
Britain, in this case the 1924–25 Empire Exhibition, and London's
Limehouse district. Each of these books is representative not just of
their authors, and their constituencies, but also of genres that crossed
media: Rohmeresque works appeared on stage and screen, in music
hall song, and even in the marketing of a brand of perfume. These
authors too wrote in various media: Simpson wrote ten novels on Chinese themes, Bland wrote verse and treaty port light fiction, Gilbert
penned a novel, and all three were well known and respected journalists; Rohmer wrote reportage, Maugham produced plays, novels and
sketches, and Miln too had worked as a journalist. Fictions overlapped
with, informed, and were fed by news reporting on the fact of Chinese
life in Britain.

It may be objected that, Smith excepted, there are no missionary
texts here, no academic studies, or works by Chinese. These were certainly published, and available, but many such works failed to travel
beyond their constituencies: fellow missionaries and supporters, scholars and students, sinophiles or political sympathisers with (most especially) Nationalist China. Treaty port recruits were unlikely to have
been recommended missionary authors or works by Chinese, and these
alternative authorities were damned relentlessly by the spokesmen of

Britain in China. Moreover, as I argue in chapter 3, settler ideology had achieved a hegemonic position within the broader context of British society in China, and the minority sectors (missions especially) were complicit in the structures and *mores* of Britain in China. By extension many missionary texts, or works by academics, read little different from books by treaty port writers. By the 1930s things had changed and new voices communicated China to Britain. That change forms one key to the argument in my conclusion, but even with that shift the missionary influence on British attitudes to China was never in any way comparable to its influence on the United States.[5]

We should remember too that books were not the only source of information and views on China: Britons of all classes and from all parts of the country, urban and rural, north and south, might encounter friends, relatives, neighbours or acquaintances who had experience of China. Retired treaty port residents apart, there were former soldiers, Royal Navy and merchant seamen. There were up to 13,000 Britons in China at any one time writing letters (most missionaries wrote circular letters to friends and supporters) or similarly communicating with relations and friends. Indeed, this volume is partly built on such archived correspondence. There were missionary and secular lectures, and mission support groups. New recruits sought information from these sources as well: a prospective policeman interrogated an aunt who worked as a nurse in Shanghai, a newly appointed naval adviser corresponded with a retired customs official before he sailed to China.[6]

We have some clues as to what people learned verbally before they went, but we have many more clues about the books they were recommended, and read. These works certainly appeared on real lists of suggested reading: the War Office's 1928 pamphlet about Shanghai, for example, prepared for the men of the Shanghai Defence Force, recommended Gilbert's *What's Wrong with China* and Bland and Backhouse's *China under the Empress Dowager*, while an appendix listed 'Some Chinese characteristics'.[7] Fictional works were frequently recommended as sources of information about China's past and present. The *China Christian Year Book* regularly included fiction in reviews of literature on China in English. Those going to China often read novels in preparation, or were recommended to. Richard Dobson of BAT prepared himself for business life in China in the 1930s by reading Pearl Buck's *The Good Earth* and Alice T. Hobart's *Oil for the Lamps of China*.[8] Sax Rohmer would not have been thus recommended, but it is unlikely that many British men reached adulthood in the two or three decades after 1913 without having read works like his Fu Manchu novels.

## *Arthur H. Smith,* Chinese Characteristics *(1890)*

We begin with the acceptable, unusual missionary voice, and the genre dedicated to explaining the Chinese *qua* Chinese. More than sociology or anthropology, or socio-economic analysis, the dominant paradigm through which the Chinese were approached was through the analysis of their 'character'. Through understanding the Chinese character Britons learned that they ought to interact with Chinese as master to servant (and knowing was mastering), and as ruler to subject.

While experience was highly regarded in treaty port society, it was believed that there was little about the Chinese that could not be encapsulated within the covers of a book for handy reference. National 'character' or 'race' analysis was a widely used and largely unquestioned mode of discourse, its scientific patina largely unchallenged until the experience of Nazism discredited it. 'Race' was often substituted as a word for 'national', although specific racial theories were also developed.[9] What was important was that national character was portrayed as a constant. This view of Chinese civilisation in particular, though hardly new as a paradigm in the early twentieth century, became an important tool in the describing of a superficially fast-changing country. As a republic succeeded the Qing dynasty it became even more important.

The small body of literature which dealt solely with analysis of the Chinese was influential, and was often recommended as a starting point for the inquisitive. An American missionary, Smith (1845–1932) wrote the most prominent, and longest-lasting, such analysis; one survey as late as 1925 rated it top of a list of 'The Most Helpful Books on China' and second best-seller in three Shanghai foreign-language bookstores.[10] Smith's object was to analyse defects in the Chinese that Protestantism would remedy. The work was critically dismissive of Chinese civilisation and culture, concluding, in short, that the Chinese lacked 'character and conscience' and that the solution was reform from outside, through the introduction of 'Christian civilisation'.[11]

He wrote with humour and a light touch, and the chapter titles give the flavour of the book: 'Face', 'Economy', 'Industry', 'Politeness', 'The disregard of time', 'The disregard of accuracy', 'The talent for misunderstanding', 'The talent for indirection', 'Flexible inflexibility', 'Intellectual turbidity', 'The absence of nerves', 'Contempt for foreigners', 'The absence of public spirit', 'Conservatism', 'Indifference to comfort and convenience', 'Physical vitality', 'Patience and perseverance', 'Content and cheerfulness', 'Filial piety', 'Benevolence', 'The absence of sympathy', 'Social typhoons', 'Mutual responsibility and respect for law', 'Mutual suspicion', 'The absence of sincerity', 'Polytheism, pantheism, atheism', 'The real condition of China and her present needs'. The importance of *Chinese Characteristics* was that it codified a set of pervasive but previously disparate characterisations, and supplied a recognisable construct of the Chinese character which other commentators referred to, as well as a model of analysis which they could follow. Smith's remedies for China were not the point for many of the book's readers: he told them what the Chinese were like, and this told them how the Chinese should be handled. Perhaps the single most important characteristic was 'face'. Although certainly a valid feature of Chinese social interaction, the foreign emphasis on 'face' in fact served to feed a heightened sense of foreign individual and national prestige. 'Knowing' the importance of face to Chinese, the treaty port Briton was ever in fear of compromising his own dignity in public.

Other texts in this vein included J. Dyer Ball's *Things Chinese* (1892, fifth, revised, edition 1925), which was still advertised by the publisher, Kelly & Walsh, in 1929 under the heading '5,000 Things You Ought to Know About China ... How Many Do You Know?' This combined analyses of the Chinese character with an almanac. The sections on 'Riots', 'Suicide', 'Time', 'Topsyturvydom' and 'Chinese people, Characteristics of' owed much to Smith.[12] Knowing these things Chinese, even if only a portion of the required 5,000, served to underpin the creation of alterity, the otherness of Chinese. 'Topsyturvydom' was the vulgar definition of Chinese otherness: everything in China, or that Chinese did, was 'backwards about',[13] upside down or back to front. Topsyturvydom also rendered China as comic, and not to be taken seriously. A satirical *Child's Primer of Things Chinese* (1923) laid this out in its introduction:

> I do not hesitate to say
> That Life, for me, in far Cathay,
> Is like a Circus ev'ry Day.[14]

## Rodney Gilbert, What's Wrong with China (1926)

China's occasional newsworthiness encouraged the publication of new China-related commentaries, or the reprinting of existing ones, and many such works incorporated this discourse on characteristics. It also prompted vivid press debates which reprised many of these notions about the Chinese. Many writers took as given the viability of Smith's analytical model; some even borrowed his catchy title.[15] Much of this discourse naturally came from the pens of those with direct experience of China. These were the books available for those who wanted to understand and know what was happening in China at that moment.

Rodney Gilbert (1889–1968) left the United States for China as a youthful medical salesman in 1912; switching to journalism he was later (acting) editor of Shanghai's *North China Daily News* during its most virulent phase in 1927, when it lambasted Chinese nationalism and the Chinese character.[16] Founded in 1850, the paper was the premier English-language publication in China. That a man like Gilbert, with little experience, and less talent, could become acting editor at a time of crisis for Britain in China was not at all unusual, merely indicative of the power that could accrue to treaty port activists. He was filling in for O. M. Green, himself of indifferent talent, and also a diehard, who was eventually prised out of his position in 1930, having edited the paper since 1911. Treaty port journalism was not highly regarded by the diplomatic establishment, but journalists invariably saw themselves as community representatives, and activists, so the damage they could and did do to Chinese and domestic views of British diplomatic policy could be great.[17]

*What's Wrong with China* (1926) was largely predicated on identifying the faults of the Chinese character and did so using, or referring to, racial theories. The absence of the question mark in the title, easily overlooked, was deliberate: Gilbert set out to describe China's faults. This was a hugely popular polemic, anchored on the claim that China 'is already spoiled and capricious beyond words, simply because she has been consistently overpraised and overrated when she should have been spanked'. Gilbert warned that unless the 'Anglo-Germanic' people solved the political problems of Asia and Africa, there would be race war.[18] By no means an original premise, it owed much to popular anthropology and the influential work of American publicist Lothrop Stoddard and other writers on 'race' questions.[19] Grafted on to this scenario was a body of opprobrious comment about Chinese (they were unmanly, docile, mendacious, idle, intolerant), and Chinese society, which was based on the fundamental premise that 'the Chinese are children'.[20] These were themes found daily in the *NCDN* under Gilbert and Green, despite the fact that the newspaper had a substantial Chinese readership. The portrayal of a non-European society as infantile or, more politely, at a lower stage of development, was common in texts like this, and deeply complicit in paternalistic imperialism, including Japanese imperialism.[21] Gilbert's pandering to extreme racism was not wholly unusual, and was certainly representative of comments published and recorded during the period of crisis for the treaty ports in which he wrote.

The average commentary recounted recent events more or less as they were understood by foreign observers to have happened. Explanations and analysis would usually be rooted in a crude race/character analysis, which reduced all political activity to the innate corruption of Chinese, and the innate cowardice of their soldiers.[22] The fate of the suffering mass of peasant China – innately dirty, diseased, degenerate and superstitious, but also industrious, thrifty and good-natured – would be lamented. Comparisons with the West would be drawn, principally with the West in China. Chinese municipal inadequacy as compared with the sanitary, administrative, engineering and policing record of the foreign concessions would be outlined. The necessity of bringing Chinese up to the Western 'level' would be posited – but the problem of deracination and Westernisation would be demonstrated. Foreign tutelage, and foreign discipline, would be urged. Sometimes the Chinese – and this was a common image – needed chastisement as if they were naughty children, both individually and as a nation. Consul Meyrick Hewlett felt that six months as a prep school master taught him 'lessons which were of real value in my subsequent relations with the Chinese'.[23] It comes as no surprise to find him in his memoirs caning a chair-bearer, who thanked him, manfully, for the punishment. This was the language used by General Dyer to justify the 1919 Amritsar massacre.[24]

The treaty port commentators appealed to history again and again; for them the pre-Nanjing Treaty world, when Europeans were still subject to Chinese law, was located not in time but in the unchanging Chinese character. With sombre seriousness, texts of the 1920s listed cruel judicial punishments inflicted on Britons in China in the early nineteenth century to underline the need to defend the treaties, and to illustrate what would happen again if extraterritoriality was lost.[25] There was an apparent contradiction in analysing both the persistence of the past (the unchanging East), and Westernisation, but the latter was always represented as superficial, as a veneer, while contradiction itself provided few discomforts for the experts: both images served a useful purpose.[26] More broadly, of course, the British empire reacted badly to the fruits of its own Westernising efforts. African and Indian professionals – middle-class, educated and 'Westernised' – were subjected to vituperative abuse.[27] In China, too, there was ambivalence about the 'modern', which was equated with 'Westernisation', or Western (usually missionary) education. This distaste was shared by many Chinese thinkers; Jerome Ch'en has identified a 'curious unanimity' between conservative Chinese and Westerners in their views about Chinese radicalism, especially after 1927, and also in their dislike and distrust of students educated overseas ('returned students'), or by Western institutions in China.[28] Whilst commentators asserted the necessity of foreign help, tutelage or education, they were not happy dealing with the results. The supposedly deracinated and 'half-educated' returned student was blamed for the nationalism which threatened the foreign position. In effect, the hegemonic function of Western tutelage was undermined as nationalism threatened the pupil–teacher relationship. British commentators idealised the Chinese scholar gentry and regretted the passing of the Manchus.[29] Attacking the 'returned student' was also a way of 'reasonably' attacking the notion of Chinese 'progress' itself, to which all commentators had to pay lip service. But progress threatened not just the relationship between British imperialism and China, which might be discussed in the abstract, it also directly undermined the hegemony of the treaty port experts.

With the exception, for obvious reasons, of Hu Shi, an outspoken critic both of the Guomindang, at least in the early years of the Nanjing decade, and of Chinese culture, those Chinese who could have interpreted China in person were disliked and distrusted. Their works were damned by treaty port reviewers, their motives and skills impugned. To allow the validity of their claim to interpret themselves and their society would have been to question treaty port social taboos by implying equality with the Chinese. It would also have threatened the livelihood of foreign interpreters of China. Chinese commentators would have had a head start linguistically and culturally, and would have been likely to be better educated than most of their foreign counterparts.[30] Their insights into Chinese politics would have been more direct, better informed, and less weighed down with the mental baggage of the treaty port mind. Clearly, the informed outsider often has advantages – of distance, disinterest and perspective – when it comes to analysing another culture. But the dominant treaty port commentary was not distanced, or disinterested, but propaganda in defence of the treaty system and the settler establishment.

Western stereotypes based on Chinese subordination were also threatened as the Chinese bourgeoisie grew in wealth and strength in the years before 1927 and made increasing political demands, especially concerning power within the foreign settlements. And it is also probable that the identifiably growing Western concern for the Chinese peasant – notably through such fictions as Pearl Buck's *The Good Earth* (1931) – was related to this dislike of modernised urban China and its elites; such had increasingly been the pattern in British India.[31] The Chinese peasantry was always portrayed as the passive victim of the corruption of the political and military elites. There was, of course, some truth in this; warlord warfare was not the comic opera portrayed in treaty port humour.[32]

Gilbert wrote another commentary (*The Unequal Treaties*, 1929) and on leaving China in 1929 a novel, *The Indiscretions of Lin Mang* (1929), which allowed him to cash in on the vogue for atmospheric and informed fiction about China in the late 1920s. The book was politically and culturally hostile to China and the Chinese but chose missionaries and supine foreign diplomats as villains to equal corrupt, xenophobic Chinese official-cum-banditdom. It was publicised as 'an attempt to depict the Chinese Racial Character, and it is a real contribution to our knowledge and understanding of the Chinese'.[33] Gilbert's didacticism was smoothly transferred from sober commentary to fiction, and both formats bolstered his print journalism.

The treaty port commentaries also pointed out that the Chinese were not the only enemy: the other was the diplomatic community, and the practice of diplomacy. Commentaries and fictions were explicitly critical of the conciliatory policies of the foreign powers. Histories pointed out that Shanghai was created by private enterprise, by the energetic efforts of businessmen and freelance agents working for a broader vision of Greater Britain, not by colonial or diplomatic red tape.[34] Gilbert, J. O. P. Bland and Lenox Simpson used fiction to augment the attacks they made in their more serious works against those they felt were betraying the treaty ports (including missionaries). In this way they identified what it was that marked a loyal member of the community, and which sectors of British society were always to be held suspect. Britain in China, bred in the best traditions of empire, was permanently threatened.

## J. O. P. Bland and Edmund Backhouse
## China under the Empress Dowager (1910)

Any list of readings about China ought to include a work of history. C. P. Fitzgerald (1902–92), himself later a successful historian, first discovered an interest in China through articles in The Times about the abortive Manchu restoration of 1917. Keen to know more, he wrote in his memoirs, he eventually discovered that 'there was no history of China, in any adequate meaning of the word, in the English language'. What Fitzgerald had already discovered, however, close to hand on his father's bookshelves, were two volumes co-authored by Sir Edmund Backhouse and J. O. P. Bland: China under the Empress Dowager (1910) and Annals and Memoirs of the Court at Peking (1914).[35] Hardly adequate as history for Fitzgerald, they were nonetheless well regarded by others at the time: the first volume was routinely recommended, and had made the reputations of its authors.

Ulsterman John Otway Percy Bland (1863–1945) joined the Chinese Maritime Customs in 1883, and then served as Secretary of the Shanghai Municipal Council (1896–1906) and as agent for the British & Chinese Corporation (1906–10), combining these posts with journalism and book writing. Bland translated Chinese material for G. E. Morrison, correspondent of *The Times*, and also served as Shanghai correspondent of the paper (1897–1907) and Beijing correspondent (1907–10).[36] He was a bullish protector of the SMC's interests, and no less a zealous agent, as he saw it, of British imperialism in China. Bland wrote a number of political commentaries, some light treaty port fiction, and even some verse, and his stylish prose was well regarded. In later life he became one of the bitterest of the diehards; leaving China in 1910 failed to deter Bland from denouncing it continuously from retirement in Suffolk. *China: The Pity of it* (1932) – a trenchant attack on modern China and the 'Foreign Office school of thought' which put up with it – was not necessarily high on anybody's list of recommendations. As both Lytton Strachey and Beijing journalist W. Sheldon Ridge pointed out, Bland lost his sense of humour.[37]

Ridge also admitted that *China under the Empress Dowager* would remain well known. Backhouse, a sinophile fraud, supplied[38] the forged source material for this history of the Empress Dowager's life, which focused on the Boxer rising; the innocent Bland polished and supplemented the text.[39] This China was exotic and poisonous, politics were court politics: 'the great game of ambitions, loves and hates that is forever played around the throne' (480). The book appeared in the month the anti-Manchu Xinhai revolution began, and was the only obviously authoritative work on the 'inner' workings of the Chinese throne then available, putting to shame alternative inside glimpses into the court in Beijing. Moreover, it was quite readable, and even inspired Strachey to write an indifferent play, *A Son of Heaven* (1925). Missionary historian K. S. Latourette criticised in 1930 the emphases in modern history which he felt served to exoticise China, by concentrating on its ancient philosophy, or marginalise it, by concentrating on what missionary turned historian E. R. Hughes later called the Western 'invasion'.[40] In *China under the Empress Dowager* modern history was exoticised too.

The exoticisation of the past, and the logic of this disdain for the modern evinced in Gilbert and Bland, led a core of writers to pass beyond philippics against modern nationalism to romantic support for the deposed ruling house. This led some to implicit support for Japan's policies in Manchuria after 1931, and then beyond. Sir Reginald Fleming Johnston (1874–1938) was the most notable, and naive, proponent of this trend. A colonial office official in Weihaiwei, he was seconded as English tutor to the former emperor Puyi in 1919, and held the post for five years. Johnston never disentangled himself from the Manchu court, toyed with involvement in Chinese politics after returning to Weihaiwei as commissioner, and as Professor of Chinese at the School of Oriental Studies in London (1931–37). He published *Twilight in the*

*Forbidden City* in 1934, a panegyric of the imperial world but also an apologia for the puppet Manzhouguo state. Johnston was quite willing to try to persuade the embassy in Britain to use *Twilight* for pro-Japanese 'propaganda purposes', helpfully citing the pages and chapters that he considered best put Japan's side of the argument.[41]

The exoticisation of China was hardly Bland's preserve, and hardly confined to historical writing. Fiction and reportage made great play of the exotic. The 'Peking' that developed in the British imagination in the 1930s – and which attracted literary pilgrims and sojourners – was that of Backhouse's 'Décadence Mandchoue', Johnston's *Twilight* and Victor Segalen's *René Leys* (1922): exotic, erotic and aristocratic.[42] Most of these works were elegiac and rooted in a Beijing largely of the authors' own imagination and selective experience. Exoticism could go further, into the homosexual pornography of Backhouse's 'memoirs', or the softer, more picturesque Kai Lung novels of Ernest Bramah, and those of Maurice De Kobra or Charles Pettit, which exploited exotic, and erotic, Chinese imagery and scenes. Chinese settings, like other foreign settings, were often merely a suitably distanced setting for erotica.[43]

Bland was a contradictory figure. As a hard-line activist and agitator he argued for the need to look closely and without illusion at Chinese realities. As a collaborator in the exoticisation of China he helped reinforce an unreal vision of the country, one which made it difficult for many observers to take the country seriously. Such contradiction points to the confusion which lay at the heart of the business of communicating China.

## B. L. Putnam Weale,
## Indiscreet Letters from Peking *(1907)*

A carping corrective to such exoticisation was provided by the works of Bertram Lenox Simpson (1877–1930). Born in China, he joined his father's service, the Imperial Maritime Customs, in 1896, but seems to have left it in 1901 under a cloud (possibly connected with zealous looting in the aftermath of the siege of the legations in Beijing). Simpson was the consummate treaty port jobbing hack, writing commentaries, begging for newspaper work, penning novels, a discourse on the *Conflict of Colour* (1910), the 'memoir' *Indiscreet Letters from Peking* (1907), and serving as *Daily Telegraph* correspondent in Beijing from 1911 to 1914. He worked thereafter in Chinese government or warlord employ. Again, Simpson was also an active figure in treaty port life: for example, in 1927 he worked to counter press attacks on the SMC.[44] He was murdered in 1930 after seizing control of the Tianjin customs for warlord Yan Xishan during the revolt of the Northern Coalition against Chiang Kai-shek. Always regarded as a somewhat louche figure, his last actions surprised few.[45] Simpson wrote to earn a living, like many of his fellow treaty port experts, and his correspondence with his publisher, Macmillan, shows him puffing up his expertise and the importance of sources included in his commentaries.[46] Years of talking himself up paid off, and Simpson achieved the status of a man who knew about China.

*Indiscreet Letters* is no straightforward memoir but a stylised account of the siege of the legations during the Boxer rising of 1900, and a caustic attack on the traditional treaty port target: the supine British diplomatic leadership. It conveys the voice of the imperialist, a man of action on the spot fighting for what is right, and betrayed by diplomacy. The threats are not just Chinese but also the competing imperial powers, especially Germany and Russia, and in his numerous later commentaries – often in fact 'pro-Chinese' by treaty port standards – the enemy is Russian, and latterly Japanese, imperialism. And the threat is to Britain. The tone of *Indiscreet Letters* is of imperial adventure, and the achievement of great things. This rugged individualism was a characteristic virtue incorporated into the self-image of Britain in China.

In memoir, fiction and popular memory the Boxer rising served as Britain in China's equivalent of the Indian 'mutiny', and thereby almost as a rite of imperial passage – although it also prompted one of the great attacks on British actions in China: G. Lowes Dickinson's *Letters from John Chinaman* (1901). Dozens of memoirs and commentaries were published in its aftermath, and the events were swiftly fictionalised in adult and children's fictions such as G. A. Henty's *With the Allies to Peking* (1900). Popular novelists and the popular voice also recast later events – the 1927 Nanjing Incident, for example – in the shadow of the Boxer.[47] The Boxers came to represent the 'Yellow Peril' (this was a fluid category, of course, later filled by Japan, and by the Red Guards).[48] Britain in China achieved imperial respectability through the Boxer rising – indeed, felt itself incorporated into the empire as a result. At the same time, as James Hevia has shown, missionary martyrdom in China can also be seen as having incorporated China into Christendom.[49] Other fictions depicted, in epic and propagandistic form, the development of the foreign presence in China, in sagas of company histories from the Opium Wars to the 1920s, or else covered its 'daily round'.[50] Such fiction complemented the more straightforward propaganda histories, or commentaries, and Simpson was not alone in fudging the boundaries between genres.

Simpson's first formal fiction – *The Forbidden Boundary* (1908) –

was derivative of W. Carleton Dawe, who wrote, in a sub-Conradian fashion, about sex between white men and Asian women. Simpson's novels dealt with a variety of political topics, such as missions and financial imperialism,[51] but always with the position and attitudes of the foreigner in China. His was topically opportunistic fictional discourse (he published none between 1920 and 1927, when the vogue for books on China prompted a resumption) which complemented his commentaries, often allowing him freedom to make harsher judgements on his contemporaries than might otherwise have been possible.[52] These novels relied on their romantic interest and their appearance as *romans à clef*. The preface to *Wang the Ninth* (1920) declared that it had the 'quality of being true and should therefore be known'.[53] Two novels contrived to describe the setting and working out of the 1911 revolution, whilst a later trilogy followed the career of a Chinese peasant from Boxer era infancy to a successful career as a warlord.[54] This was history in digestible form, and Simpson's sympathies (though slowly eroded by the end of the 1920s) meant that, although his portrayal of the working of imperialism in China was positive, his comments on foreign behaviour were different. Simpson is the earliest source yet dated for a story that did irreparable damage to the reputation of the Shanghai Municipal Council and to Britain in China. In a 1914 novel one of his characters notes that:

> There has just been a fierce controversy in the newspapers ... over the notices put up in the public gardens here. Some fool in the municipality had signboards painted with – 'Dogs and Chinese Not Admitted'. Rather rough I call it. If I were one of them I should kill some foreign devil just to equalise matters.[55]

Simpson's ambivalence about imperialism stemmed partly from his settler loyalties but also from the ambivalence of a journalist, of a man who knew a good story and how to tell one. Other journalists wrote more bluntly, with more passion and distaste for the treaty port world.

## *Arthur Ransome,* The Chinese Puzzle *(1927)*

The only successful alternative discourse before the 1930s that reached beyond its receptive constituency was one which attacked the treaty port world in the aftermath of May Thirtieth and during the high tide of the Nationalist revolution (1925–27). The treaty port British took a battering in the foreign press. The story of the Shanghai park sign was one big headache, Arthur Ransome was another. Sent to China as special correspondent for the *Manchester Guardian* in 1926–27, he took badly against what he saw. Somerset Maugham poked fun unkindly at the sad loneliness and insularity of British life in China and noted that Britons had left their manners at home; Ransome launched a pithy attack on the 'Ulster of the East', whose inhabitants were possessed of the 'Shanghai Mind'. Their thinking was anachronistic, thoughtlessly imperialistic and bellicose. 'Nothing,' he pointed out, 'could be further from the truth than to imagine that the Englishmen in Shanghai represent an English outlook or share the English point of view ... their primary allegiance is to Shanghai'.[56]

Ransome's was not the only hostile public voice. 'It is high time that the six thousand odd British in Shanghai faced the situation like the British gentlemen they claim to be,' announced Bertrand Russell and Dora Black, for instance, but Ransome did most damage.[57] His work was well timed: the Nationalist revolution was at its peak, the Shanghai settlements were on the defensive and the 20,000 British troops of the Shanghai Defence Force were the focus of world-wide media and public attention. The emergency in 1926–27 prompted a number of metropolitan newspapers to send out special correspondents, thereby breaking – temporarily – the grip of Gilbert, Bland, Simpson, Green and co. on news reporting.

Britain in China had to contend with two kinds of foreign attack: popular reportage which portrayed Shanghai life in particular as immoral, and political attacks which lambasted the treaty port British as parasitic and cruel exploiters of Chinese labour and as violent defenders of their privileges. Sleaze could be laughed off, or even incorporated into the city's guidebooks as a tourist asset.[58] Maugham could be dismissed as an ungrateful guest, or threatened with legal action (as he was by Hong Kong officials for his novel *The Painted Veil* (1925)[59]). But there was no quarrelling with the actual facts of Ransome's analysis. By 1927 the SMC's image in the world press was hardly positive: it practised racially discriminatory policies affecting its parks – international publicity about the issue had been snowballing since Simpson's comments in 1914 – and municipal employment; it had failed to implement measures to counter widely publicised abuse of child labour and it ineptly countered unarmed demonstrations with excessive armed force. Shanghailander ratepayers made things worse: they voted against the child labour by-laws, and in 1927 postponed measures to open the parks and council membership to Chinese.[60]

There was also insecurity in the discourse of the treaty port experts. After the onslaught they faced in China itself, and in the foreign press after 1925, their works achieved a bellicosity that was unusual, but they also acted to recruit more responsible and neutral voices in their support. Although, as we shall see, their writings served to incorporate Britain in China into the imperial epic, they felt imperial voices failed

**Figure 3** 'I believe in Shanghai'. From a real estate brochure issued by the Asia Realty Company in 1928

to stand by them and attempted to recruit more heavyweight voices in support. Two moves in particular underline this. The first was the recruitment by a loose consortium of London-based companies of Sir Frederick Whyte, former MP for Perth City (1910–18) and President of the Indian Legislative Assembly (1920–25), as an emissary and go-between to liaise between Britain in China and the Guomindang. Whyte's 1927 *China and Foreign Powers* was an acute survey of Sino-British relations. So successful an intermediary was he that he was recruited as a political adviser to the National government. Meanwhile an alternative China-based lobby, more closely allied with the SMC, managed to co-opt the interest of Lionel Curtis, 'the prophet of Commonwealth', in 1929. Curtis took up the Shanghai cause in particular, was active through the Royal Institute of International Affairs, and published a rather wayward volume, *The Capital Question of China* (1931). He also engineered the appointment of a senior South African judge, Justice Richard Feetham, to write a report to the SMC on its situation and future. On two levels these moves came to nothing. Whyte eloped with a Belgian baroness in 1930, the scandal neutralising any progress he was making. Feetham seems to have been corrupted by the cosiness of a Shanghai appointment. His *Report* (1931) was a damp squib, obscurely written and inconclusive; no amount of puffing by O. M. Green in *The Times* could pretend otherwise. The imperial voices failed to produce the goods for the treaty port experts.[61]

The treaty port experts, for all their lapses into insecurity, believed they had an impact on British policy; they certainly aimed to, and their writings were often interpreted by the Chinese as being officially inspired. But there is little evidence that treaty port lobbying had much influence when it strayed from issues concerning the treaty port *status quo*. The demand for a Yangzi protectorate in 1898–99 came to naught.[62] Instead the works of the China experts were aimed at populist audiences, at the British community in China, of which they were a part, at new recruits to their community to introduce them to treaty port thinking, and at those in the community of China-interests at home. Implicitly, and after 1925 especially, explicitly, these lobbyists attempted to communicate directly with public opinion in Britain and thereby, as they saw it, outmanoeuvre the diplomats. The lobbyists both informed and represented the mentality of the treaty port foreigners, and worked to protect treaty port interests. There were, of course, exceptions, but it is clear that more people read Rodney Gilbert than the sinophile alternatives.

## *F. L. Hawks Pott,* A Short History of Shanghai *(1928)*

Treaty port insecurity was not on view in the histories written of Britain in China. There were two types of work that our treaty port recruit might have been guided towards: popular monographs on Sino-Western relations, or the lighter-written history of the treaty ports themselves. The former category would usually recount a saga of 'British energy and enterprise' opening up the Far East to 'Anglo-Saxon ideals of freedom and the square deal'.[63] There was usually little about the opium trade, but much on other commerce and on Chinese isola-tionist arrogance. It was a tale of empire: if not formally included in the British empire, the treaty port communities at least looked and acted as if they were, feeling vital to its defence, specifically of India.

The latter category would certainly include a history of Shanghai, the community the majority of Britons actually joined.[64] Self-conscious pride led the International Settlement to celebrate its fiftieth anniver-sary with a triumphant jubilee celebration in November 1893; proces-sions, parades and fireworks marked the event, and hymns to the city's cosmopolitanism were sung.[65] The council decided in 1906 to com-mission the writing of its own history. During its slow gestation George Lanning's volume became a *History of Shanghai* (volume I, 1921), and thereby appropriated the pre-treaty history of the area, and the non-settlement part of the city, into the tale, which was barely taken into the 1860s. The second volume was printed but suppressed by the SMC as too tediously written, but also politically too dated for publication to be sanctioned. They held to this view despite the pub-lisher accidentally printing fifteen times too many copies. These sat in a warehouse for five years and were then pulped.[66] Settler pride had its limits. Instead, F. L. Hawks Pott, President of St John's University in Shanghai, penned his *Short History*.

Pott's book appeared at a moment of some change, and his epilogue acknowledges that 'co-operation and friendship between foreigners and Chinese' are the key to the future. Still, his tale is one not only of the development of the city of Shanghai but also of the 'growth and devel-opment of the International Settlement', and of the foreign enterprise in the city. As in other accounts there is a core belief in the unilateral achievements of 'the men from the West who built Asia's greatest city' – Shanghai – out of barren mud flats, and by implication were respon-sible for the thriving modern commerce and industrial production of Hankou and Tianjin and other centres.[67] There was usually little inter-est in the romance of the great trading companies, but great attention was paid to men of empire and warfare such as Sir Robert Hart, Sir Harry Parkes and General Gordon. The burghers of Shanghai and Tianjin built statues of them and named streets and communal buildings after them.[68] In this manner the communities asserted their membership of the British empire and their aspiration to be perceived as contributing to that wider imperial mission and community. Following from this was the interest shown in the history of the military entanglements and conflicts between the British and the Chinese and, of course, the Boxer rising and its suppression. Shanghai had its battle of the Muddy Flat (1854), when a hastily organised Volunteer corps joined British troops in attacking Chinese soldiers whose activities during the rebel Small Sword Society's occupation of the Chinese walled city threatened the settlement's security. One foreign civilian Volunteer died in this battle, which was taken as the founding date of the Shanghai Volunteer Corps (SVC), and the founding victory of the International Settlement. The emphasis on military history was boosted by accounts of the activities of Gordon and the anti-Taiping 'Ever Victorious Army'. These recurrent themes argued for communal self-protection (and helped to popularise the importance of the SVC, and to draw in recruits) and the idea that China deserved the odd bloody nose to make it see sense: 'We've always Traded at the point of the Bayonet, and we shall have to go on doing it, or clear out altogether. These people require to be taught a lesson about every ten years!' was a blunt but typical statement from a Jardine's employee in 1927.[69]

Pott's is also a tale of the civilising activities of Britain in China. The history of Shanghai – Britain in China's 'model settlement' – is certainly a history of war and trade, but it is also the history of settler initiatives, of educational and cultural activities and organisations, of the colleges and schools, the library, the North China branch of the Royal Asiatic Society, the municipal band and orchestra, and public gardens, especially the Bund-side park established on land reclaimed from the Huangpu river. Foreign Shanghai's opponents painted them as philistine reactionaries, but the settler response was to outline their record of charity and cultural activity. History was important because the imagining of community required affirmation through founding myth and the subsequent narratives of growth and development.[70] If Britain in China had a history, that justified its present, and naturally underwrote its future, for Britons in China therefore had 'birthrights'.[71] Shanghai from at least as early as 1859 was imagined as the 'model settlement'. History served to inform new recruits of the birthright they had acquired, and their status as model settlers.

# H. G. W. Woodhead, ed.,
## The China Year Book (1912–39)

Treaty port hegemony extended to the standard reference works. Any search for basic information about China in the standard sources would lead readers straight back to the treaty ports themselves. The basic reference journal was the annual *China Year Book* (1912–39), edited for most of its editions by H. G. W. Woodhead. It published documents relating to the year's events in China, providing information on the country for the treaty port man. Woodhead edited the *Peking and Tientsin Times* from 1914 to 1930 before moving to Shanghai to write for the *Shanghai Evening Post and Mercury* and later edit his own journal, *Oriental Affairs*. 'Admitted one of the ablest [foreign] writers in China', noted the US consul-general on his move to Shanghai, his appointment was 'received with bitterness by the Chinese press'.[72] Woodhead's trenchant defence of the treaty port *status quo* in his newspaper and journal columns was matched by his activism in public life, notably his role in the founding of the Shanghai British Residents' Association. This body was formed in 1931 to resist changes in British diplomatic policy as they affected Britain in China, notably the threat to end extraterritoriality.[73]

There was no core of China experts in Britain, or organised collection of information, and the treaty port propagandists filled the gap. Processes of mapping and ordering, such as those instigated by the government of India, were not copied in China, although, as we shall see, much of Britain in China was pastiche Raj.[74] China was after all a sovereign independent state. There was no systematic British attempt to map, to describe or to order China in the manner derived from Victorian concerns with taxonomy and government. Certainly, Britons and others catalogued China's plants, or junks, or Shanghai's country walks.[75] The Royal Navy's China station mapped the coast, literally, and military intelligence attempted to keep abreast of events and personalities. The China consular service was reasonably well informed, and an efficient information-gathering machine, but most of this we know only from the archives, apart from trade reports issued through the Board of Trade. Knowledge, and the translation of information from the Chinese, was organised privately, through the Royal Asiatic Society in Shanghai, for example. There were also the networks of missionary and other correspondents who supplied provincial information to the *North China Daily News*. The British press also usually relied on its Chinese counterpart for information about Chinese affairs. British firms of all sorts relied on their compradores to tap into business information networks, which was one of the key points of having compradores in the first place. Academic provision for Asian studies was woeful, and concerned with China's distant and exotic past rather than its present; only during the Pacific War was an established leading Chinese national appointed to a senior academic post in a British university for the first time, ending the long traditional run of former consuls, missionaries and customs men.[76] The Chinese Maritime Customs (notably its Statistical Department) enumerated and analysed China's foreign trade and related issues, and current or former customs men were prominent among the treaty port experts (Bland, Simpson).[77] But the British never even remotely set out to create a cadre of China experts along the lines of the 3,652 graduates of the Japanese Toa Dobun Shoin (East Asia Common Culture Academy) in Shanghai (1901–43). The students trained at this specialist college went into all fields – commercial and official – and comprised an invaluable source of expertise for Japan, not least because their training included in part the collection of material in the field.[78] For the British, the cult of the amateur, and the practice of learning on the job, prevailed. After all, China was far from being a British priority. Up to a point Britons in China were as informed as they felt they needed to be to continue functioning. But the experts' roles were filled by the publicists, apologists and activists of Britain in China who justified Britain in China, and demonstrated their own utility by representing themselves as the sole commentators on China to the West. Having hustled to get their jobs and acquire prestige, having come to China as medicine sellers or lowly customs clerks, they jockeyed to protect their jobs and the treaty port structure which facilitated their employment in China.

What Smith, Gilbert, Bland, Simpson and Woodhead demonstrated was that the essential elements of the Chinese character, essential in dealing with China, could be described and ordered. Less obviously the case with Smith than with the others was the logical corollary: only they could view the country and the people objectively. Missionaries had their own agenda, while academics' 'Vocational enthusiasm [was] apt to outweigh the teachings of direct experience and to produce results of a nature to mislead the uninitiated', according to Bland, one of the initiated.[79] The obvious contradiction was that it was on Chinese themselves that most Britons in most fields actually relied for information, in trade, or in evangelical mission work. This was met by the routine claim that they were hopelessly ensnared in corruption, or allegiance to party, or faction, or deracinated by Western education. Simpson argued in his first book that knowledge of the Chinese language and Chinese history was vital for those who wrote on China. He laid stress on 'modes of thought', but most of all on 'the "atmosphere" of the country', for in China '"atmosphere" is of the utmost importance'.[80] And of course atmosphere could be grasped even, but implicitly especially, by those with no Chinese language skills. One of Simpson's obituarists described his novels as 'almost unrivalled in respect to Chinese "atmosphere"'.[81]

Treaty port writers wrote with prescriptive intent. By demonstrating that Chinese could be described, they provided a tool for treaty port Britons who, if they learned well from the experts, could quickly become capable of handling Chinese. Also running through all the analyses of the experts was the idea that, by identifying what was Chinese, they identified what was British, and what was acceptably British in the treaty port world. They taught Britons how to behave, and fostered a sense of community rooted in the treaty ports and attacked by Bolsheviks, Chinese, British diplomats and indirectly by the well meaning 'idiocies' of the missionary enterprise.

Perhaps, having run through a bit of Putnam Weale, Bland and Woodhead, our figurative traveller to China might seek relief from this humourless bellicosity with a little light reading. The traveller might select a thriller, some middlebrow reading, or a light romance, possibly a text recommended, or equally possibly an ordinary text encountered in any library or bookstore. Sometimes the choice might be deliberate, a work chosen from a list of suggested readings, but others might have been hit on by accident, the choice indicating the place of China in the British popular imagination.

## Sax Rohmer, The Mystery of Dr Fu Manchu (1913)

No circulating library could afford not to stock books by Sax Rohmer (Arthur Henry Sarsfield Ward, 1883–1959) – and a ship's library might well follow suit.[82] Chinese themes always had their place in collections of mysteries and thriller novels, but Rohmer's were by far the most successful. Rohmer was a hack writer whose inspiration was purely opportunistic: 'Conditions for launching a Chinese villain on the market,' he is reputed to have said, 'were ideal.'[83] The first Fu Manchu story was serialised in the wake of the Xinhai revolution in 1912-13 and launched a villain with all the:

> cruel cunning of the entire Eastern race, accumulated in one giant intellect, with all the resources of a wealthy government – which, however, already has denied all knowledge of his existence ... Dr Fu Manchu, the yellow peril incarnate in one man.[84]

The caricature was hardly new; Guy Boothby employed it to successful effect in Dr Nikola (1896), but Rohmer crystallised it, and some twenty Fu Manchu books appeared during the next five decades, their popularity exploited and reinforced by film adaptations and by the copyists of the 1930s.[85] Most of the stories were set in London's Limehouse district, long the subject of Victorian literary interest, whose increased post-World War I notoriety Rohmer took advantage of – and thereby further boosted – to write works in which drug smuggling, 'white slavery' and opium dens played a major role. His fiction intentionally had the appearance of reportage, while his savvy marketing of things Chinese further extended to music hall songs, and even to the creation of a perfume, called 'Honan', manufactured by a Chinese work force in Limehouse, and launched with opium-redolent packaging and publicity in 1919.[86] Rohmer's timely opportunism mirrored that of another 'Yellow Peril' pioneer, M. P. Shiel. Asked to 'do a war serial' when 'some trouble broke out in China' in 1898, he wrote what became *The Yellow Danger* (1898), a tale of a Chinese invasion of Europe.[87] Such apocalyptic fictions were a familiar and continuing genre, their rooted insecurity also related to pre-World War I invasion stories about Germany. Yellow Peril fears also lay in the sense that European colonialism might one day have a price to pay, and start paying it in Asia. The Japanese victory over China in 1894–95, and more dramatically over Russia in the war of 1904–05, shocked Western assumptions to the core. The Boxer rising located these fears squarely on the Chinese, on the perceived mass 'fanaticism' of the ordinary people, and on the alleged 'treacherous duplicity' of China's leaders.[88]

Different Chinese and a different Limehouse, more realistic, sentimental and interracial, was a major source of inspiration for Thomas Burke's hugely successful works. These books, some nine in all, beginning with the best-selling *Limehouse Nights* in 1917, were not thrillers but dealt in a 'realist' fashion with much the same drug-filled settings as Rohmer's, and were also seized upon as film material. 'The Chink and the Child' was filmed as *Broken Blossoms* in 1919 and 1936, and *Twinkletoes* in 1927. Burke's Chinese were invariably more human than Rohmer's, were usually poor and usually sexually attracted to 'white' women. Most writings inspired by the Fu Manchu vogue, however, were thrillers. Edgar Wallace, one of the best-selling popular authors of his day, devoted a tiny but telling proportion of his immense output to Chinese themes: the sadistic cruelty and sexual salaciousness which infused *The Tomb of Ts'in* (1916) were characteristic.[89] In pulp thrillers Chinese were represented with notable frequency. Motives and meanings varied, verisimilitude was sometimes sought, sensation more usually targeted. Other nationalities or communities were represented as well: Huns, Irish and Jews, to take but three letters of the alphabet, formed significant portions of the British diet of stereotypes and villains. Most of these writers were concerned with writing saleable books, and Chinese themes, or Chinese variations on well known themes, were recognised sellers. The use of 'local colour' by Rohmer, Burke and 'Eastern' novelists was praised by creative writing guides, and welcomed by the circulating libraries.[90]

Other contemporary thriller writers successfully exploited and extended this genre; often loading their works with explicitly political messages, and often relocating the Limehouse or Fu Manchu genre to China itself, or parts of the British empire with Chinese populations (Malaya or Borneo). Even novelists who claimed direct experience of China, and interwove fact into their narratives, took on board the Yellow Peril theme in its Limehouse guise: it sold. In this manner, having described Limehouse, Rohmer also described China, and Chinese wherever they were.[91]

Rohmer's own theatrical activities were unsuccessful, but 'crook' plays were a popular early twentieth-century genre, and Chinese villains became something of a cliché on the professional, provincial and amateur stage.[92] In early 1928 London theatregoers had the choice of five different plays featuring Chinese villains on in the West End at the same time, which was somewhat excessive and led the charge d'affaires of the Chinese Legation to make an official complaint.[93] The crucial figure here was the role created by Matheson Lang in 1913: Mr Wu. The instant success of *Mr Wu* (403 performances from 1913, and 114 in 1922) provided the model villain, despite being conceived originally as a realistic antidote to 'the usual stage Chinaman', because it portrayed a Western-dressed and educated Hong Kong Chinese. Like many novelists, the authors were at pains to point out the truthfulness of their portrayal, with asides in the script justifying their portrayal of Wu's actions.[94] *Mr Wu* relied on two aspects of the villain's character that were shared with Rohmer: ingenious cruelty, and control of a powerful organisation. Matheson Lang reprised his role in films of *Mr Wu* (1919), and reformulated it in *The Chinese Bungalow* (1926, 1930). The film was remade in 1927 in the United States and a BBC radio version was broadcast in 1928.[95] This play, like many similar ones, would also have toured the British provinces, and may also have been performed by amateurs.

The prevalence of the Chinese villain gave rise to equally prevalent complaints. Missionary texts satirised the 'the slander of the silent-gliding, inscrutable villain, or the idealisation of romance and oriental splendour'.[96] Another contemporary critic charged Sax Rohmer with spreading 'race-suspicion and contempt' and was equally critical of the sentimentality and lack of realism in Louise Jordan Miln's 'China'.[97] There were Chinese protests against *Mr Wu* before it was performed because:

the plot is unchinese and we were afraid that this attempt to foist it upon the British public as a specimen of modern Chinese civilization might engender prejudices unfavourable to the Chinese in their midst.

Chinese students who were asked to assist the production refused when changes they asked for were rejected, and attempts to have the Lord Chamberlain ban the play were rebuffed.[98] The Chinese Legation's complaint in March 1928 was also dismissed. The British would have been quite happy to comply if there were 'objectionable political references' (in 1933 they abetted the withdrawal of one commentary from publication because of hostile references to Chiang Kai-shek) but in such cultural matters there was nothing they were prepared to do.[99] These were not isolated cases of protest. In fact after 1928 they became more frequent as the diplomatic relationship between Britain and China changed and an increasing tendency to accept the need for sensitivity in such matters gained ground. Most famously, in China, the novelist Lao She (pen name of Shu Qingchun or Sumuru (1899–1966)) who lived in England from 1924 to 1929, wrote a London-based novel, *Er Ma* (The Two Mas, or Ma and Son) (1929), which satirised the cultural sinophobia of the Limehouse genre.[100]

Fiction was a source of revenge, too. J. W. Bennett and A. H. Mills's fictional heroes wreaked imaginary revenge on Chinese nationalists and their alleged co-conspirators, Bolsheviks and Eurasians. In the adventure novels Chinese master criminals, bandits, pirates and communists were always defeated. In reality, of course, Chinese nationalism triumphed and the European powers retreated: but the Chinese remained the villains in this tale.

## W. Somerset Maugham, East of Suez (1922)

Britons viewed China from a distance; not least, as chapter 3 will show, when they were actually there. For treaty port residents China was a spectacle they viewed from the safety of their settlements, through newspapers, newsreels and reportage. For Britons at home it was a spectacle they might view on the stage, at the theatre, the opera, or the ballet, or else might seek in the streets of east London or at exhibitions.

Spectacle had a long history on the British stage, and 'oriental' spectacles blended in smoothly. Traditional Chinese customs, language, clothing and scenery were viewed as picturesque, as the Lord Chancellor's Department noted in 1928 when rejecting the Chinese Legation's complaints about stage portrayals.[101] When Somerset Maugham deliberately decided to write a spectacle he did so with *East of Suez* (1922), which had an opening, dialogue-free scene representing the hustle and bustle of a Beijing street. Forty Chinese actors played stall-keepers, and rickshaw men, while a 'Chinese' orchestra played the accompanying 'oriental' music.[102] China, as the title points out, is not the point of the play; Maugham's Orient starts much closer to home. Nevertheless Maugham drew his 'oriental' imagination from his China visit of 1919-20.

Oriental spectacle on stage could be much hollower, and grew out of a popular tradition that included Gilbert and Sullivan's *The Mikado* (1885) and Hall's *The Geisha* (1896).[103] Oscar Asche's *Chu Chin Chow* was the record-breaking musical of its time. First performed in 1916, and running a record 2,238 performances, this piece of affable nonsense was actually an Arabian Nights tale of robbers in Chinese disguises set in a mythical Baghdad. Its success was heightened by two film adaptations.[104] The genre was a perennial favourite.[105] Such operas as Puccini's *Turandot* (1926), which had its first performance in London in 1927, and ballets such as Bartok's *The Miraculous Mandarin* (1926) also owed something to Rohmeresque stereotypes. For related reasons, there were attempts to bring Chinese drama itself to the London stage, or drama by Chinese, or using Chinese conventions; such plays included *The Yellow Jacket* (1922), *The Circle of Chalk* (1929 and 1931) and S. I. Hsiung's *Lady Precious Stream* (1934). Their successes were, in part, due to the scope for spectacle and the exotic involved in the stagings, costumes, customs and stories.[106] By rendering China as a spectacle so relentlessly – and press coverage of the country's affairs as much as *East of Suez* did just that – Britons were distanced from it in reality as much as in the imagination.

*East of Suez* (1922) also taught distance of another kind. Maugham's middlebrow imagination decked out a conventional plot – a decent man marries a woman who, though he is ignorant of the fact, was once the lover of his best friend; the lovers' relationship is then rekindled. This plot was 'oriented', however, and a play which in a domestic setting would concern questions of class became a study of race: the woman is a Eurasian. The husband is socially ostracised for the marriage, and his wife plots his death to ease her illicit relationship, but events unravel, and as her lover shoots himself 'China takes back its own'. The Eurasian abandons Western clothing and makes herself up to emphasise her Chinese ancestry. The didacticism – about duty, race, distance – is intentional, and was read as such at the time.[107] Maugham ran through other familiar clichés, and in *The Letter* (1927, for 338 performances; filmed in 1929) the leading Chinese character was a Western-educated blackmailer.

Maugham produced works in various keys stemming from his China visit of 1919-20, but he was not an artist who restricted his use of a trick to one genre, and *On a Chinese Screen* (1922), a collection of

fifty-eight prose sketches and stories, began with an exact prose equivalent of the first scene of *East of Suez*. Set at the gate of a Chinese city,
it also evokes China as spectacle. A later sketch of an 'opium den'
notes that 'On the stage it makes a very effective set' but then recounts
its dull ordinariness. The volume is rather evenly composed of a largely
unsympathetic portrayal of treaty port life and residents, who are
nonetheless portrayed as distinct individuals, and visions of China and
Chinese, the massed indistinct humanity of coolies, or peasants, and
'types' such as scholars. There is a lurid feel to the book, which has all
the power of what Orwell labelled good 'bad' writing,[108] but there are
also home truths about Britain in China on many of its pages: the sex
taboos discreetly breached in the observance, the maintenance of class
and caste, *arriviste* self-importance, and above all hatred of Chinese,
and of being in China.

Apart from the works of Pearl Buck, Maugham's novel *The Painted
Veil* (1925), André Malraux's *Storm over Shanghai* (*La condition
humaine*) (1934), Malcom Lowry's *Ultramarine* (1933) and Denton
Welch's *Maiden Voyage* (1943) are possibly the only works of China
fiction still well known today. In Maugham and Lowry, however,
China was a background of little importance to the themes of the book,
although both visited the Far East in search of material, or found it
there. André Malraux's fiction dealt sympathetically with the Chinese
communists and unfavourably with the treaty port communities.[109]
Malraux apart, the dismissiveness with which these writers treated
Chinese characters was in itself telling. China never was the location
for serious fiction, perhaps because the dominant popular fictional dis-
courses made it impossible to take the country seriously as a setting;
there is no equivalent of E. M. Forster's *A Passage to India* or Doris
Lessing's *Martha Quest*. Moreover, as chapter 3 will show, Britain in
China was not staffed by first-rate Britons, let alone the second-rate –
and the same went for its writers; perhaps it got the fiction it deserved.

## Louise Jordan Miln, Mr Wu *(1918)*

Interracial sex, and the fact that it was taboo in the treaty ports, was a
key ingredient of much fiction on Chinese themes. Sometimes the
intention was merely the salacious or sensationalist exploitation of
taboo, in other books it was incidental, an essential piece of background colour to books on foreigners and China. In the works of Louise
Jordan Miln (1864–1933), it was the vehicle for an unforgiving, didactic prescription for distance, and difference.

Hailed after her death as Pearl Buck's 'nearest literary parallel', Miln
specialised in tales of the wealthy and aristocratic in China.[110] Her suc-

cess began her novelisation in 1918 of the play *Mr Wu*; for all her empathetic writing and criticisms of individual Western behaviour, Wu was a caricatured Chinese sadist who also owed much to the then fashionably formulaic 'Eastern' novels, with their rape-inclined Arab sheiks.[111] Sino-British romantic and sexual incompatibility and a horror of Eurasian children were themes which dominated her seventeen novels. 'Not every White and Yellow marriage is a failure,' notes the opening sentence of *By Soochow Waters* (1929), but the book set out to prove otherwise, as did her other writings on 'an adamant prejudice that was also a wholesome common sense'.[112] The stress on the taboo was so common that it became a clichéd ingredient of the tragic novel of treaty port life. The middle-class man became undone or might go astray unless he caved in to peer pressure and kept his distance, while of lower-class men nothing more could be expected than that they should make functional sexual compromises.

Miln wrote with an eye to the market (including her own Limehouse book, *Red Lily and Chinese Jade* (1928)), to popular theories on race and to a readership receptive to her romantic tragedy. But she also wrote as a sympathetic novelist of the politics and history of treaty port China. Her fictional account of the events of 1927 brought out the Raj motif: 'there were Englishmen in Shanghai who thought of Lucknow ... and where was our Residency here?'[113] She had many copyists, such as Mrs P. Connellan who set *Ten Thousand Yesterdays* (1932) among anti-Manchu intrigues in the early years of the century; it was a familiar story of failed inter-ethnic marriage and the undesirability of Eurasian children.[114] For other romantic writers China was a convenient exotic backdrop, one known from personal experience, or one which offered a little geographical variety after the fashionable and salacious 'desert' novels. Joan Conquest's *Forbidden* (1927) offered a blatantly pornographic exploration of the theme by a one-time Beijing resident.[115] Floridly speaking Chinese characters and gushing enthusiasm for the splendours and mysteries of Asia characterise most of these books, except those written for missionary purposes.

One of the strengths of popular literature lies in its ability to confirm widely held attitudes whilst imaginatively flouting them, the most obvious case being the consistent denigration of sexual and marital relations between Britons and Chinese whilst sensationally representing them.[116] Here China – as India – was feminised, and portrayed as a temptation, bluntly sexual most of the time (though as we shall see Chinese women were not perceived as being sexually attractive until at least the 1930s). Rarely was China directly portrayed as an arena which facilitated the moral corruption of Britons; John Lambourne's 1935 novel *Squeeze: A Tale of China*, an account of the temptation and decline of a young businessman, was an exception. The lesson, practical and metaphorical, was about the maintenance of distance.[117]

## Wembley

Distance was in a sense subverted by the superficial familiarity of China to the British, who grew up at the turn of the century, and grow up still, with China as an integral part of their imaginative world – what Harold Isaacs labelled the 'familiarity of Chinese strangeness'.[118] It was also already concretely present in the elite *chinoiserie* left over from the eighteenth century, and in its hand-me-down ceramic and wallpaper designs; and in other items: the Pagoda at Kew Gardens, and other architectural fancies, opium pipes brought back by friends or relations, Nankeen cottons, lacquer ware. The British drank tea, wore silk and ate rhubarb. China was further represented through the vulgar *chinoiserie* of willow-pattern, dragons and topsy-turveydom. Chinoiserie's star rose and fell in the late eighteenth century, but it left its mark on design, while trade with China left its mark on the British diet.[119]

'Chinese' played notable roles in the lore, rhymes and games of schoolchildren, as Iona and Peter Opie demonstrated. They were a 'perennial fascination' for children, forming one of the most consistent 'others' in games, sayings and other playground activities.[120] In one extreme case in 1929 a young shoplifter's legal defence rested on his dual personality and 'peculiarities', which began with 'his liking for Chinese images' but which became an obsession with meeting real Chinese, mostly laundrymen.[121] The appeal rested on 'topsy-turvey-dom', and on Chinese 'cruelty'. Adults too might also play at being Chinese, perhaps before they went to China. Theatrical Chinese villains were popular with audiences and with amateur performers. The amateur dramatic society at the headquarters of the Asiatic Petroleum Company in London produced two such plays in five years, possibly watched, or acted in, by staff members bound for China in the future. The 'characteristics' displayed were widely recognised as well: an actor in *Mr Wu* was congratulated for a 'fine character study, perfect in every detail, of the suave, impassive Chinese magnate' whose 'assumption of a Chinese accent (not that we have any pretensions to expert knowledge of the subject)' was 'exceedingly well done'. In an earlier production of *The Chinese Puzzle* the leading actor 'had no difficulty in creating the requisite Oriental atmosphere and fired off his inexhaustible supply of aphorisms with perfect aplomb'.[122] Adult and infant Britons knew how to be Chinese.

Britons were, on the whole, as ignorant of the reality of China as they were of many other places and topics; and the deficiencies of British education were frequently commented on in this regard.[123] As John M. MacKenzie has shown, even the efforts of the Imperial Institute to educate the British about the empire were never very successful, although the 1924–25 British Empire Exhibition at Wembley provided at least one treaty port resident with his earliest memories of 'China'.[124] There, two years after Somerset Maugham created a Beijing street scene on the London stage, a 'Hong Kong Street' was recreated, with 'the Chinese people living and working in it'. The spectacle could now be walked through. Starting at a 'gate which is perhaps a little more reminiscent of Peking',

> The visitor finds himself really in China. The bewildering, bright signs indicate in Chinese characters, the names of the shopkeepers and the wares for disposal, and the proprietors of the shops, pigtails and all, are smiling at their doors, ready to supplement – in what English they may know – the invitation of these signs.[125]

'Pigtails' (thirteen years after the revolution abolished the queue) and curios, with silks, incense shops and a dealer in 'Human Hair goods', joined sharks' fins and birds' nest soup served by 'genuine 'Chinese boys' in the Chinese restaurant, to the accompaniment of a Chinese orchestra, in a gamble exactly calculated to convey a frisson of the dangerous East, easily reachable in ten minutes from Piccadilly.[126] The street, squeezed between exhibition halls for Ceylon and the West Indies, was constructed in mock Chinese style, with Chinese roofs; some 200 Chinese worked in the exhibit. A 20ft by 15ft scale model of the whole colony served to remind visitors that Hong Kong was itself the nominal subject of the exhibit, and accompanying models of two British-owned dockyards served a similar purpose. But the Wembley exhibition – to which Britons made just over 27 million visits – served to advertise not Hong Kong but the incorporation of Chinese into the British empire.[127]

## Limehouse

Wembley's Hong Kong street was also a deliberately pointed appeal to the popularity of Limehouse. By 1924 the notoriety of the district, thanks to the efforts of Sax Rohmer, Thomas Burke, the popular press and the Metropolitan Police, was at its highest. Britons might not go to Wembley, but many of them visited 'Limehouse' in fiction and the press, and some even visited the district itself, braving the mysterious and dangerous Orient on a day trip to Wapping. Akira Iriye identified

Chinese in America and Americans in China as representative Chinese and representative Americans respectively for the host population in each country: the impact on attitudes to the other's country and inhabitants was strongly influenced by the immigrants.[128] The China-born population of England and Wales was hardly large – 1,100 in 1911, 2,400 in 1921, and 1,900 by 1931 – but it was tremendously 'representative' in Iriye's sense.[129]

There were three distinct groups of Chinese in Britain: students, mission activists and the Chinese communities of Limehouse, Liverpool and scattered concentrations elsewhere. The latter category wrote nothing, but much was written about it by journalists and novelists and it had a presence in the press and in reportage far greater than its numbers justified. This was mostly a transient population of seamen, although a smaller, more permanent presence developed, performing services such as lodgings, catering and provisions, and also slowly offering services to European customers. Laundries and restaurants became the two main occupations. Limehouse was orientalised, and China often seen through constructs of Chinese derived from imaginative re-creations of the tiny district. Three events raised the public profile of the Chinese in Britain: the kidnapping of Sun Yatsen by the Chinese legation in 1896, the 1906 election, fought by the Liberal Party partly, but prominently, on the issue of Chinese labour in South Africa, and the criminalisation of opium during World War I.[130] Other issues which exercised the Home Office were allegations of organised illegal immigration, disputes with British seamen about Chinese labour, and issues of sex between Chinese men and British women.[131] On Home Office instructions, on the night of 31 August 1921, and at 10.00 a.m. on 23 February 1928, police forces nationwide visited all Chinese boarding houses, laundries and homes, with a view to checking immigration status. A similar series of co-ordinated raids in Wales was launched on 4 November 1924. No other immigrant alien community in Britain has been subject to such concerted and co-ordinated police action in peacetime.[132]

Chinese and illegal drugs were undetachable in both the popular and the official mind. Opium use, and allegations of cocaine smuggling, became big issues for the popular press and the Home Office alike after World War I. There was a series of high-profile cases, notably the death of an actress, Billie Carleton, from a drug cocktail in 1919, and the trial and jailing of a Hong Kong Chinese known as 'Brilliant Chang'. Rohmer used the Carleton case, thinly disguised, in *Dope: A Novel of Chinatown and the Drug Trade* (1919). Chang, jailed for possession of cocaine and trafficking in 1924, was reputed, on little evidence, to be (in the words of the *Daily Express*) the 'Yellow King of the Dope Runners' and the man suspected by police of having supplied a dancer, Freda Kempton, with the drugs which had killed her in an equally sensational case in 1922.[133] The threat these Chinese males posed to white women was a relentlessly reiterated theme. Chang was alluded to in fiction and in *Cocaine*, a film made shortly after his arrest – and media attention continued after his release from jail and deportation. In the aftermath of his arrest there was a barrage of press reports into the drug 'scene' in London, and alleged Chinese involvement. Other alleged 'dope kings' with links with West End drug markets were jailed, deported or refused re-entry to the country.[134] The stereotypes used to portray these men were consistent, and the evidence was usually slender, rooted more in Sax Rohmer's Limehouse than east London's. Popular fiction quite obviously informed factual reportage, and certainly infiltrated the language of police and Home Office officials. At the same time it fed off the scandals of the early 1920s. Rohmer's caricature of the Chinese mastermind had a circular relationship with the truth: 'Mr King' in *The Yellow Claw* (1915), followed by Sin Sin Wa in *Dope*, found his 'factual' expression in the constructed figure of Rohmer's 'Mr Big' and then in Brilliant Chang, and was promptly re-fictionalised as Burma Chang in *Yellow Shadows* (1925).[135]

Popular culture rewrote the history of Sino-British relations. Tellingly, the subject of opium, and of poison, surfaced again and again. The issue of opium had dominated British relations with China throughout the nineteenth century, and residual embarrassment about the Opium Wars can easily be found, in school textbooks, and in some histories of Sino-British relations.[136] In the twentieth century British popular culture turned the issue around: Chinese opium smuggling into Britain, and the entrapment of British youth in the process, became the paradigmatic representation of opium. Opium pipes were a favourite present brought or sent back by visitors to Britain to titillate their friends or family with a frisson of the forbidden.[137] The history of Britain in China itself became divorced from the history of British involvement in the opium trade and instead became an epic squarely in the genre of imperial myth-making, a constant struggle against Chinese xenophobia, violence and corruption.

Chinese students were a more activist body than other members of their community in Britain. As well as producing between them a handful of volumes on contemporary China – the works of Tang Liang-li, for example – or of memoirs, there were occasions when they actively lobbied against offensive portrayals of Chinese.[138] Political activism of a limited sort was undertaken during the Nationalist revolution. Chinese resident in Britain were too few to have the impact on British relations with China that communities in the United States did: anti-Chinese pogroms in California especially, and the Chinese exclusion Acts, as Michael Hunt has shown, drew the United States into a closer and closer relationship with China itself. The caveat here is that Limehouse acquired a prominence in British popular culture, in the press, and in the Home Office and police mind, out of all proportion to its size, and influenced British perceptions of Chinese behaviour, and of China.[139] In that sense Chinese in Britain were 'representative' of Chinese and China.

## *Revd C. E. Darwent*, Shanghai: A Handbook for Travellers and Residents *(second edition, 1920)*

Closing in on the Chinese coast, our recruit might leave Limehouse, shelving his novels and starting to read his guidebooks more closely. These were aimed at residents as well as travellers, and C. E. Darwent's handbook to Shanghai was the obvious choice for those travelling there. Darwent was a settler clergyman, minister at the dissenting Union Church for twenty years before moving to Tianjin five years before his death in 1924.[140] Three themes would emerge from his detailed survey and these reinforced many of the issues already discussed. First, there were prescriptions for individual behaviour towards the Chinese; second, China in the flesh was itself a spectacle; third, foreign Shanghai was a civilised community.

'The visitor must see that he is not imposed on,' notes Darwent in the section on 'Jinrickshaws', adding shortly later that the 'passenger ought in his own interest to watch the coolie and in a way assume command of him'. To aid this assumption of command there is a short vocabulary of pidgin English imperatives: stop, go faster, be careful.[141] There is little indication in this book that Chinese will ever be anything but servants and guides. In its account of the activities of the Shanghailander it is clear that the environment, disease threats and military threats had all been mastered, and the Chinese too. The individual's smallest contribution to that process was important; not being imposed upon was vital. After all, the 'price of empire is that the bones of its soldiers and sailors lie on every foreign shore'; the old British cemetery in the French concession contains the graves of the British dead, and 'All British subjects must feel moved when they visit it'.[142] Shanghai demanded allegiance and the honouring of this blood debt.

The text also abounds with interest in the Chinese, their social customs, architecture, activities and wares, or rather with instructions on where to get a good photograph, or view, of Chinese life, business, architecture, or boats, for sketching or painting. For Darwent, as for Maugham, as for visitors to Wembley or charabanc tourists to Lime-

## "Weedy-women"

The sun is shining,
Hurray—hurray!
That means the weeders
Will come today.
They'll sit on the lawn
In a long blue row,
And chatter like monkeys
As hard as they go.
—The gardener says
They dig up the weeds,
But Father is certain
They're after his seeds!

**Figure 4** 'Weedy-women': settler rhymes for children. From Patricia Allan, *Shanghai Picture-verse* (Shanghai, 1939)

house, China was a spectacle: festival days are good for catching the Chinese *en fête* and dressed up; the filling in of Shanghai's Yangjing-bang creek between the French concession and the International Set-tlement was 'ruinous' for those interested in 'picturesqueness'; good curios can be bought in such-and-such a district; Shanghai has a pagoda in the vicinity; this 'characteristic' Chinese architectural feature is actually scarce and the Longhua pagoda ought to be visited.[143]

Darwent's guide served to further emphasise the key theme found in Hawks Pott that Shanghai was a 'civilised community'. 'It is doubtful whether any place in the world has as many books per head to its pop-ulation as Shanghai', boasted the guide (meaning the foreign popula-tion),[144] while attention was drawn to the public gardens and to the municipal orchestra, an icon of Britain in China's integrity as a com-munity.[145] The band playing on summer evenings in the public garden at the end of Shanghai's Bund has often been the subject of florid rem-iniscence; the ceremony of attendance, in 1919 often by over 2,000 res-idents, was symbolic of the wholesomeness of the community, and also its civilised nature. There was more to life in Shanghai, this ritual announced, than making money: theirs was a community which really existed, and in which the full range of human behaviour was present, and appreciated, a community which had an integrity of it own. Shang-hai was not a larger version of the smaller treaty port enclaves, or of Shameen island at Canton, replete with the privations of life in the old traders' Factories.

The handbook sets out to reassure visitors that Shanghai is not dan-gerous, or unhealthy, and that with a little foresight, and the assump-tion of authority over the Chinese they would meet, they might view the city safely, and enjoy the spectacle of China. Like other guides, or sets of instructions, it aimed to introduce Britons to the life they were expected to live. They might view China, and Chinese – but perhaps not often, as the text admits foreign residents rarely venture into Chi-nese suburbs – and they will be assimilating themselves into Britain in China. 'There is a good town club with a fine library and the Race and Recreation Club is said to be the best in the East,' noted some 1928 instructions for consular clerical officers heading for Hankou.[146]

None of this is or should be surprising. Clerical officers might well ask about recreational facilities, about whether they ought to bring a morning coat and top hat, or some prints to decorate their quarters, or extra underclothes (advisable, 'local prices are prohibitive').[147] But guidebooks overlapped with histories, and with commentaries, and served, like them, as prescriptive manuals, not as guides to Shanghai, but as guides to being British in Shanghai, and guides to staying British in Shanghai, in the manner criticised by Ransome, and noted by Miln:

a heightened Britishness which underpinned a new identity. This new identity was a settler identity.

## First impressions: Britons in China

Having read their commentaries, histories, novels and guidebooks, or else having seen China recreated on the stage, having walked through China at Wembley, or in Limehouse, British recruits to the treaty ports set out to China itself, passing through British colonial possessions where they would meet their first Chinese. What happened, then, when fiction met fact? The following chapter will examine the process of socialisation into treaty port society, and the creation of the treaty port man. In this section we look briefly at first impressions. In tandem with public and official concern about the impact of fictional portrayals of the Chinese it is clear that individual behaviour and attitudes were also influenced by the China of the British imagination.

Evidence from letters and diaries shows Britons reading and digesting Rodney Gilbert ('he ... has buttered it on hot and thick; but with it all much nearer the mark than anybody else with his ideas on this uncivilised race of degenerates'[148]), sending the treaty port facts home, and also drawing upon fiction, consciously or otherwise, when articulating their experiences and mentally ordering their new world and their relation to it. A naval officer attended a meal 'which recalled "A Treaty Port Dinner" in Somerset Maugham's ... "On a Chinese Screen"'.[149] A ship's pilot had 'a large moustache ... just like Fu Manchu'. R. V. C. Bodley described meeting in China a Daoist priest with 'a moustache suggestive of Chu Chin Chow'. In 1924 Charles Drage recorded visiting a temple in China, viewing a Buddha and imagining human sacrifice: 'one could easily imagine oneself plunging a knife into some weak, struggling body bound and prone before that remote indifferent figure'. There was more Sax Rohmer here than Gautama. A *Daily Express* correspondent in 1928 wrote on Shanghai with 'hazy ideas of Sax Rohmer's Chinese underworld and opium den life flitting through' his mind. Malcom Lowry boasted imaginatively about being wounded by crossfire in an underworld gun battle in Shanghai in 1927. First impressions lasted, too. Nineteen-year-old Shanghai-born John Thorburn had various schemes of adventure, including fighting pirates with a Q ship at Bias Bay, and joining the Chinese army to fight communists and bandits. He left Shanghai in May 1931 in an attempt at 'adventuring' which went fatally wrong. 'Everyone has heard of the Chinaman's cunning, silence and inscrutability,' mused ex-Shanghai Municipal Police Sergeant E. W. Peters. 'After spending several years in close contact with them, these three brief words seem to me to describe them better than any others'. Peters's repertoire of ignorant clichés prevented empathy and possibly helped create the attitudes which led to his arrest and trial for the gratuitous murder of a Chinese beggar.[150] The connection between the Chinese and poisons – pervasive in fiction – surfaced in reality. The wife of a returning trooper of the Shanghai Defence Force claimed in court that he had brought back poison and tried to administer it to her; a medical orderly in Weihaiwei feared for his life; historian H. B. Morse's wife hated the Chinese, and assured John Fairbank that they would poison him.[151] When naval officer H. C. Simms saw his first pagodas from the Yangzi he wrote that 'it was the first bit of the real China I had seen'.[152] The perceived reality of China was strongly rooted in fictional representations and clichés. China without pagodas was not China.

Analyses of Chinese character were as symptomatic as they were formative. The market for them already existed but characteristics 'observed' tended to be self-fulfillingly prophetic; Britons saw in the Chinese what they expected to see. They used the vocabulary supplied to articulate their own feelings and impressions and so consciously or unconsciously accepted and reinforced the validity of the notions outlined. The discourse of Chinese characteristics offered a dismissive and distancing vocabulary for articulating experience: 'Often I feel that one experiences in China the things that one only reads of in novels at home,' remarked one Quaker missionary, William Sewell. For Sewell life in China actually revealed 'that side of the Chinese character which is so grossly exaggerated in the cinema and in the cheap magazines at home'.[153] Memoirs written by residents of China refer often enough to such comments to show that accepted notions were internalised, and to show how clichéd a vocabulary it was. What was more important was the pervasiveness and ordinariness of the discourse of characteristics in British print and related cultures. Richard Wilhelm wrote of the revelatory nature of his insight that the abstract term 'coolie', over whom the Revd Darwent had instructed him to 'assume command', had prevented him from seeing Chinese labourers as human beings with human relationships.[154] Novelist and treaty port resident Stella Benson (1892–1933) wrote of one of her acquaintances in England that she 'had donned an armour of false facts about everything' to do with China, a metaphor which suggests both aggression and self-protection.[155] Some fiction, such as Pearl Buck's, could also enable people to understand, empathise and articulate; for then British Minister Sir Miles Lampson seeing the summer flooding of 1931 from the air 'Reminded one forcibly of the opening passages of Mrs Buck's *Good Earth*.[156]

Raymond Dawson's 1967 study, *The Chinese Chameleon*, dismissed popular culture as a topic of interest; it was 'little more than a blend of *Chinoiserie* quaintness and "heathen Chinee" oddness and inferiority'.[157] It does, however, need investigating closely: together with the treaty port-dominated discourse on China in the press and in commentaries, it served to construct a China that British recruits to the foreign presence would have found different and dangerous but which they would naturally have been able to 'handle'. Moreover, the influence of this dominant discourse can be seen in the way those treaty port residents who were initially sympathetic to Chinese political aspirations or to the Chinese themselves grew disillusioned and adopted the clichés and virulence of the experts.[158] The 'China hands' knew their market well: the effect on individual behaviour of lessons rammed home daily in the pages of the *North China Daily News* was marked.

## Conclusion

There was no structured attempt by the British government to create a body of knowledge, or experts, to facilitate its engagement with China. Instead, British settlers in China dominated the British discourse, not missionaries, academics or those actively interested in Chinese culture and society. As the treaty ports had 'made good', and made themselves, so the treaty ports wrote and rewrote their own history, and wrote and rewrote China. The experts were mostly self-made men, the same types identified by Warren Cohen as influential in US–Chinese relations. The pervasiveness of 'knowledge' about China and the Chinese, the facility with which knowledge was acquired and disseminated, and the static nature of the stereotypes involved in all media served to provide a basis for, or to reinforce, the foreign sense of superiority and domination. Sir Frederick Maze, Inspector-general of the Chinese Maritime Customs from 1929 to 1943, was fond of repeating the claim that his predecessor Sir Robert Hart's success in taking over and running the service was due to his 'unparalleled knowledge of Chinese psychology'.[159] An understanding of diplomatic, military, economic or political considerations was seen to be of secondary importance. The experts had reputations to create and jobs to do, to justify and to protect, as individuals and as a community. 'He talks and writes merely to keep his precious job,' wrote Maze in 1929 of E. M. Gull, Secretary of the China Association.[160] Bland, Woodhead, Gilbert *et al.* all had precious jobs to protect, which explains the especial virulence they reserved for the largely better-educated returned students who challenged their interpretations and competed for their interpretative roles.

The treaty port hegemony in the representation of China, and of Sino-British relations served to buttress Britain in China. The function of the barrage of propaganda in all media, explicit or implicit, was twofold. First, Britain in China attempted to sideswipe its (British) diplomatic enemy by asserting its own incorporation into the greater British imperial world, and its irreplaceable centrality to the Sino-British relationship. Second, it served to introduce readers and recruits to the *mores* of the treaty port world. British literature on, or dealing with, the Chinese ultimately taught one major lesson: the necessity of maintaining distance between Britons and Chinese. The language used was similar to that used about other British-dominated nations and peoples and by colonial rulers. Here it underpinned the fact that Britain in China was a real community, by imagining it, its social *mores* and its structured relations with the Chinese, with non-settlers and with other foreigners in China. Our traveller's books and experiences articulated and confirmed degrees of difference and domination, and suggested principles of behaviour: firmness, condescension and the need for supervision, maintaining one's own aloofness and untainted correctness – in short, the need for distance. These principles both rationalised and informed the social structure of, and socialisation within, the British communities in China, to which we now turn.

## Notes

1   Warren Cohen estimated that 'fewer than 100 American men and women regularly had the opportunity to offer their opinions on issues relating to East Asia' between 1900 and 1950. By far the majority of these were journalists; missionaries and academics made up the remainder. Warren I. Cohen, *The Chinese Connection: Roger S. Greene, Thomas L. Lamont, George E. Sokolsky and American–East Asian Relations* (New York, 1978), 2, 293–303.

2   Henry Hodgkin, *China in the Family of Nations* (London, 1928), 244–5.

3   Joshua A. Fogel, *The Literature of Travel in the Japanese Rediscovery of China, 1862–1945* (Stanford CA, 1996); Stefan Tanaka, *Japan's Orient: Rendering Pasts into History* (Berkeley CA, 1993).

4   An exception is John M. MacKenzie, *Orientalism: History, Theory and the Arts* (Manchester, 1996).

5   Michael H. Hunt, *The Making of a Special Relationship: The United States and China to 1914* (New York, 1983); Harold Isaacs, *Scratches on our Minds: American Images of China and India* (New York, 1958).

6   F. G. W. interview with author, 13 September 1996; National Maritime Museum, Greenwich (hereafter NMM), H. T. Bailie-Grohman correspondence, *passim*.

7   War Office, *Notes on Shanghai* (London, 1928).

8   *China Christian Year Book, 1928* (CCYB), 380-1; CCYB, 1929, 546-8; CCYB, 1931, 421–3; Richard Dobson, *China Cycle* (London, 1946), 7.

9   Ivan Hannaford, *Race: The History of an Idea in the West* (Washington DC, 1996), 325–68.

10  *Chinese Recorder* (May 1925), 299–305.

11  Arthur H. Smith, *Chinese Characteristics* (Shanghai, 1890), 396, 404. For an analysis see C. W. Hayford, 'Arthur H. Smith and his China Book', in S. W. Barnett and J.

K. Fairbank, eds, *Christianity in China: Early Protestant Missionary Writings* (Cambridge MA, 1985), 153–74.

12 J. Dyer Ball (revised by E. T. C. Werner), *Things Chinese; or, Notes Connected with China* (Shanghai, 1925); *NCDN*, 2 May 1929, 1.

13 Imperial War Museum, London (hereafter IWM), J. M. Philips papers, letter to P. S. Jones, 15 December 1924. Philips was a salesman for the Asiatic Petroleum Company.

14 R. R. Le Fernbach, *A Child's Primer of Things Chinese* (Tianjin, 1923), Introduction.

15 Department of Overseas Trade, *China: Notes on some Aspects of Life in China for the Information of Business Visitors* (London, 1934), Chapter VI, 'Chinese Characteristics'; O. M. Green, *Discovering China* (London, 1938), 5–6.

16 Cohen, *Chinese Connection*, 296.

17 'Mere stupidity' was 'the cause of most of our trouble with the British press in China and Hong Kong, which is naturally run by third rate men – otherwise they would not be doing that sort of work' – Sir Erich Teichman minute on Canton No.178, 30 November 1929, PRO, FO 228/3987/2 22g.

18 Rodney Gilbert, *What's Wrong with China* (London, 1926), 7, 199.

19 On the influence of these writers see Hannaford, *Race*, 325–68.

20 Gilbert, *What's Wrong*, 45–9, 166–200.

21 Thomas R. Metcalf, *Ideologies of the Raj* (Cambridge, 1995), 25, 192, 229; Mark R. Peattie, 'Japanese Attitudes toward Colonialism', in Ramon H. Myers and Mark R. Peattie, eds, *The Japanese Colonial Empire, 1895–1945* (Princeton NJ, 1984), 92–6.

22 E. M. Gull devoted chapters of *Facets of the China Question* (London, 1931) to 'Nonpractical China' and 'The Sinister Side'. Hong Kong University lecturer J. N. Smith began *China's Hour* (London, 1930) with a chapter on 'The Chinese Mind'.

23 Meyrick Hewlett, *Forty Years in China* (London, 1943), 1–3.

24 Hewlett, *Forty Years*, 148; D. Sayer, 'British Reaction to the Amritsar Massacre, 1919–1920', *Past and Present*, 131 (1991), 146.

25 W. E. Soothill, *China and England* (London, 1928), 32–41; Putnam Weale, *Why China sees Red* (New York, 1926), 323–32; H. G. W. Woodhead, *A Journalist in China* (London, 1934), 261.

26 A similar contradiction between ideas of Indian 'race decline' and 'institutional changelessness' is noted in Metcalf, *Ideologies of the Raj*, 84.

27 Kennedy, *Islands of White*, 163–4; G. D. Killam, *Africa in English Fiction, 1874–1939* (Ibadan, 1968), 71–81; Metcalf, *Ideologies of the Raj*, 105 6.

28 Jerome Ch'en, *China and the West: Society and Culture, 1815–1937* (London, 1979), 52, 169–73.

29 H. A. Giles, *Chaos in China* (Cambridge, 1924), 36–8; W. E. Soothill, *China and the West: A Sketch of their Intercourse* (London, 1925), 192.

30 Hu Shih and Lin Yu-tang, eds, *China's own Critics: A Selection of Essays* (Peking, 1931). Elected in 1928, Hu Shi was the first Chinese appointed to the council of the Royal Asiatic Society (*Journal of the North China Branch of the Royal Asiatic Society*, 59 (1928), viii).

31 F. G. Hutchins, *The Illusion of Permanence: British Imperialism in India* (Princeton NJ, 1967), 156, 187.

32 Waldron, *From War to Nationalism*, 144–5.

33 Rodney Gilbert, *The Indiscretions of Lin Mang* (London, 1929); *Mr Murray's Notable New Books*, autumn 1929.

34 C. A. Middleton Smith *The British in China and the Far Eastern Trade* (1920), 140.

35 C. P. Fitzgerald, *Why China? Recollections of China, 1923–1950* (Melbourne, 1985), 13–14.

36 Thomas Fisher Rare Book Library, University of Toronto, Ms. 81, J. O. P. Bland collection, Box 27, 'Memoirs' (unfinished) of J. O. P. Bland (hereafter Bland papers, 'Memoirs').

37 See Strachey's review of *Li Hung-Chang* (1917) in 'A Diplomatist: Li Hung-Chang', in *Characters and Commentaries* (London, 1933), 233; and Ridge's fragmentary manuscript note on Bland: School of Oriental and African Studies, London (hereafter

SOAS), PP MS 30, W. Sheldon Ridge papers, Box 5, folder 2.

38 Literally, of course, as he either forged it or was party to a fraud of which Bland was entirely innocent; see Hugh Trevor-Roper, *Hermit of Peking: The Hidden Life of Sir Edmund Backhouse* (Penguin edition, Harmondsworth, 1978), 225–64.

39 Trevor-Roper, *Hermit of Peking*, 68–91.

40 Michael Holdroyd, *Lytton Strachey* (Vintage Press edition, London, 1994), 547-50; K. S. Latourette, 'Chinese Historical Studies during the Past Nine Years', *American Historical Review*, 35 (1930), 748; E. R. Hughes, *The Invasion of China by the Western World* (Oxford, 1937).

41 Robert Bickers, '"Coolie work": Sir Reginald Johnston at the School of Oriental Studies, 1931–1937', *Journal of the Royal Asiatic Society*, Series III, 5 (1995), 385–401; Thomas Fisher Rare Books Library, University of Toronto, J. O. P. Bland papers (hereafter Bland papers), Box 19, Johnston to J. O. P. Bland, 28 March, 9 April 1934.

42 Harold Acton, *Memoirs of an Aesthete* (London, 1948); John Blofeld, *City of Lingering Splendour: A Frank Account of Old Peking's Exotic Pleasures* (London, 1961), 13; Osbert Sitwell, *Escape with Me! An Oriental Sketchbook* (London, 1939); Victor Segalen, *René Leys*, translated by J. A. Underwood (London, 1990).

43 Edmund Backhouse, 'Decadence Mandchoue', and 'The Dead Past', Bodleian Mss. Eng. Misc. d. 1223–2; Maurice Dekobra, *His Chinese Concubine* (London, 1935); Charles Pettit, *The Son of the Grand Eunuch* (London, 1927).

44 See PRO, FO 395/419 *passim*.

45 He had many enemies: *North China Star*, 2 October 1930, 1, 15 November 1930, 1; Bland papers, Box 4, Bland to Bell, 23 June 1906; Fitzgerald, *Why China?*, 144–50.

46 See, for example, British Library, Manuscript Collections (hereafter BL), Add Ms. 55023, Macmillan & Co. Ltd, publishers, Simpson correspondence.

47 Alice Tisdale Hobart, *Within the Walls of Nanking* (London, 1928).

48 Colin Mackerras, *Western Images of China* (Hong Kong, 1989), 197.

49 James L. Hevia, 'Leaving a Brand on China: Missionary Discourse in the Wake of the Boxer Movement', *Modern China*, 18 (1992), 321.

50 Dorothy Graham, *The China Venture* (London, 1929); Alice Tisdale Hobart, *Pidgin Cargo* (London, 1929); Veronica and Paul King, *The Commissioner's Dilemma: An International Tale of the China of Yesterday* (London, 1929), 'Forward'.

51 *The Unknown God* (London, 1911); *The Human Cobweb: A Romance of old Peking* (London, 1910); *The Eternal Priestess: A Novel of China Manners* (London, 1914).

52 The critical approach to missions in *The Unknown God* is echoed in his *Why China sees Red*, 115–17.

53 *Wang the Ninth: The Story of a Chinese Boy* (London, 1920).

54 *The Eternal Priestess* (1914) and *The Altar Fire, or, The Story of the Chinese Revolution* (London, 1917); *Wang the Ninth, Her Closed Hands* (London, 1927), and *China's Crucifixion*.

55 Putnam Weale, *The Eternal Priestess* (London, 1914), 26. On the genealogy of this story and its resilience see Bickers and Wasserstrom, 'Shanghai's "Chinese and Dogs not Admitted" Sign'.

56 A. Ransome, *The Chinese Puzzle* (London, 1927), 28–32.

57 In a letter to *The Nation and Athenaeum*, 5 February 1927, p. 619.

58 *All about Shanghai and Environs: A Standard Guide Book* (Shanghai, c. 1934), 43–4, 73–7.

59 Preface to the Penguin edition, *The Painted Veil* (Harmondsworth, 1952), 9–10.

60 Robert Bickers, 'Shanghailanders: The Formation and Identity of the British Settler Community in Shanghai, 1842–1937', *Past and Present*, 159 (1998), 200–2.

61 Endicott, *Diplomacy and Enterprise*, 10; Fung, *Diplomacy of Imperial Retreat*, 276 n 60; SMP D5265; Deborah Lavin, *From Empire to International Commonwealth: A Biography of Lionel Curtis* (Oxford, 1995), 239–52.

62 Pelcovits, *Old China Hands and the Foreign Office*, 220–59; Darwin, 'Imperialism and the Victorians', 633–4.

63 Middleton-Smith, *British in China*, 24, 26.

64  For those heading to Tianjin there was O. D. Rasmussen, *Tientsin: An Illustrated Outline History* (Tianjin, 1925).
65  *The Jubilee of Shanghai, 1843–1893* (Shanghai, 1893).
66  Shanghai Municipal Archives, Shanghai (hereafter SMA), Shanghai Municipal Council secretariat files, U 1–3–164, 'The History of Shanghai'; Bland papers, Box 19, G. Lanning to J. O. P. Bland, 28 November 1906.
67  This was how a later contribution to the genre put it, J. V. Davidson-Houston, *Yellow Creek: The Story of Shanghai* (London, 1962), dedication; *NCH*, 3 March 1928, 336; Gilbert, *What's Wrong with China*, 291; War Office, *Notes on Shanghai*, 6, 16.
68  'Shanghai's Cemeteries and Monuments', *Oriental Affairs* (June 1938), 313–16.
69  As recorded in NMM, Sir Louis K. Hamilton papers, Journal, 27 May 1927.
70  Benedict Anderson, *Imagined Communities: Reflections on the Origin and Spread of Nationalism*, revised edition (London, 1991).
71  Bickers, 'Shanghailanders', 202–3.
72  Woodhead, *Journalist in China*, 62, 242–3; US National Archives and Records Administration (hereafter NARA), Record Group (RG) 84 Tianjin Post Files, Decimal File 800, August Report, Shanghai, 1930.
73  *NCH*, 30 November 1932, 334.
74  Metcalf, *Ideologies of the Raj*. See also, in particular, C. A. Bayly, *Empire and Information: Intelligence Gathering and Social Communication in India, 1780–1870* (Cambridge, 1996)
75  I. A. Donnelly, *Chinese Junks and other Native Craft* (Shanghai, 1924); E. S. Wilkinson, *Shanghai Country Walks*, second and revised edition (Shanghai, 1934).
76  Poor eyesight meant that he did not stay long, but the pattern had been broken (T. H. Barrett, *Singular Listlessness: A Short History of Chinese Books and British Scholars* (London, 1989), 103). See also Bickers, '"Coolie work"'
77  On the Statistical Department see J. K. Fairbank, M. H. Coolidge and R. J. Smith, *H. B. Morse: Customs Commissioner and Historian of China* (Lexington MA, 1995), 175–8.
78  Douglas R. Reynolds, 'Training Young China Hands: Toa Dobun Shoin and its Precursors, 1886–1945', in Duus, Myers and Peattie, eds, *Japanese Informal Empire in China*, 210–71.
79  J. O. P. Bland, *China: The Pity of It* (London: 1932), 163.
80  B. L. Putnam Weale, *Manchu and Muscovite* (London, 1904), xii.
81  Herbert Chatley, 'Obituary' of Lenox Simpson, *Journal of the Royal Asiatic Society (North China Branch)*, 62 (1931), ii.
82  Joseph McAleer, *Popular Reading and Publishing in Britain* (Oxford, 1992), 88–9.
83  Quoted in R. E. Briney, ed., C. Van Ash and E. S. Rohmer, *Master of Villainy: A Biography of Sax Rohmer* (Bowling Green KY, 1972), 75; on Rohmer see Clive Bloom, 'West is East: Nayland Smith's Sinophobia and Sax Rohmer's Bank Balance', in C. Bloom, ed., *Twentieth Century Suspense: The Thriller comes of Age* (London, 1990), 22–36.
84  *The Mystery of Dr Fu-Manchu* (London, 1913), 23.
85  Briney, *Master of Villainy*, 112–16; William F. Wu, *The Yellow Peril: Chinese Americans in American Fiction, 1850–1940* (Hamden CT, 1982), 183–206.
86  *Dope: A Story of Chinatown and the Drug Traffic* (London, 1919).
87  M. P. Shiel, 'About Myself', in A. R. Morse, *The Works of M. P. Shiel: A Study in Bibliography* (Los Angeles CA, 1948), 5.
88  Raymond Dawson, *The Chinese Chameleon: An Analysis of European Conceptions of Chinese Civilization* (London, 1967).
89  E. Wallace, *The Tomb of Ts'in* (London, 1916), 54, 77, 160, 282–5; M. Lane, *Edgar Wallace: The Biography of a Phenomenon* (London, revised edition, 1964), 233–6.
90  Michael Joseph, 'Short Story Writing for Profit', *Complete Writing for Profit* (London, 1930), 192, 139.
91  J. W. Bennett, *Dragon Shadows* (1928), *The Yellow Corsair* (1928), *Manchu Cloud* (1929), *Son of the Typhoon* (1929), *Chinese Blake* (1930), *Spinach Jade* (1939); 'Warren Hill' (probably a pseudonym), *Yellow will Out* (London, 1929), *That which*

*is Crooked* (London, 1930), *The Crystal Skull* (London, 1930); A. H. Mills, *The Yellow Dragon* (London, 1924), *Intrigue Island* (London, 1930), *Stowaway* (1931).

92 P. S. Barry, *How to Succeed as a Playwright* (London, 1928), 61.

93 PRO, FO 228/3801/1 23J, W. C. Chen to Sir Austen Chamberlain, 7 March 1928.

94 *Who's Who in the Theatre*, fourteenth edition (London, 1967), 1535; Matheson Lang, *Mr Wu Looks Back: Thoughts and Memories* (London, 1941), 112; British Theatre Association Library, Theatre Museum, London, *Mr Wu*, Script, H. Owen and H. Vernon, Note, 16.

95 *CET*, 19 January 1928, 38.

96 John Foster, *Chinese Realities* (London, 1928), 160.

97 Paul Linebarger, Jr, 'Western Fiction about China: General Misconceptions and Misrepresentations', *Chinese Nation*, 10 December 1930, 602, 617.

98 M. C. T. Z. Tyau, *London through Chinese Eyes, or, My Seven and a Half Years in London* (London, 1920), 293–97; BL, Lord Chamberlain's Correspondence, 1913/2028, W. Langley [FO] to The Comptroller, Lord Chamberlain's Department, 25 November 1913 (enclosing, The Chinese Minister to Sir Edward Grey, 21 November 1913, and Y. T. Tang and W. L. New to the Chinese Minister, 20 November 1913), and D. Dawson to Under Secretary of State, Foreign Office, 27 November 1913. In fact an earlier version of the play, in which Wu's revenge was carried out, was vetoed by the censor, see the correspondence in BL, LC Play Scripts, 1913/2028.

99 The commentary was Ada E. Chesterton's *Young China and New Japan* (London, 1933); see the file in PRO, FO 395/502, P2394/2394/150.

100 See my 'New Light on Lao She, London, and the London Missionary Society, 1921–1929', *Modern Chinese Literature*, 8 (1994) 21–39.

101 PRO, FO 371/13225, F1341/F1190/10, Major C. L. Gordon to Under Secretary of State, 19 March 1928.

102 W. Somerset Maugham, *Collected Plays* III (London, 1952), Preface, ix–x.

103 Dance and Talbot's *A Chinese Honeymoon* was a similarly successful spectacle in 1901 and ran for 1,075 nights after 1915, while another 'Chinese' musical, *San Toy*, ran for 768 performances after 1899. *Who's Who in the Theatre*, 1530, 1537.

104 *Who's Who in the Theatre*, 1530; *Chu Chin Chow: A Musical Tale of the East*, Oscar Asche and Frederic Norton [1916] (London, 1931).

105 W. C. Duncan and L. Wylie, *Shanghai: Spectacular Operette* (1918); Edgar Wallace, *The Yellow Mask* (1928); *Kong: A New Chinese Drama* (1931); Franz Lehar, *Land of Smiles* (1931); *San Toy* (1932).

106 G. C. Hazelton and [J. H.] Benrimo, *The Yellow Jacket: A Play in the Chinese Manner* (1922); Klabaund, *The Circle of Chalk* (1939), S. I. Hsiung, *Lady Precious Stream* (London, 1934).

107 A. Curtis and J. Whitehead, (eds), *W. Somerset Maugham: The Critical Heritage* (London, 1987), 238–41.

108 In his 1942 essay 'Rudyard Kipling': George Orwell, *Collected Essays* (second edition, London, 1961), 179–94.

109 *The Conquerors* (London, 1929); *Storm in Shanghai* [*La Condition humaine*] (London, 1934).

110 S. Kunitz and H. Haycroft, eds, *Twentieth Century Authors* (New York, 1942), 964.

111 Billie Melman, *Women and the Popular Imagination in the Twenties: Flappers and Nymphs* (London, 1988), 90–6.

112 *By Soochow Waters* (London, 1929), 1; *Ruby and Ivy Sên* (London, 1925), 14.

113 Louise Jordan Miln, *The Flutes of Shanghai* (London, 1928), 153.

114 Mrs Percival (Marguerite) Connellan, *Ten Thousand Yesterdays* (London, 1932); Edith Wherry, *The Red Lantern* (London, 1911).

115 On the 'Eastern' novelists see Melman, *Women and the Popular Imagination*, 89–104.

116 J. G. Cawelti, *Adventure, Mystery, and Romance: Formula Stories as Art and Popular Culture* (Chicago, 1976), 35–6.

117 Metcalf, *Ideologies of the Raj*, 101–2.

118 Isaacs, *Scratches on our Minds*, 70; William W. Appleton, *A Cycle of Cathay: The*

*Chinese Vogue in England during the Seventeenth and Eighteenth Centuries* (New York, 1951); Dawson, *Chinese Chameleon.*

119 Appleton, *A Cycle of Cathay*; Dawson, *Chinese Chameleon.*

120 Iona and Peter Opie, *The Singing Game* (Oxford, 1985), 465–7; see also Lachlan Strahan, '"The Luck of a Chinaman": Images of the Chinese in Popular Australian Sayings', *East Asian History*, 3 (1992), 68–9.

121 *CET*, 28 February 1929, 142.

122 *The Pipeline*, 9, 27 November 1929, 380; 4, 30 January 1924, 32.

123 Sir John T. Pratt, *War and Politics in China* (London, 1943), 19–20; John Blofeld, 'Sino-British Cultural Relations', *China Society Occasional Papers* (London, c.1946), 2–3.

124 John M. MacKenzie, *Propaganda and Empire: The Manipulation of British Public Opinion, 1880-1960* (Manchester, 1984), 107–12, 122–43; SA, transcripts of interviews with ex-Swire employees. These have been quoted anonymously, but are numbered consecutively in surname alphabetical order of interviewee, followed by the page of transcript, hereafter: SA. ST [Swire Transcripts] – 6, p. 5. ST – 5, 2.

125 *The Times, British Empire Supplement*, 23 April 1924, xv; *British Empire Exhibition 1924 Official Guide* (London, 1924), 77.

126 *British Empire Exhibition 1924 Official Catalogue* (London, 1924), 66–7.

127 *The Times, British Empire Supplement*, 23 April 1924, xv; *The Times, British Empire Supplement*, 24 May 1924, xiv. See also, in this regard, Timothy Mitchell, *Colonising Egypt* (Cambridge, 1988).

128 Akira Iriye, *Across the Pacific: An Inner History of American–East Asian Relations* (New York, 1967), 33–9. Jerome Ch'en's *China and the West* is structured on the same premise.

129 Colin Holmes, 'The Chinese Connection', in Geoffrey Alderman and Colin Holmes, eds, *Outsiders and Outcasts: Essays in Honour of William J. Fishman* (London, 1993), 74. The figures are impressionistic, and do not indicate periodic swings: in 1917 there were, for example, an estimated 4,000 Chinese in Limehouse alone: PRO, MEPO 2/1629, 988692/7, 'K' Division Metropolitan Police Report, 30 June 1917.

130 Sun Wen, *Kidnapped in London* (Bristol, 1897); J. Y. Wong, *The Origins of an Heroic Image: Sun Yatsen in London, 1896–1897* (Hong Kong, 1986); Graham Wallas, *Human Nature in Politics* (London, 1908), 107; A. K. Russell, *Liberal Landslide: the General Election of 1906* (Newton Abbot, 1973), 106–8, 196–9; Peter Richardson, *Chinese Mine Labour in the Transvaal* (London, 1982); Virginia Berridge, 'East End Opium Dens and Narcotic Use in Britain', *London Journal* 4 (1978), 3–28; Holmes, 'Chinese Connection'.

131 See PRO, HO 45/11843, for various papers on these issues from 1906 to 1935.

132 PRO, HO 45/11843, 139147/169; MEPO 3/311, 650/2/36; HO 45/11843, 139147/276.

133 For files on Chang see PRO, MEPO 3/469, 216/unc/511, 201/sd/63 and 216/unc/200.

134 See the files PRO, MEPO 3/469, 221/unc/39; MEPO 3/433: MEPO 3/1049, 216/unc/901, 216/unc/459, 216/unc/1459.

135 See Rohmer's letter to the *Daily Express* in PRO, HO 45/11843, 139147/157.

136 Kathryn Castle, *Britannia's Children: Reading Colonialism through Children's Books and Magazines* (Manchester, 1996), 122–32.

137 Strahan, '"The Luck of a Chinaman"', 75; policeman Maurice Tinkler sent one home to his sister; his colleague Frank Peasgood brought one back for his.

138 Marek Kohn, *Dope Girls: The Birth of the British Drug Underground* (London, 1992), 137–9.

139 Hunt, *Making of a Special Relationship.*

140 *NCH*, 18 October 1924, 97.

141 C. E. Darwent, *Shanghai: A Handbook for Travellers and Residents* (Shanghai, 1926), xiv, iv.

142 *Ibid.*, 76.

143 *Ibid.*; Carl Crow's *Handbook for China* (fourth edition, Shanghai, 1926) recommended that 'The visitor [to Shanghai] who cannot visit any other city in China should see the Loonghwa Pagoda', 149.
144 Darwent, *Shanghai*, 125.
145 SMA, U 1-1-130, Orchestra and Band Committee Minutes, Chairman A. Howard, 9 March 1923.
146 PRO, FO 369/2018, K6175/6175/210, A. Veitch to W. C. Scott, 28 March 1928, 'Report on Conditions in Hankow affecting Clerical Officers'.
147 *Ibid.*
148 NMM, Hamilton papers, Letter to Freddy, 13 June 1927.
149 NMM, Hamilton papers, journal, 24 February 1928.
150 ST – 21, 41; R. V. C. Bodley, *Indiscreet Travels East* (London, 1934), 187; Drage papers, Diary, 20 May 1924; 'As others See us: Typical Misdescription of Shanghai', *NCH*, 14 July 1928, 82; Douglas Day, *Malcom Lowry: A Biography* (London, 1974), 91; Robert Bickers, 'Death of a Young Shanghailander: The Thorburn Case and the Defence of the British Treaty Ports in China in 1931', *Modern Asian Studies*, 30 (1996), 271-300; E. W. Peters, *Shanghai Policeman* (London, 1937), 34.
151 *CET*, 25 October 1928; IWM 87/22/1, F. W. Bunter papers, Memoir, 11; J. K. Fairbank, *Chinabound: A Fifty Year Memoir* (New York, 1982), 21.
152 IWM, H. C. Simms papers, Journal, 15 May 1925.
153 Friends' House Library, London, Friends Service Council archives (hereafter FSC), CH/6, Rose Tebbutt to Bertha Bracey, 13 September 1931; CH5/4, W. G. Sewell, journal letter, 4 December 1926.
154 Richard Wilhelm, *The Soul of China* (London, 1928), 22–4.
155 Benson Diaries, 5 April 1929.
156 Lampson Diaries, 28 July 1931.
157 Dawson, *Chinese Chameleon*, 165.
158 India Office Library and Records, London (hereafter IOLR), J. Bazalgette papers, letter to parents, 11 May 1927.
159 See his comments on a letter received from L. A. Lyall: SOAS, Sir Frederick Maze papers (hereafter Maze papers), Confidential Letters, Vol. 2, 28 May 1927, and Confidential Letters, Vol. 3, Maze to Charles Addis, 22 February 1929.
160 Maze papers, Confidential Letters, Vol. 3, Maze to W. F. Tyler, 10 July 1929.

# CHAPTER THREE

# Britons in China:
# a settler society

A recruit to Britain in China arrived in Hong Kong by sea some five weeks after leaving Britain, and usually sailed on up the coast to Shanghai, or transferred at Hong Kong to another ship. The first part of China our traveller physically saw, smelt, felt and heard was a British colony. The first Chinese would already have been glimpsed some days back in Singapore or Penang: colonial subjects in another British possession. Unless they travelled west over Canada or the United States and the Pacific to Japan, and then Shanghai – which was most unusual for new recruits on company tickets – they literally came into China through British empire. There was no innocent port of entry.

Hong Kong and Shanghai formed the twin hubs of Britain in China, headquartering between them nearly all Britain in China operations. Hong Kong covered south China, Shanghai the north and centre. Tianjin sometimes formed a third node. From the APC office in Hong Kong a recruit might shift on up to a branch office in Canton; from Shanghai a China Inland Mission (CIM) recruit might move on to a training college in central China. These cities and these networks serve as one way of delineating Britain in China's identities. More important, though, were the broader communities the new recruits joined. Four overlapping but clearly differentiated groups comprised this British presence in China: settlers, expatriates, missionaries, and officials. The largest sector is labelled here the settler community, and it is part of the argument of this book that settlers should be clearly distinguished from the other sectors, and that the settler problem lay at the heart of Britain in China. Settlers (who in Shanghai even fashioned a moniker for themselves: 'Shanghailanders') were united economically in their common dependence on the existence of a foreign-controlled society in the Chinese treaty ports. This dependence informed their responses to all issues involving reform of the fundamental treaties, and served to foster a strong common identity out of their common predicament.

They saw themselves, and were seen by observers, as a coherent group, sharing a coherent local identity.

Of course, all Britons in China possessed multiple identities: British, imperial and local. All three identities were ever present, and criss-crossed the different sectors, but depending on the circumstances one identity might become more prominent. The local identity was the most troublesome for the British state's efforts to renegotiate its relations with China. A British identity might be taken here as given – although these individuals came from rural and urban Britain, from north and south, Wales, Scotland, Ireland and England – and an imperial identity might likewise be assumed for the inhabitants of a state with an imperial culture. This chapter explores in particular, then, how the local identity was acquired and inculcated, and whose purposes it served, and how it was protected through formal and informal socialisation, through the institutions of treaty port life, and by the policing of behaviour to maintain racial, sexual and class taboos. These features and fractures were shared with other British (and European) colonial societies, as a growing body of literature has shown, although maintenance rather than replication has been the central focus of such works. What emerges clearly, however, is the hegemonic position of the settler community in British treaty port society. Settler institutions and social practices vital for settler survival, whilst certainly often exaggerations of domestic models, established new patterns of behaviour that influenced recruits and members to other British sectors, to missions, and to expatriate business. The underlying insecurity of their position led settlers to demand the complicity of the other sectors in the mock Raj that was created in China. More than their settlements and concessions, with their administrations and resources, the mentality of the British in China reveals that Britain in China was a concrete entity, a mental and physical state within a state. Settlers had a past history, a present identity and, as far as they were concerned, future prospects to protect from the Chinese and from the British state alike.

This chapter first examines the communities which operated in China under the British flag in the treaty ports and beyond them, wherever Britain in China was to be found. It then looks at the recruitment and socialisation of recruits into treaty port society, and the strategies employed to maintain social and sexual distance between Britons and Chinese, as well as the punishments handed out to transgressors. Peer pressure and an emphasis on individual character were the nuts and bolts of this process, and individual experience is the focus of this analysis. The chapter then outlines the 'imagining' of the treaty port community, and in particular the identity, practices and beliefs of settler society. Although the British enterprise in China was ever Sino-British, and reliant on Chinese personnel, collaboration, business and finance, at the heart of the settler identity lay a root fear of Chinese, a belligerent antipathy that found expression in moments of crisis such as May Thirtieth.

## British subjects in China

British communities were spread throughout China. In 1900 there were concessions (with elected British-controlled municipal councils) in Hankou, Jiujiang, Tianjin, Zhenjiang, Shamian (Guangzhou) and Xiamen; British-dominated International Settlements in Shanghai and Gulangyu (Xiamen) and the more formally colonial Weihaiwei and Hong Kong. Shanghai was much the largest settlement, followed by Tianjin: the others – the 'outports' – contained hundreds of Britons at the most, usually only scores; many of them were formally outside the treaty system. Outside these communities the pattern of settlement was dictated by trading networks, notably along the China coast, in Manchuria and along the Yangzi at Yichang and Chongqing, and by patterns of missionary evangelisation. Albert Feuerwerker calculated that in 1919 only 106 (about 6 per cent) of China's 1,704 *xian* (counties) were without some form of missionary presence. Almost 2,000 Britons worked for British missionary societies in China in 1919, running 384 mission stations.[1] Britain in China extended beyond the treaty ports, then, but, as we shall see, was dominated by the *mores* and disciplines of urban settler life. The British inhabitants of these communities comprised settlers, expatriates, missionaries and official personnel, as well as the 'other British', groups with various categories of British-protected status: Sephardic Jews, Eurasians, overseas Chinese and British Indians.

Settlers typically fell into three categories of occupations. The range is covered by the Skinner clan, active in Shanghai across three generations. George Lowday Skinner arrived in Shanghai in 1866 as a seaman, joined the police, summoned his betrothed from Somerset, and spawned descendants who remained in the city until 1949. First, there were those Britons who worked for the treaty port service industries, the Shanghai Municipal Council or the Shanghai Municipal Police. Skinner's daughter Evelyn, for example, worked for the council as a typist, while his son-in-law's sister married the future Secretary of the British council in Hankou. Foreign missionaries and mission workers in Shanghai would also fit into this first category, although the broader mission presence was different; another Skinner relative married a German missionary. Some in this category worked for the expatriate

China companies as locally recruited staff, or in non-managerial positions – seamen, for example – as did Skinner's son-in-law, W. E. Kent, who worked for Swire's China Navigation Company before becoming a Shanghai harbour pilot. The bulk of people in the treaty port service trades were working-class, or lower middle-class. The personnel files of demobbed soldier Maurice Tinkler and his companions who went out in 1919 to join the police force show them to have been farm hands, labourers, porters and soldiers. Two, only, seem to have come from middle-class backgrounds.[2] Secondly, settlers were property owners and land speculators, such as those who controlled the Shanghai Land Investment Company, or Algar & Co., founded by Skinner's son-in-law Albert Algar, and managed from 1928 to 1949 by Algar's nephew, Noel Kent, a third-generation Shanghailander.[3] G. L. Skinner's son Charles worked in shipbuilding, and rose to become director of a shipbuilding company.[4] Thirdly, they were small businessmen and women, they ran boarding houses or shops, tuned pianos, sold books or ran dairies. None of these jobs or opportunities, or possibilities of access to them, would have existed without the treaty port system. Although actual occupational statistics are hard to obtain, by far the greater proportion of the British community in Shanghai in particular at any one time was composed of settlers. Much smaller settler communities with similar socio-economic identities were located in Tianjin and Hankou.

The second group of Britons in China was the expatriate businessmen who dominate accounts and representations of the treaty port era. Again, this label is not common in secondary literature, but it was clearly visible to participants at the time, and the distinction was also apparent within the Japanese community, the presence most closely resembling the British. A division between the 'company' and 'native' factions dominated Japanese treaty port politics in Shanghai.[5] This group includes the traders, bankers, manufacturers and those working for, running or representing mining, shipping or railway interests. They were employed by the largest China companies, by Jardine Matheson, or Butterfield & Swire, or by the multinationals: British American Tobacco, Imperial Chemical Industries, Asiatic Petroleum Company. They were geographically far more dispersed than the settlers, and much more likely to be moved from treaty port to treaty port, or into the interior. Thirdly, there were British Protestant missionaries of various denominations, Plymouth Brethren to Anglican, involved in educational, social, medical and evangelical institutions. Although there were urban concentrations in the treaty ports, the missionary community was by far the most dispersed group spatially. The fourth group includes those in British government service: diplomats, diplomatic staff (policemen, archivists, etc.), consuls and servicemen. There were troops at Tianjin, Legation guards in Beijing and gunboats on the Yangzi and Pearl rivers.

The British community was diverse, and varied in composition geographically. But the large settler community in Shanghai, the sojourning businessmen who worked for Jardine's or Swire's, and the mission staff up country were all British nationals, although this shared identity was fractured by class, and by strong conflicts of interest between settlers and expatriate businessmen who might just as easily have sojourned somewhere else. These conflicts were played out in treaty port municipal politics, and in the press, and we shall return to them. However, the rhythm of the employment was similar: recruitment, socialisation, two or three decades' active service punctuated by lengthy periods of home leave, concluded by retirement to an unfamiliar 'home', or staying on in the known comfort of China, or moving to the dominions. Increasing numbers of treaty port families stayed on in Shanghai for more than one generation. Two generations were not at all uncommon, three by no means unusual – but settlers were still more often made than born. British nationals were seen as a homogeneous community by visitors and by the Chinese and were expected to act as such by the British Supreme Court in Shanghai, under whose jurisdiction they lived and worked, and by the Legation, which sometimes chastised or deported troublemakers, and which co-operated with charitable groups in assisting the passage home of the indigent.

While colonial and dominion nationals – Australians or Canadians, for example – were subsumed, identifiable groups under British protection were excluded in varying degrees from this community as it defined itself, or remembers itself. Baghdadi Jews (who called themselves Sephardic) – from Bombay in particular – identified themselves as British, but as Jews and as Asians they were doubly excluded by Britons.[6] For Eurasians with British protection the same applies: poorer Eurasians were regarded as a singular nuisance by British officialdom, although consuls were more sympathetic if they were of 'good character [and] British education'. Wherever possible, protection was withheld or withdrawn if found to have been mistakenly given, and in any case only those born in Hong Kong were recognised as British protégés.[7] There was also a large Indian community, mostly policemen or nightwatchmen, but also including merchants.[8] Like Hong Kong or Straits Settlements Chinese, who were also British protégés, they were excluded. Except in so far as they impinge upon British nationals from the metropole, those groups will not be discussed here, where the defining constant, as it was in Britain in China, is 'race' (although religion, language and dress also partly served as subsidiary markers). It was important for Britons' self-ascribed identity to draw the distinction with regard to Asians who shared British protection in China. Popular culture and treaty port propaganda returned relentlessly to this distinction, damning sexual transgressions above all. Communal identity and solidarity in Britain in China, as we shall see, were located most visibly in questions of race, and the polarity between a constructed 'white' British presence and the other 'races' it encountered in China. British Asians or Eurasians muddied these waters and threatened not only that identity but that very presence.

These 'other Britons', and Chinese, were differentiated by their 'race' from the Britons discussed here, although it could be translated into the legal realities of twentieth-century treaty port life only as nationality. Where Britons might see only 'orientals', the treaty port system accommodated on a technically equal level Japanese, Chinese with British or Japanese protection and Eurasians with all manner of nationality. For example, only Chinese nationals could actually be excluded from the Shanghai International Settlement parks. The boundary between British and Chinese was a difficult one to fix, and was subject to negotiation in which, as I shall show, the undoing of even the smallest constituent part of what was considered British threatened the undoing of the whole. Bolstering 'race', then, a culturally defined Britishness became vital for identity, and also as evidence of the maintenance of distance from the Chinese. We know, of course, and the evidence shows, that men and women of all classes broke all the rules outlined below, again and again. But we also know that they knew that what they were doing was rule breaking: they knew that there were rules, and they knew what they were.

'Race' may rightly be queried as the benchmark of 'Britishness' because after about 1917–18 Britons also began to define themselves against another group in Shanghai, and the treaty ports generally: the White Russians. Destitution and desperation forced many Russian men to take menial or mercenary jobs, and Russian women to work in the sex trade, or the entertainment field. The Russians were seen by Britons and others to undermine 'white prestige' by the employment they took, their lifestyles, their homes, but mostly by the sheer poverty of the majority. In this sense the Russians were the exemplars of 'poor white' behaviour as it was perceived, and, as will be shown below, taboos about specific forms of interaction with the Russians were as strong as those for Asians. The marginalisation of Russians was compounded by the fact that they were stateless refugees from the civil war, or the USSR, or from the Russian communities in Manchuria, cut adrift from their metropolitan centre. Theirs was a refugee culture: they could not go on from China except through luck, craft or marriage, and most could not go back to the USSR. British settlers had also basically come to stay, but they remained linked to their homeland, and retained their multiple identities. The Russians had only one, and that was a negative identity: unless they took Chinese citizenship (as more and more did in the 1930s), they had no legally recognised existence at all.[9]

Quite apart from racism or popular notions of race degeneration, prestige, internal social solidarity and hierarchy, the narrow definition of 'British' served a concrete purpose. Treaty port residents always had the example of Macao to mull over. 'Portuguese' in treaty port terms meant Portuguese Eurasian (today termed Macanese). The restricted definition of 'British', bolstered by the sex and marriage taboos outlined below, served to prevent the 'Macanisation' of Britain in China. The continued support of the British government depended on the continued ability of settlers in particular to demonstrate not only a commitment to British institutions and social practices, but also that they were still 'ethnically' British. Given the strength of racist attitudes in metropolitan society, British diplomats in China were hardly likely to bestir themselves to support a community which had lost all trace of its identity. In formal colonies we know that European colonialism fixed racial boundaries by banning mixed marriages between settlers and natives in periods of colonial reconstruction after rebellion (in German South West Africa, East Africa and Samoa), or it might define different 'racial' categories in law (the Dutch East Indies).[10] In informal empire, self-regulation was the only strategy that could be resorted to, especially as protection by the British state was dependent not on race but on nationality.

## Why go to China?

Conceptually, going to China was no great move. Recorded motivations mirror those which sent people to work in the British empire, or other informal zones of influence and settlement. Emigration was common – some 17 million people left Britain between 1815 and 1914 – while working abroad was a perfectly routine part of the British experience. Britons sought work in a world-wide labour market into which China was integrated. Advertisements for the Shanghai Municipal Police (SMP) in the working-class Sunday newspaper *The People* between March and May 1919 were lodged among calls for men to work in Uganda, the West Indies and Britain itself. By 1922 the Shanghai Municipal Council had some 600 mostly British employees in its secretariat, and in the revenue, public health, public works and police departments, and had become by far the biggest employer of British personnel in the International Settlement.[11]

[ 73 ]

**Figure 5**  Inspector E. W. Everson and family. From Putnam Weale, *Why China sees Red* (1925), p. 34

Expatriate businessmen often had no choice: those who joined multinationals such as BAT or APC 'simply got [their] marching orders'.[12] Some joined companies especially to go east, hoping to achieve greater wealth, comfort and importance faster than would be possible in Britain. Some went back to where they had been brought up, others came from families with a tradition of imperial service. It may be that, for some, service overseas provided a way of escaping the perceived greater competition for jobs and position that mass education and a democratic mass society were slowly bringing about in Britain. Dane Kennedy has certainly identified such rationales behind contemporary emigration to Kenya, for example, but most migrants just needed work.[13] Some drifted to China because their record made returning to Britain difficult: C. Y. Jones went to Shanghai direct from prison in Nyasaland in 1930. Some went after demobilisation at the end of World War I – among them some expressly leaving the Europe of the trenches behind. Novelist Graham Greene saw the prospect of working in China for BAT as a means of escape from thwarted love and quotidian pettiness in Britain. Others with a taste for adventure and fighting, possibly inspired by fictional characters or real-life figures who surfaced in the newspapers, like General 'Two-gun' Cohen or Frank 'One-arm' Sutton, came – like C. Y. Jones – to work for 'the local Chinese warlord'.[14] Military visitors often bought their discharge and stayed on after the Boxer War, or after service in the Shanghai Defence Force: eighty six soldiers left it for the SMP in 1928–29. Others came on regular army postings and stayed: in 1928 a lance corporal looked for a job as a warehouse manager, while W. R. Giles became Beijing correspondent of the *Daily Mail*.[15]

For those who thought about it at all, or who had read the commentaries of the settler propagandists, the myth of making a quick fortune in China had evolved into a desire to enjoy the other, more reliable benefits of the foreign but familiar treaty port world. 'China' was socially more open, easier to enter and less competitive than the more prestigious apparatus of the Raj and other services in the empire, or commercial employment elsewhere. Others opted for the Chinese consular service because it was easiest to get into, or because they failed diplomatic service exams. The benefits were tangible and immediate. There were servants – consul Meyrick Hewlett was issued with his 'boy' on day one of his four-decade stint in China in 1898, as was a later consul, J. A. Sinclair. Even A. H. Rasmussen, a customs 'outdoorman' and lowest of the foreign low, inherited his predecessor's servant in 1905. There was perhaps more spacious living, and probably a higher standard of living. Better promotion prospects were offered in some professions; journalists acquired positions of authority and respect much faster than they could ever have hoped to in Britain: their Chinese pond was small.[16] Those who left the treaty ports sometimes returned to China for precisely these reasons. China itself was as incidental to these considerations as it was to the treaty port world, although some, brought up on a diet of literary adventure, or newspaper reports, retrospectively saw this wider setting as a source of excitement and interest. But the choice was frequently accidental: H. G. W. Woodhead escaped an unhappy job and home life, consul J. T. Pratt happened by chance upon an announcement of the consular examinations, Meyrick Hewlett was bullied into keeping a childhood decision to go. J. O. P. Bland was in first year as an undergraduate at Trinity College Dublin when his father announced that the family finances could no longer support his education and that he would have to seek employment. Using the Ulster connections which provided so many other recruits for the service, Bland was placed in the Chinese Maritime Customs.[17]

As Jonathan Spence has rightly noted of his 'China helpers', 'implicit in most of their actions is … a desire not so much to help China as to help themselves.' They left for China to avoid 'feared or experienced frustrations at home.' There were certainly those who went who hated British society because it was too reactionary and those who felt it was too democratic, but in the wider materialistic sense, of course, the British were there to help themselves; that is, to earn a living.[18]

## Socialisation

The China they went to, Britain in China, was an improvised construct whose institutions, affectations and aspirations were more or less consciously derived in equal measure from the specific features of foreign life in China, of Britons abroad elsewhere (and at home), particularly the British in India. The last is a recurring theme: the assumptions, structures and even the vocabulary of British India (tiffin, lakh, shroff, godown, coolie, bund, boy, chit), as well as some of its inhabitants (Sikhs mostly, as security personnel), were carted off to China. British India set the standard for imperial culture; its customs, argot, even the construction of its history, served as a model for real and aspirational colonialism alike. Britain in China, and Britons in China, swaggered at times as if they were a Raj in China. 'Having been in India,' remembered one Swire's employee, 'I had an idea of what Eastern life was like.'[19] Furthermore, as we have seen in chapter 2, on the voyage out to China Britons would have passed through territories where Chinese formed part of the formal imperial subject population. On arrival they would often have found Sikhs recruited into British-controlled police

forces as a visible colonial affectation. The effect of the Indian example
on their perception of the nature of their relationship with the Chinese
in China was tangible, and the impression this must have made on the
Chinese might also be remembered. Another Swire's employee in later
life recalled that 'the way we treated the Chinese ... [was] a relic of
India rather'. This was a contemporary criticism. Lionel Curtis felt
that 'The British ... are badly handicapped by traditions established in
their earlier contact with India.'[20] There were big differences, of course,
notably the fact that Britons in India were under the heel of the Raj
themselves, and no settler society developed there.[21] What mattered,
however, was not the Raj as an actual political structure but the Raj as
mentality, as decoration, and style.

This Chinese Raj sat a little awkwardly at times, for the broader foreign presence in China was nominally international; in Shanghai, especially, the British shared municipal power. After 1900, in every treaty
port, official relations with the Chinese were co-ordinated with the
other consuls, but the British remained the preponderant non-Asian
presence, and set the tone, while their institutions were the models
of treaty port life. Surrounding, and encompassing, the British
community itself, then, was a nominally cosmopolitan world, the
international presence in China, and then China itself. The British
communities kept their distance from cosmopolitanism. This was true
of the smaller ports especially, but was a common feature of expatriate
life.[22]

The surrounding milieu, of course, was overwhelmingly Chinese;
resistant as they were to the claims of cosmopolitanism, the British
were even more strongly resistant to China. Ignorance beforehand, or
the misinformed notions derived from treaty port propaganda and fiction, were reinforced by what was learnt, and how, when Britons
arrived:

> Captain Miners ... gave me a friendly welcome and that first evening we
> sat on his verandah while he informed me of the prevailing local condi-
> tions and gave me a preliminary briefing on my new duties. I remember
> feeling a little surprised to learn that social contacts with Chinese were
> rare and were not encouraged by either the Chinese or the Foreign com-
> munity.[23]

W. J. Moore's reception on his arrival in Shanghai as a young merchant
navy officer was not unusual, even if it was a little explicit, and the
insularity of Chinese society was frequently cited as the justification for
such behaviour. Most institutions 'met' their new arrivals and showed
them the ropes. Meyrick Hewlett and fellow consular novices were met
at Beijing station in 1898 by an earlier draft who 'although they had only

preceded us by five months ... made us feel that they were old hands'; the students were immediately issued with room, servant and teacher. Whilst such education was more often implicit than in the lessons given by Captain Miners, one consul, for example, was still bluntly warned against sinophilia: 'Don't forget you're British'.[24] Distance was the credo inculcated into recruits – social distance, sexual distance, even distance from Chinese food, and the Chinese language.

The inculcation was verbal. Socialisation into treaty port society required those already socialised to pass on the values acquired, and so the myth of the 'China hand' was born. Information about China, the Chinese and the British position in China circulated verbally as it circulated in print. British 'knowledge' of China and events in China was acquired in the *ad hoc* way examined in the previous chapter, and was transmitted in equally *ad hoc* ways. It is possible to follow the flow of information and its reception, digestion and regurgitation in letters and diaries as men talked and new men listened. And talking 'shop' excessively was perhaps natural in a community so replete with 'experts', where time hung heavily after the day's work. One impressionable naval officer, Louis Hamilton, arriving with the Royal Navy in April 1927, imbibed truths about the Chinese republic at dinner parties and clubs up and down the Yangzi, soaking up theories, explanations, justifications and arrant nonsense. His informants were books, consuls, customs officials and businessmen.[25]

Everyone, then, was an expert, and talked, and talked: 'there is never any lack of things to say', wrote missionary William Sewell.[26] Surviving correspondence from China is astonishingly didactic, and many of the potted histories and explanations similarly so, and derived directly or indirectly from the treaty port experts. The very profusion of China memoirs is also related to this. Men made sense of their new world by describing it, and their new place in it, and at the same time found themselves constructing both their British identity and a new local identity. Recruits learned the British–Chinese map: 'China', for most, was the treaty ports; other cities and provinces did not exist. They learned a pidgin-English-derived argot ('maskee', 'can do'), and such dehumanising and distancing designations as 'boy', 'amah' and 'coolie' for their servants.[27] If they did not know them already they were directed to sound authors (Gilbert, Bland, Putnam Weale), to the *North China Daily News*, and they were reminded that nobody at home knew Chinese realities. They learned the key Britain in China dates (1900, 1927), and were directed to the correct historians, consigning China's living and past culture to the dustbin; they read them well.

Most arrivals in China would be male, young, single (by company or mission society regulations) and leaving home for the first time. Start-

## Amah

Amah's very useful (and doesn't scold a bit!)
I *never* have to dress myself and Mother needn't
knit.
She gets through all the mending (but darns blue
socks with gray!)
And washes all our dresses and irons them right
away.

When her work is over and Amah's in the mood,
She shows me to her husband and lets me taste his
food;
She gives me sticky candy, and curls my yellow hair,
And says I'm much more handsome than little girl
downstair'.

Amah says she's getting old—I *really* think it's true,
She's awf'lly round and wrinkled and walks quite
slowly, too.
She's going to the country while we are by the sea,
But Mother thinks it's just as well because she's
spoiling me.

**Figure 6** 'Amah': settler rhymes for children. From Patricia Allan, *Shanghai Picture-verse* (Shanghai, 1939)

ing on the boat out, men teamed up; later on, in bachelor 'messes' or more informally in clubs, they lived, worked, ate and played together. It was in the short and long-term interests of 'griffins' (new staff) to fit in immediately. It helped them overcome lonely disorientation, and ensured a smooth professional future. As one businessman recalled, 'First class travel for juniors was an introduction to the life they were expected to lead as a form of education. A bank needed its young to circulate, play games, etc., and often the friends one made rose with you to high seniority'.[28] Second-class Britons travelled second class – policemen, missionaries and their like – but the same principles applied. Peer solidarity was a general prophylactic. For example, firms required their staff not to compromise or bankrupt themselves in pursuing the delights of being monied and abroad for the first time. To that end, the new Masonic club opened in Shanghai in 1928 was intended as 'a social hall, where the younger masons could associate and spend happy evenings together rather than that they should be forced to seek relaxation in less favourable places'.[29] Worried about the fact that 'Shanghai for a young man fresh from home is the devil', one Swire director started an employee's riding club in 1925, hoping to influence new arrivals with a 'very good riding clique', who 'go to bed early and ride before breakfast, keep fit and do not waste their money on wine women and song'. Riding before breakfast often paled in comparison with such pleasures. A newspaper in 1928 lamented that employees 'once of excellent character ... have had to be shipped home, simply because they have gone to pieces from night life and easy credit'. Even the threat of civil action for debt might ruin a career, especially as the bad publicity in a small, acutely self-conscious community was felt to be 'letting the side down'.[30] The cashless 'chit' system was often blamed, a practice rooted in affected colonialism. Residents refused to carry cash on their person and instead signed IOUs, which were often not paid until presented at their homes. 'I felt like a plutocrat,' remembered A. H. Rasmussen on first signing a chit: others spent like one. Getting into debt was also often a process of transgression of racial boundaries and prestige, as Britons would borrow from Chinese colleagues, superiors or employees, or from Indians – especially in the SMP. The race hierarchy was thereby compromised in British eyes.[31] Probationary sergeant S. G. N. Bailey resigned in 1924 when facing court writs for payment of bills for 'clothes, liquor and motor cars'.[32] Sergeant James Douglas, on his sudden death in 1926, owed a third of his estate to three tailors, two garages, his shoemaker, four cafés, the SMP and Municipal Service Club bars, a watchmaker, as well as an unpaid newspaper bill. The total was equivalent to about five times his probable monthly salary.[33]

[ 80 ]

Despite these problems, and to counter the treaty ports' much maligned reputation, it was asserted that the quality of the British in China was up to empire standards. There was repeated stress on character. Manly and other virtues were identified in the 1928 obituary of a twenty-six-year-old banker, E. E. Tricker: horseman, shot, Volunteer, 'a true presentation of the standard Englishman, for he was bluff honesty personified'. A commentator in the China Inland Mission (CIM) journal *China's Millions* claimed that 'the average businessman in China today is a specially selected man, a man who has learnt to play the game in the public schools and universities of his homeland'. This idealised description of the young Briton – fair, firm, sporty, imperialist[34] (and, one might add, middle-class) – was hardly matched by the reality. British residents were not 'specially selected' and many did not 'play the game'. The quality of the British, while not easily quantifiable, was not highly regarded by observers: for Stella Benson they were 'tenth-rate'.[35] And as for middle-class, the British establishment needed its cadre of working-class British nationals: seamen, soldiers, policemen and labour overseers. These groups of men presented special problems of their own, but they could be subject to a harsher regime. Like many other British organisations in China, the SMP took what it could get, and lived with the high turnover of men, but it also arranged in 1906 for the men to be subject under Orders in Council issued by the Legation, to a military style discipline which meant men could be tried and jailed for infractions.[36] Character, if not internalised, could be disciplined, although the dead were beyond chastisement: 'bluff honesty's' debts, for example, far outweighed his estate.[37]

Not surprisingly, then, for observers such as the missionary E. R. Hughes – who launched an effort to improve these matters in 1932 – British businessmen did not live up to the gentlemanly standards they claimed, notably in their relations with the Chinese.[38] Visitors remarked on the impatient and violent behaviour of foreigners towards the Chinese, and diplomatic reports record it. Violence was common enough to enter Chinese Shanghai slang; eating *waiguo huotui* (foreign ham) meant receiving the all too frequent kicks aimed at rickshaw pullers by foreign passengers. The fabled cheapness of human life in China could be 'catching', as evidenced by the famous 1936 trial of SMP sergeant Peters for the murder of a sick Chinese beggar. With British public opinion in his favour he was acquitted despite the evidence, and it was not an unexpected result. Of an earlier case the Shanghai Consul-general remarked, 'that the jury would never bring in a verdict of 'guilty' against a 'white' British subject charged with murder or manslaughter of a Chinese'.[39] Suspicion and insecurity, and saturation in cultural portrayals of Chinese as a threat, and as responsive only to force, or the threat of force, contributed singularly to this situation. It would be wrong to caricature all Britons in China as belligerently racist all the time – as many historians do – but it would be equally incorrect to ignore the extremism of thought and action displayed in times of crisis, and, above all, it would be incorrect to ignore the facts of treaty port life, which bear little relation to the sentimental portrayals common in memoir literature. Repeated stress on the character of the treaty port British alerts us to both the bad public image of Britain in China and to its underlying insecurity.

These are the men who went; how did they structure their time when they arrived in their new environment? For many people it was their first taste of life outside school, or beyond a brief apprenticeship at offices in London. Missionaries had usually spent a year or two studying before being sent. Companies wanted efficient, hard-working and playing recruits: missions wanted energetic and linguistically capable evangelists; new arrivals wanted to find their place and establish themselves quickly. They did so by joining a club, a Volunteer corps (a 'social unit which partakes very largely of the nature of a club'[40]), the police specials, a Masonic lodge, a sports club, an old boys' association or a church. These institutions formed informal and formal networks of association and they shaped the community. Some were extensions of home networks – schools or lodges – which provided a ready entrée into society, and sometimes introductions to work. With such a variety of competing and differing reasons for being in China, it is clear that only through the institutions of the society, and processes of socialisation, could a sense of community have been established and maintained.

Britain in China was Anglican, and established churches where it could. Men might actively attend church according to their denomination (but not a church shared with Chinese converts, only with fellow treaty port residents); at the very least they marked births, weddings and death with Christian ceremonial. Being Christian also marked them out from Chinese who were not, or who, if they were converts, were felt by non-mission Britons to have effectively deracinated themselves. This functional Anglicanism also provided self-reassurance: in Shanghai's Holy Trinity Cathedral Shanghailanders asserted their decency, and humanity, and the organic completeness of their real community. Church organisations served social functions as well from the earliest days, running a seamen's hostel in Shanghai from 1859, while the Salvation Army ran a hostel for homeless foreign men in the city, and opened another in Hankou in 1935.[41]

More than the church, however, it was the club which structured treaty port life. The club provided accommodation and recreational facilities, a library, a bar, a meeting hall, and so on; most of all it provided company, new or familiar. Shanghai was a 'city in which a man is lost if he has not at least one club at his disposal'.[42] Exclusion of Chinese, club servants apart, served to distance Britons from their hosts, and from the unavoidable Chineseness that assailed their five senses outside the club doors. British exclusivity at the Shanghai Club contrasts with the Cercle Sportif Française, to which access was much less restricted, the American Club (Chinese members from 1929) and the German Club Concordia (Chinese members from 1917.[43] In the main, other foreign communities also kept themselves separate from the Chinese, except professionally, but those national clubs which were more cosmopolitan, such as the Cercle Sportif Français, were widely disliked by Britons for their 'mixed and dubious' company.[44] As important, clubs were socially segregated; exclusiveness was guaranteed by the high cost of membership and by the nomination system. Most ordinary Britons would never have set foot inside the Shanghai Club, mixing, instead, in the police canteens or in Masonic lodges. Clubs put people in place according to their nationality, race, class or sex. Women were excluded from the Shanghai Club, but most concessions also had a recreation club which admitted both sexes. The recreation clubs served the double function of sociability and sport, but club rules and conventions also imposed a discipline on social interaction and personal behaviour participation in club life meant participation in communal life, and playing by communal rules.

Freemasonry performed a similar function, and was extremely popular among foreign men. The first lodge was founded in 1849, and by 1928 the eleven lodges of the North China District had 850 members, including a cross-section of treaty port society. Some lodges were more fraternal than others: the Union Lodge Tientsin had a recognisably purely lower middle-class membership, while others were socially more refined. Membership was frequently plural and lodges would visit each other; policeman Maurice Tinkler described one such visit of his Shanghai lodge to the Doric Lodge, Chinkiang (Zhenjiang). For Tinkler lodge membership represented social advancement, enabling him to join a better club and cement himself further into Shanghai; in 1923 he was acting secretary of the lodge and in 1925-26 master. A. H. Rasmussen's climb from customs outdoorman to business manager was accompanied by enthusiastic Masonry.[45] Others, already Masons, found assimilation into treaty port society made easier for them.

Another forum for integration was the national society – St George's, St Andrew's, St David's or St Patrick's. The importance of such societies was bolstered by the premium placed on patriotism and

British identity. In the theatre of treaty port life Britishness was often reinforced by demonstrative national patriotism, particularly Scottishness or Irishness, and by that of dominion nationals too. National societies provided another forum for integration (and for organising the repatriation of the indigent). There was a Scottish Company of the SVC, and the annual St Andrew's Ball was a grand affair. National identity within Britishness could also abet fracture, of course: tension was visible over a Scottish preponderance in the SMP (although the Scottish presence in the empire generally was disproportionately large).[46]

The communal structures of treaty port life reinforced values acquired in Britain such as those associated with public schools – imperialism, militarism and sportmanship – and the ethos of public service.[47] Doctrines of service and militarism were also catered for by volunteer corps, which in Shanghai in 1928 comprised one-third of eligible British men – the highest national percentage. Informal pressure to join from superiors or peers remained strong into the 1930s.[48] There were Volunteer corps in Tianjin and Hankou, and small self-defence units elsewhere. Volunteering in Shanghai demanded a night's drill once a week, an annual camp, occasional parades and inspections. As well as performing a self-defence and public order role (the SVC was called out sixteen times between 1900 and the end of 1938), volunteering provided company, a mess and exercise. It was also an affectation. The annual inspection and the annual church parade of the SVC involved route marches through the settlement, whilst corps members were usually given ostentatious funerals with full military honours. These were public shows of British and communal confidence for the benefit of the participants but also served as a reminder to Chinese of where effective military power lay. Military spectacle also contributed to aggressive insularity in the British community itself, encouraging strains of paramilitarism and belief in seeking solutions though action, as opposed to diplomacy. For example, British civilians not under SVC control took an active part in the fighting that took place in Shanghai in the days after 30 May 1925.[49]

Sport was an integral part of treaty port life from the earliest days, and laying out a racecourse a primary ritual through which the British marked their new arrival and remade their new environment. The Hankow Race Club was the 'crown of Hankow' for one visitor; its 'long shady drive seems to transport you from China to the homeland'. Sporting ability was highly valued; companies sometimes asked their London branches to send out new staff with specific sporting talents, and a sense of a broader treaty port identity was partly boosted by 'inter-port' sports fixtures in rugby, hockey or cricket. Sport was a relaxation, but it was also a communal event – foreign businesses largely closed down on race days – and it was also an arena of social advancement, and of conspicuous consumption to advertise social arrival. The elite sport of paper hunting – fox-hunting without the fox – demonstrated mastery over the Chinese landscape near Hankou or Shanghai, as did shooting, another favoured recreation, which was less ostensibly elitist because cheaper. Shooting was at once exercise and relaxation, as men hired houseboats and were rowed out on to canals and waterways; it was also very much a social affectation, part of the cod-colonial middle-class lifestyle that even members of the SMP indulged in. Most events and clubs were strictly racially exclusive until the late 1920s, and only nominally desegregated thereafter.[50]

Patterns of sociability stretched out beyond social and sports clubs. Night life and informal socialising were important expressions of social status and interaction. Both consumption and participation were meant to be conspicuous, and productive and protective of status. In Shanghai, for example, foreign lifestyles followed patterns set by the settler elite, which were directly and speedily informed by New York, Paris and London. They were also structured by the peculiarities of extraterritoriality; in Shanghai in particular gambling was an ostentatiously popular illegal pastime. By no means could most residents afford such a lifestyle, but many still lived it anyway. Going to China involved going up a class in both lifestyle and aspirations. A man like Maurice Tinkler was mesmerised by the things he saw when he arrived in Shanghai in 1919. The son of a downwardly mobile Lancashire ironmonger, Tinkler had joined the army on leaving school in 1915, served on the western front for some three and a half years as private and NCO, and was in officer training when he was demobbed. After failing to find work in Britain, and feeling cut off from his family and home by the war experience, he applied to join the SMP. On arrival in Shanghai in August 1919 he wrote an excited letter home:

> Shanghai is the best city I have seen and will leave any English town 100 years behind – that's not exaggerated. It is the most cosmopolitan city of the world bar none and the finest city of the Far East. At night it is lit up like a carnival, and an orchestra plays in the Public Gardens along the river front. (Fountains beautiful trees etc.) ... There is a splendid electric car service and everyone seems to own one of the latest type of American cars.[51]

For Tinkler Shanghai meant, not the 'East', but modernity and the 'West': consumption, light, electricity. Bottom of the foreign pile, and bitter about it, he lived a life largely unthinkable in his native northwest England but wished the Chinese 'would have a real good riot, and murder a bunch of the petty, arrogant, local millionaires and profiteers. Then they might realise that the police force is here.'[52] While waiting for the bloodbath he consumed leisure activities and goods in Shanghai, going to night clubs, dance halls, the cinema. A sense of his worth as a man, and as a 'white man', as much as a taste for a good time was invested in this activity – Tinkler spent and talked his way off the bottom in 'white' company. Even on a low police salary he could afford to spend the time and the money: he had a string of White Russian girlfriends and took them out to places where he would be seen: for male company he joined the Freemasons. He consumed leisure by travelling for his own amusement, on shooting trips inland, and on trips abroad. As a detective Tinkler often used cars, and his letters recount how he strutted the lobbies of Shanghai's hotels, conscious of his swagger, his smart clothes, his shoes and his freedom to perform. He was also being self-consciously modern – peppering his letters with American slang, picked up from detective fiction, and idealising the United States as a modern go-getting meritocracy – more modern by far than his provincial English background. Throughout all this Tinkler lived a lifestyle pointedly at odds with the economic and social reality of foreign working-class life in Shanghai or other treaty ports.[53] In the 1930s especially in Shanghai there developed a hedonistic night club and cabaret culture which was used to market the city in guidebooks and damn it in *exposés*. For most settlers, however, with families to support, it was an irrelevance.

Irrelevant or otherwise, such *exposés* had their costs: they politicised the communal and social institutions and practices of the treaty port world, and condemned the character of the treaty port Briton. Shanghailanders had in fact largely lost a propaganda war by the end of 1927. Arthur Ransome's strictures on the 'Shanghai mind' and the 'Ulster of the East' did much damage to their international public image. These were the people, it was widely believed, who were, in the self-caricature of one council member, 'Die-hards of the most virulent and bloodthirsty type; ... all suffering from a chronic species of Brain fever known as the "Shanghai Mind" and ... we spend our time deliberately insulting our Chinese friends and our money on the up-keep of huge orchestras to which no one ever listens.'[54] The imaginary 'No dogs or Chinese' sign, alleged to have been placed by the council at the entrance to the public gardens on the Bund, finished off Ransome's work, a myth still officially perpetuated in mainland China despite the evidence collated even by its own historians that there was no such sign.[55] Foreign attacks on the settlement's handling of political and socio-economic issues had to be taken more seriously. The SMC followed a non-intervention policy with regard to social and industrial matters long after this was politically acceptable in the 1920s. The council provided few services, and those few mostly geared to its minority foreign residents until well into the early twentieth century. Arguing that to interfere with Chinese social problems or the economic status quo would be exceeding its powers, and claiming that measures of reform were likely to prompt civil or political disturbances,[56] the SMC had usually opted to do little. In the eyes of the British and US press by the end of 1927 Shanghailanders were exploiters of Chinese labour, which if it demonstrated against them was shot down in the streets.

A more positive identity for Britons in China was actively fostered through a constructed treaty port character that was described and reiterated in memoir after memoir. According to this self-image Britons in China were self-reliant, charitable, hospitable, convivial, meritocratic, brave, public-spirited; they were 'bluff honesty personified', fairminded and generous. They did what they had a right to do, no more, but certainly no less. These virtues were trumpeted in prose, as chapter 2 showed, and newsprint, to dissuade readers of notions of decadence or diehard reaction.[57] They did not deny, and were rather proud, that fortunes might be made in China; 'rags to riches' stories contributed to the legends through which the foreign community characterised itself.[58] Nor did they deny that life could be comfortable; but hard work and the 'frontier spirit' deserved rewards as long as treaty port Britons remained conscious of their duties and obligations neither to let the side down nor to show it up.[59] This stress on character also underlay the identity of the settler communities, which marked themselves off not by their socio-economic position (and thence drew attention to their insecurity), but by their imagined communal identity. In effect, they attempted to hijack the idea of a 'Shanghai mind' to their own use.

As well as reconfirming existing British and imperial values, these communal institutions and practices inculcated new values into recruits: physical isolation from the Chinese, distance from other national groups, loyalty to the local community, the firm, to the British enterprise in China, and to the 'race'. The intent was prescriptive, and the heightened Britishness of the treaty ports was a rejection of the Chinese world which otherwise swamped them, physically as much as metaphorically. Apart from going to seed, rack or ruin, the clichéd danger was of 'going native'. The danger was twofold: eccentricity and 'deracination'. Consular recruit J. A. Sinclair was warned against losing the right perspective when his enthusiasm for the language seemed to be getting the better of him: those who went Chinese were 'no use to us'. Popular mythology held that such enthusiasm was dangerous, as was study of the language itself, and Reginald Johnston was frequently pointed out as the prime example of such eccentricity. 'They lived pleasant lives,' wrote Richard Dobson of those who 'went Chinese', 'yet were never much good to the tribe any more.'[60]

## Women

Missionaries apart, society was predominantly male even after the turn of the century, when the proportion of British women residents started to rise as a variety of factors made life for foreigners in Asia easier, more comfortable and safer. Improvements in steamship services and other communications, in sanitation, disease prevention and medical treatment, and the introduction of the telegraph, electricity, refrigeration and so on, all made it easier and less risky for men to bring their wives out with them, to bring out women to marry and to raise young children. Wives were usually met in Britain on leave or were the daughters or other relatives of treaty port families. There were very limited employment opportunities for single women as secretaries such as Phyllis Harrop, who went to Shanghai as a single woman in 1929 and worked first for the telephone company and then as secretary to Sir Victor Sassoon, or as teachers or nurses with the SMC and in private hospitals; these women formed a marriage pool for institutions like the SMP.[61] By 1928 only four foreign women in Shanghai were of sufficient seniority to sign official correspondence for their companies. Employment opportunities were increasingly monopolised by the daughters of treaty port families, while lower-class women could be found running boarding houses or cafés: in 1934 there were two recorded British cabaret dancing partners in Shanghai's International Settlement. It is possible that there were more, and that some British women were employed by the foreign brothels in the city earlier in the century.[62]

Stella Benson felt that British 'Women are never apropos or relevant in China – they are never people – only ladies – a sort of social backwater.'[63] Benson, former suffragette, active snob and working novelist, was married to a CMC official, Seamus Anderson. A series of dreary postings in south-west China and Manchuria – recorded in her voluminous diaries, and in some travel sketches and novels – were enlivened by a sojourn in Hong Kong, where Benson became involved in social welfare activism. Her continued independent career was at odds with treaty port society, and with the CMC.[64] For most middle-class women in the larger settlements there was no question of work nor was there any question of access to any real community or political power or influence. Public life was structured around the Tientsin

Women's Club or the British Women's Association (BWA) in Shanghai, which catered for the 'social backwater', while journals such as *Social Shanghai* or *The China Journal* were developed for a foreign English-speaking female readership. Charitable, religious, sporting or theatrical organisations were also numerous, and on a smaller scale these patterns were copied in the outports if numbers were sufficient. Mostly, however, their relationships were more informal and centred on club life. Very little in their public life brought women into direct or more than token contact with Chinese. The Social Service Division of the BWA, for example, was 'for the relief of needy British women stranded in this port'. These clubs, associations and committees existed to provide something for the women to do as well as a mutual support structure, and they were also expressive of broader communal values and ideas, including distancing from Chinese.[65] It is hard to accept the applicability here of the claim that British women, in Malaya for example, because of their different educational experience, were less infused with imperial ideas than men. Nor were all the men there, or in Shanghai, 'subject to a narrow, standardised public-school training' so that the women were therefore 'more open-minded and adaptable ... to the realities of the colonies'. Socialisation took place in China itself among the British communities and was a very effective finishing school. Women were no worse and no better than men.[66]

Living, as did Chinese of similar social standing, in compound housing to protect themselves from the sights, sounds and smells of China, the home-making duties of the British wife in Britain in China certainly echoed those of British women in India. There the home was the Raj in miniature, and the woman's duty was often to manage this state and her subjects, the servants. Also, it was on women disproportionately that the duty fell of recreating Britain in the home, both as a source of psychological relaxation, and also as a statement of identity and purpose. On women too fell the duties, outlined by public health officials in Shanghai, of guarding the family, and children, from the dirt and disease of China, imported by servants or by their lapses into 'characteristically' filthy habits. It was the 'Missee' who fought the war of attrition against the assumed 'characteristic' dishonesty of the Chinese servant, and who saw that dignity (face) was maintained and that peculation (squeeze) was kept within a mutually acceptable range. Children were also to be protected from the servants into whose charge they were delivered, from learning bad habits (such as masturbation) and from developing emotional ties.[67] The quotidian reliance of Britain in China on Chinese even in the home was fraught with tension and insecurity, and men and women were ever engaged in policing the encounter.

## The outports

Treaty port life had its variations – urban Shanghai, calmer Tianjin – and then there was the comparative quiet of the 'outports': the smaller treaty ports, settlements and outposts scattered through China along the railway and river networks. Some Britons found the quietness and the opportunities for social status, sport and saving money agreeable. Others found them claustrophobic and petty, full of what has been called the '*misery of empire*'. 'Thence to the gunboat for a drink,' wrote a Swire's employee in Yichang in 1935, 'Oh, what boredom is expressed in those simple words.'[68] The average outport consisted of a club, some sports facilities, a few foreign business compounds outside the city and a nearby site chosen as a 'hill station'. In memoirs, letters and journals these often come across as lonely, empty places – empty, that is, of Europeans.

Expatriate businessmen on arrival in China often began in the 'up country' distribution agencies; the experience involved a great deal of rough living and functioned as a rite of passage in which men learnt their business, basic Chinese, and how to negotiate with Chinese; it also explains, partly, the marriage ban. Men were usually based in large towns from which tours of inspection of Chinese agencies were made. J. M. Philips joined the APC in 1923, serving in Canton, and then in Wuzhou, with three other secular foreigners (enough for bridge) who were shunned by the missionary community, and then at equally lonely Nanning. His letters record his glum experiences with verve and good humour, dampened for the reader by the knowledge that he died a lonely death at the hands of bandits in 1926, aged twenty four.[69] BAT's Richard Dobson, who survived his salesman's days in China to write an engaging memoir, started at Zhengzhou in 1936, with one colleague, a Belgian, a Scot and the inhabitants of a mission, then at Changsha with the eighteen-member Changsha Club. John Logan, another tobacco salesman, was based at Shijiazhuang in 1930 and described the foreign community as containing himself, his superior (an eccentric, 'gone native' English bachelor) and fifteen Frenchmen, each with his concubine. Death was ever a persistent partner of Britons' activities in China, and much more visible in these smaller outposts, and this is reflected in the memoirs: 'Six died in my second year,' noted Rasmussen of his spell in Zhenjiang.[70]

Loneliness made young newcomers more than anxious to fit in when they graduated to larger communities. After his up-country experience Dobson's early disdain for treaty port society was replaced with affection, and political upheaval cemented such loyalties. Most expatriates working for foreign-based companies were also moved around the county frequently, thereby gaining broad experience, but this was also useful for cementing men's loyalty firmly towards the company itself and to the small and similarly peripatetic British communities in which they lived and through which they moved as they were promoted. For many missionaries, too, based permanently 'up-country', it could be an intensely lonely experience: F. J. Griffith of the Church of England mission in Shandong did not see another European for eighteen months in 1915–16. Confrontation with the novelty and unfamiliarity of place and language – and isolation – could never adequately be prepared for beforehand.[71]

Missionaries apart, other Britons whose jobs were static became fiercely loyal to, and protective of, their own communities. In the first instance local identities evolved and were maintained. The most obvious was the Shanghailander identity; Tianjin residents evolved a less stridently publicly separatist identity in a concession that was smaller, staider and much more relaxed.[72] In both cities cosy coteries among the settler elites and the expatriate business community ran the institutions of public life, nominating each other for election to the councils, co-opting each other on to municipal committees, and appointing each other to positions in social, national and other societies. The smaller sites had their recognisable 'Pooh-Bahs'. U. J. Kelly in Zhenjiang provided one example in 1925: 'Secretary of the Doric Lodge, Chief of Police, Fire Dept., Public Works Dept., Waterworks, Sanitation, Secretary of the British Municipal Council and of all the clubs'. Swire's Shantou manager, Hance, ruled the roost in that port as other long-time residents did in theirs.[73] Consuls tended to fill this role in the smaller ports, although there was always an element of competition with the Customs Commissioner, who, as a Chinese government official, nominally led the wider foreign community. For all the differences, British life in the outports still worked to many of the same rules, with the same intent as in the larger cities. It remoulded new Britons into the treaty port style. Moreover, it emphasised class distinctions, and accentuated 'race' barriers.

The rhythm of treaty port life was punctuated annually by at least one long leave. When it could afford to do so, Britain in China took to the beaches at Weihaiwei, Beidaihe or Qingdao, or else to 'hill stations' – developed out of necessity, but also as a pseudo-Raj affectation. Every large settlement developed its favoured locale. It might be rented Chinese temple buildings or bungalows built at an upland site (Beijing's Western Hills, Chengdu's Bailuding or Guanxian), or *faux* – India style settlements complete with bungalows bought and developed by savvy foreign speculators. The largest of these were Guling and Moganshan.[74] Here were established clubs, churches and schools. Treaty port segregation was re-created as missionaries and commercials took to their own valleys, and there was national segregation too between Americans and Britons. As in India the resorts provided 'physical and psychical relief',[75] while educational provision for children there became important.[76] What was important for India was important here: the removal of children from the influence of Chinese servants, the excising of whatever Chinese dialect they had learnt, and a culturally 'British' education in what was assumed to be a healthy climate (and one more akin to 'home'), where parents might visit for their annual leave. For urban missionaries, too, boarding their children in these locations removed them from the moral threats of city life, and the spoiling life of settler culture.

## Missions and Missionaries

Segregating themselves even on holidays, missionaries formed an identifiable sub-community within the wider British community. Unlike most treaty port Britons they went to engage with and change China, although China itself was not necessarily important in itself. It was a 'heathen' field ready for conversion, and the criteria for the assessment of candidates for the China Inland Mission, for example, placed evidence of a 'call' to serve in China in particular only fourth among its requirements in 1931.[77] Some went out expressly to offer their professional skills to the Chinese – doctors and teachers, for example – whilst others felt a religious vocation for working in China that usually defied secular interpretation.[78] Some saw even mission service in China as social advancement. For Gladys Aylward Britain meant being 'consigned eternally to "servants' quarters"' in a rigid caste system. In China her status was immeasurably and instantly improved.[79] Most missionaries, after training in Britain for a year or two, went first to the North China Union Language School in Beijing, an American school in Nanjing, coastal schools at Xiamen and Shantou or the CIM Training Schools in Anping and Yangzhou.[80] After this language training they were sent either to their designated station, where most learning was done on the job, or first to a different nearby station for further language study. Although there were significant urban presences missionaries settled farthest out from the urban concentrations of foreign residents, but it is clear that until the late 1920s they mostly still lived in treaty port society. They lived in small isolated groups, and stayed within those communities, although each society had its own district organisations and these held monthly, quarterly and annual meetings. 'Itinerating', or trekking out into the countryside either to unevangelised areas or to check on converted ones, was the equivalent of the businessman's 'up country' tour and no more comfortable.

Missionaries had some of the closest continual links with all types of Chinese communities of all foreign groups in China, but the pattern of missionary life was hardly dissimilar to the rest of Britain in China. The structures of mission organisation and its social life institutionalised distrust of the Chinese and the acceptance of Chinese difference, and the need for segregation. Foreign-staffed missions generally ran Chinese church organisations, where Chinese Christians were usually in subordinate positions to Europeans. Most British staff lived in large foreign-style houses in mission or educational compounds. They had their servants and employed a variety of Chinese auxiliary staff in their schools, hospitals and church and residential compounds, just as businessmen did. In the LMS the experience of Marjorie Clements, who served in China from 1930 to 1936, was quite obviously a liberation from a dull and predictable existence in Britain, and a jump up a class in lifestyle. In her year of language training at Beijing there were holidays: the 'whole of August free. Absolutely. It's a thing I have never had in my life before.' There was a servant (at one point she had no idea if the servants went home or slept somewhere in her house) and responsibility both to the local communities and to the wider Christian enterprise in China.[81] For an ex-shop assistant and domestic help from a working-class family in south London this was revelatory, and there is a clear sense from her letters of a struggle between the temptations of treaty port life and her commitment to the mission. Some gave up the struggle. Her aged colleagues' frosty reaction to her taste for golf was one of the symbolic reasons for the speedy resignation of Miss J. M. Dixon from the LMS in Hong Kong in 1931.[82]

For the evangelical workers (that is, the active proselytisers and preachers) much of the hard work of evangelising was undertaken in the Chinese countryside, often in rough conditions (the equivalent of the salesman's 'up country' tour); but there was always a compound to retreat to in which could be found a British house, British food, furnishings, company and the exaggerated trappings of a middle-class British life style. British missionaries generally socialised with each other, and not with Americans or others. This was especially true of their holidays in Guling, Mogan Shan, Beidaihe, and so on, retreats of Britishness which, together with regular district meetings and conferences, punctuated missionary life.[83] Then there were the generally seven-yearly year-long furloughs, which would 'help to restore the sense of mental equilibrium … dislocated' by working in China.[84] In the larger treaty ports, such as Shanghai, Tianjin and Hankou, some missionaries were members of Masonic lodges and generally took part in the social and institutional activities of the British communities, and many openly identified themselves with the business communities and the political *status quo* of the treaty era. There were exceptions: Ronald Rees of the WMMS worked to foster better relations in Shanghai during the crisis of early 1927 by organising informal Sino-British discussion groups with British officers, businessmen and other non-missionaries.[85] An Anglo-American missionary coalition forced the SMC to close down brothels in the International Settlement in the period 1920–24. However, for many, the treaty port lifestyle and expectations were seductive.

It was widely accepted by the 1920s that missionaries had segregated themselves socially from their Chinese equivalents, and that this was a structural result of mission socialisation. Students at the North China Union Language School in Beijing, for example, like Marjorie Clements, only met Chinese servants and teachers and generally socialised with other foreigners.[86] Distance was reinforced in other ways. The adoption of Chinese children by missionary women was usually deprecated by mission boards; the WMMS refused to permit such children to live in mission bungalows. Such adoptions could not be prevented but the society refused to pay travel expenses and also refused to accept them as *bona fide* adoptions.[87] Intermarriage with Chinese was not condoned and was very rare (only one LMS woman married a Chinese man between 1875 and 1917). Refusal, or inability, to learn Chinese, notably by medical or educational workers, was also distancing, while formal language training for missionaries was still in its early days.[88]

Most businessmen paid public lip service to the rightness of the mission enterprise but there was much hostility. Missions were blamed for creating Chinese nationalism through their educational efforts. Evangelical Protestants from the United States were the main target of this abuse, and inevitably anti-American bias played a role. This was a mantra learned early in a businessman's career. 'Very poor fish,' wrote J. M. Philips, who later elaborated: 'Unconvincing, jealous, bickering, bigoted, Pharisaical and, on the whole, unchristian.'[89] The teetotal, anti-smoking and pious rigidity of many Protestant missionaries accounted for part of the social gulf – tensions that existed within missionary societies too. The problem was also partly a matter of class perceptions; the claim that the London Missionary Society (LMS) were 'usually people who got jobs as office boys or clerks' in Britain was characteristic, and missionaries were hardly free from making such claims themselves.[90] There was also the question of money. Missions could ill afford to pay their workers anything excessive, and staff generally travelled second-class on trains and ships in and to China, thereby segregating themselves from other foreigners and compromising, it was felt, British dignity by doing so.

Dislike was mutual if equally predictable and ritualistic. William Sewell was shocked by the behaviour of the foreign community in Shanghai towards Chinese; Marjorie Clements recorded drunkenness and abusiveness among American train passengers; T. Biggin feared for the morals of young police recruits. Revd Hope Moncrieff vividly complained about business life: 'the amount of money wasted on gambling, wine, cigars, horse and dog racing, and social vice, would meet the salary of most missionaries two or three times over.'[91] Still, army officer Jack Bazalgette developed a liking for CIM workers, whose aggressively fundamentalist approach to Chinese society appealed to many foreigners. In 1928 he found a kindred spirit in an ex-SMP officer turned CIM who put down 'the trouble to the foreign education of Chinese'.[92] Roman Catholic missionaries also tended to be admired for similar reasons, notably their success and, by inference, their doctrinal confidence. Theirs, in fact, was the 'missionary muscularity' so approved of by the pro-imperialists. Ultimately businessmen and others resorted to cliché. 'We are all missionaries,' declared banker Charles Addis at a London Missionary conference in 1934, whilst O. M. Green lauded their 'altruism'. In return the head of the CIM was keen to point out that 'the fact of our being missionaries does not make us less loyal Englishmen'.[93]

Missionary loyalty is in fact the reason for the inclusion of missionaries in the discussion at this point. Despite the obvious differences in training (and in geography, income, interaction with Chinese), the mission community was still subject to many of the same social and socialising practices to be found in secular Britain in China. As chapter 5 shows, it took the emergency of the Nationalist revolution to force mission societies to rethink their social practices, and indeed to rethink almost on a case-by-case basis the suitability of individual personnel remaining in China. Many missionaries and mission workers, including educational, health and other professionals, behaved and thought little differently from British settlers and expatriates. In the larger metropolitan centres outside Shanghai (which remained an exception) mission staff were more integrated into local foreign society than mutual hostility might suggest. And missionaries were also subject to the same taboos concerning their personal behaviour and relations with non-Britons.

## Boundary maintenance

We now turn to look at the core practices felt to be necessary to maintain and replicate the identity of all these 'loyal Englishmen', in particular the barriers of class, race and sex. This identity was represented and nurtured by the institutions of treaty port life, but it was also guarded from the threat that was China, and from the threats of the spoilt life lived by many Britons. To ensure the reproduction of the British community as it existed Britons needed, first, to replicate their society through socialising new recruits and children; thereafter they regulated themselves and each other. The function of this self-regulation was to define the group, protect it and punish transgressors.

Not forgetting one was British lay at the core of the new identity acquired by recruits and by children. Children were educated to be British, not cosmopolitan, and were either sent 'home' for their education, if their parents could afford the expense, or to schools in the treaty ports, some of which barred non-British children, and most of which barred Chinese. For settlers, education in Britain served to refresh and reinforce core British identity, and it often made children more acceptable for employment by expatriate companies in China on their return. These companies were often loathe to employ the 'Shanghai-born', unlike most settler firms. For expatriates it gave their children the education they would have had anyway, and trained them for entry to the labour market from or in Britain. For both it enabled the withdrawal of children from the inappropriate influence of Chinese servants, or unwelcomely cosmopolitan friends. At Tianjin's Gordon School one former pupil remembered that 'the walls were hung with pictures of English scenes' and portraits of the King and Queen. The aim of the school was to give its pupils knowledge of the 'British way of life', and there was a pointed absence of education about China, the Chinese and their languages.[94] Empire Day was celebrated with sports and Scout parades; the annual round of ceremonies, celebratory days and marches was important for children. These were the socialising methods common in Britain and more important in China if children were going to maintain, or indeed acquire, a British identity.[95]

For adult recruits education took place in the bar and the dining room, but also in the manager's office. Meritocracy was the stuff of the treaty port self-image, as it was in settler communities elsewhere, but hierarchy remained vital and prominent. As in Britain class awareness was accepted and acceptable. In the absence of a governing class which might snub 'commercials' as it did in the empire there was a greater degree of meritocracy among the elite than might otherwise have been the case, but there was still an observable and observed social hierarchy. A. H. Rasmussen wrote of 'a reality that none could escape' and later found it 'hard to conceive of a bigger change than that of an outdoor staff man in the Customs suddenly finding himself in the merchant class'. C. E. Temlett remembered being cut dead in mid-dance when his partner learnt that he was a customs outdoorman. There were two clubs in Zhenjiang earlier in the century, one for the outdoor customs staff and one for the consul, the indoor staff, and the merchants. The Shanghai Light Horse (Figure 8, p. 129) was the elite unit of the SVC and had a membership application procedure akin to that of a social club.[96]

The social status of a British businessman in China was probably greater in China than it would have been at home, but Stella Benson considered them 'converted kitchenmaids and promoted commercial travellers' (whilst the navy usually looked down on all British residents). The prospect of committing himself to a career in China surrounded by men he considered socially inferior caused Graham Greene to resign from BAT.[97] Expatriates considered themselves socially superior to the Shanghailanders of all classes, who were often described by expatriate businessmen and consuls as 'low whites' or 'lesser Europeans'. Expatriates attended different clubs and different Masonic lodges, and often lived in different parts of town, and were more likely to enjoy (and more able to afford) the night life Shanghai was supposedly famous for, than was the 1930 letter-writer: 'Clerk and family: 25 years and no home leave'.[98] Even in death there were distinctions: Jardine Matheson's had its own war memorial and Armistice Day ceremony. Class tensions could be divisive and prompted bitterness. Tinkler ranted in his letters about the Shanghai elites. In Warren Hill's novel The Crystal Skull (1930) a lower class Briton uses the mind reading powers of the skull to extract revenge for the snobberies of Shanghailander society. The author used a pseudonym but obviously knew Shanghai well, and hated it too.

For British settlers, their assumed social status was even more tenuous, especially among lower middle-class Britons in regard to the Chinese, and was seen by some as a cause of the perceptibly high level of racist aggression: 'they take it out of the Chinese so as to make themselves feel big,' claimed William Sewell. As he admitted, most of the Chinese the British community came into contact with were lower-class – servants, clerks, rickshaw men and coolies.[99] Those that were met at business or official functions – compradores, merchants – were rarely socialised with. Class prejudice was often used to articulate race prejudice: all Chinese were socially inferior. But the element of race was further emphasised in the question of sex.

The sexual taboo, as has been shown, was an important and conspicuous theme in fiction about China. In reality it is difficult to know whether the taboo was honoured more in the breach than in the observance, but it was certainly honoured in public and institutional observance, particularly when it came to marriage. 'Bluff honesty personified' did not betray the tribe by marrying out. Abroad has always been associated with sexual opportunity, and certainly not just by the British, frequently for the banal reason that this was how many young people left the security and restraining influence and presence of family and home society.[100] Social pressure and company regulation attempted to replace that lost external restraint.

In the earlier stage of the British presence concubinage with Chinese women was common, and not considered abnormal; indeed, it appears to have been encouraged, as a sort of release. Robert Hart had three children with his partner Ayaou; Bland was tempted more than once but claimed to have resisted.[101] The twentieth-century treaty ports were still largely bachelor societies, although the proportion of families settled there grew steadily. As elsewhere in the colonial world, British men took native partners when there was a shortage of fellow Britons or other Europeans.[102] The presence of European women – and after 1917 especially the influx of White Russian refugees – made stable sexual relations with Chinese as much 'unnecessary' as taboo. This at least was the public view: 'most of us preferred Shanghai because the girls were white,' recalled one sailor, although that still leaves a minority who 'tasted some of the fruits'.[103] There was a class qualification to this taboo, however. 'They were a bit more funny about their office staffs, because they came into the social life of Hong Kong much more than we did,' remembered one seaman of his employers.[104] Lower-class men were subject to a looser regime up to a point: Chinese prostitutes were provided for the troops of the Shanghai Defence Force in 1927, when brothels were taken over as *maisons tolerées* to curb the spread of venereal diseases among the force. Military efficiency, then, was the reason for fewer strictures over sexual behaviour, as was often the case elsewhere in the empire.[105]

Chinese women were still formulaically represented as unattractive in letters, diaries and memoirs. There is little evidence here before the 1930s of the sexualisation of Chinese women in the European male gaze, such as has been noted in other colonial contexts: real Chinese women were not considered sexually desirable.[106] Literary denigration did not always survive real meetings unchanged, although one commentator was apt to believe that prettiness among Chinese women was due to their having some 'white blood' - a rationalisation, perhaps, of a disquieting attraction. Colonial administrator, and later Cambridge university scholar, Victor Purcell (1896–1965) was unusual in admitting to having set up a Chinese mistress in Guangzhou in 1921–22 at the start of his career; a desire for a 'sleeping dictionary' and 'a bourgeois hankering after a regular establishment in place of brief encounters' were given as the reasons. While Britons often lived with Russians – it 'was fairly common ... and the Japanese seemed to be quite popular' – few lived with Chinese.[107] Sexual relations with Chinese women, then, seem to have been perfunctory matters of curiosity, middle-class 'psychic health', and lower-class libidos. Homosexuality, a double (and illegal) taboo in this context, is much less well documented.[108]

Sex, then, was probably all very well. But, to maintain its national and racial identity, British society in China operated a strict policy of race-determined endogamy for middle-class men – those it idealised as its representative leaders. A confidential circular was issued in the consular service in 1908 strongly deprecating marriages with Chinese, and threatening permanent exile away from the larger centres for those who did marry outside the group.[109] There were mixed marriages in all sectors of the community, but pressure was exerted by relatives, peers and superiors to make sure that expatriate businessmen and consuls did not get permanently involved with Chinese, Eurasians or Russians: 'Foreign, native, half-caste, are definitely taboo,' wrote the Hongkong & Shanghai Bank's chief manager in 1937. If men did thus marry, their 'services were normally dispensed with immediately' by companies such as Swire's, Jardine's and APC. The element of paternalism had three purposes: subordinating the individual to his company, protecting him in the expatriate society he had chosen to live in, and protecting that society from convention breakers.[110] The community's elite, as elsewhere in colonial societies, was expected to show restraint, judgement and that character they were boasted to possess. Unorthodox unions were 'letting the side down'. Of those who married Russians one woman remarked, 'they were not quite as good as they should be'.[111] Unsurprisingly, given their prominent denigration in fiction, Eurasians were widely disliked, both as partners and as issue; the language used to describe them was often strong, indicating how deeply the taboo was felt. Eurasians physically blurred the racial boundary, as well as demanding by their very presence responsibilities and attention.

Again, class differentiation was a factor. Marriages with Russians did occur, and, as in India, so did marriages between Eurasians and lower-class Britons. Of 249 marriages registered at the British Consulate-general in Tianjin between October 1919 and April 1934 fifty three were to Russian women, and four to Chinese. The great majority of the British husbands in question were customs officers or servicemen, or else were otherwise employed in lower-class or lower middle-class positions. In Hankou similar marriages accounted for twenty nine and four out of 150 registrations between 1917 and 1936. In passport-hungry Shanghai the motive could also certainly be mercenary. This class divide was also present among the US armed forces, whose officers would have ruined their careers but many of whose enlisted men did marry Chinese, at least before the Russian influx.[112] The marriage taboo grew in force throughout the twentieth century before declining gently towards the end of the 1930s. The registers of Shanghai's Holy Trinity Cathedral show no Anglo-Chinese weddings for the period 1923–41.[113] Other sources show that such marriages occurred, but the privacy of the consulate-general was preferred, presumably because of public distaste. Marriage to Chinese still rankled. Banned in the SMP until 1927, it was permitted thereafter only if the fiancée was investigated and proved to be of good class background, while continued restriction of the right to marry to men who had completed one term's service was designed to encourage them to try out the marriage market at home while on long leave. Allowances were made for lower-class sexuality, then, which were not tolerated in their superiors. For reasons of the efficiency of the men (to avoid administratively paralysing levels of venereal disease), their unimportance in the treaty port hierarchy, and because of the difficulty of policing their sexuality, lower-class Britons were allowed to marry notionally unacceptable partners. Sergeant Parker of the SMP was given permission to marry a Chinese woman in 1927: she was recognised by the commissioner to be of 'respectable parentage'; and he was 'unlikely to rise to the more senior ranks of the Force'.[114] In the flexibility of the marriage taboo the treaty port hierarchy was reinforced.

The taboo was also gendered. Women's sexuality was a point of explicit concern. By the 1920s non-Russian foreign prostitution had largely been suppressed, and women's marriage options became even more circumscribed.[115] Social pressures in the treaty ports against unions between foreign women and Chinese or other Asian men were extremely strong. The marriages that did take place occurred outside China between British women and overseas Chinese students.[116] This was a familiar colonial pattern. Moreover, British women who intended to travel to China to marry Chinese men were interviewed by the Far East Department of the Foreign Office in an endeavour 'to persuade [them] to give up the idea of such a marriage'. An official leaflet pointed out that the consequent loss of British nationality meant that British law could not 'protect [them] in China from treatment which does not conform with the rules applicable in Christian countries in regard to marriage'.[117] Treaty port opinion always had examples of this to present to unbelievers, quite apart from the lessons to be learnt from novels. Naval lieutenant Hilken's letters to his sister in 1930 detail his attempts to dissuade her from marrying a Chinese man: 'you would find the situation here very embarrassing if you came here [Hong Kong] together. Except in business, and on official occasions, the two races do not mix at all.'[118] Hilken's point is valid and worth remembering as a general principle: mixed marriages would have necessitated a greater amount of mixed socialising than the demands of British self-ascription accepted on any except formal occasions. This was partly because 'race' could not serve as the legal marker for British-controlled institutions. Exclusion of Chinese from the parks and swimming pools of the Shanghai International Settlement had to make exceptions for Chinese with British, or other foreign, nationality. A Chinese wife took her husband's nationality, and could not therefore be excluded – although she was issued with special passes and would be instructed to wear European dress.[119]

It is necessary to remember here that a recurring theme in correspondence from men in China is fear of male Chinese sexual desire for 'white' women. Prejudice against black male sexuality is well documented, and as Ann Stoler has demonstrated in her works, sex is 'a crucial transfer point of power, tangled with racial exclusions in complicated ways'.[120] Chinese men were excluded from close physical proximity with foreign women, for example in swimming clubs, and were kept out of European brothels and massage parlours until the 1930s. Naval officer Charles Drage recorded unease at familiarity between an American missionary woman and her Chinese landlord: 'it will always seem queer to me to hear a coloured man call a white girl by her Christian name'; the subtext is clearly sexual. Marjorie Clements reported the horrified reaction of American soldiers at her intention to spend 'a night alone with the "Chinks"' in a second-class railway carriage. For related reasons William Sewell and others decried the effect of the portrayal of European women in Western films as corrosive and dangerous. The dress and dancing of European women in China also came in for such criticism. This taboo was characteristic of European colonial societies.[121] For all the talk of the character, masculine virtues and restraint of men like E. E. Tricker, the upholding of prestige and protection of identity were highly gendered. Women's bodies were the chosen repository of British morals in Eastern places.

Social and sexual isolation and improvisation were compounded in the outports and mission stations. Stella Benson described the Nanning foreign community in 1929 as 'nine missionaries, three unregenerates'. The Swedish customs outdoorman was ill with syphilis contracted from a Chinese prostitute, while young Humphreys of APC, 'rather obsessed by his physical loneliness', pinned his hopes unrealistically on his missionary neighbours. Fear of syphilis kept him away from Chinese prostitutes. His predecessors in Nanning in the early 1920s, reported another of them, J. M. Philips, had included one suicide, two alcoholics, one murder victim and a man who took a Chinese mistress; another, 'Mercifully for him, was married just before he arrived here and left within four months.'[122] Other nationals were more open – remember John Logan's fifteen French engineers, each with his concubine – but if Nanning is at all representative then it would appear that the British were just more discreet, as they were elsewhere, in the light of greater social taboos, and that most sexual relations with Chinese women were considered a matter of contingency and necessity.[123]

Britons maintained their Britishness and distance from Chinese and China in other ways – through their diet, clothing, habits and language. They ate their domestic cuisine, reproducing as far as possible the tastes of home with Chinese or imported ingredients, and they mostly found Chinese food disgusting.[124] The preparation of British food – which usually meant teaching Chinese cooks approximations of familiar dishes – and the eating of it served as daily domestic rituals, involving the maintenance of 'standards'. Personal papers show Chinese food being eaten only on ritual social occasions, or sometimes out of curiosity.[125] The difficulties Britons had were not merely to do with familiarity and health – the latter a real fear as many young lives were lost to diseases such as typhoid – but were also to do with prestige. They also retained prestige by not wearing Chinese clothing, except perhaps as a joke. Missionaries who did so for real were disdained by many of their colleagues, let alone other British communities. A mannered eccentric like Reginald Johnston certainly enjoyed the shock value of posing in Chinese clothing, but on the whole it was not done, and the fact that Chinese men traditionally wore gowns also made such clothing unmanly. Britons took rickshaws, not trams, in Shanghai, conscious in these small details of personal and what was called 'racial' prestige. Tinkler learnt quickly to 'go about in rickshaws mostly and throughout the East they get to be a habit with everyone'.[126]

Not wishing Chinese food to enter his mouth, the treaty port Briton also tried to keep Chinese words out of it too. In this China followed the colonial pattern, which made language a positive and necessary barrier, and a marker of difference.[127] Obviously Britain in China was rooted in exchange and interaction between Britons and Chinese, exchange which required levels of understanding, including language and social customs. But for most Britons this was facilitated by Chinese agents, or by a small minority of their fellow nationals. Superficially, language acquisition was not a necessity. English so dominated treaty port commerce that even treaty port German was heavily affected in diction and vocabulary.[128] Linguistic limitations forced direct communication to be undertaken in pidgin English, a language of demand and command, which also served as a vehicle for ridicule of the Chinese. Otherwise communication was reduced in English to 'friendly noises' between fellow businessmen, and Britons were forced to rely on Chinese translators. Chinese still had to be learnt by many British employees, but the rule was more honoured in the breach. It was unpopular, and was considered demeaning or deracinating. Transfers around the country militated against expatriates spending their time learning a dialect unintelligible elsewhere in China, and companies unrealistically expected staff to study in their leisure time or on the job. For other British employees, such as policemen in Shanghai, promotion and pay were linked to passing language exams, and the job itself would have been impossible without some grasp of the language. But few linguists would willingly have chosen to join the SMP. Pidgin, gesture and a limited vocabulary of loud imperatives were the sum of the communication skills of many, particularly those who filled supervisory roles.

Insularity and self-protection led the British community to close ranks against perceived transgressors of its rules. 'The community usually cured them, but if it didn't it broke them,' remembered G. H. Gompertz, a Jardine's employee.[129] Sir Frederick Maze was the target of one particular communal exclusion during his struggle with the British Legation for the post of Inspector-general of the CMC in 1929, and men were informally drummed out of the treaty ports. This was not specifically a British trait but the British made a greater virtue of national solidarity and prestige (especially in criminal cases) than other national groups in China professed to. In times of crisis this sensitivity led individuals who were not in favour of 'gunboat' policies to be accused of being 'pro-Chinese'. The application of this term in particular was peculiarly indicative of the community's insularity and hostility to the Chinese community. To a very limited extent the British also tried to regulate entry, and continued residence in China, by their fellow nationals. Obviously, all companies and organisations attempt to regulate entry to those who, fulfilling organisational needs, will best be able to operate. The Legation could refuse its good offices to shady businessmen, and Orders in Council regulating business were issued in 1915, partly to try to introduce some checks on *bona fides* and behaviour. There never was a crook on the scale of the American Frank Raven, whose group collapsed in May 1935, but the threat remained that abuses of extraterritoriality could go well beyond the acceptable.[130]

Although settler society quite obviously developed through neglect rather than design, the British state and treaty port leaders did attempt at least to prevent the growth of a white underclass, or class of poor whites. But this initiative was not born of altruism: the fear was that such a class would be detrimental to the 'prestige' of the British, bothersome to its consulates and Legation, and liable to confuse Sino-

British relations. Unlike in India, where the numbers and government powers over British subjects were greater, this was a haphazard process.[131] Dismissed lower-class men were shipped home from China, where possible. In particular the SMP, the largest cadre of working and lower middle-class Britons – and the group of men who may have built up the worst of non-British contacts – was the focus of attention. SMC policy was to attempt to persuade policemen to leave Shanghai through contracts which provided free passage home. The record of those who stayed tended to show that this was a sensible policy. Poor whites compromised 'white prestige', not only through public drunkenness or indigence, but through the very fact of their poverty and the compromises they had to make with their British cultural identity, such as living in Chinese houses and neighbourhoods, and eating Chinese food.

The external function of these taboos was also to maintain distance. Close contact with the Chinese was felt to be corrupting of British character, and not just for those whose linguistic or cultural interests got the better of them. Taboos bolstered the theatre of official and municipal life which demonstrated distance, prestige and visible power. The public parades of the SVC and foreign defence forces, and the use of Sikh policemen, were expressions of this, as was the gunboat. The need here was to believe, despite the reality, in a public school-educated leading class which ought to know how to restrain itself, and to discipline the lower classes. These taboos were important, and were prominently visible. They stemmed from the very insecurity of the British presence. In terms of numbers, even in Shanghai, the largest concentration of Britons in China, they never exceeded their 1871 highpoint of 1.16 per cent of the International Settlement's population.[132] Insecurity was also rooted in the total reliance of the British on Chinese, as their servants, compradores, colleagues, workers, employees, and on the treaties. To maintain and replicate their community, and their identity in the face of those – British and Chinese – who opposed it, required strong wills, clear boundaries and harsh justice.

## Believing

It was important for Britain in China to demonstrate its commitment to the various strands of its identity: imperial, British, local. These were matters of patriotic communal demonstration and individual internalisation. It is important to take seriously their 'imagined community', and their self-ascribed incorporation into the larger British imperial diaspora and the 'Britains over the seas'.[133] On Empire Day in

1928 at the Shanghai Club Sydney Barton, Shanghai's Consul-general, declared that he hoped that 'the spirit which animated our Empire had not been wholly absent from the representatives of the Empire's people who lived here.' Empire was present in more than spirit, as Barton continued: 'In Shanghai, though outside the bounds of the Empire, we had concrete evidence of the privileges of citizenship in the Empire in the presence of His Majesty's naval and military forces, who had come from many corners of the Empire for the protection of this community.' Others explicitly claimed that theirs was an imperial role. Frederick Maze, Inspector-general of the Maritime Customs, claimed that he was playing a 'lone hand' in an 'Outpost of Empire'. 'The Flag at Chinkiang' was how the *North China Herald* chose to announce the reopening of the consulate there in 1928, emphasising the patriotic and imperial element.[134] If the empire stood for anything immediately tangible to the Shanghailander then it stood for the expansion of British influence, culture and trade. How better to promote trade with China than through the creation of a city run by institutions created on British lines and staffed by Britons? They believed that their very autonomy and their imagined identity served imperial interests. Empire Day, coronations and jubilees were celebrated with all the pomp the community could muster. Writing and thinking themselves into the empire was an insurance policy: if the British state believed that Shanghai, Hankou and Tianjin were imperial assets their longer-term future might be assured. So at times of crisis (1925–27, the late 1930s) the rhetoric gained added urgency. The Britons lionised in treaty port legend were not the free-traders whose activities had established the British in China but men of war and empire: Gordon, Parkes and Hart. The settler communities in particular saw their forebears as men who fought, advised, saved and organised the Chinese in such a way as benefited the foreign presence. Mostly individuals, their legends stressed the importance of individual character, behaviour and endeavour to Britain in China. Patriotism could be exaggerated, as it was in Jiujiang in 1927:

> After the Parade foreigners and everyone adjourned to the consulate where we drank the King's Health after the consul had made an excellent Imperialistic speech, this part of the programme finished off by singing God Save the King – a thing one would look on as somewhat theatrical if done at Home, but then an Englishman has got to go abroad before he realises what the King stands for and means to him personally.[135]

The annual royal birthday celebrations in Shanghai saw impressive displays of national sentiment and military force, as did, of course, the national days of other foreign states. Showing off was *de rigueur*. In

1928 3,000 troops and SVC members paraded, a twenty-one-gun salute was fired, every seven shots being interrupted by a rifle fusillade from the SVC and the singing of a verse of the national anthem.[136] Such clumsily pompous rituals were conducted on Armistice Sunday, St George's (Patrick's, Andrew's and David's) Day and usually involved cenotaph ceremonies, church services, march-pasts, receptions, dinners and balls. Most communities had a cenotaph, or at least a war memorial.

'Citizenship of the empire' might be demonstrated in this way, and many believed in it, but it also served as a gloss over a much stronger strand in the triple identity of the treaty port British. For settlers, more than any other community, their local identity was paramount. British and imperialist identities came to the foreground in emergencies of their own devising (May Thirtieth) or of those facing the British state. Hundreds returned to Britain to join up in World War I; among the dozens killed were thirty seven members of the Shanghai Club alone.[137] The acting Captain Superintendent of the SMP had resigned in October 1914, and gone to join the 10th West Yorkshire Regiment. On 15 December 1914, having met them on arrival in London, he marched about two dozen of his former Shanghai charges in column up to the Central Recruiting Office in Whitehall, where many of the men volunteered for service in his regiment. 'I left Shanghai to fight for my King and country and the cause of freedom,' wrote one of the men, SMP Sergeant Grimble. 'I can assure you I put one or two in for Shanghai,' he continued, of his bayonet. But he left his legs in France, and at least fifteen SMC employees were killed.[138]

Putting one or two in for Shanghai was important. Settlers were Shanghailanders, or residents of Tianjin or Hankou, first and foremost. Local identity was rooted in the mental appropriation of the history of 'Shanghai' or 'Tianjin' or 'Hankou' by Britons for themselves. The development of these ports was portrayed as solely their creation. Nothing was there before them, and no one helped them in their work of creation. Like other British settlers, or the Boers in South Africa, and Deliaan planters in Sumatra, they saw themselves as having moved on to 'empty' land.[139] They also had founding legends, the empty mudflats on which they had been allotted their concessions and settlements had turned to mercantile gold at their touch, and like many aspiring nations they had founding victories, notably the SVC's battle of the Muddy Flat (1854). In this way they asserted their independence, self-reliance and communal spirit.[140]

As in British literature and popular culture, the Boxer rising remained central, and many of the participants were still alive and working in China in the late 1920s. In 1924 Charles Drage was entertained at dinner by Meyrick Hewlett's account of the Legation Siege, whilst one young banker was often told similar first-hand stories in 1929. The treaty port press kept memories active. On 'Siege Day' in 1931 a memorial service was held at the Canton Road cemetery in Tianjin. Consular representatives, military detachments and a band gathered with other foreign residents for a ceremony which took in a 'Memorial Prayer', the singing of Kipling's 'Lest we forget' and the decoration of the pertinent gravestones by Boy Scouts and Girl Guides.[141] Here again we see the importance of the Raj: the Boxer rising was Britain in China's 'Mutiny'; 1900 was its 1857, its 'Red Year'. We see this too in the memorials they fashioned for themselves, the 'Lest we forget' wall at the British Legation, which visitors were often shown, or a memorial at the Shanghai Consulate-general to five consular casualties of the Beijing siege, and in the continuing discourse on modern China.[142] In the face of 'Chinese fanaticism' Christian foreigners were always 'besieged' in the metaphorical Legation compound. Of all things, the Boxer rising actually made the British enterprise in China respectable. There was little profit to be found in the two conflicts invariably and unhappily termed the 'Opium Wars', however often treaty port Britons demurred that free trade and diplomatic equality had been the issue. But with the Siege of the Legations the British in China acquired a thoroughly respectable imperial blooding, and imperial incorporation. A modernised version of the Boxer 'outrages' may be seen in the reaction to, and the totemic use of, the Nanjing incident in 1927. Nanjing was just what the foreign community was waiting for: when Nationalist troops took the city a number of foreigners were roughly treated and six were killed. Rumours spread of rape and murderous xenophobia, and the events were swiftly mythologised in the press, in club talk and in Nora Waln's fiction *Within the Walls of Nanking* (1928). Re-articulating recent events in the language of a heroic past and a pan-imperial present conveniently simplified recent political history for new arrivals, expressing Britain in China's situation in the language of empire. Such beliefs provided rationales for attacks on government policy and the activities of British officials in China. 'Our diplomats of the Victorian era were of a different mettle,' thundered 'British Trader' in a 1927 letter to the *North China Daily News*.[143] John M. MacKenzie has shown how the British empire's heroic myths were in fact 'primarily military'; these local variants emphasise the assumed imperial mantle of Britain in China.[144]

## Conclusion

Britain in China, then, maintained itself through the treaty system, through the British military presence, and through effective socialisation of newcomers, and regulation of the private and public lives of its members. An incoherent assemblage of conflicting and competing interests, permitted to function in China by virtue of British protection, fashioned itself into a whole. Britain in China's wholeness lay not so much in any broad communal identity as in the shared process by which specific values were disseminated, and modes of behaviour were regulated and replicated. What coherence there was lay in the settler community. Settler hegemony in the institutions and social practices of the treaty port world ensured complicity in the Chinese Raj from the distinctively different British communities of expatriates, missionaries and officials. By flexibly incorporating itself into the mental world of empire, by stridently protecting and asserting the three strands in its identity – British, imperialist, local – this fractured society of competing interests preserved its *bona fides* in the eyes of the British state, while at the same time protecting its difference from Chinese and foreign society. In this way a community some 13,000 strong (1930) maintained and replicated an identity increasingly at odds, as we shall see, with the currents of Sino-British relations, and British 'national interests'. 'One thought instinctively of Lucknow,' wrote the Revd Scott when he saw APC's Chongqing installation surrounded by Chinese troops, but flying the flag, in 1926.[145] The next two chapters will show how attempts were made by various official and private individuals to stop people instinctively thinking of Lucknow, and to make them think of China, the Chinese nationalist present and the future. In the following chapter we turn to the attempts at the re-establishment of control by the British state over Britain in China after 30 May 1925, when the mock Raj and modern Chinese nationalism were shown to be incompatible.

## Notes

1 Albert Feuerwerker, *The Foreign Establishment in China in the Early Twentieth Century* (Ann Arbor MI, 1976), 39, 46–7.

2 Forty-five of these files were examined among the SMP's papers in the SMA U 1–9$_3$ series, SMP Personnel Files.

3 In 1933 some 76 per cent of the land in the International Settlement was registered in British names (in 84 per cent of the total land value). British ownership was often merely (but profitably) nominal; actual ownership lay in the hands of Chinese, who were forbidden to own land under the land regulations, but did so through British agents. I owe these calculations to Christian Henriot's unpublished analysis of the SMC's cadastral register for 1933.

4 Information on the Skinners comes from family-held sources.

5 Joshua Fogel, 'Shanghai–Japan: The Japanese Residents' Association of Shanghai', paper prepared for the conference 'Wartime Shanghai, 1937–45', Lyon, October 1997, 8.

6 Lachlan Strahan, *Australia's China: Changing Perceptions from the 1930s to the 1990s* (Cambridge, 1996), 105–6; Maisie J. Meyer, 'The Sephardi Jewish Community

of Shanghai, 1845–1939: The Question of Identity' (London School of Economics Ph.D. thesis, 1994). Chiara Betta, 'Silas Aaron Hardoon (1851–1931): Marginality and Adaptation in Shanghai' (School of Oriental and African Studies Ph.D. thesis, 1997).

7  PRO, FO 228/4324/2 84x, Legation to FO No.162, 13 February 1930.
8  Markovits, 'Indian Communities in China, c. 1842–1949'.
9  On the Russians see Wang Zhicheng, *Shanghai E'qiao shi* (History of the Russian Émigré Community in Shanghai) (Shanghai, 1993), and the work in progress of Marcia R. Ristaino: 'Port of Last Resort: The Diaspora Communities of Shanghai'.
10  Lora Wildenthal, 'Race, Gender, and Citizenship in the German Colonial Empire', in Frederick Cooper and Ann Laura Stoler (eds), *Tensions of Empire: Colonial Cultures in a Bourgeois World* (Berkley CA, 1997), 268, Stoler, 'Rethinking Colonial Categories'.
11  Robin Cohen, *Global Diasporas: An Introduction* (London, 1997), 68; *The People*, 16 March 1919-25 May 1919; *Directory and Chronicle of China and Japan ... 1922* (Hong Kong, 1922), 808–11.
12  John Logan, *China: Old and New* (Hong Kong, 1982), 3.
13  Leslie Gill interview, BBC 'Lion and the Dragon' (hereafter [name], BBC 'Lion and the Dragon'); Kennedy, *Islands of White*, 46–7.
14  NARA, RG 263, Shanghai Municipal Police Special Branch records (hereafter SMP) D3002; Norman Sherry, *The Life of Graham Greene*, I, *1904–1939* (London, 1989), 194–210. Daniel S. Levy, *Two-gun Cohen: A Biography* (New York, 1997); Charles Drage, *General of Fortune: The Story of One-arm Sutton* (London, 1963).
15  *BCCJ*, March 1928, 72; *NCH*, 10 March 1928, 388.
16  Hewlett, *Forty Years*, 3; J. A. Sinclair, BBC 'Lion and the Dragon'; A. H. Rasmussen, *China Trader*, 8–11; Woodhead, *Journalist in China*, 49; W. F. V. Pennell, *A Lifetime with the Chinese* (Hong Kong, 1974), 89.
17  Woodhead, *Journalist in China*, 13; Pratt, *War and Politics*, 9; Hewlett, *Forty Years*, 1; Bland papers, 'Memoirs', chapter 1, 1.
18  Jonathan D. Spence, *The China Helpers: Western Advisers in China, 1620–1960* (London, 1969), 292.
19  ST – 5, p. 2.
20  ST – 19, p. 13; SOAS, Royal Institute of International Affairs. Far East Department papers (hereafter RIIA), Box 8, Lionel Curtis, 'Notes on China', 20.
21  R. K. Renford, *The Non-official British in India to 1920* (Oxford, 1987); P. J. Marshall, 'The Whites of British India, 1780–1830: A Failed Colonial Society', *International History Review*, 12 (1990), 26–44.
22  For British influence on the American community see James Huskey, 'Americans in Shanghai: Community Formation and Response to Revolution, 1919–1928' (University of North Carolina Ph.D. thesis, 1985), 35–7. On the influence of the Indian pattern see Callaway, *Gender, Culture and Empire*, 70–5; on that pattern see Dane Kennedy, *Magic Mountains*, passim.
23  W. J. Moore, *Shanghai Century, or, 'Tungsha Flat to Soochow Creek'* (Ilfracombe, 1966), 31.
24  Hewlett, *Forty Years*, 2–3; J. A. Sinclair, BBC 'Lion and the Dragon'.
25  NMM, Hamilton papers, Journal, 11, 27 May 1927.
26  SOAS PPMS, W. G. Sewell Papers (hereafter Sewell papers), Box 16/3, journal letter, 9 September 1928.
27  For African parallels see Kennedy, *Islands of White*, 155.
28  Maurice Lister, unpublished 'Memoirs', 13; Christopher Cook, *The Lion and the Dragon: British Voices from the China Coast* (London, 1985), 17–18; C. King, 'The First Trip East – P & O via Suez', in F. H. H. King, ed., *Eastern Banking: Essays in the History of the Hongkong and Shanghai Banking Corporation* (London, 1983), 212–13.
29  *NCH*, 28 January 1928, 140.
30  SOAS, John Swire & Sons papers (hereafter SP), ADD 1079, J. K. Swire to G. W. Swire, 11 May 1925; *NCH*, 30 June 1928, 551.
31  A. H. Rasmussen, *China Trader*, 4.

32  SMA U 102–5–156, file on S. G. N. Bailey (SMP: 1921–24).
33  PRO, FO 917/2656, James Douglas, probate file.
34  *NCH*, 14 January 1928, 54; *China's Millions*, August 1929, 123. See Mangan, *Games Ethic and Imperialism*, 18–19.
35  Benson Diaries, 19 April 1930.
36  'King's Regulation No. 1 of 1906: Regulations for the Shanghai Municipal Police, 12 October 1906', in G. E. P. Hertslet, *Treaties, etc. … between Great Britain and China*, II (third edition, London, 1908) 1080–1.
37  HSBC Group Archives, London (hereafter HSB), LOH I 103.243, Semi-official letters from Shanghai, F. E. Beatty to A. Moncur, 7 February, 30 March 1928.
38  PRO, BT 60/31/5/65, E. R. Hughes to Crowe, 15 December 1932.
39  Innes Jackson, *China only Yesterday* (London, 1938), 32; PRO, FO 228/4312/164 84, W. Russell Brown to Lampson, Hankow S/O, 18 February 1930; Yan Fusun, *Shanghai suyu dacidian* (Dictionary of Shanghai Colloquialisms) (Shanghai, 1924, facsimile edition, Tokyo, 1971), 30–1; N. F. Allman, *Shanghai Lawyer* (New York, 1943), 96; Peters, *Shanghai Policeman*, 233–322; PRO, FO228/3980/3 20k, Shanghai No.172, 1 June 1929.
40  *NCH*, 22 June 1928, 503–4.
41  George Lanning and S. Couling, *The History of Shanghai*, I (Shanghai, 1921), 435; *Central China Post*, 7 February 1935, 9.
42  *NCH*, 18 August 1928, 287.
43  G. H. Gompertz, *China in Turmoil: Eye-witness, 1924–1948* (London, 1967), 80; Huskey, 'Americans in Shanghai', 173; Françoise Kreissler, *L'Action culturelle allemande en chine: de la fin du XIX$^e$ siècle à la Seconde Guerre Mondiale* (Paris, 1989), 15–16. For details of the institutions available in two treaty ports see O. D. Rasmussen, *Tientsin: An Illustrated Outline History* (Tianjin, 1925), 304, and *Shanghai Commercial and Shopping Pocket Guide* (Shanghai, c. 1935), 391–409.
44  Gompertz, *China in Turmoil*, 80.
45  Lanning and Couling, *History of Shanghai*, I, 435; F. M. Gratton, *The History of Freemasonry in Shanghai and Northern China*, revised by R. S. Ivy (Tianjin, 1913), 303; *Calendar of the District of Northern China (E.C.)* (Shanghai, 1937), 14; *Freemasonry in Northern China, 1913–1937*, 107, 139, 207, 319; Christopher Haffner, *The Craft in the East* (Hong Kong, 1977), 169–70; Christopher Haffner, *Amoy: The Port and the Lodge: The Corinthian Lodge of Amoy No. 1806 E.C.* (Hong Kong, 1978), 102; W. S. Sims, *The Story of Union Lodge No. 1951, E.C., Tientsin, North China* (Tianjin, 1931), Appendix 'A'; IWM R. M. Tinkler papers (hereafter Tinkler papers), letters, 27 November 1921, 10 October 1923, 16 December 1925.
46  Strahan, *Australia's China*, 108–12; John M. MacKenzie, 'On Scotland and the Empire', *International History Review*, 15 (1993), 714–39.
47  See Mangan, *Games Ethic and Imperialism*.
48  *NCH*, 16 June 1928, 467; 16 May 1928, 455. Woodhead, *Journalist*, 15; W. H. Evans Thomas, *Vanished China: Far Eastern Banking Memories* (London, 1956), 50.
49  The same thing happened in Hankou: IWM 89/21/1, J. E. March, memoir, 71.
50  Austin Coates, *China Races* (Hong Kong, 1983); Gretchen Mae Fitkin, *The Great River: The Story of a voyage on the Yangtze Kiang* (Shanghai, 1922), 59–60; C. Cook 'The Hongkong and Shanghai Banking Corporation in Lombard St', in F. H. H. King, ed., *Eastern Banking: Essays in the History of the Hongkong and Shanghai Banking Corporation* (London, 1983), 200; *Central China Post*, 7 February 1935, 9; C. Noel Davis, *A History of the Shanghai Paper Hunt Club, 1863–1930* (Shanghai, 1930).
51  Tinkler papers, letter, 22 August 1919.
52  Tinkler papers, letter, 27 November 1921.
53  This paragraph is based on Tinkler's papers at the IWM.
54  SMC, *Municipal Gazette*, 19 April 1928, 159c. Ransome's articles were published as *The Chinese Puzzle* (London, 1927).
55  See Bickers and Wasserstrom, 'Shanghai's "Chinese and Dogs not Admitted" Sign'.
56  They had a point; see Tim Wright, 'Shanghai Imperialists versus Rickshaw Racketeers: The Defeat of the 1934 Rickshaw Reforms', *Modern China*, 17 (1991), 76–111.

57 O. M. Green, *The Foreigner in China* (London, 1943), 14.
58 'A Great Romance of Shanghai: Death of a Resident who once Slept on the Bund and who Gave £50,000 to a Museum', *NCH*, 21 April 1928, 104.
59 FSC CH/5/4, Sewell letter 19 February 1927.
60 J. A. Sinclair, BBC 'Lion and the Dragon'; Dobson, *China Cycle*, 50.
61 Phyllis Harrop, *Hong Kong Incident* (London, 1943), 7–12.
62 *NCH*, 28 July 1928, 149, 153; 19 May 1928, 307; on the cabaret dancers see NARA SMP D5695, report dated 9 March 1934. On foreign prostitution see Eileen P. Scully, 'Taking the Low Road to Sino-American Relations: "Open Door" Expansionists and the Two China Markets', *Journal of American History*, 82 (1995), 62–83.
63 University of Cambridge, Add. 6798–6802, Stella Benson Diaries (hereafter Benson diaries), 21 February 1930.
64 Susannah Hoe, *The Private Life of old Hong Kong: Western Women in the British Colony, 1841–1941* (Hong Kong, 1991), 247–65; Perry Anderson, 'A Belated Encounter', *London Review of Books*, 20:15, 30 July 1998, 3–10, 20:16, 20 August 1998, 28–34; Joy Grant, *Stella Benson: A Biography* (London, 1987).
65 O. D. Rasmussen, *Tientsin*, 257–8; *NCH*, 21 January 1928, 83; 11 February 1928, 243; 24 March 1928, 489; 2 June 1928, 367, 371; *BCCJ*, December 1931, 310–11.
66 J. Brownfoot, 'Sisters under the skin: Imperialism and the Emancipation of women in Malaya, c. 1891–1941', J. A. Mangan, ed., *Making Imperial Mentalities: Socialisation and British Imperialism* (Manchester, 1990), 49.
67 See, for example, Cook, *Lion and the Dragon*, 56–8, 116–17; see, also, Jane Hunter, *The Gospel of Gentility: American Women Missionaries in Turn-of-the-Century China* (New Haven CT, 1984) 128–73.
68 R. Hyam, *Empire and Sexuality* (Manchester, 1990), 89–90; SOAS, PP MS 49 Scott papers, Box 2, M. W. Scott Diary, 7 May 1935.
69 IWM DS/MISC/99, J. M. Philips Papers, Letters to P. S. Jones.
70 Dobson, *China Cycle*, 15–16; Logan, *China*, 54; A. H. Rasmussen, *China Trader*, 26.
71 Dobson, *China Cycle*, 13, then *passim*; SOAS, PP MS 49 Scott papers, Box 1, file 2, F. J. Griffith to Miss Heathcote, 11 January 1917.
72 Similar differences have been identified in the Japanese communities in Tianjin and Shanghai, Fogel, 'Shanghai-Japan', 22–6.
73 Tinkler papers, letter, 16 December 1925; Charles Drage, *Taikoo* (London, 1970), 273.
74 *China Year Book*, 1936, 180–1; Crow, *Handbook for China*, 169, *NCH*, 18 August 1924, 274.
75 Tess Johnston and Deke Erh, *Near to Heaven: Western Architecture in China's old Summer Resorts* (Hong Kong, 1994); Kennedy, *Magic Mountains*, 8.
76 Kennedy, *Magic Mountains*, 130–46.
77 SOAS, Overseas Missionary Fellowship papers, archives of the China Inland Mission (hereafter CIM), London Council Minutes, volume 16, 13 May 1931, 317.
78 See for example Ronald Rees, *Life in China 1922–1947* [Harrow, 1971], 1 (Sewell Papers, PPMS 16/38); Sewell himself went 'in response to the promptings of our Chinese student friends': PPMS 16/18, 'Early Days of Medical Education in China', talk given at the ECA summer school, Oxford, 1929, 1.
79 Alan Burgess, *The Small Woman* (London, 1957), 56.
80 *CMYB 1918*, 311–20.
81 SOAS, Council for World Mission archives, London Missionary Society (hereafter LMS), China Personal Box 13, Clements to Mrs May, 2 August 1931; Candidates' Papers 1900–1950, Box 8, M. G. Clements.
82 LMS, South China (hereafter LMS SC) Box 27, Dixon to F. H. Hawkins, 5 August 1931.
83 *CMYB 1911*, appendix VII, xxiii–xxviii.
84 LMS North China (hereafter LMS NC) Reports Box 11, A. P. Cullen, 'Annual Report 1931'.
85 SOAS, Wesleyan Methodist Missionary Society Archives (hereafter WMMSA) South China (hereafter SC) fiche 582, R. Rees, circular letter, 30 March 1927.

86 LMS Central China (hereafter CC) Reports Box 11, David F. Anderson, 1930, 'Report of the First Year's Work in China, 9th December 1929 to 31st December 1930'.

87 WMMSA Synod fiche 198, WMMSA to the SC Missionaries' Meeting, 28 November 1929; , WMMSA WW Hupeh, fiche 126, [?] to Miss Long, 20 January 1932; WMMSA WW Hupeh, fiche 117, Nora Booth to Miss Heller, 23 March 1924; SOAS PP MS 49 Scott Papers, Box 3, file 22, F. J. Griffith to Miss Heathcote, 24 April 1929.

88 Rosemary Seton, '"Open Doors for Female Labourers": Women Candidates of the London Missionary Society, 1875–1914', in Robert Bickers and Rosemary Seton, eds, *Missionary Encounters: Sources and Issues* (London, 1996), 67; K.S. Latourette, *History of Christian Missions in China* (London, 1929), 640–1.

89 J. M. Philips papers, letters, May 1925, 7 April 1926.

90 ST – 19, p. 6.

91 FSC CH/5/4, W. Sewell, circular letters, 25 March, 1 June, 2 July 1927; LMS China Personal Box 13, M. Clements, Letter to Mrs May, 23 September 1933; LMS NC Reports Box 10, T. Biggin, 'Report for Year 1928'; SOAS, Presbyterian Church of England Archives: Foreign Missions Committee and Women's Missionary Association (hereafter EPMA), Fukien Box 19, Revd Hope Moncrieff to P. J. Maclagan, 31 July 1928.

92 IOLR, J. Bazalgette letters, 23 July 1927, 17 October 1928.

93 Dobson, *China Cycle*, 32; J. M. Philips Papers, letter, 7 April 1926; Sir Erich Teichman, *Affairs of China* (London, 1938), 291–3; Mangan, *Games Ethic and Imperialism*, 168–75; Roberta Dayer, *Finance and Empire: Sir Charles Addis, 1861–1945* (Basingstoke, 1988), 251; Green, *Foreigner in China*, 90; PRO, FO 670/220/56, Revd D. Hoste to Prideaux Brune, 20 January 1928.

94 Brian Power, *Ford of Heaven* (London, 1984), 142–3; Mark J. Gayn, *Journey from the East* (New York, 1944), 132–3.

95 On Empire Day see MacKenzie, *Propaganda and Empire*, 232–6.

96 Rasmussen, *China Trader*, 5, 75; C. E. Temlett, BBC 'Lion and the Dragon'; IWM 89/21/1, J. E. March memoir, 94, March papers. On meritocratic myths and realities among Kenyan and Rhodesian settlers see Kennedy, *Islands of White*, 182–6.

97 Benson Diaries, 21 February 1930; Hamilton papers, Journal, 4 October 1927; Sherry, *Life of Graham Greene*, 200, 205–9.

98 A revealing slice of this life is caught in Cook, *Lion and the Dragon*, and in the transcripts of the oral history project Cook undertook for Swire's: SA, ST; *NCDN*, 26 January 1930, 4.

99 FSC CH5/4, W. G. Sewell, journal letter, 25 March 1927.

100 John Pemble, *The Mediterranean Passion: Victorians and Edwardians in the South* (Oxford, 1988), 99–102; Paul Fussell, *Abroad: British Literary Travelling between the Wars* (Oxford, 1980), 113–16.

101 Dayer, *Finance and Empire*, 13–14; Katherine F. Bruner, John K. Fairbank and Richard J. Smith, eds, *Entering China's Service: Robert Hart's Journals, 1854–1863* (Cambridge MA, 1986), 151–4, 230–2; Bland papers, 'Memoirs', chapter 2, 8–12.

102 Kennedy, *Islands of White*, 178.

103 ST – 18, Reel 2, p. 11; Caulton, BBC 'Lion and Dragon'.

104 ST – 1, p. 45.

105 *CWR*, 18 February 1928, 300; *CET*, 26 January 1928, 55; PRO, WO 191/43, 'No. 3 British General Hospital 1927 January–July, War Diary'; Ann Laura Stoler, *Race and the Education of Desire: Foucault's History of Sexuality and the Colonial Order of Things* (Durham NC, 1995), 179; Kenneth R. Balhatchet, *Race, Sex and Class under the Raj: Imperial Attitudes and Policies and their Critics, 1793–1905* (London, 1980).

106 Stoler, *Race and the Education of Desire*, 184–90; Malek Alloula, *The Colonial Harem* (Minneapolis MN, 1986).

107 IWM, Charles Drage papers (hereafter Drage papers), Journal, 17 October 1923; Victor Purcell, *The Memoirs of a Malayan Official* (London, 1965), 129–33; ST – 1, p. 38; Bland papers, 'Memoirs', chapter 3, 4–16.

108 But see Anne-Marie Brady, 'West meets East: Rewi Alley and Changing Attitudes

towards Homosexuality in China', *East Asian History*, 9, (1995), 97–120.

109 PRO, FO 369/133, Circular, confidential, 26323/08, 15 August 1908; P. D. Coates, *The China Consuls: British Consular Officers, 1843–1943* (Hong Kong, 1988), 441–3.

110 F. H. H. King, *The History of the Hongkong and Shanghai Banking Corporation*, III, *The Hongkong Bank between the Wars and the Bank Interned, 1919–1945: Return from Grandeur* (Cambridge, 1988), 285–9.

111 ST – 8, p. 35.

112 PRO, FO 674/321–324; FO 666/18–20 *passim*; Cook, *Lion and the Dragon*, 26.

113 Lambeth Palace Library, London, Mss. 1567–72, Holy Trinity Cathedral, Shanghai, marriage registers.

114 SMA U 102–5–471/1, Extracts from the Watch Committee Minutes, 11 Feburary 1927.

115 Scully, 'Taking the Low Road to Sino-American Relations', 65; Christian Henriot, *Belles de Shanghai: prostitution et sexualité en Chine aux XIX$^e$–XX$^e$ siècles* (Paris, 1997), 319–39.

116 Prominent Chinese families were not necessarily in favour of such unions either: Shanghai Academy of Social Sciences, Chinese Business History Resource Centre, Liu Rongsheng archives, 14–014, Liu Rongsheng to his sons, 18 August 1933.

117 Callaway, *Gender, Culture and Empire*, 51; Butcher, *British in Malaya*, 185–6. PRO, FO 372/3139, T10589/10589/378, E. S. Harris, minute, 4 September 1935, on Cadogan to Foreign Office, No. 1231, 31 July 1935.

118 NMM T. J. N. Hilken papers, letters to Kathleen Hilken, 21 January, 22 December 1930.

119 The issues are dealt with in SMA U 1–3–868, 'Admission of Chinese to Parks (1920–25)', and SMA U 1–3–2434, 'Public swimming bath and pool – Misc. (1923–30)'.

120 Stoler, *Race and Education of Desire*, 190. See also Kennedy, *Islands of White*, 138–41, and Callaway, *Gender, Culture and Empire*, 237–40.

121 Drage papers, Diary, 21 October 1925; LMS China Personal Box 13, Marjorie Clements, letter to Mrs May, 20 June 1931; W. G. Sewell, *Land and Life of China* (London, 1933), 130; Ann Stoler, 'Making Empire Respectable: The Politics of Race and Sexual Morality in Twentieth Century Colonial Cultures', in Jan Breman, ed. *Imperial Monkey Business: Racial Supremacy in Social Darwinist Theory and Colonial Practice* (Amsterdam, 1990), 46–8.

122 Benson Diaries, 24 March; 9, 11, 16 February 1930; J. M. Philips papers, letter, 7 April 1926.

123 Callaway, *Gender, Culture and Empire*, 48–51.

124 Hamilton papers, Journal, 11 June 1927.

125 See also Carl Crow, *Foreign Devils in the Flowery Kingdom* (New York, 1940), 254–65.

126 Tinkler papers, letter, 22 August 1919.

127 Kennedy, *Islands of White*, 155–60.

128 Kreissler, *L'Action culturelle allemande en chine*, 20.

129 Gompertz, *China in Turmoil*, 54.

130 W. Stark Toller, *Handbook of Company Law* (Shanghai, 1923); on Raven see *Oriental Affairs* (March 1936), 118–22.

131 Kennedy, *Magic Mountains*, 135–6; David Arnold, 'European Orphans and Vagrants in India in the Nineteenth Century', *Journal of Imperial and Commonwealth History*, 7 (1979), 104–27. See also Kennedy, *Islands of White*, 168–70.

132 You Yiren, *Jiu Shanghai renkou bianqian de yanjiu* (Research into Population Change in old Shanghai) (Shanghai, 1980), 145.

133 Wright, *Twentieth Century Impressions*, preface.

134 *NCH* 26 May 1928, 334; 8 September 1928, 403; Maze papers, Confidential Letters, Vol. 3, Maze to A. J. Toynbee, 6 January 1930.

135 Hamilton papers, Journal, 3 June 1927.

136 *NCH*, 9 June 1928, 426–7.

137  *NCH*, 11 February 1922, 378.
138  SMC, *Annual Report*, 1918, 21a–23a; SMA U 102–5–23, A. F. Grimble to K. J. McEuen, 1 April 1926, 6 April 1916.
139  Stoler, 'Rethinking Colonial Categories', 150.
140  Robert Bickers, 'History, Legend, and Treaty Port Ideology, 1925–1931' in Robert Bickers (ed.), *Ritual and Diplomacy: The Macartney Mission to China, 1792–1794* (London, 1993), 81–92.
141  Drage papers, Journal, 24 September 1924; HSB, S16.1 Personal Narratives, B. C. Allan, Narrative, 11 May 1963; 'British Memorials in Peking' in *NCDN*, 13 August 1927, 11; 15 August 1927, 7; 'Shanghai's Cemeteries and Monuments', *Oriental Affairs* (June 1938), 316; *Peking and Tientsin Times*, 18 June 1931, 4.
142  Simms papers, Journal, 17 January 1925, see also 2 June 1925. Paul A. Cohen, 'The Contested Past: The Boxers as History and Myth', *Journal of Asian Studies* 51 (1992), 92–6; J. E. Hoare, 'The British Embassy in Peking 1861–1991', unpublished Ms., 1991, chapter 5, 5–6.
143  C. Martin Wilbur, *The Nationalist Revolution in China, 1923–28* (Cambridge, 1983), 91–2; *China in Chaos*, 1; see also Rodney Gilbert in *NCH*, 16 April 1927, 114. Drage papers, Journal, 24 September 1924; see Bland on the 'Foreign Office school of thought', *China*, 176–97; *NCDN*, 15 August 1927, 4.
144  John M. MacKenzie, 'Heroic Myths of Empire', in MacKenzie, ed., *Popular Imperialism and the Military, 1850–1950* (Manchester, 1992), 113, 134.
145  IWM W. F. Scott papers, Letter to his sisters, 23 October 1926.

# CHAPTER FOUR

# Dismantling informal empire

We now turn to look at the early days of the journey from Hankow 1927 to Hong Kong 1997. The acute crisis of the mid-1920s, prompted by May Thirtieth, and deepened by the Nationalist revolution, forced British diplomats to begin reconfiguring the British presence. This chapter explores the problems they faced and the resistance they met, and narrates the slow process of change down to the commencement of the Pacific War in December 1941. Reform of diplomatic practices and pretensions was allied to structural reform of the treaty port system (treaty revision, for example) and a concerted diplomatic drive to revamp the rump settler communities. The chapter then looks at settler resistance, before turning to the final victory of the diplomats. Three distinct phases can be seen: crisis management and profound reform in the aftermath of revolutionary upheaval (1925–31), a quiescent period of deceptive normality for the remains of the treaty port system (1931–37), and then a renewed diplomatic drive to nullify settler power (1937–41). During this period British diplomats abandoned their long-term allies, the treaty port settlers, and chose new collaborators: an alliance of expatriate interests and selected leading China companies. Despite active and artful resistance, and despite the entrenchment in mentalities and structures identified in the previous chapter, the settler grip on the British presence in China, and on the British imagination, was broken. By the outbreak of the Pacific War the British state had nationalised Sino-British relations.

Britain in China was a complex, overlapping community of sectors often at odds with one another, as we have seen. It took for its public style a pan-imperial pomp common east of Suez and originating in India. In the bar, in the office, on the streets and in the bedroom, Britons in China also acquiesced in a network of taboos and restraints that served to maintain the cohesion and claims to legitimacy of just one sector: the settler community. This distortion of British economic relations with China provides the key to an understanding of the difficulties facing the British state's China policy in the early twentieth century. Settlers could not just be ignored, or wished away. Moreover, they had the potential, demonstrated by May Thirtieth, to spark conflagration. This chapter explores the range of tactics employed by British diplomats to reassert control. Theorists of imperialism argue that persistent instability in a situation of informal influence often brought about formal intervention, and this certainly happened in China. But, instead of backing up the British presence, the diplomats came to pack it up.[1] Although the events of 30 May 1925 forced British diplomats to begin attempting to disengage China policy from acquiescence in settlement, it took the best part of the next two decades. Early British efforts to abandon extraterritoriality were thwarted by a lack of will in the face of organised settler resistance in 1931, and the Japanese invasion of Manchuria provided an excuse for shelving such efforts and lessened Chinese enthusiasm for antagonising possible diplomatic allies in its struggle with Japan. Even so, through collaboration with expatriate business figures, and other allies – including non-British nationals – radical changes were introduced to those municipal administrations which survived the 1920s, while the character of the British economic relationship shifted towards transnational companies, and a core of settler China companies that were able to adapt. But it was only during the build-up to the Pacific War that British diplomats managed to seize effective control of the SMC – the last but strongest bastion of settler power – and it was only with the Pacific War itself that the settler issue was finally resolved. The Sino-British treaty of February 1943 abolished extraterritoriality and the remaining concessions: the foundations of the settler world were destroyed.[2]

Dismantling the settler presence required two broad movements in British diplomatic activity in China, which built on the broad-brush policy initiatives generated by the December Memorandum and the January Offer, notably renegotiation of the British stance on customs tariffs, and extraterritoriality. High policy apart, the diplomats needed on the one hand to dismantle the settler power structure and, on the other, to reform the settler mentality. The two moves were certainly interconnected: they hoped to foster changes in attitudes by reforming concession life and influencing the personal behaviour of individual Britons and, by altering their behaviour, to reinforce alterations in the political structures of treaty port life.

Reform led to the formal re-entry of the British state into the private sphere of Sino-British relations after 1925, in an attempt to undo the damage carried out by its previous neglect. The Foreign Office, in alliance with a core of expatriate business interests, began to identify, in effect, which British interests in China it was prepared to support. Other sectors of the British presence were then categorised, in principle, as, if not expendable, then of little priority because of the political difficulties they posed. Even so, it still had these other interests on its hands, of course, and untangling the Shanghai knot, for example, would be no easy matter. In its dealings with Britain in China the Foreign Office, and its Legation, laid urgent stress on reforming treaty port institutions, attitudes and expectations. Mending fences with the Guomindang would have few results if treaty port Britons kept punching holes in them. Here began in earnest the drawing together of the expatriate China interests, prioritised by London and the Legation – and by themselves – and the British government. This process reached its climax in the years after 1937, but characterised British diplomatic attitudes throughout the Nanjing decade.

'British interests' were also, of course, and continued to be, strategic: Britain's military presence played a role in imperial defence schemes; questions of 'prestige' were constantly factored into China considerations; there was the question of Anglo-Japanese relations, while China was one front line in the struggle of the empire against the USSR and its support for anti-colonial movements and Asian communism. These factors all informed China policy, including the dismantling of the treaty port system, but on the whole that process was carried out with little disruption of these other national interests.

## The British establishment in China

To start with, diplomats had to begin acting like diplomats. They had to reform their own patterns of behaviour and come to terms with losing the prestige of proconsularity, and also some real control over key revenue-raising organs of the Chinese state. The Legation and the consular service were both heavily implicated in the mock Raj, and disengaging them from it – without unsettling diplomatic dignities – was a key aim and feature of British Minister Sir Miles Lampson's regime (1926–33). The emphasis on British 'prestige' in private life was discussed in chapter 3, but it was also a constant theme in public life. Empire depended on prestige, and with men like Sir John Jordan as British Minister (1906–20) it was hardly surprising that the British diplomatic establishment affected proconsular airs after 1900, and particularly after the collapse of centralised political power in the early republic. This was partly based on effective British control of the Chinese Maritime Customs after 1911–12 – a key source of central government income already partly in British hands – and this was bolstered by the establishment of foreign administration in the Salt Gabelle in 1913.[3] Holding the purse strings gave British diplomats an unhealthy close interest in the activities of the various Beijing governments of the 1920s.

But prestige was more than just the exercise of power: it also lay in the theatre of diplomatic life. The 1901 Boxer Protocol saw the creation of an extraterritorial Legation Quarter in Beijing, governed by the diplomatic body in committee, which exercised full administrative rights in the heart of China's nominal capital. The consulates and consulates-general scattered throughout China fulfilled similar functions.[4] Diplomatic airs were also based on the grand physical reality of the Legation compound itself, and Britain's leading role in legation life, and the maintenance of these appurtenances was instinctive. The Legation itself, a 'city within a city within a city', accommodated some 2,000 people: 'There is no other Legation that can compare with it; either for beauty or for dignity,' claimed Lampson in March 1927.[5] The Guomindang set up their capital in Nanjing and changed Beijing's name to Beiping to expunge associations with the corrupt Northern governments and their subjection to the foreign powers, but British diplomats stubbornly remained in Beijing until 1935, and it is clear that despite 'practical' reasons elaborated against any earlier move, the motive was prestige. A new legation would have had none of the dignity or the historical associations – of the Boxer siege and the victory of the powers – of that in Beijing. Beijing was also perhaps symbolic of the warlord years when the British successfully handled relations with the Northern governments in what one China merchant described as a 'hopeless atmosphere of fatuous note-writing to Chinese ministers who probably don't exist'.[6] Nanjing had acquired humiliating overtones as a result of the 1927 Nanjing incident, and scuttling down to the Yangzi looked uncomfortably like kow-towing to a Nationalist whim. Scuttle down to Nanjing the Minister eventually did, however, in 1935 – and as an ambassador, to boot, although the Beijing compound was not given up until 1959. Ritual and symbol characterised the new Chinese republic after 1912, and continued to do so under the Guomindang.[7] The battle over symbol was readily joined by British diplomats.

Imperial *hauteur* was not confined to the insular symbolism of the Legation district and its walls. Lampson admitted in 1927 that 'the Legation has of recent years had practically no contact of the human kind with the Chinese', and embarked on 'serious dinners for all Chinese of note' including a rather gratuitous 'gala show' for the doomed warlord Zhang Zuolin. A Sino-British Club was formed in 1928 in pursuit of such gastronomic *détente*, whilst the Peking Race Club held its first joint meetings with the local Chinese club.[8] Innocuous as they seem, such new efforts to interact with Chinese administrators and politicians on an informal level marked the opening of a different relationship, and an inversion of the attitudes and preconceptions of the British: distance became a disability, *hauteur* hamstrung good relations. No longer was it sensible to act out fantasies of proconsular grandeur, and so diplomats and consuls became mere diplomats and consuls. Some found it just as interesting; in Nanjing the convivial consul-general, Sir Meyrick Hewlett, lubricated relations with senior government officials through alcohol and bridge. Consuls all over China were enjoined to be less distant, and more engaged with their Chinese peers, after 1927. Efforts were made to rid the service of diehard settler supporters, such as Sir Sidney Barton in Shanghai, who was kicked upstairs to become Minister in Abyssinia. At higher levels personal relations improved to the point that, despite wide differences in diplomatic stance, the 1931 negotiations on extraterritoriality were conducted on a houseboat on a waterway near Nanjing, and Lampson's personal relations with Chiang Kai-shek were good. These attempts to ease social relations between leading Chinese and diplomats were also important because of the leading role consuls played in British treaty port society, and the example they could set. They were largely initiated by Lampson and the new career diplomats he requested from the Central Department of the Foreign Office; these were not men from the China establishment.[9] The changes were made much easier for the British by the fact that the men they were now dealing with were nearly all Western-trained, and the quality of officials in the Chinese Ministry of Foreign Affairs was high. Negotiating unresolved treaty issues – as well as the negotiation of quotidian affairs between consuls and Commissioners of Foreign Affairs – became much more difficult, but it also became much more challenging.[10]

The quality of British officials looked distinctly poor by comparison with the new breed of Chinese diplomat. One of the first things Lampson did on arrival in China was set up a Legation committee to investigate the state of the consular service and suggest reforms.[11] Despite some improvements many problems remained unresolved, and amalgamation of the service with the general consular service in 1935 was partly concerned with making sure that China recruits would be spending at least a quarter of their career to come outside China, keeping them fresher and more attuned to life outside the treaty port world.[12] The onset of war, and the end of the treaty system, rendered such reform redundant.

The consular service was an organ of the British state, but it was also part of the British community. As might be expected, instructions to student interpreters going to Beijing laid most stress on the sporting accessories and social outfits needed for treaty port life, whilst clerical officers going to Hankou were told about the club and sporting facilities. Many consuls, or their relatives, married into treaty port families, and all lived and worked among them; this and the fact that consuls spent their careers in China often caused conflicts of interest, and explains why the odd man – such as Sir Sydney Barton – 'went native', and threw his lot in with the settler interest.[13] Consuls also acted as the leaders of the British communities, in Shanghai and in the smaller ports. They took a wider lead in the communities honorarily presiding over chambers of commerce, for example, whilst in 1928 Barton in Shanghai was president of the Boy Scouts' Association (Shanghai branch) and the Shanghai Horticultural Society, among other posts. There were national celebrations to preside over, and troops to review: many, in fact, were the occasions for consular plumage and gravitas. Dressing up to inspect the Boy Scouts was hardly discontinued, but in their relations with local Chinese authority (normally through the Commissioners of Foreign Affairs) consuls had to change their behaviour and the character of their response to many issues and their relationship with the local settler interests. A rigid official stance and direct consular intervention in cases involving British nationals, over taxation, in shipping disputes, or over the forcible occupation of mission premises, for example, which were once routine, began to be recognised as anachronistic. Such an approach was also increasingly ineffective: the time for '"incidents" and "teach them a lesson" is definitely past' reported one consul-general in May 1928; 'direct co-operation' was now necessary.[14] The time was past, too, for acting out the pomp of empire beyond its bounds.

### The Chinese Maritime Customs

It was certainly time to face up to the inevitable loss of influence over Chinese government bodies such as the Customs, Posts and Salt. Under Sir Robert Hart, Inspector-general of the service from 1863 to 1908, British hegemony in the CMC was kept functionally and nominally understated. Hart worked to keep the service independent of foreign power and overbearing influence, and to instil this ethos into his subordinates. The capture of a controlling interest in the service in 1911–12 by the foreign powers, who were keen to ensure smooth repayment of foreign loans in the new era of apparent turbulence and provincial autonomy, quickly became a fixed part of the proconsular landscape. The foreign inspectorate took over collection of the revenues and their deposit in foreign banks, while an International Commission of Bankers – appointed by the Diplomatic Body in Beijing – assumed control of loan repayments, passing the surplus over to the

Beijing government.[15] A major source of Chinese revenue now lay in foreign hands, and the 'surplus' was not automatically handed over.

There were two issues facing the British by the end of the 1920s: control of the inspectorship-general and related personnel matters, and the 'threat' to business practice and European jobs posed by 'sinification', or, as one consul-general put it, 'infiltration of Chinese' into the service.[16] The service had been built up on British lines, argued the British, and only Britons would be able to keep it running effectively. Hart had been succeeded by Sir Francis Aglen in 1911, who was dismissed by the government of Zhang Zuolin in 1927. A struggle in 1928–29 between two Britons, A. H. F. Edwardes and Sir Frederick Maze, for the top post, left vacant during the Nationalist revolution, was badly mishandled by the Legation, which backed the loser, for the wrong reasons, and vilified Maze as a deracinated traitor who thought nothing of swearing an oath of loyalty to the National government.[17] This curious episode contrasted strongly with the pragmatism starting to be shown elsewhere. The necessity of safeguarding the service for the protection of Chinese trade and the vital role the foreign staff played in bolstering the 'moral flabbiness of the Chinese mind', as represented by morally weak Chinese customs officials, was the stated motivation. An altruistic appeal was also made to the financial needs of the National government which, it was claimed, could be secured only by the CMC as it stood. Lampson later described his misgivings as an 'instinctive mental reserve' about Chinese corruption and inefficiency. The contradictory internal logic of this prejudice later led to complaints that Chinese customs examiners were over-diligently applying the letter of the regulations to foreign merchants, as a result of their instinctive xenophobia, whilst foreign customs officials were also 'held down to strict instructions' for fear of disciplinary action.[18] Opposition to sinification more generally stemmed from the entanglements of empire, and was partly motivated by the desire of consuls to protect the livelihoods of friends and relations who participated fully in the activities of their local foreign communities.

Maze claimed all along that he intended to preserve the foreign element in the Customs, and he largely succeeded, remaining head of the service until 1943.[19] Although control of the service and its revenues passed effectively into Chinese hands its character did remain semi-British, with enough concessions to satisfy the demands of Chinese staff and the propriety of the National government.[20] Chinese started entering the higher ranks of the service in more than nominal numbers in 1928, and the character (and language) of the service was altered from British (English) to Chinese.[21] Similar unsuccessful arguments were used against sinification of the CMC as were heard from defend-

[ 121 ]

ers of the effectively foreign-run Salt Gabelle, a more recent addition to the diplomatic portfolio.[22] In all these cases the Legation and consuls attempted to preserve as much of the *status quo* as possible by claiming that the running of these foreign-staffed and structured services was incompatible with the loyalties of Chinese social life and individual characteristics. In fact the British presence in China functioned as smoothly without British predominance in the CMC as it had done with it.

By acquiescing in the inevitable surrender of squatters' rights to the highest levels of the service the Legation and the Foreign Office divested themselves of high-profile areas where they had become embroiled in conflict with the Guomindang. The actions of British CMC officials during the Nationalist revolution had more than once served to sour, or threaten to sour, British relations with Chinese authority.[23] By allowing, or conniving in, the over-extension of the British reach into Chinese government and public affairs the Legation exposed the British presence generally to the mobilised anti-imperialism and nationalism of the mid-1920s. Relinquishing control was partly a matter of accepting that the Guomindang's finance policies and its commitment to servicing foreign debts made the initial justification of control redundant.[24] But it was also a matter of dismantling the *imperium in imperio* that was Britain in China.

### Britain in China

The CMC was an institution at the heart of Chinese government, and the Shanghai Municipal Council was a body at the heart of Britain in China; but if customs issues served to sour Sino-British relations, Shanghai questions threatened to poison them. By the late 1920s British diplomats privately admitted that the situation in the concessions had long been in need of reform. However, the inertia of the *status quo*, and the gulf between private liberalism and public policy, had encouraged complacency on the issue until the Nationalist revolution. In the treaty ports the various British or international administrations had not accommodated to shifts in economic power in their communities, or in China generally. The SMC, for example, failed to adapt to the emergence of an economically powerful urban Chinese business elite in the city during and after World War I. The concessions had never been intended to be the European quasi-colonies that many residents evidently thought they were. Nor were they intended to be examples and schools of municipal behaviour for the Chinese, nor could they be in fact while they excluded Chinese from active participation in municipal affairs and took little interest in the welfare of Chinese residents. Nor, indeed, had they been intended to facilitate the profitable business whereby foreign landholders rented to Chinese tenants (or for them, as Chinese were forbidden to own or rent land in the settlement) – although this had been a steady source of British fortunes in Shanghai, for example, since the Taiping rebellion. Defence of this profit mechanism was an implicit theme throughout the history of the concessions. Zhenjiang, for example, was described in 1929 by one diplomat as 'a concession of absentee rent-collecting landlords, the *reductio ad absurdum* of the object of holding concessions in China'.[25]

By creating a council in the old British concession at Hankou in 1927 that included three British members, the Chen–O'Malley agreement raised false hopes that British residents might also be allowed representation on other retroceded authorities, and that a precedent had been set for future agreements. In Tianjin Consul-general Sir James Jamieson was so surprised that he raised the issue of 'most favoured Concession treatment'.[26] In Jiujiang in 1928 the British community refused to pay any local taxes, except as voluntary contributions, without equivalent and adequate representation. This 'settler mentality' had to be disabused. The Legation issued King's Regulations ordering them to pay up, whilst Consul-general Brenan starkly told the Shanghai British Chamber of Commerce that British subjects in China 'who are pursuing legitimate interests other than trade ... as far as they look to support from the home country ... are inevitably subordinate to the exigencies of trade'.[27] The concessions were irrelevant as far as the exigencies of trade were concerned, claimed Sir John Pratt, a former consul who had transferred to the Foreign Office's Far Eastern Department, and who laboured intensively to change the *status quo*.[28] 'Trade' here was meant broadly, in opposition to settlement and land investment, and it signified not just the process of trade but the trading interests, in opposition to settlers, whatever their 'legitimate interests'. The new diplomatic priorities dictated the need, immediately, for compromise and reform in the British concessions. The aim, generally, was to protect essentials but to reform where necessary and where unavoidable. Gradual reform and long-term positioning for the inevitable sinification were preferable to risking recovery by force, or other measures that would threaten British trading interests.

We now turn to look at those legitimate interests, roughly in order of size, sketching out their development and the measures taken by the diplomats to reform, redirect, or abolish them.

### Shanghai

The English, later the International, Settlement at Shanghai was established in 1843.[29] The foreign residents were allowed to rent land in a strip alongside the Huangpu river outside the Chinese walled city of

Shanghai. The land regulations which underpinned the settlement were first drawn up by the local Chinese administrator, the Daotai; later versions (1854, 1869, 1898) provided the basis on which the mainly British Land Renters elected a committee to maintain order and construct roads and jetties. In 1854 this became the Shanghai Municipal Council (SMC), and the Land Renters also established a Shanghai Municipal Police Force (SMP), having the year previously, in response to the seizure of the Chinese city of Shanghai by rebels, formed a Shanghai Volunteer Corps (SVC).[30] Chinese were forbidden from renting land in the demarcated settlement area.

Foreign Shanghai's imagined history had the new settlement arise from marshy swamps through foreign enterprise, and in truth a new town was constructed: the riverside was bunded, roads were built, a public garden was established on reclaimed land opposite the British consulate. Smart merchant houses in the neoclassical style that came to characterise British Asia were constructed. The new settlement attracted Chinese residents, especially during the Taiping rebellion (1850-65), and a largely unplanned melange of Chinese housing and Western housing developed – there was no singularly European district. Land and property speculation made many fortunes. In time the old core of the British settlement became the business district, residential areas were found to the north and to the west, and industrial development after 1895 took place mostly in the north and east. Developments in Shanghai largely set the fashion for the second wave of concessions and settlements established in 1861, and the 'Model Settlement' largely supplied the people as well, even Chinese servants for those pioneering residence in new cities with no tradition of dealing with Europeans.[31] Utilities were developed through private or municipal initiative: gas lighting for the streets (1865), telephones (1881), electricity (1883), water (1883), tramcars (1902). Other services speedily developed: a (British) Shanghai Club (1862), newspapers (notably the weekly *North China Herald*, 1850, and the *North China Daily News*, 1864), a branch of the Royal Asiatic Society (1857) and, even before the SMC, a racecourse (1850 in its earliest incarnation and location).[32]

Table 4 indicates the speed and pace of the number of the residents in the settlement, and Britons in the city generally. As the British population grew (and the population of transients such as seamen was always high), and as society in the new treaty port became more complex, the SMC had to extend its range of activities, and British diplomats had to extend theirs. A 'Mixed Court' developed out of the posting of a Chinese official, later a deputy magistrate, in the settlement as a representative of the Shanghai magistrate, to deal with police cases against Chinese residents, and other disputes involving Chinese. A British consular official sat with him to oversee foreign interests, to ensure as far as possible that International Settlement laws were implemented, but also to confront any extension of Chinese sovereignty back into the settlement through the court. A British Supreme Court was established in 1865 to deal with civil, criminal and Admiralty cases in China and Korea.[33]

**Table 4:** Number of British residents in Shanghai, 1851–1936

| | International Settlement | French concession | Chinese jurisdiction | Chinese in International Settlement |
|---|---|---|---|---|
| 1851 | 256 | | | |
| 1871 | 894 | | | 75,047 |
| 1876 | 872 | | | 95,662 |
| 1880 | 1,057 | | | 107,812 |
| 1885 | 1,453 | | | 125,665 |
| 1890 | 1,574 | | | 168,129 |
| 1895 | 1,936 | | | 240,995 |
| 1900 | 2,691 | | | 345,276 |
| 1905 | 3,713 | | | 452,716 |
| 1910 | 4,465 | 314 | | 488,005 |
| 1915 | 4,822 | 681 | | 620,401 |
| 1920 | 5,341 | 1,044 | | 759,839 |
| 1925 | 5,879 | 2,312 | | 810,279 |
| 1930 | 6,221 | 2,219 | 891 | 971,397 |
| 1932 | | 2,684 | | |
| 1934 | | 2,630 | 1,153 | |
| 1935 | 6,595 | | | 1,120,860 |
| 1936 | | 2,648 | | |

Sources NCH, 3 May 1851, 159, and SMC, *Annual Reports*, 1871–1935; H. G. W. Woodhead, ed., *The China Year Book, 1931* (London, 1931), 694; Zou, *Jiu Shanghai renkou bianqian de yanjiu* (Research into Population Change in old Shanghai) (Shanghai, 1980), 145–7.

Clearly, the modern city of Shanghai grew up around, and because of, the self-administered foreign enclaves in its centre. The self-image of the 'model settlement' was first posited in the late 1850s, and was ever after at the heart of the constructed history and the active policy of the SMC and its settler constituency.[34] The enclaves themselves grew in size after 1854. In 1899 there had been significant extensions of the areas controlled by the French municipality and the SMC. As part of a policy of further expansion thereafter the SMC developed a road-building programme into Chinese-administered areas, hoping to

**Figure 7** 'Shanghai's armour'. From I. I. Kounin (ed.), *Eighty-five Years of the SVC* (Shanghai, 1939), facing p. 202

incorporate them at a later date. Efforts were made to extend SMC control in 1909, and at various moments thereafter. Extra-settlement roads were still being built in 1923.[35] Parallel to this the council over the years progressively hardened its active opposition to the exercise of Chinese authority in the settlement over Chinese residents. The SMC arrogated to itself more than just extra land. In conjunction with the Shanghai consular body during the chaos of the revolutionary transition in 1911 it actually took over and greatly extended the powers of the Mixed Court in the settlement.[36] This was certainly a step too far. Not only was it an arrogation of Chinese sovereignty beyond that ever taken in peacetime, but Chinese lawyers were to prove a formidable and active body of informed and articulate resistance to the SMC – and the court was an issue that affected them directly.[37]

The government of the International Settlement was a complicated affair, an accretion of precedent over thin legal foundations. 'Sound considerations of political and practical expediency rather than abstract legal rights' – as the Secretary-general admitted in 1930 – underpinned the SMC's 'consistent and strenuous resistance' to the collection of revenue within the settlement by Chinese authorities, and the same considerations led it to resist any Chinese government

[ 126 ]

claims to functioning within the settlement.[38] There was no direct Chinese representation on the council until 1928, and no Chinese electorate either. The SMC was elected annually on a property-based franchise that excluded most Britons even from voting, and even more from standing for election, while others held multiple votes, depending on the number of properties they represented. In 1854, when the council was formed, there were some thirty to forty Land Renters out of a foreign (mostly British) population of about 250. Only in the late 1930s did more than one-sixth of the British community get the vote. The Land Renters (and ratepayers) met once a year in full session, to vote on the budget, and also on substantive issues put forward by the council, or by other Land Renters. The nine members of the council (five British, two American, and two Japanese after World War I) met regularly in full session but delegated much of their work to committees of elected councillors and co-optees. All these men were usually drawn from the ranks of the managers of the bigger expatriate and Shanghailander companies. The very first council appointed a Secretary to oversee the embryonic administration, and by 1922 some 600 mostly British employees were employed in the secretariat, and in the revenue, public health, public works and police departments, supervising a far larger number of Chinese. The SMC had become by far the biggest employer of British personnel in the settlement.[39]

Individual Britons in Shanghai were subject, like all Britons in China, to the jurisdiction of their consuls. The SMC, however, was constitutionally responsible only to its electorate, and not to any direct consular or diplomatic authority (unlike its French neighbour). Shanghailanders were fond of reminding themselves, and the world, of this fact. Exactly who the SMC was answerable to always remained unclear. The British Minister in Beijing could not formally order the council, as a body, to do anything, although the land regulations themselves were subject to diplomatic agreement, and the SMC was subject as a body to claims made against it in a Court of the Consuls (instituted 1869), convened when necessary, of those foreign powers with interests in the settlement.[40] The chief administrator of the council – the Secretary before 1925, supplemented by a Secretary-general concerned with political matters, thereafter – occupied a powerful position within this 'dictatorial' bureaucracy. The councillors were elected annually, and many stayed barely long enough to get to grips with policy. A forceful individual with an imperialist agenda like J. O. P. Bland could keep the SMC lobbying hard for expansion. Only in the 1920s did the secretary start to lose his freedom of action to new committees of councillors and co-optees.[41] The secretariat files for the 1920s show again and again how the bureaucracy itself set the tone of

[ 127 ]

administration's relations with Chinese residents and interest groups; in particular, the SMP set their own political agenda. Before the SMC could reform its behaviour after May 1925, it had in fact to be taken in hand, and also had to take itself in hand.[42]

The population of the International Settlement, then, was predominantly Chinese, and substantial holdings of property were owned by Chinese too, and these residents remained subjects of the Qing and the republic. Despite this the SMC worked hard to exclude Chinese authority from the settlement and to extend its own authority over its Chinese subjects. In the settler imagination Chinese residents became native subjects. Just as colonial regimes ordered and catalogued subject populations, so the SMC, through the SMP in particular, regulated the city and its residents, constructing a zone of European law and social practice. Ultimately, settler control rested on the acquiescence of the Chinese, and on an implicit accommodation between settler needs (order, health, revenue) and Chinese local society. Where and when the SMC abused that acquiescence – for example, by insulting local elites over access to the public gardens, or through imposing unpopular regulations – the council met protest or opposition: the wheelbarrow riot (1897) over an increase in licence fees, or the Mixed Court riot (1905) over SMC interference with the court. The latter saw loss of life and the destruction of a police station; on the whole, however, the accommodation worked until the 1920s.

The SMC derived its revenue from rates, from licence fees, and from bond issues. Chinese residents provided by far the bulk of this revenue.[43] In return they got precious little in the way of services, let alone representation. Arguing into the 1920s that the International Settlement functioned as a safe haven, and that in return for security Chinese residents ought to accept the status quo, the SMC and its supporters had obstructed reforms of the administration that might have co-opted leading Chinese residents. In the aftermath of the 1905 Mixed Court disturbances a Chinese Consultative Committee was formed to keep the council 'informed of Chinese public opinion in all important matters', but it was vetoed by the ratepayers.[44] Although a Chinese Advisory Committee was grudgingly formed in 1920, to placate demands for Chinese representation after a rates strike, the dinner at the Astor House Hotel and guided tour of the SMC's administration building that they were given were no substitute for a fully representative council.[45] Not surprisingly, this body was a failure, and became defunct with the wholesale resignation of its members after May Thirtieth 1925.[46] On top of the political exclusion of elite Chinese, and the absence of Chinese from the council's administrative staff, the SMC fought a long campaign, with the full support of the ratepayers and set-

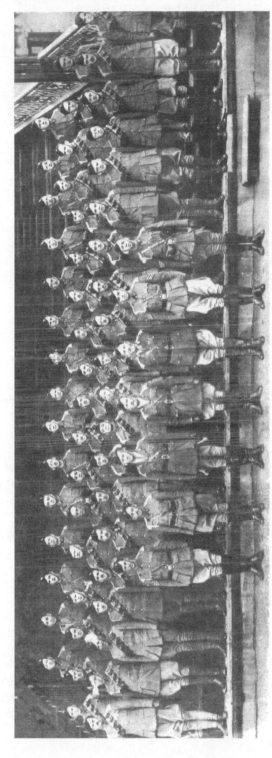

**Figure 8** Settlers in uniform: the Shanghai Volunteer Corps' elite Light Horse Company in 1931. From I. I. Kounin (ed.), *Eighty-Five Years of the SVC* (Shanghai, 1939), p. 158. John Hay Thorburn (see pp. 148–9) is fourth from left in the back row, his father Mansel Hay Thorburn is on the far right of the front row.

tler opinion in the settlement, to keep Chinese nationals – other than servants or local officials by arrangement – out of the public parks from which they had been barred (amahs excepted), since 1889. Meanwhile its police force maintained a licensing regime that discriminated against Chinese free association in the settlement. The foreign administrators of the heart of China's most important city gave their Chinese residents much cause for angry complaint.

The administrative division of Shanghai, complicated by the international status of the International Settlement, fostered the activities of the sleazy and the crooked in the city, Chinese and foreign alike.[47] The 'model settlement' appeared in the international public eye as a rotten settlement. Quite apart from illegal gambling, or opium trafficking, child labour and the 'white slave trade' were perceived as ostentatiously flourishing whilst the city fathers cheerfully amused themselves by listening to their municipal band playing in a public garden that was off-limits to Chinese. The SMC was cajoled into cleaning itself up, or made efforts to do so on its own initiative. Local Anglo-American missionary pressure forced an unwilling SMC slowly to close down all brothels between 1920 and 1924, while hitherto legal opium shops in the settlement were suppressed in 1917. The SMC never abandoned its sovereignty to Chinese organised crime, as its southern French neighbour was to do in 1930-32, but the battle against corruption was hard, and more than once, over opium and gambling, the situation almost got out of hand.[48] Extraterritoriality, Chinese organised crime and its relationship with the Guomindang state made for a heady brew.

The SMC presented British diplomats with a number of problems, but they may be summed up in the fact that it provided a sitting target. By its very existence, by the range – the ever-increasing range in the twentieth century – of its intervention in settlement life and business (Chinese and foreign), the SMC served up provocations on a plate for local and national Chinese authority, and for the Chinese populace in the settlement. These problems constantly threatened to infect Sino-British relations generally. Settler self-aggrandisement apart, the acquisition of greater powers was forced on it by the need to administer efficiently a rapidly growing and constantly changing urbanising environment, and to prove itself a 'model settlement'. By governing the heart and the guts of China's most industrialised, urbanised city, the powerhouse of new culture and an educational centre, the SMC was drawn into conflict, or the possibility of conflict, with Chinese residents, students, business elites and politicians, moral reformers, social or political activists. There was no unbroken history of Chinese resistance to the exercise of SMC authority – and like many colonialisms its power was often appropriated and used by its local collaborators for their own ends – but the potential for disaster was there.

Identities overlapped, of course, and settlers, with their multiple allegiance to Shanghai, to Britain in China, to the British empire and to Britain, were far from backward about calling for military or diplomatic support from the British state when they needed it. When it suited self-made and self-reliant Shanghailanders they became occupants of an outpost of empire well deserving of, for example, the 20,000 strong Shanghai Defence Force despatched in 1926–27, or a battleship or two moored off the Bund. But when the emergency was over they expected the empire to leave them alone again while they paid public obeisance to it on Empire Day and royal anniversaries. During the global emergencies which faced Britain in 1914 and 1939 settlers certainly returned to fight for the empire – but many left behind argued from Shanghai's uniqueness that regulations about trading with the enemy, for example, were rather more complicated than might be thought. The Britain in China settler was not a part-time imperialist, but was clearly a part-time member of the British empire.

Diplomatic acquiescence in settler assumptions, throughout the decades of its growth, served to bolster the view that the moral rights of the British residents of the treaty ports ought somehow to be paramount, their wishes heard and respected, and that they had a 'birthright'.[49] Occasionally the diplomats would veto settler plans – the attempt in 1906 to completely replace the Chinese members of the SMP with Sikhs was rejected as being tantamount to British military occupation of the settlement.[50] But the perceived implication of the municipal structures created was that the financial security of landlords, bondholders and British municipal employees was of singular importance. One school of thought in Shanghai, popularised notably by O. M. Green and by R. Huntley-Davidson of the Shanghai Publicity Bureau, was that the foreign residents had every right to demand the establishment of a free port akin to Danzig – a view which in one form or another can be dated back to at least 1862.[51] In fact the jurisdictional powers of the SMC within the settlement were so vague that the Legation and Foreign Office worried about actions of the council which exposed that vagueness to Chinese criticism, and possible official or popular retaliation. It appeared to the diplomats that the SMC was deciding the limits of its own powers.

## Reforming the Shanghai Municipal Council

In pursuit of its reformist agenda the Legation, sometimes directly, but mostly working through the Consul-general, attempted to influence the composition of the SMC and urge it to reform. Consul-general Sir

Sydney Barton, whose behaviour during the May Thirtieth emergency had been heavy-handedly reactionary, was slow about reform in the calmer atmosphere of 1928, but subsequent officials were more active.[52] In 1930 the new Consul-general, Brenan, announced that 'Four out of the six British members are old personal friends of mine and I think that all six will work well together and with me.' Old personal friendships became important conduits for encouraging reform and impressing on the SMC the need for various policies or concessions to the Chinese. Progressive younger figures in the expatriate community, such as the Keswicks at Jardine's, were systematically courted and encouraged.[53] Co-operation began with tentative contact between the Shanghai community leaders and the National government in 1928 when R. Calder-Marshall, chairman of the British Chamber of Commerce, met Nationalist Ministers Song Ziwen (T. V. Sung) – who was dined at the Shanghai Club, a specifically symbolic location – and Kong Xiangxi (H. H. Kung).[54]

There was also symbolism in the fact that the 1930 election saw the defeat at the poll of H. E. (Harry) Arnhold, chairman of the council – ironically for being too reformist. Arnhold was a Hong Kong-born British subject, educated in Britain, but his firm, Arnhold Brothers, had been the German-registered Arnhold Karbeg & Co. in 1914. Reconstituted as a British company after 1919, it was taken over by Sir Victor Sassoon in 1923. Arnhold's served as a front for Sassoon's political interests in the International Settlement – Harry was his man on the SMC. Sassoon's interests in China were varied, but they were predominantly Shanghai-based. Arnhold's defeat was warmly welcomed, as the diplomats disliked him. 'Not an attractive personality,' noted Lampson. He also attracted antisemitic and anti-German hostility. Arnhold was to re-emerge as a settler community leader in the 1930s, serving on the committee of the British Residents' Association, and then back on the SMC from 1932 to 1937, chairing it in 1934-37. One of the winners in 1930 was Butterfield & Swire's Shanghai manager, N. S. Brown, whose activities encouraging reform in the settlement, boasted Arnhold, rendered him *persona non grata* with many influential members of the community'.[55]

Appeasement of Chinese residents and opinion also began in 1928 when three Chinese councillors were finally allowed on to the council.[56] In 1929 pressure for a further increase was resisted by the foreign councillors, who, Garstin complained, 'have some difficulty in realising ... that ... "there is a world elsewhere", besides Shanghai or even China'. In January 1930 they bowed to foreign and Chinese pressure, and announced the intention of the council to propose an increase.[57] The ratepayers' annual meeting, however, was roused by a prominent settler extremist, British lawyer Ranald G. McDonald, into overthrowing the motion. This was precisely the kind of trivial-seeming incident the diplomats feared most, one where settlers could do much potential harm. The Consul-general panicked and suggested the forcing through of the change by the Consular Body in Shanghai and the Diplomatic Body in Beijing. In the event all passed peacefully: an emergency meeting was called instead, and intense lobbying engaged in to bully the British community into accepting the seriousness of the matter. Fear of the possible Chinese reaction was the motivating force, and memories of May Thirtieth were fresh. The motion was passed, but the episode revealed a new dynamic in internal settlement affairs: the active and uncompromising intention of the diplomats to unpick the Shanghai knot.[58]

There was more to the problem than democratic representation, of course. 'If only we could reach the terms of dining together and slapping one another on the back, so to speak, so many of these things become so much easier to handle,' mused Lampson in 1929.[59] Such back-slapping, as we have seen in chapter 3, was not facilitated by the isolation of the British and the exclusiveness of their social structures. Foreign Shanghai's public image was also irredeemably harmed by the parks issue. Objectors to Chinese use had their way at the ratepayers' annual meeting in 1927 but the issue was resolved, and the parks opened to ticket-buying Chinese, in 1928.[60] Encouraging elite Britons to mix socially with their Chinese peers was more difficult, but the diplomats accorded it importance and pushed people to work at it. Where British clubs relied on Chinese goodwill to function, such as the Boat Club, with its regatta at the punningly named Hen-li, or the Paper Hunt Club, but instead began to meet official obstructions, limited concessions and compromises could be, and were, extracted. Attempts were made to maintain racial and class taboos. Swire's Shanghai manager, N. S. Brown, took a lead in such moves, and was instrumental in getting the Paper Hunt Club to make an effort to enrol more 'Chinese gentlemen riders' as a *quid pro quo* for the rescinding of restrictions on hunting in the countryside around Shanghai in 1930.[61] The Boat Club was asked the same year by Education Minister Wang Zhonghui to make the regatta 'less European'. It took steps to 'induce Chinese educational establishments locally to train for and take part in the regatta'. Actual membership of the club for Chinese was refused, because it would have raised the issue of the club's mixed bathing facilities, Chinese participation in which remained a social taboo.[62]

The need for co-operation was often stressed, and ritualistic get-togethers were held, but the British peevishly complained that they were 'expected to do all the co-operating, and the Chinese do not do their share'. [63] Progress was made, however, where it mattered to the diplomats: at elite levels. British business leaders learned the value of friendly social intercourse with their Chinese counterparts in the 1930s, although there were still divisions. N. S. Brown provoked resentment, even 'disgust', among other Shanghailanders as a result of his 'fraternisation' with the Chinese.[64] Swire's made moves to 'entertain more Chinese' and recognised that there were other advantages to mixing with them. 'It won't be a case of everlasting shop with these people, who have more to talk about than the foreigners here.'[65] By 1937 the Bank of England's representative in Shanghai felt progress on the issue great enough – but, more tellingly, pertinent enough – to report to his superiors.[66] These moves dealt with elite interaction, with those sections of the British community that the Foreign Office threw its weight behind: expatriates, and not settlers. This interaction served to commingle leading British figures and the interests they represented with the new Chinese ruling class, and with their Chinese competitors and business associates; it also served to detach the expatriate and to a lesser extent the settler elites from the insular settlement interests of the bulk of the Shanghai British.

Cocktails, paper chasing and Chinese crews in the Hen-li regatta were hardly going to solve the Shanghai imbroglio, which was an issue of Chinese sovereignty. The SMC in 1927 issued a 'Manifesto' declaring that it was 'fully alive to the fact that the rapid growth of the Chinese population of Shanghai has rendered an alteration in its constitution desirable'. This acknowledgement that the accommodation underpinning the Shanghai bargain was unbalanced had wide-ranging implications.[67] The council set up an economy committee in 1927 which concluded that more could, and should, be done to employ Chinese municipal staff and to make the SMC more aware of its new Chinese electors, and its Chinese ratepayers and residents.[68] The printing, in Chinese, of the annual report, and a weekly summary of the *Municipal Gazette*, was begun as was a programme of translation of municipal regulations. Efforts were also made to improve the Chinese language skills of the council's foreign employees, whose efforts had previously been nominal and poor, but which were compulsory by 1930. In December 1930 the council announced that no new foreign employees would be appointed unless it was clear that the posts involved could not be 'satisfactorily filled by Chinese', and Chinese cadets were appointed as engineers, health inspectors and to the fire brigade.[69] This process, examined in depth as it affected other sectors of the British presence in the next chapter, would later acquire the name 'localisation': the economic and political imperatives of British trade, missionary activity, and later British administration in Hong Kong, made it vital to make the agencies of the British in China less British, and more Chinese. The short cut taken was to employ Chinese personnel at all levels.

Chinese education was a contentious issue, especially given its expense, but in 1931 the council chairman announced that 'it is the duty of this Settlement to provide improved educational opportunities for the children of Chinese residents'. Similar noises were made about health provision, previously concerned mostly with the foreign population.[70] Concern about the social conditions engendered by Shanghai's rapid and ruthless industrial development had prompted a well publicised investigation into child labour in the settlement in 1922–25, much to the detriment of the image of the SMC. The reforms then attempted had been derailed by events, but thereafter the SMC had to begin engaging in social and economic work. In 1932 it set up an Industrial Section to enforce Guomindang factory legislation in the International Settlement, and this also became a research and mediation body.[71] There were, of course, limits to how much the SMC could achieve in this sudden engagement with Chinese society, but the effort was real.

The council's police force was also reformed under the guiding hand of an officer recruited from an Indian police force – to make it more efficient, and less likely to spark off, or inflame, a future May Thirtieth. There was a new structure, there were new weapons for riot control and there was a trained riot squad together with a drive for new, better-quality recruits. Old corruption or inefficiency was purged.[72] There was also an element of reaction to the establishment of the Shanghai Public Security Bureau (Gong'anju), one of the aims of which was the recovery of the foreign concessions, and to the bad example set by the French concession. A leaner and more efficient SMP had to be created to cope with the moral threat this possibly successful police force posed. The council was also forced to abandon its hold on Chinese courts in the settlement: under the Provisional Court agreement of September 1926 the old Mixed Court was abolished and replaced by a branch of the Jiangsu provincial court. This remained partly under SMC control, but in 1930 the court was fully rendited.[73] Much of the impetus to reform also stemmed from the establishment of the Chinese Special Municipality of Greater Shanghai (Da Shanghai tebie shizhengfu), which set out to turn the 'model settlement' idea on its head by undertaking in its zone the social, educational, health and other activities so patently ignored by the SMC in the International Settlement.[74] To fend off this criticism, the SMC had to engage with Chinese society, otherwise it lost one of the few rationales for its continued existence. The SMC itself was also a constantly evolving institution, trying to keep up with the city and society. As late as 1915 the administration had largely been a 'one-man show' in the hands of the Secretary.[75]

Seemingly the most important and constructive move in the publicity campaign waged by the SMC after 1925 was the commissioning of the Feetham investigation in 1930, through the auspices of Lionel Curtis (see chapter 2). Sir Richard Feetham was instructed to advise the council 'with a view to assisting them in formulating some constructive plan or scheme' which would satisfy Chinese aspirations and protect (foreign) business interests in the settlement.[76] The report itself, published in late 1931, was an irrelevant and arcanely constructed restatement of the conservative case against any speedy retrocession.[77] Its importance was that it could be pointed to as evidence of a sincere desire on the part of the SMC to reform, especially as it was critical of many aspects of the council's relationship with the Chinese population. In fact the spirit of the investigation and report clashed with the spirit of the extraterritoriality negotiations then under way between Lampson and Wang Zhengting. Feetham's sponsors and supporters felt that Shanghai should be excluded from the negotiations.[78] The Manchurian crisis rendered both projects obsolete.

The SMC's bold attempt to recreate itself was by no means as complete a surrender as it might appear. 'Looking to the time when Municipal Administration of the International Settlement would pass into Chinese hands', the council sold off its power department to an American consortium, and the waterworks to a British company, to 'protect' the Western capital invested, and also the standard of service. It is also notable that the council's pension list, for foreign, mainly European, staff, began to lengthen rapidly after 1925. That year there were barely fifteen pensioners; by 1939 there were 203.[79] In this way the 'self-controlling bureaucracy' protected the interests of its staff, whilst privatisation protected the utility supplies from a new Chinese-controlled council which in British minds threatened inefficiency or political misuse.[80] Throughout the 1930s the SMC was slowly developing into a body much more representative of the interests of all the residents of the settlement. The Japanese invasion of Manchuria, and the outbreak of the Sino-Japanese War in July 1937, put further reform on hold, but, as will be seen below, the struggle for control continued.

On the eve of the war, in May 1937, Harry Arnhold, who had just stepped down as SMC chairman, penned a newspaper article on the SMC to mark the coronation of George VI.[81] His vision of Shanghai was largely undented by reform, or by the continuing assault on SMC autonomy by Chinese authorities. Where Lanning and Couling had merely appropriated the whole of the city into their history of the International Settlement, Arnhold upped the ante, and described it as 'the cradle of freedom of modern Chinese thought, speech and press', incorporating 'China's modern culture' wholesale into his version of SMC history. The long battle against the 'irregularities' of the pre-1911 Chinese administration had been fought by the SMC, and fought by it alone, armed merely with 'common sense'. Arnhold certainly articulated the beliefs of Britain in China about its achievements, and its impact on Chinese society, politics and culture, and he spoke in the settler terms which incorporated settlers into the wider British empire story. But he also spoke for Sassoon's, and for local vested business interests fighting a rearguard action in the unresolved struggle over the existence of the settlements. Likewise, other constituents of the International Settlement who were threatened by reform appropriated its 'model settlement' and cosmopolitan rhetoric for their own purposes. White Russians in particular zealously incorporated themselves into the settlement polity.[82] British settlers were happy to have such support: they turned to cosmopolitanism when it suited them, and when the language of empire failed to strike the right note, but after 1937 the language of empire was to become the language of their survival.

## Tianjin

Opened as a treaty port in 1860, a British concession in Tianjin was leased shortly thereafter by the British government. Land regulations, first promulgated in 1866, regulated land purchase, and established an elected municipal council with tax-raising powers. Chinese were forbidden from directly owning land in the concession. The settlement was extended in 1897, and again in 1903, while the British Municipal Council developed, although somewhat in miniature, a full panoply of utilities and services, as in the International Settlement in Shanghai, including a 700 strong police force (1940) and a Volunteer corps equipped with a field battery. Fourteen hundred Britons (1938) lived side-by-side with some 4,000 other non-Chinese and 72,000 Chinese residents – the latter paying in property taxes and licence fees very much more than 50 per cent of the council's revenue.[83] Situated side-by-side with eight other foreign concessions in Tianjin – when at their most numerous – the British area contributed to the development of a substantial foreign-controlled zone, replete with foreign-style buildings compromising very little with their location – faux-classic banks, a crenellated municipal building (Gordon Hall) and a public garden, Victoria Park.[84]

Tianjin had the real siege history that Shanghai affected. In June 1900 the foreign areas had been besieged by Boxers and Chinese troops, an event still commemorated, as we have seen, as late as 1931. But in Tianjin reform ran more smoothly than in Shanghai. This was partly because of the greater direct control consuls had in smaller concessions: the Tianjin Consul-general, for example, presided over the annual ratepayers' meeting and had a right of veto over all decisions taken and by-laws issued.[85] Moreover, it was less prominent in Chinese and foreign eyes than Shanghai. The British Municipal Council in the Tianjin British concession installed a Chinese representative after 1919. In 1926 it threw open its parks to all residents, regardless of nationality, and in 1927 it decided (in Lampson's words) to 'eliminate all discriminatory provisions against the Chinese' and to appoint five Chinese councillors; new land regulations to that effect were drawn up in 1928, though not without some reservations, especially over the example being set to Shanghai.[86] A British advisory committee had been set up in response to Chamberlain's 'January offer' on retrocession, and this body, which included the municipal chairman, reported various measures aimed at the 'maximum of generosity, while safeguarding fundamental British interests.' Retrocession negotiations did begin, with the Northern government, and a treaty was initialled, but quietly abandoned in favour of municipal reform. One vital concession involved increasing the number of Chinese appointed to the council's staff. In 1930 the position of vice-chairman was given to the Chinese, but this was merely nominal as the chairman had, by regulation, to be a British subject, as did anyone standing in for him. A Chinese Deputy Chief Inspector was appointed to the police, and the forty (1922) Sikh constables were removed. The minutes of the annual meeting of ratepayers were in future to be published in Chinese.[87] Small as they seem, such packages of measures served to unravel the fabric of the mock Raj.

This progress gratified the Legation and generally pre-empted criticism; the Chinese business community thanked the British with a celebratory dinner in 1929. As in Shanghai, it was no surrender: many ratepayers were disenfranchised at the same time, to restrict the vote to the wealthier Chinese and British and, in effect, to depoliticise the more communally representative structure that was created. 'We must guard against the "low-white" danger,' wrote Sir John Pratt to Warren Swire. Pension schemes were rapidly introduced for British staff, as in Shanghai, to protect them 'from being wrongfully dismissed without adequate compensation by any authority to whom control of the area might in future be surrendered'.[88] Treaty-backed legalism was ingrained, but protection of British interests was actually achieved by reaching an accommodation with those elements of local Chinese society which mattered, in partnership with the expatriate leaders of the British community, not the British community as a whole. In this way Tianjin's settlers were marginalised. Partly by way of response, an *ad hoc* body, the Tientsin British Committee of Information, started publishing 'memoranda' from 1926 onwards which largely contained propaganda, some of it virulent, against treaty reform.[89] Such expressions of settler discontent were to become familiar as Sino-British negotiations on extraterritoriality got under way in 1931.

### Hankou

The British concession at Hankou dated from the 1858 Treaty of Tianjin, and was established in 1861 (extended 1898). A Municipal Council, pointedly on the SMC model (complete with the same odd translation of 'Municipal Council' as its official Chinese name: Gongbuju (Works Department Bureau)) was immediately instituted, and the business of settlement undertaken. As well as bunding, road making and policing, there was a racetrack to be constructed, and a club, a Volunteer corps to be formed, and a newspaper instituted.[90] The concession was subject to strong pressure for change after the Chinese municipality took over the former German and Russian concessions as Special Administrative Districts (SADs) after World War I. These were run by a Chinese director and Sino-foreign councils of elected representatives. Points of contention included the Hankou International Hospital (funded by the SADs and the Concession Councils), which barred Chinese, and the question of Chinese representation on the Hankou British Municipal Council as a *quid pro quo* for foreign representation in the SADs. After disturbances connected with May Thirtieth, in which four Chinese were killed on 11 June 1925 in Hankou by the Hankow Volunteer Corps, the British Municipal Council began planning reforms in response to the country's changing political atmosphere. Chinese residents in the small, symbolically walled-in area had to register yearly for a residence permit and formed a quarter of the population. Despite some diehard resistance, it was decided to allow two Chinese representatives on to the council, increasing its number to six. This was the logical outcome of permitting residence; it was also felt that it was 'best to work with the persons among whom we live', while for the Chinese representation would also have 'an educative value'.[91]

This small community attempted to secure the *status quo* with the minimum concessions acceptable to the local Chinese authorities, but such moves were superseded by the seizure of the concession in January 1927, and by the Chen–O'Malley agreement which ratified and legalised the transfer. Under the agreement Hankou had been immediately retroceded and a municipality created to administer it under a Chinese director and six elected councillors, three Chinese and three Britons. The Sikh constables were, as elsewhere, dismissed, and a tablet commemorating the hand-over was placed on the Municipal

Building. The bitter atmosphere in Hankou was not conducive to municipal success, despite the fact that British residents were allowed to be involved in local municipal affairs, a concession they never appreciated as such, preferring to see it as a right.[92] Taxation was the usual cause for complaint. But parts of the community were apt to respond in diehard terms about British prestige and still hankered for reoccupation by force. Hankou thereafter drifted into the decent obscurity of a post-treaty port community; nothing much happened there to bother British diplomats or upset their new dispensation, though occasionally they had to lecture residents mildly on the need for mutual co-operation

This situation lasted until the Sino-Japanese War. As the Japanese army approached Hankou in the summer of 1938 diehard settlers demanded that British forces should reoccupy the former concession, as the 1927 treaty gave no third party a right to ignore the special position of the British. When Nationalist troops abandoned the city a British director was briefly reappointed by the Chinese authorities and British marines landed to police the area, home in normal times to 700 foreigners and 8,000 Chinese. Director W. S. Dupree, CBE, issued a strong protest to the Royal Navy when the marines handed policing over to the Japanese six days later, and Hankou's brief return to British administration was terminated.[93]

### The smaller communities

The smaller communities faced more immediate threats of retrocession. There was little point in keeping hold of them, as their political disadvantages far outweighed their utility; it was better by far to withdraw, in effect, from the periphery, to the Shanghai centre. Jiujiang (Kiukiang) was seized back the day after Hankou fell in 1927. A Special Administrative District was set up, but abolished, with little British opposition, in January 1930, authority devolving on the Jiujiang municipality. Tiny Zhenjiang (Chinkiang), another 1861 concession, was handed back in 1930, as were the Xiamen concession and the leased territory of Weihaiwei. The latter was the only port whose rendition had broader implications, as it was the summer base of the Royal Navy's China station. The 1930 agreement safeguarded this function for ten years (with a renewal option hereafter), and the loss of a Colonial Office backwater whose sole recent function had been to keep Reginald Johnston, its Commissioner, out of harm's way, was not regretted by the Foreign Office.[94] Spurious municipal structures elsewhere based on purchase or custom rather than treaty were eventually also dispensed with. A Sino-foreign committee for the foreign area in Ningbo ceased to exist in 1927; the 'Chefoo International Committee' ceased to exist in 1930; Jigongshang was 'returned' in 1935, and the hill station of Guling passed from the hands of its 'Estate Council' (complete with constitution and a 'Kuling Hymn') to the local Chinese authorities in 1936.[95] The process unpicked the structure of Britain in China in symbolic ways well publicised by the settler press. The Bund at Zhenjiang was used for public executions in 1928, and this was considered 'undesirable from the point of view of British prestige'. 'New use for Kiukiang Bund' was a droll *North China Herald* caption to a 1929 front-page photograph of Nationalist troops squatting there (expressly to show their contempt for the foreigner, claimed another witness); William Sewell complained in 1928 that the Hankou Bund was 'no longer a very nice place to walk as it is so unsanitary and smelly'. Bunds remained symbolic of the Western space created and maintained among Chinese chaos, and of the remaking of the Chinese environment by Western technology and enterprise. The symbolism was lost on neither Chinese or Britons.[96]

Elaborate preparations were made for protecting as much as possible of the remaining symbolic structures of treaty port life, especially in these smaller communities which, unlike Shanghai or Tianjin, would have little recognisable identity after retrocession. This applied to cemeteries and war memorials, but also where possible to segregated recreational facilities; the Bund in the Hankou British concession had previously been reserved for foreign use, as had the municipal school. The Chinese authorities were unwilling to continue funding the school unless it admitted Chinese pupils – so the school became a private institution funded by British and American companies.[97] In Jiujiang the public gardens had become part of the Kiukiang Club grounds, and the club was sold by its owners, the 'foreign lotholders', to the Kiukiang Club & Recreation Ground, a British-registered company. This procedure removed the gardens from municipal control and left them open only to club members, that is, to Europeans.[98] When the 'Chefoo International Committee' was abolished the same protective action was suggested for the recreation grounds there. Similar measures were taken to safeguard British cemeteries from spoliation.[99]

On the island of Shamian in Guangzhou, home to a tiny British concession complete with council and police force, plans were laid in 1929, as 'If the Council became a Sino-Foreign body as at Hankow it is feared that their controlling vote may be used to throw the Swimming Bath Club open to Chinese and other Orientals and so render it practically useless to the present white membership.' The club leased land from the council, which in turn leased it from the consulate. It was decided that the council should divest itself of the lot, which would be leased directly to the club from the consulate via a trust fund. The threat of forced assimilation was thereby removed. Similar measures were taken to protect the public gardens, which were to be included in the consulate's own lot, whilst the tennis and football clubs were transferred to the Shameen (Canton) Club. 'It is most desirable to have all this sort of thing fixed up well ahead of any talk of rendition,' minuted the Legation's Chinese Secretary, Sir Erich Teichman, in 1929, 'Certainly: most wise,' commented Lampson.[100]

The treaty port universe shrank, and British attitudes towards it altered. Maugham had woven an embittered world of hard, dyspeptic British residents, but as the 'outports' were abandoned nostalgic affection became the dominant theme in memoir and fiction, and the central inscription in the literature of colonial nostalgia. Far from being remembered as frustrated imperial bridgeheads, or in the case of Hankou as the first unavenged defeat of the British empire in Asia, they were re-imagined as the eccentric locations of a vanished way of life.[101]

Hong Kong alone remained almost completely untouched by these debates. The Nanjing regime, whose sway in south China was hardly substantive before Chiang's extension of the regime's power there in 1936, made few efforts to extend discussions on treaty revision to the Crown colony.[102] In retrospect this was surprising, as the actions of the Hong Kong government during the Guomindang's tenure in Canton in the period 1917-26 had constituted, according to Sir John Pratt, 'a series of foolish and provocative acts which it is difficult to justify'. Provocative was certainly the word, as they had prompted the Canton regime in 1925 to formulate long-term strategies for war with Britain.[103] The Hong Kong administration was weaned off making its own foreign policy to China through Lampson's efforts, and later made its own peace with the new regional authorities in its Chinese sister city. It remained important for the reconfigured British presence in China largely because of its military functions: it was the only British naval base in the Far East, the site of a major signals intelligence outpost, and after 1929 the site of HQ China Command.[104] Hong Kong mostly served British peace of mind, as a bastion of British prestige, power and law in East Asia. The latter aspect slowly became more important in the face of the National government's commercial legislation in the 1930s, which led many British companies to shift the legal base of their operations to Hong Kong.[105]

The reform or dismantling of the institutions of British treaty port life was certainly patchily accomplished, but by the end of 1930 the map of Britain in China had been physically and mentally redrawn. Broader strategic interests were preserved at Weihaiwei, or imperial interests at Hong Kong. The International Settlement at Shanghai and the Tianjin British concession remained outside the Crown colony as *de facto* British possessions, with all the appurtenances of treaty port administration. Only in parts of Shanghai, Tianjin and Xiamen did Sikhs still police the streets and Britons dominate municipal councils. The tiny Shamian concession, the Legation quarter in Beijing, and the Xiamen Gulangyu International Settlement were also retained. British prominence, but above that the character of its presence caused it to lose, or to abandon, these smaller enclaves when the less politicised presence of the French allowed them to maintain their concession at Shanghai and smaller zones at Tianjin, Hankou and the Guang-zhouwan leased territory. Even Japan was able to keep its concessions in Suzhou, Hangzhou, Hankou and Chongqing.[106]

## Changing British behaviour

While attempting to overhaul its own personnel and their attitudes, the British establishment also attempted to reform its charges. In its bluntest form this meant impressing on some individuals that they had better leave China. Individual behaviour was felt to affect and, at times, threaten the safety of whole communities, whether it was occasional boorish vandalism or engaged resistance to Guomindang activity. Consuls and others lectured and harangued their nominal charges, or lobbied to have men recalled or sent elsewhere in China.

Keeping the communities calm was important. In Shanghai, especially with the heightening of jurisdictional disputes with Chinese authority after the founding of the Chinese Special Municipality, and its Public Security Bureau in 1927, the atmosphere was at times tense. 'The foreign community ... are mostly in that state of mind which considers it derogatory to foreign prestige to be ordered to do anything by a Chinese,' explained the Consul-general in December 1930, discussing foreign responses to Chinese police activity on the extra-settlement roads.[107] In a related issue, Lampson sent all consuls a telegram instructing them to try and avoid incidents involving cars by discreetly persuading British citizens not to drive their vehicles themselves in Chinese territory, as accidents quickly became incidents. These instructions were passed on to individuals by companies and councils, to the contemptuous amusement of the press.[108]

On less tangible issues there was the problem of restraining the settler community, which was apt to be swayed by diehard activists such as by Ranald G. McDonald in 1930 over the issue of increasing Chinese representation on the council. The fear of causing Chinese public disorder through such injudicious foreign collective or individual behaviour was real. The danger was twofold: firstly the threat of civil disorder; secondly the fear that the Guomindang could use such an opportunity as a pretext for either unilaterally seizing the settlement or forcing an immediate agreement on the issue. This insecurity was constant and called for vigilance and faster and better reactions than had been evidenced by May Thirtieth. Better relations with Chinese community leaders were required and sought. In the case of the 1930 ratepayers' meeting Brenan quickly arranged a meeting with the prominent Shanghai businessman and community leader Yu Xiaqing to try and head off any agitation.[109] Better relations would emerge only from the sustained efforts of those in authority to set a good example to the British communities. This required, of course, such relations to have palpably successful diplomatic and commercial results.

Longer-term thought was given to these issues. Businessmen and diplomats came together in London in 1932 to discuss ways of improving 'Anglo-Chinese relations' – by which they meant the behaviour of Britons in Shanghai and elsewhere. The initiative was led initially by former missionary E. R. Hughes, who had the backing of N. S. Brown, among others. While the result – some meetings of diplomats and businessmen, and the commissioning of a slim handbook for young business recruits, published by the Department of Overseas Trade – was hardly dramatic, the episode was still important. The crux of the matter had been identified. Wherever possible – in China, in the treaty port press, and now in London with new recruits – diplomats and their allies tried to change the tone of relations between Britons and Chinese and inculcate 'a somewhat better conception of, and attitudes towards, the Chinese and China'. Undoing the impact of British culture's portrayal and re-creation of China was the task they had in mind.[110]

Britain also played a role in the 'international cultural rivalry' played out in China as an adjunct to political and economic competition, and which was designed to cement ties with the new elites.[111] It was widely felt, for example, that the growing primacy of American influence in China was a direct result of the large number of Chinese students who studied in the United States. Dislike of Britain, British methods and moderation was thought to be instilled by an American cultural environment, with its republican and democratic ideals. The situation was also bad for trade, which it was felt would 'follow' the student.[112] The biggest single innovation was the remission of the Boxer indemnity. A 'China Indemnity (Application) Act' was announced in 1922 and passed into law in 1925. It allowed receipts collected after 1922 to be used for educational or other purposes 'beneficial to the mutual interests' of Britain and China. A Boxer Indemnity Commission – including Dame Adelaide Anderson, W. E. Soothill, Hu

Shi and Ding Wenjiang – visited China in 1926 to investigate areas where subventions could be made. Amongst other proposals it recommended the establishment of a programme of scholarships for Chinese students to study in Britain, but stressed that the desired emphasis should be 'more cultural than technical'. A programme of academic exchanges and scholarships began in 1932–33. The Federation of British Industries (FBI) and the China Association also put forward a technical training scheme, and their selectors were told to 'pick future leaders'; efforts were made to keep in touch with them when they returned to China through garden parties for the British Returned Students' Union, for example.[113] The widespread personal bias of Britons against the Westernised students may well have remained, but it was no longer politically expedient and grew increasingly anachronistic.

Hong Kong University was, theoretically, a more cost-effective way of inculcating such cultural influence. However, according to its former Chancellor, it suffered in recruitment because mainland Chinese students apparently resented discriminatory treatment in the colonial atmosphere of Hong Kong, whilst British firms in China were wary of employing the university's graduates. They were thought too bookish, and too many of them were Straits Chinese and not, therefore, 'gentleman's sons'.[114] Much of this educational debate remained theoretical, however, as financial constraints on British schemes were strong. By 1939 only fifty-eight students had arrived on the FBI scheme; between 1925 and 1931 an estimated 5,700 Chinese students went to study in the United States. A Sino-British Cultural Association was set up in Nanjing in 1933 to facilitate academic and cultural links but there were to be no funds from a British government whose more immediate priority was the countering of German and Italian anti-British propaganda. Meanwhile more Chinese students went to Japan than to either Europe or the United States, although Japanese education was not highly regarded. But it was cheaper, and there were more scholarships available.[115]

The issue of education was closely allied to that of British advisers to China. The British Naval Adviser of 1931–33 certainly felt that his chief duty was to alleviate British unemployment by selling battleships (a recurring salesman's dream), but he also constantly stressed the value of British training for Chinese naval officers, as these things brought British influence. But as far as the Legation was concerned his chief duty was to prevent any other nation filching the position.[116] There was no proof that foreign advisers were influential or that they at all strengthened the position of their home nation in the eyes of the National government. Sir Meyrick Hewlett was allowed to retire early from the consular service to become an adviser to Chiang Kai-shek, but once installed he was never used and left China in disappointment. But the need to cultivate closer relations kept the British angling for advisory positions. Advisers such as Sir Frederick Whyte did provide a channel through which personal relations could be further eased, but Britain's share of advisers was not large and only the Leith-Ross mission in 1935-36 had any major impact.[117]

### Opposition to reform: the British Residents' Association

The pattern of this reform of the municipalities is clear: squatters' rights in municipal administrations, associations and committees were jettisoned by the British state in collaboration with its allies in the treaty ports, in particular the expatriate business community. The aim was to whittle the British presence down to core national interests, defined specifically in opposition to the settler pretensions of Britain in China. It is also clear that, without the Japanese invasion of Manchuria, this process of retrocession would have developed further more quickly. Shanghai, already the subject of a battle for administrative, as well as moral, sovereignty, would have been negotiated away. In tandem with this series of moves was an attempt by the diplomats to protect some elements of British communal life – notably recreational, or symbolically memorial, locations. The old affectations were subordinated to the 'exigencies of trade', although small pockets of exclusion of Chinese were perpetuated wherever possible.

Protecting foreign sports grounds from Chinese athletes was no substitute for protecting foreign livelihoods. British settlers reacted bitterly to this diplomatic offensive because they could see quite clearly that it signalled their redundancy. As indeed it did – the thrust of the diplomatic process was to engineer a collaboration between the new Chinese ruling elite and its chosen British partners, thereby jettisoning the small treaty port people. For their part, settlers' relentless barrage of propaganda about the Chinese maintained that every such concession threatened British lives. New tactics were employed to spread the settlers' message, as public opinion abroad seemed to have turned against them. The self-styled 'Tientsin British Committee of Information' churned out its *Memoranda*. In June 1927 a Shanghai Publicity Bureau was set up to disseminate pro-SMC and anti-communist propaganda. In a page-long letter to the *North China Daily News* in 1927 on 'The need of making facts known', Rodney Gilbert had suggested changing the function of an existing 'Constitutional Defence League' – which aimed to counter communist activism among Chinese workers – to the dissemination of propaganda about Shanghai abroad, to counter allegedly erroneous views held abroad about Shanghailanders. The bureau was originally a quasi-municipal body, with offices in the

SMC administration building and an SMC representative on its committee, and it aimed to 'explain the functions of municipal government, and to foster a Sino-foreign public opinion in favour of the gradual development of the Shanghai administration'.[118] It published and circulated a *News Bulletin*. Lampson initially recommended 'Close, but unofficial liaison' to the Shanghai Consul-general.[119] But Swire's, for example, refused to distribute the bulletin because of its 'critical, if not unfriendly tone towards matters Chinese'.[120] By early 1929 this was also the feeling of the Chinese, who made requests to the SMC to suppress it.[121] The calibre of those involved was not rated too highly, and it quite plainly represented local interests: the Shanghai Land Investment Company (which housed it), Arnhold's (and therefore Sassoon interests), Teesdale's (treaty port lawyers) and Gibb Livingstone, a long-established agency house. R. Huntley Davidson, its secretary, took its case to Britain and the United States in 1929, representing the British and American councillors on the SMC, and the chairman of the British Chamber of Commerce, in discussions with politicians and diplomats in a 'personal capacity'. He presented a memorandum calling for the establishment of a free port, under League of Nations mandate, at Shanghai. The proposal was not well received; Huntley Davidson, reported one Swire director, appeared 'to be doing the Shanghai Community incalculable harm'. At the Royal Institute of International Affairs in London the impression he left behind was that 'if that is really the frame of mind and outlook of the Shanghai Community, Heaven help them.' It was also plain that the bureau was representing large land interests, hardly ordinary members of the community.[122] By the end of 1929 the bureau was effectively played out, but publicity moves continued. The SMC, for example, created an official publicity post in 1931, in response to ratepayers' pressure, to publicise its new policies and activities. The move was initially intended to influence foreign opinion but the council came to feel that the overriding need was for better publicity in China because the existing inadequate system led to 'misunderstandings' on the part of the Chinese. This was hardly surprising: only after 1930 were the gazette, annual reports and other council material published in Chinese translation. The press post was abolished as an economy measure at the end of 1936, but it dutifully released communiqués and greeted visiting foreign journalists with 'a short history of the Settlement, a statement of its financial position, and an outline of Council activities'. It also produced sections on the city for guide books.[123]

Accompanying these efforts of the publicists and the land oligarchs was strong resistance to reform from those who ultimately had most to lose from the erosion of these structures: the employees of the concession administrations or utilities, the Maritime Customs, and those who serviced such communities: the small treaty port British. Where they could occasionally protest they would: they voted Harry Arnhold out for not being diehard enough in 1930, and disrupted reform plans at the 1930 SMC ratepayers' meeting but mostly they were marginalised or, as in Tianjin, disenfranchised. They felt that they were being betrayed by the diplomats, and their hostility even embraced the SMC itself. The council was compromising its Britishness, while other bodies lobbying for British interests in China such as the China Association or the British Chamber of Commerce were hand in diplomatic glove.

China coast lobbying pre-dated the treaty system, of course, although the activities of the free-traders in the 1830s marked perhaps the historical high point of lobbying success. In the treaty era itself the lobbying for a forward policy in the 1890s by the China Association (founded in London in 1889) or its more activist offshoot the China League (1900) had borne very little fruit.[124] Settler agitation had, however, certainly succeeded in expanding the size of the settlement at Shanghai – and the potential for land investment there. The chambers of commerce had been established in their modern form under diplomatic patronage in World War I to help counter German trade – and were hardly independent community representatives. Although some local branches of the China Association in China were apt to be more activist than the parent body in London, there was little scope within the existing organisations for radical dissent from British China policy. As the SMC, that 'old friend' of British consul-generals, supped with Chinese nationalism at the Shanghai Club and abandoned its fixed opposition over the parks, Chinese representation and the Provisional Court issue, settlers had no forum left by 1931.

They got their forum, however, in the formation of the Shanghai British Residents' Association (BRA; later styled the British Residents' Association of China). In early summer 1931 the British communities in China felt threatened by treaty reform. Well publicised – but confidential – negotiations were then under way between Sir Miles Lampson and Wang Zhengting, and the SMC and other interested parties were lobbying hard against reform. With the aid of Lionel Curtis, the council had commissioned the Feetham report, published in April and mid-June, which garnered a great deal of publicity. Against this background the experience in early June of an ordinary young Shanghai Briton, John Hay Thorburn, provided a chilling counterpoint to the supposed safety offered by extraterritoriality, let alone the post-extraterritorial system that Lampson was negotiating to put in its place. Thorburn, a somewhat immature nineteen-year-old fantasist, secretly left home to 'make good', setting out, it seems, on an attempt to join Guomindang forces engaged in the first encirclement campaign against the CCP in Jiangxi province. In a night-time melee on the Shanghai–Nanjing railway line he fatally wounded two Chinese gendarmes, and was subsequently seized and later secretly executed – just two days after Lampson had initialled a draft treaty he fully expected to return and sign. Although much of the case was quickly uncovered by the SMP, by British diplomats and by other searchers, the affair was hushed up by the military unit responsible and it was not until mid-November that Thorburn's fate became definitely and publicly known – meanwhile Shanghai newspapers publicised his disappearance, and their reports dwelt on the manner of his presumed grisly end. The *Shanghai Evening Post and Mercury* kept a daily tally on its front page of the days since he disappeared.[125] This was a potent mix. Thorburn's fate resonated with individual fears for personal safety and for the safety of family and friends in China, while the contemporaneous threat of treaty reform threatened livelihoods and futures – at a time when the world economic situation was bleak.

The response to this crisis from the 'small treaty port people' was the formation of the BRA. Prominent leaders of this organisation included Woodhead, Green and Ranald G. McDonald (apparently regarded by 'the small person ... as his special representative on the committee')[126] It was established by a mass meeting of British residents in November 1931, which was fuelled by opposition to the extraterritoriality negotiations and particularly by outrage over the Thorburn case. Membership speedily grew among the British communities in China, as the organisation represented those whose employers discouraged or forbade political activism in the treaty ports. The association opposed further concessions to the National government, and attempted to bypass the Legation by appealing directly to parliamentary and public opinion in Britain through a full-time London office. It also attempted to influence the composition of the SMC by indicating to members which British candidates to vote for in elections. It was, in essence, an admission of the impotence felt by the bulk of the British community in the face of the diplomatic assault on their position, and an indication that their interests really had been 'subordinated' to the exigencies of trade and pragmatic diplomacy.[127] Companies like Swire's, tellingly, refused to have anything to do with this desire of 'the small treaty port people' to 'go backwards'. The company was more concerned with 'bigger national interests'. The BRA for its part recommended its members not to vote for Swire's man on the SMC in 1933, and N. S. Brown lost his council seat as a result.[128]

This was not a new phenomenon at a time of crisis. In August 1927 a 'Shanghai Fascisti' had been organised, to 'support the authorities in the present crisis, and to act in the interests of the entire community', and there had been a great rush to enrol.[129] It is clear, from letters and diaries, that disillusionment with the Foreign Office, the Legation, the SMC and business elites was thorough, and that the appeal of a para-military organisation tapped into the rich vein of subdued violent discontent – so much so that council leader Sterling Fessenden took pains to urge great caution on the organisation for fear of incidents. The Fascisti were one of the precursors of the BRA, their leadership was mainly British, and there was some overlapping in the personalities involved. The organisation was moribund by 1928, as the immediate emergency appeared to be over. The BRA needed different tactics to deal with a much more tangible threat, and with the fissure that had developed in the British presence in China as settlers found themselves marginalised by the strengthening relationship between British diplomats and expatriate firms.[130]

British resentment in 1931 was also displayed through widespread support for the Japanese in the aftermath of the invasion of Manchuria. Japan's strong-arm action appealed to those who felt betrayed as the British Legation oversaw the dismantling of the structure of informal empire in China. Ordinary Britons, as well as some of the most prominent treaty port figures, such as Woodhead, voiced such opinions. For one man they were 'one of the greatest hopes for the Far East'; another declared, 'We have one consolation and that is that Japan is out to teach [China] a much needed lesson.'[131] As the informal empire was dismantled those who lost out dreamt dreams of violent revenge. A. H. F. Edwards, disbarred by the Guomindang from taking over the CMC, ended up working as a publicist and adviser to the Japanese embassy in London. Bitter at events generally in China since the end of the Qing, Sir Reginald Johnston urged the same embassy to use his *Twilight in the Forbidden City* (1934) as pro-Manzhouguo propaganda.[132] Support for Japan also represented a last surge of perhaps unconscious belief in the united front of the 'powers' in China. Although rivalry between the powers had always, and continued, to be a key feature of the foreign enterprise in China (and one which Chinese nationalism exploited profitably – especially the isolation of the British), the rhetoric of shared interests still lingered. Even, ironically, at the very moment when those rivalries moved into their final, and most destructive, phase.

Did settler opinion matter? It certainly sent out the wrong messages to Chinese observers, and through its grip on China news reporting in Britain it also peddled its jaundiced views to the British public. The potential of the community for belligerence certainly forced British diplomats to be cautious about provoking confrontation, or even noisy encounters, with the press: they worried constantly about settlers' ability to ratchet up tension. Settler mobilisation though the BRA alone did not force British diplomats to shelve extraterritoriality negotiations in 1931: but when the opportunity arose to evade confrontation they leapt at it. The settler problem was still extant in 1937, however, and caused terrible tensions on a new front – with the Japanese.

### The press

The diplomats tackled treaty port structures, but they were also concerned with the question of publicity and the media discourse on China. They worked hard at reining in the treaty port English-language press, which was a continual catalyst of minor disputes with the Chinese authorities but also a short cut to influencing the behaviour of the wider community. An uncircumspect press might undermine what privileges remained. The practice of designating specific newspapers, such as the *Central China Post* (Hankou) or the *North China Daily News*, as the sole publisher of official consular notifications gave rise to confusion, as some foreign readers interpreted this as meaning that those papers expressed official views in their editorials.[133] Chinese political opinion viewed the *North China Daily News* as an official British mouthpiece (the 'kept lady of the Bund'), a claim not helped by the Foreign Office's policy of refusing to censure the press directly for criticism of foreign governments.[134] This was unfortunate, given the paper's deservedly diehard reputation and hostility towards British policy. O. M. Green was frequently called upon to mend his ways on both counts; in 1929 the paper was temporarily banned from the Chinese mails for criticism of the Guomindang, and Green was advised by the Consul-general to tone things down. 'If anyone would murder Green,' wrote Warren Swire, 'I would gladly pay for his defence *and* the education of his orphans.' Similar problems were presented by H. G. W. Woodhead and the *Peking and Tientsin Times*. In 1927 Woodhead was asked to 'exercise discretion' in reports on the Hankou agreement and subsequent events. At the same time journalists perceived as pro-Nationalist were also restrained informally, if possible, whilst in early 1927 Lampson asked the Foreign Office News Department to divert press attention to the virtues of Zhang Zuolin. One such journalistic bugbear was Arthur Ransome; another was a young Australian, F. B. Riley, pro-Nationalist special correspondent of *The Times*. The unfortunate Riley was kidnapped and killed by Chinese soldiers in late 1927. 'Thank God', minuted Swire.[135]

As we have seen in chapter 2, the real problem lay in the treaty port press, rather than in occasional visiting correspondents, because treaty port editors usually doubled as correspondents for the domestic press, and had, thereby, two channels in which to do their damage. Correspondent Rodney Gilbert was packed off in 1929, and Lampson used all his influence to 'get a different and better type' to replace Green in 1930, to the point of seeing the proprietor to impress on him the 'need for a change of policy by the paper'. He had already received a deputation, containing Lionel Curtis and Swire's N. S. Brown, suggesting a better man. In this he seems to have succeeded. Green was replaced in 1930 by a former information officer from the India Office. Three years earlier Chamberlain had persuaded Geoffrey Dawson, editor of *The Times*, to seek Lampson's help in getting a correspondent for the paper to replace Green, whilst in January 1930 Lampson lectured Fraser of *The Times* 'about the advantages of taking a somewhat more sympathetic attitude' in his messages home to the paper.[136]

This activity was important; the depoliticisation of the British treaty port press was never completely realised, but in the 1930s it certainly became less rancidly inflammatory than in the days of Green and Rodney Gilbert. Smaller settler fry, such as William Bruce Lockhart, louche owner and editor of an obnoxious Shanghai bi-weekly, *The Showdown*, had the book thrown at them. Brought up in China (his father was born in Shanghai in 1850), Lockhart had arrived in Shanghai in 1905, making an erratic living as a salesman before launching *The Showdown* in mid-1928. The paper was popular in the city for its aggressive tone towards the Chinese. On Lampson's orders Lockhart was hauled up in front of the Consul-general after complaints from the Nationalist Minister of Foreign Affairs in 1929. After a further offence he was found guilty of contempt of court.[137] Paradoxically, growing international interest in events in China served to undermine the treaty port journalistic establishment. The political situation in the 1930s, and the keener interest taken in China, saw more foreign journalists stationed in Shanghai, and they were more concerned with Sino-Japanese relations, or the Guomindang–CCP struggle, than with what were increasingly seen as local squabbles, unless these were internationalised. Settlers lost their hegemony, and the *North China Daily News* in particular became more and more a community newspaper in the 1930s than the 'thunderer' on the Bund that it had been.

## The Foreign Office regains control, 1937-41

The Japanese invasion of Manchuria in 1931 put the process of diplomatic change on hold, but in the years before the outbreak of the Sino-Japanese War the culture of British business and diplomacy in China changed drastically. Big business made its own peace with the National government, and – as the following chapter shows – with the Chinese market, while the British government together with British bankers played useful roles in currency stabilisation in 1935–36. The measures taken in the years 1927–31 had done much to defuse immediate tensions with the Guomindang, but Manchuria had given a short lease of life to the settler establishment as reform of extraterritoriality was shelved and as the National government sought allies. The Marco Polo bridge incident on 7 July 1937, however, and the developing Sino-Japanese war saw a renewal of the drive by the Foreign Office to regain control, not control of China or any part of it – there was no 'forward policy' aimed at rehabilitating China under British tutelage – but control of Britain in China.[138]

Growing Anglo-Japanese tension, not only over China but also over Japanese economic relations with the British empire, developed steadily through the 1930s. Vacillating attempts to devise a new relationship were mounted by the Treasury after 1935 against the opposition of the Foreign Office, which remained immune. Any resolution of Anglo-Japanese tension would be bound to undermine Sino-British relations spectacularly, and instead the diplomats attempted to tread a middle path while nudging both sides to reach a settlement. The long-term calculation was based not on support for Chiang's National government but on fear of the power of China's mass nationalism. Even the increasingly sound strategic demand for the neutralisation of Britain's possible East Asian difficulties, to enable it to focus better on Europe, could not surmount this fear. Moreover, popular support for China in Britain grew throughout the 1930s, and especially after the outbreak of war in 1937.[139]

The war itself put the British in a quandary. Rushing to the support of Chiang Kai-shek did not exactly appeal, and would hardly improve relations with Japan, but it was impossible for the British to see the Japanese action as in any way acceptable, not only to British interests in China, but by international standards in state-to-state relations. Having let China down in 1931-32, to the extent that the legitimacy of the League of Nations had been resoundingly undermined, a middle way had to be negotiated to avoid provoking conflict with Japan while not alienating Chinese opinion too far.[140] Moreover, as chapter 6 will show, the suspicion and hostility towards Chinese and China that had so marked British culture as late as the end of the 1930s had been quite significantly supplanted by a much more positive attitude. Public opinion in Britain was significantly pro-Chinese.

The war disrupted British economic interests in China, and in Japanese-controlled areas there were concerted moves to discriminate against and drive out British trade.[141] In fact, overall, the years after 1937 were particularly good for British trade: anti-Japanese boycotts, and the emergency needs of the National government, stimulated the trade of other powers. In these circumstances the remaining British coastal concessions and Hong Kong became much more important as safe havens for British economic interests, but they also became increasingly, and increasingly hotly, contested by the Japanese, collaborationists and the National government. The unoccupied cities became key points in the survival tactics of the regime, and they also served to undermine Japanese economic warfare tactics, through their continued use of the National government's currency, the fabi.

Japanese advances after 1931 had served to put pressure on the British position. The Japanese development programme for Manzhouguo made it no realm for non-Japanese trade interests.[142] Japanese-sponsored smuggling into north China undercut British interests too. In Shanghai the Japanese had never quite removed their military forces from the Hongkou district of the International Settlement. The Japanese attack on the Chinese-administered Zhabei suburb was launched from Hongkou on 28 January 1932, strictly a violation of the neutrality of the settlement. After the cease-fire a naval landing party was stationed in barracks in Shanghai's 'little Japan', and the military presence gave a fillip to the Japanese community in Shanghai.[143]

In both Tianjin and Shanghai Japanese troops occupied the Chinese-administered zones of the cities in 1937, in the latter case after a particularly bloody and destructive campaign which drove hundreds of thousands of refugees permanently into the International Settlement.[144] The settlement also became a relatively safe haven for anti-Japanese and anti-collaborationist terror units. The SMC lost effective control for good of the northern districts of the settlement to the Japanese military, and in the face of unrelenting Japanese pressure resigned areas of police sovereignty to the Japanese and collaborationist regime. The deteriorating situation after 1937 saw Chongqing and pro-Wang Jingwei units fight a terror war within the settlement which tested the SMP and British military to their limit. 'It is horribly worrying,' wrote the Secretary-general to the British ambassador in 1940, after yet another assassination of a collaborator. 'I wonder if you can yet once again try to get Chunking to give orders to do the killings outside the settlement.'[145] As a result of the wartime crisis, and the strained relations with the Japanese, the Foreign Office extended its reach into remaining treaty port institutions and freedoms. For example, to prevent Chinese use of the British flag to attack the Japanese through publications printed in the unoccupied concessions, British subjects were forbidden from printing non-English publications without ambassadorial consent.[146] The diplomats also became involved in SMC business in new ways, and this saw the culmination of British diplomats' attempts to bring the council to heel. The Foreign Office telegrams and despatches piled up in London, where they still lie in the archives, dealing with rice supplies, municipal elections, SMC sovereignty, the composition of the SMP, the political and ordinary crime crisis, individual murders and other incidents, including the terror campaigns which involved, among other things, assassination attempts on leading British SMC personnel.

Through all this, British residents, buoyed by the suspension of treaty renegotiation at the onset of the decade, continued living as if little was going to change, and most of the 3,000 British women and children evacuated to Hong Kong by 21 August 1937 were back by Christmas. There was at the individual level as well an attempt to perpetuate normality, which involved the reassertion of civilised achievement. The core of Shanghailander identity lay in the claim to be a real community in which people lived and worked, and created and consumed culture. The defeat of moves to shut down the municipal orchestra in 1938 – the 'greatest cultural asset east of Suez' – clearly indicates this aspect of settler morale, and the desire to act as if Shanghai was still a communal home where some compromises just could not be made. Life in the city was saturated with such symbolism.[147] Morale could not stay high indefinitely, and Britons started leaving when the European war began. Army reservists in the SMP resigned to rejoin their units. Others, scenting the wind, resigned, shipped their families to Australia and joined up, and some men were pulled out by the British government. To stem the flow the SMC persuaded the Foreign Office to instruct its staff to remain at their posts as their contribution to the war effort.[148]

Desperate to maintain the 'neutrality' of the settlement, the SMC itself bowed to Japanese military pressure to censor or suppress anti-Japanese activity.[149] The SMP Special Branch files chronicle quietly the scale of 'Assistance to Japanese Gendarmerie' in 1939: 'arrest of suspected members of Shanghai Anti-Japanese Special Service Corps', 'Two male Chinese ... loaned to the Japanese Water Police for ... the purposes of interrogation', 'Arrest of two Chinese members of guerrillas unit'. The SMP had rendered such 'assistance' to the Nanjing government's Shanghai Public Security Bureau and thereby ravaged the Shanghai Communist Party. The routine was ingrained. Opinions were fairly clear, however: 'Sir, for information. A congregation of scum,' noted the Special Branch chief to his superior over a report on a meeting of a collaborationist 'peace assembly'. 'Yes,' was the reply.[150] The council also accepted the replacement of existing Guomindang inter-

[ 155 ]

ests in the settlement by the Japanese or collaborationist regimes, although it resisted challenges to the pre-war *status quo* over police sovereignty where it could, and for as long as it could. Caught between the Guomindang and the Japanese, and later the Wang Jingwei regime, the SMC earned few plaudits for its stance, which was regarded as simple collaboration by many observers, a difficult charge to rebut when the SMP assisted the Japanese in the arrest of opponents in the settlement. After the onset of the European war the isolation of the council became more pronounced.

The key issues which undid the autonomy of the SMC were the composition of the elected council itself (and its administration) and council finances. Electoral struggles with the Japanese began in 1936, when the Japanese Residents' Association breached the convention that only two Japanese candidates would stand for election to the SMC, whereupon all British electors would vote for them to ensure that both would be elected. Three Japanese stood that year, but mobilisation of British voters through the British Residents' Association defeated the move. Although this tactic was considered again in 1938, in 1939 it became clear to British observers that the number of Japanese electors was growing at a rapid rate through vote splitting: property was being nominally subdivided into parcels big enough to warrant qualification for the franchise, and these lots were registered in the names of Japanese residents.[151] The SMC secretly lobbied the British consulate-general to urge a vote-splitting rejoinder in July 1939. Official co-operation was needed in the shape of a lower consular fee for the nominal transfers which were planned and put into effect in time for a bitter municipal election in 1940.[152]

'No doubt another Thorburn case or Hankow incident would revive public interest' in the British Residents' Association, commented H. G. W. Woodhead in January 1936, as its activists worked solidly but undramatically to put the settler case in London.[153] Chinese nationalism was not the catalyst, however. The Japanese threat prompted collaboration between the BRA, the China Association and the British Chamber of Commerce in Shanghai through a Joint Election Committee after 1936. The BRA's membership was China-based, and younger than that of the China Association, which was also mostly male. A China Parliamentary Group in the British Parliament had become the BRA's main publicity forum. BRA members could vote only in Shanghai or Tianjin, however, and mobilising them to protect British dominance of the SMC became the association's chief function.[154] The duplication of representative groups irritated Swire's, who talked about uniting British efforts, but who remained wary of being 'terribly damaged by Shanghai local policy'.[155]

Anglo-Japanese tension developed swiftly after the onset of the war. The Tianjin crisis in 1938-39 saw Japanese troops blockade the British concession partly in an ultimately successful bid to force the concession authorities to hand over Chinese guerrillas held in police custody.[156] On other fronts Japanese agents sponsored the anti-British activities of such collaborationist bodies as the Daminhui (Great People's Movement) which agitated against British economic interests in Shanghai – seizing control of a strike at a cotton mill in Pudong in June 1939. The strike was dragged out for six months, and two Britons died in related violence.[157] The Daminhui also conducted anti-British activities in Tianjin and Xiamen. The latter, even, was the subject of tension in 1939 over the assassination of a collaborationist official, a pretext used by the Japanese to escalate pressure on foreign interests.[158] The council, deciding that 'a policy of realism was in the best interests of the settlement', had already appointed a Japanese-speaking unit in early 1939, but settlement of the assassination issue saw their acceptance of the appointment of two senior Japanese policemen from the Shanghai Municipal Police into the force.[159] By 1940 the Japanese presence in the settlement was decisive, while the refugee problem and economic disruption left little room to debate issues of sovereignty. In Tianjin the police riot squad kept up a steady patrol to prevent 'unneutral activity' – and thereby make the concession 'as attractive and pleasant as possible'.[160]

Japanese hostility hardly made concession life pleasant after 1938, and it altered its character in a number of ways. Not least among these was a swing away from the settler brio so smoothly articulated by Harry Arnhold, towards the language of Britishness. Being blockaded by Japanese troops and electric fences, as in Tianjin, quite literally forced a sense of community back on to the British. The Japanese did not differentiate between settler or expatriate. Communal defence and solidarity in the face of the threat meant a greater sense of solidarity among all Britons. This unity was fractured and fragile, and it barely lasted until the end of the Pacific War. But it shows how the multiple strands in the identity of Britain in China constantly shifted, and also how contingent was the settlers' sense of imperial citizenship: they were British by choice.

Electoral gerrymandering, sanctioned and aided by London, prevented the Japanese achieving a majority on the SMC in 1940, but in August British councillors talked about 'going into opposition' on the SMC by accepting Japanese demands.[161] Vote-rigging worried the diplomats, however. They knew it was indefensible, and that the Japanese actually had a very good case for increased representation in all aspects of Settlement life. In this small area, of course, as in bigger issues in

Anglo-Japanese relations, Japan's claims were far from illegitimate. The fear was that overt involvement would provoke unilateral Japanese action. The rancour which accompanied the election, and which partly lay behind a murderous assault on SMC chairman W. J. Keswick by the president of the Japanese Residents' Association in January 1941, proved deeply worrying.[162] In the almost immediate aftermath of that event, with another council election looming, the Consul-general, British councillors and the Secretary-general, Godfrey Phillips, met to find ways to avert 'the possibility of bloodshed on a serious scale'. The situation was 'untenable and unjustifiable'.[163] To avert the feared crisis British councillors began planning for a 'government by commission' that became the hastily cobbled together Provisional Council agreement in April 1941. This suspended the land regulations and the electoral process, and introduced a consular-appointed Shanghai Provisional Council with a reduced Anglo-American presence.[164] In many other areas – especially over policing, and the suppression of anti-Japanese activities – the SMC had already capitulated to Japanese demands. This agreement had the merit of meeting the Japanese part of the way over the question of seats by diminishing the overt British presence on the SMC and diluting it by appointing Dutch and Swiss members. It also sealed British consular control of that very presence. The long cherished and protected autonomy of the settler British was abolished.

At the same time as British diplomats had secured their long-sought control over settler politics, growing tensions led to the effective abandonment of this policy of overt involvement in the affairs of the International Settlement. As London was blitzed Shanghai's shrill cries for special treatment – calls for negotiations leading to the establishment of neutral status in the event of conflict, for example – raised diplomatic hackles. 'Shanghai have been the spoilt child of this country too long. They will have to stand on their own feet more in future,' minuted one London diplomat in March 1941, a widely held view.[165] Why not let the Japanese take over the International Settlement altogether, mused a Foreign Office committee in April 1941? Then they would have to worry about feeding it and maintaining order, and it would weaken them militarily.[166] By this point the priority was no longer combating Japanese encroachment, but positioning for the expected wider conflict in the Pacific. The stricter definition of British imperial interests drawn up excluded China; Hong Kong became the new front line of the British empire in East Asia, but the key to imperial defence was actually identified as Singapore, guardian of communications with the south-west Pacific; even Hong Kong was merely an 'outpost'.[167] Shanghai passed beyond the bounds and care of empire. There was little contradiction between the close support the diplomats gave the SMC to counter Japanese belligerence and the longer-term aim of getting rid of Shanghailanders. There was every expectation that a final resolution of the Sino-Japanese crisis would precipitate a resolution of treaty port issues between Britain and China. Protecting the SMC against Japanese demands after July 1937 was a long-term negotiating tactic. Certainly real questions of British prestige were felt to be at stake, but the aim was to survive, and to preserve the pre-conflict *status quo* to get as good a deal as possible in the inevitable aftermath. Whatever the Japanese acquired, diplomats knew, would not easily, if at all, be returned to British hands after the war.

The key feature of the diplomatic encroachment on the active governance of the International Settlement was that it happened in partnership with big business. Companies such as Jardine's, Hongkong & Shanghai Bank, ICI, BAT, the Calico Printers' Association and Swire's got involved because they could see that the old settlement days were finished, and so they struggled to buy time, and position themselves for peace. In 1935 when a joint BRA-China Association group was mooted Swire's planned to include ICI, BAT, Jardine's, APC and Arnhold's, as well as 'a local vested interest' such as land or broking. In late 1937 one emergency meeting of Anglo-American interests consisted on the British part of Swire's, Hongkong & Shanghai Bank, APC, Jardine's, ICI, BAT and Godfrey Phillips for the SMC. Settlers lost control of the SMC to this active coalition of the diplomats and the 'British hongs on the Bund' – eight of which alone held 5,127 British votes in February 1941 (out of a total of 12,500 British votes). The local democracy of the self-styled 'model settlement' became irrelevant.[168] A long-looming financial crisis faced by the council was another cause behind the loss of SMC autonomy. 'Bad finance', inflated sterling commitments, a declining revenue base due to the Japanese occupation and other factors squeezed the SMC, not merely resulting in problems with possible general repercussions on its autonomy and status but also seriously impairing its operational efficiency. A life-saving loan was negotiated by the SMC from the Hongkong & Shanghai Bank in 1940, but it was brokered by the diplomats and was another example of the extension of Foreign Office control. Negotiations over this, and over the elections and the Provisional Council,[169] drew diplomats and expatriate businessmen closer together and away from the 'community', as they termed the settler interest – consciously distancing themselves from it in the process. It is also clear that they blamed Shanghailanders for many of these problems.[170] The European war itself cemented the relationship between expatriate interests and the British state. 'Firms of good repute', such as ICI or CPA, were aided in their efforts to import

**Figure 9** Jardines in the chair: the Shanghai Municipal Council, 1940–41. Chairman W. J. Keswick sits in the centre of the front row, with Yu Xiaqing on his left.

raw materials from the United States; smaller interests were squeezed out. Senior businessmen – of 'good repute', one assumes – such as Tony Keswick of Jardine's, or Valentine St John Killery of ICI, took on important positions in the Ministry of Economic Warfare or Special Operations Executive – from where they could, and did, lobby for their own post-war interests.[171]

The build-up to the war had seen a somewhat paradoxical situation develop: at the same time as the British empire sharply distanced itself from its possessions in China, outside Hong Kong, there was an incorporation of institutions, enterprises and individuals fully into the plans of the empire in a new way. British imperial defence schemes stopped at Hong Kong: the point was made over and over again in diplomatic minutes dealing with Shanghai questions, industrial supplies for British companies or tenders for war work from the same firms. Shanghai was not a colony, and 'wider imperial interests' were not affected by difficulties there.[172] But in the build-up to the Pacific War the British state was keen for the SMC to act as a buffer to Japanese activities in Shanghai, and it was also keen to recruit British personnel into its intelligence apparatuses.

Britons in China, who had always worn their British empire hat at times of imperial crisis, were keen as war approached to stress to the empire the utility of their activities, and companies, and the order they brought to the city of Shanghai.[173] After all, if one fear which had bolstered the sex taboos which characterised settler society was the fear of the Macanisation of the British presence, then in the two years after September 1939 the great fear was of the White Russianisation of the Britons on the China coast. If Britain was defeated in Europe, Britons feared, they would become stateless refugees, at the mercy of the Japanese but more at the mercy of the Chinese. Having seen what the Russian communities had gone through in the two decades after 1917, it was not a prospect settlers or expatriates relished. Partly with this fear in mind, the remaining Britons in unoccupied China noisily asserted their citizenship of the empire. The Japanese threat also focused perceptions sharply because it extended beyond the remaining Chinese treaty ports, and paid no heed to settler and expatriate conflicts: all British presences in East and South-east Asia were threatened by Japan. All British presences then had an essential British identity rudely thrust back on them.

## Conclusion

The newly developing relationship between the British state, or its diplomatic and military agents in China, and British business interests there emerges as a key to an understanding of Sino-British relations after 1925. Broader issues of Anglo-Japanese relations, and British relations with the United States or the USSR, were important, and issues of imperial defence, and questions of imperial prestige, became prominent, but for the British relationship with China we have to look most closely at Sino-British relations *in* China. Having acquiesced in the growth of the treaty port system, which had developed a sophistication and ambitions far in advance of the imaginings of early lobbyists for a 'factory' on the China coast, or of the treaty makers themselves, British diplomats had to set about dismantling their settler monster. The personal relations of consuls, traders, settlers and diplomats were enmeshed, however, and the settler mentality was pervasive, while the view from Shanghai always seemed far more complex than the view from the desks in the Far Eastern Department of the Foreign Office. Britain in China was a tangible polity that had developed largely in the interstices of the treaties, through local agreements with Chinese authority (such as the land regulations in Shanghai) or through the self-aggrandisement of the settler elites. Reform, revision or abolition was far from easy; despite the nominal subordination of individual British (or British-protected) subjects to their Minister and his consuls, Britain in China had no master.

To enable the fundamental revision of Sino-British relations mapped out by the generalities of the December memorandum in 1926, the diplomats had to assert and exercise control over their charge. To do so they had, in the end, to nationalise Sino-British relations. This they did by identifying what 'British interests' in China actually were, and then by forging an alliance with non-settler interests, an alliance which was finally cemented in the shadow of the Pacific War. The alliance was formed of an amalgam of some long-term China companies whose interests were broader than those of the run-of-the-mill China houses – notably Jardine Matheson and John Swire & Sons – and newer, largely transnational firms. Many of these companies developed their own strategies to circumvent the problems caused by the treaty system, and distanced themselves as far as they felt able from the 'small treaty port people' and the *ancien régime*. A key tactic here was to forge direct relations themselves with the National government, as Jürgen Osterhammel has shown. Diplomacy aside, British firms cut tax deals, paying hefty sums in advance for discounts, and gained government support in labour disputes.[174] The corollary was the forging of a new partnership with the British state.

This partnership was most important in Shanghai – the capital city of Britain in China. Companies like Jardine's, or the Hongkong & Shanghai Bank had long been involved in governing the International

Settlement, but in the 1930s they became involved with the aim of getting it fit for dissolution, and after 1937 with holding the line for all British interests in the face of Japanese aggression. Existing scholarship locates this shift in a victory of a big-business China lobby, but that is a fundamental misreading of the facts.[175] The high point of lobbying success over China surely lay in the pre-treaty period; big business and finance thereafter lobbied with as little success in the 1890s as in the 1930s. British settlers lobbied through the fact of their very presence, maintained their tight grip on Sino-British relations down to the late 1920s, and fought effective reform for the best part of two decades thereafter. After the late 1920s, however, it was the British state, in particular the Foreign Office, which worked to reconfigure Britain in China, and which chose its own partners.

## Notes

1  Darwin, 'Imperialism and the Victorians', 619.
2  K. C. Chan, 'The Abrogation of British Extraterritoriality in China, 1942–43: A Study in Anglo-American-Chinese Relations', *Modern Asian Studies*, 11 (1977), 257–91.
3  Fung, *Diplomacy of Imperial Retreat*, 22–4.
4  Feuerwerker, *Foreign Establishment in China*, 29–30, see also Michael J. and Yeone Wei-chih Moser, *Foreigners within the Gates: the Legations at Peking* (Hong Kong, 1993); Hoare, 'British Embassy Peking'.
5  PRO, FO 800/260, Lampson to Chamberlain, 9 March 1927.
6  SP, ADD15, J. K. Swire to C. C. Scott, 19 June 1925.
7  Endicott, *Diplomacy and Enterprise*, 98–9.
8  PRO, FO 800/260, Lampson to Chamberlain, 9 March 1927, Middle East Centre, St Antony's College, Oxford, Killearn papers (hereafter Lampson Diaries), 25 February 1927, 12 May 1928, 13 November, 20 December 1929.
9  Coates, *China Consuls*, 453–5, 461–3; 467–9; Lampson Diaries, 17 March 1927, 24 May 1931.
10  Kirby, 'The Internationalisation of China', 441.
11  PRO, FO 369/2020, K13934/12995/210, Lampson to FO, No. 1264, 24 October 1928.
12  D. C. M. Platt, *The Cinderella Service: British Consuls since 1825* (London, 1971), 225–30.
13  PRO, FO 369/2017, K8289/3238/210, Legation to FO No. 563, 29 May 1928; FO 369/2018, K6175/6175/210, 'Report on Conditions in Hankow affecting Clerical Officers'; for an indication of the network of relationships see Coates, *China Consuls*, 491–547.
14  PRO, FO 228/3880/43 67b, Chunking No. 13a, 11 May 1928.
15  Feuerwerker, *Foreign Establishment in China*, 60–6.
16  PRO, FO 228/3943/45 52, Hankow No. 103, 14 October 1929.
17  Martyn Atkins, *Informal Empire in Crisis: British Diplomacy and the Chinese Customs Succession, 1927–1929* (Ithaca NY, 1995).
18  PRO, FO 228/3741/96 5a, Chunking S/O, 13 June 1928, forwarded in Lampson to Chamberlain, 14 July 1928; FO 228/3943/34 5a, Lampson to Henderson, No. 1015, 15 July 1929; FO 228/4206/3 32g , Tientsin No. 20, 5 April 1930.
19  Maze Confidential Letters, Vol. 3, Maze to N. S. Brown, 20 January 1930.
20  In 1925 the service employed 1,260 foreigners and 7,144 Chinese; by 1937 the figures were 774 and 8,408, and foreign staff still held the majority of senior posts, CMC, *Service List*, 1925–37.
21  Maze Semi-official Letters, 9, No. 822, 8 June 1928, and No. 824, 26 July 1928; CMC,

*Service List*, 1928.

22  See Legation file 12c for 1928: PRO, FO 228/3768–70.

23  Eugene Byrne, *The dismissal of Sir Francis Aglen as Inspector of the Chinese Maritime Customs Service, 1927* (Leeds, 1995); Atkins, *Informal Empire in Crisis*, 82–3.

24  Osterhammel, 'Imperialism in Transition', 264.

25  PRO, FO 228/3998/1 29a, Teichman minute on Chinkiang No. 1, 1 March 1929.

26  PRO, FO 228/3179/60 108c, Jamieson to Lampson, S/O, 28 February 1927.

27  PRO, FO 228/3818/ 28c, Kiukiang No. 2, 18 January 1928; FO 228/3997/39 28c, Kiukiang No. 27, 6 August 1929; FO 228/4352/1 124d, Shanghai No. 100, 17 April 1930, Chairman's report, British Chamber of Commerce Shanghai, Annual General Meeting, 15 April 1930.

28  PRO, FO 228/3839/40 40a, Confidential print, F8405/67/10, 'Memorandum respecting the Hankow Agreement', 1 November 1928.

29  A French concession was also established in 1849 (and a conseil municipal in 1862); a still smaller American concession was delineated in 1854 but amalgamated with the British settlement to form the International Settlement in 1863.

30  *NCH*, 2 July 1854, 203; 2 September 1854, 18; 11 November 1854, 58–9.

31  F. M. Mayers, N. B. Dennys and C. King, *The Treaty Ports of China and Japan* (London and Hong Kong, 1867), 445.

32  Pott, *Short History of Shanghai, passim*.

33  Thomas B. Stephens, *Order and Discipline in China: The Shanghai Mixed Court, 1911–27* (Seattle WA, 1992), 44–7; Wright, *Twentieth Century Impressions*, 401.

34  *NCH*, 25 June 1859, 187. There is no adequate history of the SMC; the first decades are still best captured in John King Fairbank, *Trade and Diplomacy on the China Coast: The Opening of the Treaty Ports, 1842–1854*, Stanford edition (Stanford CA, 1969).

35  SMC, *Annual Report*, 1908, 226–35; *Annual Report*, 1909, 264–71 (including map); *Annual Report*, 1915, 105b–106b; Clifford, *Spoilt Children of Empire*, 32; Pott, *Short History of Shanghai*, 270.

36  Stephens, *Order and Discipline in China*, 48–52.

37  Alison W. Connor, 'Lawyers and the Legal Profession during the Republican Period', in Kathryn Bernhardt and Philip C. C. Huang, eds, *Civil Law in Qing and Republican China* (Stanford CA, 1994), 237–42.

38  SMA U–1–3–2484, 'Application of the Stamp Tax Law in the International Settlement', memorandum by Sterling Fessenden, 22 March 1930.

39  *Report of the Hon. Mr Justice Feetham, CMG, to the Shanghai Municipal Council* (three volumes, Shanghai, 1931), I, 80, II, 166; Zou Yiren, *Jiu Shanghai renkou bianqian de yanjiu* (Research into Population Change in Old Shanghai) (Shanghai, 1980), 141; *Directory and Chronicle of China and Japan ... 1922* (Hong Kong, 1922), 808–11.

40  Pott, *Short History of Shanghai*, 68.

41  SMA U–1–3–1974, N. O. Liddell to Chairman, SMC, 16 March 1922.

42  See, for example, disputes over the SMP's 'arbitrary and often harsh discrimination' against Chinese associations and clubs: SMA U 1-3-227, 'Chinese Clubs and Associations', minute by Sterling Fessenden, 17 August 1928, and file.

43  In 1931 Feetham reported an estimate for 1927 of 55 per cent, but decided that this was already far too low; Feetham, *Report*, II, 176.

44  SMC, *Annual Report*, 1906, 392–6.

45  SMC, *Annual Report*, 1920, 65a–66a; SMA U 1-3–1114, 'Chinese Councillors (1920–25)', SMC Minute, 27 September 1922.

46  SMC, *Annual Report*, 1920, 190a–197a; SMA U 1-3–1114, SMC Minute, 19 September 1923, and *passim*.

47  Scully, 'Taking the Low Road to Sino-American Relations', 62–83; Brian G. Martin, *The Shanghai Green Gang: Politics and Organised Crime, 1919–37* (Berkeley CA, 1996), 34–5.

48  Henriot, *Belles de Shanghai*, 319–39; Brian G. Martin, 'The "Pact with the Devil": The Relationship between the Green Gang and the Shanghai French Concession

Authorities, 1925–1935', in Frederic Wakeman Jr and Wen-hsin Yeh, eds, *Shanghai Sojourners* (Berkeley CA, 1992), 293–300.

49  PRO, FO 228/3179/67 108c, Tientsin No. 21, 1 March 1927, 'Minutes of a Joint Meeting of the China Association Tientsin Branch and the Tientsin British Chamber of Commerce, 7 February 1927', 15; FO 228/4283/22 69b, Shanghai No. 103, 24 April 1930.

50  See the discussions on the issue in PRO, FO 228/2518.

51  *NCH*, 7 August. 1862, 122–3.

52  On the SMC and May Thirtieth see Clifford, *Spoilt Children of Empire*, and Robert W. Radtke, 'The British Commercial community in Shanghai and British Policy in China, 1925–1931' (University of Oxford D.Phil. thesis, 1991).

53  PRO, FO 228/4283/15 69b, Brenan to Lampson, S/O, 13 March 1930; FO 228/4046/16 69b, Lampson minute on Shanghai No. 129, 20 April 1929; Lampson Diaries, 21 February, 27 March 1931.

54  SP, JSS II 2/7, Butterfield & Swire, Shanghai (hereafter BSS), to John Swire & Sons, London (hereafter JSL), 28 September 1928.

55  PRO, FO 228/4283/6 69b, Shanghai no. 18, 3 February 1930.

56  See Legation Dossier 69, 1928, PRO, FO 228/3883; Feetham, *Report*, I, 113–30. Five Chinese representatives were also appointed to the council's committees, one on each: SMA U-1-3-1115, SMC Minute, 18 January 1928.

57  PRO, FO 228/4045/9 69, Garstin to Lampson, S/O, 16 June 1929; Feetham, *Report*, II, 109.

58  SMC, *Municipal Gazette*, 17 April, 3 May 1930; see Legation file 69b, 1928 (FO 228/4283), in particular PRO, FO 228/4283/18 69b, Shanghai No. 71, 17 April 1930; FO 228/4370 30b, Brenan to Lampson, private, 22 April 1930.

59  Lampson Diaries, 25 February 1929.

60  *NCH*, 9 June 1928, 43; 11 August 1928, 233.

61  PRO, FO 228/4134/40 3, Brenan to Lampson, S/O, 30 October 1930, and enclosure.

62  PRO, FO 228/4285/3 69z, Ingram to Lampson S/O, 2 June 1930; FO 228/4285/4 69z, Brenan to Lampson, Shanghai No. 150, 6 June 1930.

63  PRO, FO 228/4352/1 124d, Shanghai No. 100, 17 April 1930, 'Minutes of the Annual General Meeting of the British Chamber of Commerce, Shanghai, 1930', 22.

64  PRO, FO 228/4273/24 63, Shanghai, S/O, 30 October 1930 and minutes.

65  SP, ADD 15, G. W. Swire to JSL, 8 February 1929.

66  Bank of England archives (hereafter BOE), G1/296 31, W. Kirkpatrick 'Notes for Remarks to Advisory Committee, Export Credits Guarantee Department, on 2 November 1937', 13.

67  SMC, *Annual Report*, 1927, 66–7.

68  *Municipal Gazette*, 9 February 1929, *passim*.

69  SMC, *Annual Report*, 1929, 180; SMC, *Annual Report*, 1930, 324; SMC, *Annual Report*, 1931, 310; SMC, *Annual Report*, 1931, 328. Assessing the results of these moves is not easy, since the council, probably with this very aim in mind, stopped publishing a list of its employees in the *Annual Report* after 1931.

70  SMC, *Annual Report*, 1931, 11; F. C. Jones, *Shanghai and Tientsin, with special Reference to Foreign Interests* (London, 1940), 15–18.

71  Robin Porter, *Industrial Reformers in Republican China* (Armonk NY, 1994), 117–29.

72  PRO, FO 371/13930, F3501/250/10, Lampson to FO, No. 19, 'Notes of an Informal Meeting at the Home of Mr H. E. Arnhold, Chairman of the SMC', 22 May 1929.

73  Stephens, *Order and Discipline in China*, 64–5, Frederick Wakeman, Jr, *Policing Shanghai, 1927–1937* (Berkeley CA, 1995) 70–2.

74  Not for the first time: see Mark Elvin, 'The Administration of Shanghai, 1905–1914', in Mark Elvin and G. William Skinner (eds), *The Chinese City between Two Worlds* (Stanford CA, 1974), 239 62; Christian Henriot, *Shanghai, 1927–1937: Municipal Power, Locality and Modernisation* (Berkeley CA, 1993).

75  SMA U 1-3-1974, N. O. Liddell to Chairman, SMC, 16 March 1922.

76  Feetham, *Report*, I, 5.

77 Teichman, *Affairs of China*,162.
78 PRO, FO 228/4370/84 30b, Brenan to Lampson, 12 February 1930.
79 PRO, FO 228/4047/1 69l, Shanghai No. 1, 3 January 1929; SMC, *Annual Report*, 1925, 324, *Annual Report*, 1939, 412–14.
80 The SMC knew all about the political misuse of utility supplies, having cut power supplies to, in effect, Chinese-owned factories outside the settlement during the general strike after the May Thirtieth incident; Clifford, *Spoilt Children of Empire*, 134–7.
81 *China Press*, 'Coronation and Sino-British Trade Supplement', 12 May 1937, 29, 77.
82 I. I. Kounin, ed., *The Diamond Jubilee of the International Settlement of Shanghai* (Shanghai, 1940); Jeffrey N. Wasserstrom, 'Imagining Community in the International Settlement: The Shanghai Jubilee as an Invented Tradition', paper presented at the University of California, Berkeley CA, Centre for Chinese Studies, 2 December 1994.
83 Tientsin British Municipal Council, *Report*, 1938, 9. Previous British population figures are available for 1913 (388), 1925 (682), 1929 (755), 1934 (1,451) (*ibid.*); Jones, *Shanghai and Tientsin*, 126–7.
84 O. D. Rasmussen, *Tientsin*.
85 Jones, *Shanghai and Tientsin*, 117–27.
86 PRO, FO 228/3179/101 108c, Tientsin No. 37b, 2 April 1927, 'Minutes of the Annual General Meeting of Ratepayers'. Previously Chinese were admitted to the parks only with permits, and in effect this was intended to admit only amahs (except 'quarrelsome' ones) and their European charges; British Municipal Council, Tientsin, *Handbook of Municipal Regulations* (Tianjin, n.d. [*c.* 1923]), 92–3; Lampson Diaries, 16 December 1927; HSB, LOH I, 103.243 64/44, S/O Files from Shanghai, A. B. Lowson to C. R. Rice, 21 March 1928.
87 PRO, FO 228/3637/60 39a, Tientsin No. 231, 7 September 1928; FO 228/4206/6 32g, Tientsin No. 88, 14 October 1930; FO 228/4229/3 39a, Teichman minute on Tientsin No. 35, 23 June 1930.
88 PRO, FO 228/4015/3 39a, Tientsin No. 28, 9 April 1929; SP, China Sundries, Book 1185, J. T. Pratt to G. W. Swire, 24 April 1928; Jones, *Shanghai and Tientsin*, 123; *Peking and Tientsin Times*, 18 April 1929.
89 The fullest collection of the publications of the Tientsin British Committee of Information can be found in the files of the RIIA, Boxes 7 and 10.
90 Feetham, *Report*, II, 192; Mayers *et al.*, *Treaty Ports of China and Japan*, 443–4; Wright, *Twentieth Century Impressions*, 692–3.
91 PRO, FO 228/3187/105 26, Hankow No. 30, 15 March 1926; FO 228/3187/121 26, Hankow No. 6, 4 May 1926.
92 PRO, FO 228/3839/37 40a, Hankow No. 38, 14 April 1928.
93 *Oriental Affairs*, April 1937, 181–2, July 1938, 24–6, August 1938, 98–9, December 1938, 303, January 1939, 27.
94 PRO, FO 228/4201/1 28c, Hankow No. 5, 15 January 1930. Pamela Atwell, *British Mandarins and Chinese Reformers: The British Administration of Weihaiwei (1898–1930) and the Territory's Return to Chinese Rule* (Hong Kong, 1985), 162.
95 Fei, *Zhongguo zujie shi*, 432; CYB, 1936, 180–1; PRO, FO 369/2018, K6294/6294/210, H. Phillips, 'Inspection of the Ningpo Consulate', 30 March 1928; Jeanie Woodrow Woodbridge, *Glimpses of Kuling: A Souvenir of Lushan* (Shanghai, 1904), 14–16.
96 PRO, FO 228/3819/1 29a, C-in-C to Lampson, 26 March 1928, enclosure No. 2; NCH, 27 April 1929, 1; caption by P.H.M-F., *The Pipeline*, 29 May 1929, 170; Sewell Papers PPMS 16/3, Sewell, journal letter, 4 March 1928.
97 Sewell Papers PPMS 16/4, Sewell, journal letter, 3 December 1933; PRO, FO 228/3840/1 40d, Hankow No. 50, 16 May 1928, enclosing Hankow No. 11 to Foreign Office, 11 May 1928; on the school's funding and necessity see the letter to C. C. Knight of 24 August 1928 from the Hankow British Chamber of Commerce chairman, A. E. Marker, explaining the changes, in SP, JSS II, 2/7, BSS to JSL, 31 August 1928.

98 PRO, FO 228/3997/2 28c, E. W. Mills to Commissioner of Foreign Affairs, 4 January 1929, in Kiukiang No. 1, 4 January 1929; FO 228/3997/6 28c, Kiukiang No. 6, 8 March 1929; FO 228/3818/7, 28c, Kiukiang tel., 29 December 1928.

99 PRO, FO 676/72 17b 1930, 'Chefoo Recreation Ground and Cemetery Trust'.

100 PRO, FO 228/4106/1 122g, J. F. Brenan to Divisional Architect, H. B. M. Office of Works Shanghai, Shanghai No. 2, 7 January 1929; FO 228/4106/2 122g , H. B. M. Office of Works, W. E. Jones, 9 March 1929; FO 228/4106/2 122h, Legation minutes on Inston to Bradley, Office of Works, Shanghai, 8 February 1929; H. S. S. [Smith], *Diary of Events and the Progress on Shameen, 1859–1938* (Hong Kong, 1938).

101 Cook, *Lion and the Dragon*; C. S. Archer, *Hankow Return* (London, 1941).

102 Norman J. Miners, 'From Nationalist Confrontation to Regional Collaboration: China-Hong Kong-Britain, 1926–41', in Ming K. Chan, ed., *Precarious Balance: Hong Kong between China and Britain, 1842–1992* (Armonk NY, 1994), 590–70.

103 PRO, FO 228/3724, 2B, China Confidential Print, F703/703/10, 6 February 1928; Chiang Kai-shek to 'General Galen', 26 June 1925, document No. 7, C. Martin Wilbur and Juie Lien-ying How, eds, *Missionaries of Revolution: Soviet Advisers and Nationalist China, 1920–1927* (Cambridge MA, 1989), 502–5.

104 Richard J. Aldrich, 'Britain's Secret Intelligence Service in Asia during the Second World War', *Modern Asian Studies*, 32 (1998), 186–7.

105 Robert Bickers, 'The Colony's shifting Position in the British Informal Empire in China', in Brown and Foot, eds, *Hong Kong's Transitions, 33–61.*

106 Fei, *Zhongguo zujie shi*, 427–35; Peattie, 'Japanese Treaty Port Settlements in China, 1895–1937', 174–6.

107 PRO, FO 228/4284/4 69h, Shanghai No. 329, 2 December 1930.

108 PRO, FO 228/4312/172 84, Circular tel. to Consuls No. 10, 4 March 1930; *NCH*, 25 March 1930, 466, 483.

109 PRO, FO 228/4283/13 69, Shanghai No. 104, 22 April 1930.

110 PRO, BT 60/51/3, Beale to Crowe, private, 13 June 1932; 'Memorandum by Mr G. E. Hubbard', 2–3; Hughes to Crowe, 15 December 1932; *China: Notes on some Aspects of Life in China for the Information of Business Visitors* (London, 1934).

111 Sophia Lee, 'The Foreign Ministry's Cultural Agenda for China: the Boxer Indemnity', in Duus, Myers and Peattie, eds, *Japanese Informal Empire in China*, 300.

112 See, for example, *Eastern Engineering*, 12 July 1928, 173, 'Opportunities in China'.

113 *Report of the Advisory Committee ... respecting the China Indemnity*, 5, 7, 22, 151; *Report of the Executive Council of the Universities' China Committee in London for 1932–33*, 2 6; Sir Frank Gill, 'The Chinese Engineering Apprentice and the Federation of British Industries', UCC, *Annual Proceedings, 1942–43*, 27; SOAS, China Association archives, CHAS/MCP/37, Minutes of Meeting of Joint Committee Shanghai, 19 September 1932; Delia Davin, 'Imperialism and the Diffusion of Liberal Thought: British Influences on Chinese Education', in Ruth Hayhoe and Marianne Bastid, eds, *China's Education and the Industrialised World: Studies in Cultural Transfer* (New York, 1987), 33–56.

114 PRO, FO 800/258, C. Eliot to Sir Austen Chamberlain, 19 June 1925; see an attempt to improve the perception of HKU engineering graduates by their professor, C. A. Middleton Smith, '"Practical Chinese Engineers": The Demand and the Supply', *Far Eastern Review*, July 1930, 344–8; SP, ADD 1079, JSL to BS Hong Kong, 25 February 1927.

115 Lee, 'Foreign Ministry's Cultural Agenda for China', 272–306.

116 NMM Bailie-Grohman Papers, GRO/33, Autobiography Part 2, 63, 93; the myth of selling battleships to China had a long pedigree, but it had never justified the hopes invested: Backhouse spent seven years 'selling' battleships in 1910–17; Trevor-Roper, *Hermit of Peking*, 216–20.

117 Hewlett, *Forty Years*, 248–9; Endicott, *Diplomacy and Enterprise*, 102–49

118 *NCH*, 16 April 1927, 114, 11 June 1927, 473. Details of the Constitutional Defence League from *NCH*, 6 February 1926, 235, 20 March 1926, 521, and 4 August 1928, 200.

119 PRO, FO 228/3883/3 69k, Garstin to Aveling, 5 October 1928, Lampson minute on same.

120 SP, JSSII 2/7, BSS to JSL, 31 August 1928.
121 PRO, FO 228/4046/2 69k, Garstin to Aveling, semi-official, 28 January 1929.
122 PRO, FO 228/4045/11 69, FO No. 524, 15 May 1929; SP, ADD. 15, [?] to G. W. Swire, 10 May 1929; Teichman minute, 15 November 1929, on FO 228/4046/12 69k.
123 *Municipal Gazette*, 17 April 1930, 151–6; 10 July 1931, 313, 23 August 1930, 355; *NCH*, 28 July 1931, 109, 122; SMC, *Annual Report*, 1936, 27; SMC, *Annual Report* 1935, 262.
124 Darwin, 'Imperialism and the Victorians', 631–4; for a fuller account see Pelcovits, *Old China Hands*.
125 This section is based on my 'Death of a Young Shanghailander'.
126 *NCH*, 7 June 1932, 389.
127 *NCH*, 12 November 1931, 240; *Oriental Affairs*, April 1935, 155–6. For details of the BRA see SMP D2961.
128 SP, JSS I 3/7, G. W. Swire to J. S. Scott, 27 January 193; *NCH*, 29 March 1933, 493.
129 *NCH*, 20 August 1927, 323.
130 *NCH*, 1 October 1927, 14. Arthur de C. Sowerby, editor of the *China Journal* and self-styled explorer, was replacement leader of the Fascisti and committee member of the BRA, *NCH*, 14 January 1928, 53, 28 December 1932, 498.
131 Readers' letters in *Shanghai Evening Post and Mercury*, 11 October 1931, 11, 19 October 1931, 11. See, for example, the opinions recorded disapprovingly by Lampson: Lampson Diaries, 28 October 1931; and H. G. W. Woodhead, *A Visit to Manchukuo* (Shanghai, 1932), 106–7; on this point see Endicott, *Diplomacy and Enterprise*, 28–30.
132 Endicott, *Diplomacy and Enterprise*, 74; Bickers, '"Coolie work"', 398–9.
133 Consular notifications, complete with the royal coat of arms, were often placed immediately at the head of the editorial column of the *Central China Post*, for example, *Central China Post*, 18 February 1935, 6.
134 Wellington Koo, *Memoirs* (New York, 1948), II, 46; *The China Critic*, 23 January 1930, 75; SMC, *Annual Report*, 1925, 66; P. M. Taylor, *The Projection of Britain: British Overseas Publicity and Propaganda, 1919–1939* (Cambridge, 1981), 26.
135 PRO, FO 228/3987, Legation dossier 22z 1929, *passim*; FO 228/3987/5 22z Shanghai No. 133, 22 April 1929; SP, China Sundries Book 1185, G. W. Swire to M. W. Lampson, 18 January 1927; Lampson Diaries, 12 October 1927; FO 395/419, P899/57/150, Lampson to Wellesley, 28 June 1927 and enclosures. *The Times*, 7 October 1927, 14, 11 November 1927, 16, 23; SP, ADD 1079, G. W. Swire notation on BSS to JSL, 8 July 1927. On Zhang see FO 395/419, F97/57/150, Lampson to Willert, 29 January 1927.
136 PRO, FO 228/4370 22L, Peking No. 40, Lampson to Selby, 19 January 1930; Lampson Diaries, 18, 20 January 1930; *NCH*, 25 March 1930, 464; *India Office List*, 1929. Thomas Ming-Heng Chao, *The Foreign Press in China* (Shanghai, 1931), 50; FO 800/260, Chamberlain to Lampson, 11 April 1927.
137 PRO, FO 228/3872, Shanghai No. 256, 6 December 1928; FO 228/4189/3 22, Shanghai No. 202, 25 July 1930, 'List of Foreign Newspapers in Shanghai'; FO 228/4040/3 61L, Shanghai No. 256, 6 December 1929.
138 Forward policy is the main theme of Endicott, *Diplomacy and Enterprise*.
139 Antony Best, *Britain, Japan and Pearl Harbor: Avoiding War in East Asia, 1936–41* (London, 1995).
140 Thorne, *Limits of Foreign Policy*, 367–8.
141 Best, *Britain, Japan and Pearl Harbor*, 56.
142 Nakagane Katsuji,, 'Manchukuo and economic development', in Duus, Myers and Peattie, eds, *Japanese Informal Empire in China*, 133–57.
143 William Crane Johnstone, *The Shanghai Problem* (Stanford CA, 1937), 282–91; Thorne, *Limits of Foreign Policy*, 202–10.
144 Good contemporary accounts are Jones, *Shanghai and Tientsin*, and Robert W. Barnett, *Economic Shanghai: Hostage to Politics, 1937–1941* (New York, 1941).
145 PRO, FO 676/435, G. G. Phillips to Sir Archibald Clark-Kerr, 29 June 1940.
146 Frederic Wakeman, Jr, *The Shanghai Badlands: Wartime Terrorism and Urban*

*Crime, 1937–1941* (Cambridge, 1996); *Oriental Affairs*, January 1939, 11–12.

147 SMC, *Annual Report*, 1938, 16.

148 See, Commissioner Bourne's letter to British members of the force (n.d., 1940) in PRO, FO 371/53598, F4117/44/10.

149 Barnett, *Economic Shanghai*, 25.

150 SMP D8299, 'Assistance to Japanese Gendarmerie', index; SMP D 8477, 1 September 1938; Wakeman, *Policing Shanghai*, 135–61.

151 See, e.g., PRO, FO 371/23454, F3896/84/10, G. W. Swire to R. G. Howe, 18 April 1939.

152 Barnett, *Economic Shanghai*, 29–31.

153 *Oriental Affairs*, January 1936, 6–7.

154 *Oriental Affairs*, March 1936, 112–13, May 1938, 259–61.

155 John Swire & Sons, company archives, London (hereafter SA), Misc. 121, 'China interwar Political Letters, 1925–38', JSL to BSS, 8 December 1938.

156 Lee, *Britain and the Sino-Japanese war*, 181–204.

157 Best, *Britain, Japan and Pearl Harbor*, 65–7; details of the strike are in Shanghai Municipal Police Special Branch, file SMP D6968.

158 Nicholas R. Clifford, *Retreat from China: British Policy in the Far East 1937–1971* (London, 1967), 111–12.

159 Kulangsu Municipal Council, *Report*, 1938, 5; 1939, 5–7.

160 Tientsin British Municipal Council, *Report*, 1940, 33; *NCH*, 26 June 1940, 489.

161 SA, MISC 122/I, BSS to JSL, 23 August 1940, 'Wartime SMC Letters'.

162 Best, *Britain, Japan and Pearl Harbour*, 3; Barnett, *Economic Shanghai*, 35–6.

163 PRO, FO 371/27631, F883/130/10, Shanghai No. 17, 11 February 1941, Memorandum.

164 SA, MISC 122/I, 'Wartime SMC Letters', BSS to JSL, 7 February 1941; E. M. Gull, *British Economic Interests in the Far East* (London, 1943), 47–8.

165 PRO, FO 371/27707, F1681/1676/10, A. H. Scott minute on Shanghai No. 187, 3 March 1941.

166 PRO, FO 371/27707, F2737/1676/10, FE Dept Minute, 7 April 1941.

167 Paul Haggie, *Britannia at Bay: The Defence of the British Empire against Japan, 1931–1941* (Oxford, 1981), 168, 174.

168 SA, Misc. 121, 'China interwar political letters', G. E. Mitchell to W. J. Keswick, 29 September 1935; Misc. 122/I, 'Wartime SMC Letters', BSS to JSL, 1 October 1937; PRO, FO 371/27631, W. J. Keswick to B. D. Beith, 6 January 1941; FO 371/27631, F534/130/10, Shanghai No. 11, 1 February 1941; FO 371/27632, F4054/130/10, Shanghai No. 65, 25 February 1941.

169 PRO, FO 371/27631, F883/130/10, Shanghai No 17, 11 February 1941; FO 371/27707, F2254/1676/10, W. J. Keswick to Ashley-Clarke, FO, 19 March 1941.

170 SP, Box 2063, JSL to BSS, 2 February 1940.

171 PRO, FO 371/27672, F5273/285/10, Ministry of Supply to FO, 14 June 1941; FO 371/27707, F2254/1676/10, W. J. Keswick to Ashley-Clarke, FO, 19 March 1941.

172 PRO, FO 371/27707, F534/130/10, Sir Archibald Clark Kerr to Shanghai, No. 63, 6 February 1941.

173 See file F285/285/10, PRO, FO 371/27671–3.

174 Osterhammel, 'Imperialism in Transition', 283–4.

175 Endicott, *Diplomacy and Enterprise*, 183–4.

# CHAPTER FIVE

# Staying on:
# the localisation of British
# activity in China

Staying on in China was the aim of the settler, the expatriate businessman and the missionary. Settlers' resistance to the Foreign Office's attack on the *status quo* was motivated by their desire to protect their livelihoods: settlers had nowhere else to go, whereas expatriate businesses or mission societies were already operating elsewhere outside China, and could refocus their operations if necessary. After 1949 that is what they had to begin to do as PRC policies froze them out of China. The nationalism which developed in the 1920s prompted different strategies. China, and the myth of the China market (for goods and souls), were certainly considered more important than the plain figures might demonstrate they ought to have been, however, and companies like Butterfield & Swire, or the multinational BAT, and organisations like the fundamentalist China Inland Mission or the LMS were keen to stay on in China however political circumstances might change. Successful settler adaptation to the new realities of a nationalistic China, and a new regime set on translating such feeling into legislation in a number of fields, was unlikely, despite attempts to turn the SMC, for example, into a more representative municipal administration. Many British businesses and mission societies, however, resolutely set out to transform their relationship with their respective Chinese markets: they improvised or accelerated programmes to make themselves less distinctively British, even less distinctively foreign, and to merge themselves into China. As the union jack increasingly became a target to attack rather than a source of protection, they reflagged themselves. This metamorphosis was not external, in the strict sense of passing up British protection – after all, extraterritoriality was not abolished until 1943 – but in spirit, in culture and in practice these organisations changed their identity.

As this chapter shows, sinification, or sinicisation, or what became known in Hong Kong in the late colonial period as localisation, became a key component of non-settler British strategy in China after the Nationalist revolution. British organisations overhauled structures of responsibility, purged personnel, reorientated their operations, worked to seek new partnerships with existing Chinese colleagues, or sought new partnerships where necessary, and generally tried to insinuate themselves into Chinese society and politics in ways that had previously seemed taboo. Such change was a key feature of the transition undergone by British companies in Hong Kong in the 1990s in the face of the hand-over to the PRC. It should come as no surprise to find that a company like Swire's (as Swire Pacific) sold a 25 per cent stake in its flagship company Cathay Pacific Airways in April 1996 to the China International Trust & Investment Corporation: in 1935 Swire's (as Butterfield & Swire) offered Song Ziwen a 30 per cent share in their then flagship equivalent, the China Navigation Company.[1] The intention, and the method, were the same: to cement their new relationship with Chinese authority at a time when the political map of the British presence in China was in transition. The broader colonial context is instructive. Research into British firms in India in the early twentieth century, and in the face of the rise of Indian nationalism, has shown two distinct patterns: the decline of older agency houses, and an influx from the late 1920s onwards of direct investment from multinational firms through newly established subsidiary companies. The agency houses largely declined because of shortages of capital, but also because of failures to adapt to the changing political situation.[2] It has also been argued that a complacency engendered by the political economy of the Raj before 1914 hindered adaptation in later years when the colonial state was itself in flux.[3] But the situation in China suggests instead that firms would more likely improvise and attempt to adapt themselves, with varying degrees of success, to the abandonment of the projection of British power. This was certainly the pattern elsewhere in the British empire – in Ghana or Malaya, for example. Moreover, decolonisation also masked other structural changes occurring at the same time in the post-war period.[4]

Missions and business superficially had little in common, and their personnel were often antagonistic towards each other, as chapter 3 has shown. Moreover, both sectors were hardly homogeneous – age, class and gender, as well as particular Protestant beliefs, divided the mission world, while businesses stretched from the Hongkong & Shanghai Bank to small owner-occupied shops. Nonetheless, in general both sectors shared the expectation that they could survive any political storm or change in the status of British operations in China. Neither presence was solely predicated on the maintenance of Britain in China, though both were more engaged in it than later seemed sensible. Both had benefited in China from the legal framework provided by extraterritoriality, and the freedom of action provided by the limited reach of the Chinese state in the nineteenth and early twentieth centuries, which was further restricted by the treaty system. They had both been able to operate throughout China, with British state protection, and to expand the range of activities undertaken largely as their needs, whims or interests dictated. Their personnel had benefited from the daily gunboat operations of the China station, which offered protection or punitive retaliation for attacks on Britons, or the armed might of the British (Indian) state in times of greater crisis. Similarly, after 1928 both faced a fundamental reshaping of the support offered by the British state, and both were threatened by the legislative innovations and the regulatory drives of the National government. A key feature of the new regime was its steady extension of the reach of the state into new fields, such as commerce (previously only nominally regulated by commercial legislation in 1904, and 1914) and education: the registration of educational institutions of all sorts was a key plank in the state's policy in this field. For these transnational organisations to continue operating across China's borders under the new dispensation, greater dexterity was needed than had previously been the case. Many aspects of the responses of businesses and missions to the new situation were identical, and so deserve examination together. They extended the numbers and responsibilities of their Chinese personnel, cloaked the nationality of the enterprises, set up partnerships with Chinese organisations, and built up new relationships with figures in Chinese society they had previously ignored. Moreover, older British agency houses and mission societies were both challenged and partly supplanted in this period by new transnational organisations, whether companies such as ICI or Lever Brothers, or interdenominational bodies such as the YMCA.

This chapter first examines the nature of the problem as it faced British businesses, taking as its focus the varied activities of the long established agency house, Butterfield & Swire, before looking at the range of activities it undertook to secure its place in the new order established by nationalism in China. It then turns to look at British missionary societies, the problems they encountered and the policies they adopted. In the crisis period of 1925–27 British organisations found themselves under siege, boycotted, subjected to the attentions of revolutionary activists, and often the anger of their own staff. The crisis focused minds, and external change – Anglo-Japanese trade rivalry or intellectual and social religious developments – added urgency to the changes outlined below.

## Transforming British businesses

Penetration of the China market had always involved using local inter-mediaries. This situation had evolved in two interrelated ways: first, and most obvious, there was the compradore system, whereby foreign firms located a Chinese partner who, having posted sufficient security, provided the link between the company and its Chinese customers or clients. The term compradore was applied fairly loosely and included the massive parallel organisations operating under compradores for Swire's or Jardine's, as well as the men who oversaw the Chinese employees of smaller foreign institutions; even the Shanghai Con-sulate-general had its compradore. The second outcome was that there was a great deal of masking as British of Chinese capital, ownership or other activity – share ownership, or land holding in the settlements, for example. In such cases distinguishing between what was Chinese and what was British was never straightforward. Surveys of British busi-ness, for example, which argue for seeing the Hongkong & Shanghai Bank as a 'British' institution misrepresent the nature of the treaty port world, and also underestimate the guile with which even such rep-utable offshore transnational organisations set about acquiring nation-ality for themselves.[5] But for their part British companies did not act as if this multifaceted pattern of ownership and identity was actually the case: the mental world of Britain in China kept boundaries rigid, while the perquisites of extraterritoriality were available only to those with impeccably pukka paper credentials. Moreover, at a certain level, many companies were satisfied with serving the treaty port market, or else were lulled by complacency, in the 1920s in particular, into mis-reading the dynamic changes taking place in the China market gener-ally. It took the shock of nationalism to knock business sense back into many of them.

A representative, but not unusual, example of the bad business sense engendered by treaty port *mores* can be found in the way one Butterfield & Swire subsidiary, the China Navigation Company (CNCo), treated Chinese passengers and crew on its passenger ships. This was a key sector of China's economy in which British firms were able to operate because of privileges extracted by treaty (inland navigation rights). The important emerging market in the 1920s was identified again and again by foreign observers as the modern, or Western-educated, Chinese, in effect the bourgeoisie. But conditions on board foreign-owned ships replicated and enhanced patterns of social and 'racial' division in treaty port society. What amounted to European-only bastions were literally built into them for a start, to pre-vent piracy – a growing problem throughout the 1920s. In practice, by

[ 173 ]

the late 1920s, there was segregation in nearly every part of the travelling process: passengers travelled in separate classes, disembarked in
separate ways, and were sold tickets by parallel but separate organisations; by the Butterfield & Swire Agency office for Europeans travelling
on CNCo ships, and by the compradore's office for Chinese passengers.
Foreigners were also generally not allowed by that company, or by Jardine Matheson's Indo-China Steam Navigation Company, to travel in
Chinese accommodation. In fact until 1925 all shipping companies had
farmed out their Chinese accommodation on the Shanghai to Hankou
route to the Yangtsze Passenger Syndicate, a Chinese organisation,
until this practice had been stopped by the anti-piracy guidelines of the
British government.[6]

Conditions in the different classes of shipboard accommodation
were rigidly different. Usually there was a saloon class for foreign travellers, with foreign food and furniture, and a Chinese first class, with
Chinese food and round tables. This was described, on various ships, as
being below the foreign level in 'bath, sanitary conveniences' and lacking the 'deck space and other comforts' of the saloon class. There was
also, depending on the ship, a second-class Chinese and third-class or
steerage.[7] Much of this differentiation was economically motivated
and concerned with arranging accommodation to suit all pockets. But
there was transparent indifference to the conditions in which Chinese
passengers ate, slept, bathed, relieved themselves and promenaded. On
the CNCo ships *Poyang*, *Tatung* and *Ngankin* in 1928 there were only
'two water closets, both situated on the upper deck, on which there is
accommodation for 144 Chinese passengers and ship's staff. On the
bridge deck where there are berths for 30 first class and 38 second class
passengers there is no lavatory at all'.[8] After this shipboard discrimination the final insult for Chinese passengers on CNCo ships before 1930
would have been that the Yangzi steamers berthed at the Pudong side
of the Huangpu river at Shanghai, and therefore opposite the city itself.
A launch met all steamers to land saloon – that is, foreign – passengers
'on the Shanghai side, leaving most of the better class of Chinese ... to
take a sampan ... and put up with exorbitant overcharges on the part of
sampanmen and coolies at Pudong'. Not surprisingly, 'friction has been
experienced in preventing native passengers ... from boarding her, and
resentment is often shown at this "preferential" treatment.' European
saloon passengers had also complained about 'being swamped with
Chinese' as a result of one unsatisfactory attempt at mollifying 'better
class' Chinese by allowing some passengers to use the launch service.[9]

This was by the 1920s no way to run a business; but such practices,
as we saw in chapter 3, lay at the heart of the settler social world. The
British economic presence in China was financial, industrial and com-

mercial – all three were threatened by the politics of economic nation-alism, but they were also risking their own future through inefficiency bred of the arid certainties of the treaty port system. By failing to adapt quickly enough to the rise of Chinese demand because of discrimina-tory practices British companies seemed to be abdicating their role in the China market.

As well as a developing and then triumphant Chinese nationalism, British firms faced other problems in the China market. There were new Chinese competitors, new foreign competitors, and perceptibly diminishing returns of utility from the compradore system. Although such worries were certainly not confined to the China market, British commentators moaned repeatedly throughout the early twentieth cen-tury about the lack of effective marketing of British products, although one early attempt to create a manufacturers' export association aimed at China, the British Engineers' Association (1912), proved a fiasco.[10] The 1930 Department of Overseas Trade (DOT) mission to the Far East reported that Britain's exports to China were declining rapidly, when those of the United States, France and Germany were soaring. Their explanation lay in high prices, bad marketing and poor advertising. ICI's success with its 'Crescent' brand of fertiliser, and BAT's aggres-sive marketing campaigns were the great exceptions.[11] Both compa-nies, it should be noted, were transnationals, and relative newcomers to the China market. Japanese trade rivalry with Britain was undoubt-edly strong – and the figures show Japan supplanting Britain in the China trade as the century progressed (although Japanese activities in Manchuria somewhat distort the national picture) – but the Japanese operated under extraterritoriality.[12] More worrying for British observers was German success, for example, which was based not on treaty privilege but on better marketing, better language study among foreign staff, better treatment of Chinese staff and greater interest in Sino-foreign enterprises. Although such comments and complaints about German methods were also rooted in continuing Germanopho-bia, in one sense Germany had been forced to pioneer a post-treaty system road because of the attempted dismantling of the German pres-ence in China engineered by Britain in 1918–19. The enforced repatri-ation of German nationals – which saw a fall in the number of German firms from 281 in 1916 to seventy-five in 1918 – did German trade more good than harm. Forced to reinvent their presence, and work without extraterritoriality, German firms had a ten-year head start on working under the new dispensation and casting aside 'British' meth-ods.[13] The British need, in short, was to try to follow the German lead.

However, the most damaging long-term competition came from the

Chinese. This was not just a by-product of political change, but resulted from social change in Chinese society and also from the evolution of Chinese business practice in the face of Western competition. 'Modern' Chinese firms, such as the Yong Li Soda Company, or overseas Chinese groups such as Nanyang Brothers in the tobacco trade, were beginning to operate in Western-dominated (and often Western-created) markets.[14] They were also beginning to do so with specific national or local political support, buttressed by legislation, or harassment, which aimed to disbar or hamper foreign activities. In Sichuan, for example, the development of the Minsheng shipping line – which treated Chinese and foreign passengers equally – was partly fostered by tax concessions unavailable to foreign shipping passing through Chongqing.[15] The DOT also identified as a major trend in 1933 the fact that more and more Chinese companies were trading directly with foreign firms overseas, thereby cutting out the foreign agency houses.[16] This growth of Chinese business was partly caused by, and partly caused, the growth of a largely politically nationalist Chinese middle class (although descriptions of a homogeneous and national class can be misleading). It was largely urban, frequently grew out of successful compradore businesses, and supplied the competitors, the compradores, the staff, and the increasingly vocal and discerning customers of foreign companies; those in the shipping business, where customers voted with their wallets, could not afford to ignore it.[17] It was responsible for the modernisation of towns, which caused a reassessment, for example, of insurance scope and practice among foreign companies. It also supplied the most vocal opposition, through various organisations, to the trading and other privileges of foreign business.

In the face of political and economic change, and foreign and Chinese competition, the British felt they were in danger of leaving the China market by default. Sir Miles Lampson was circumspect about the problems facing British business in China in a 1930 comment, but he easily, if ambivalently, identified areas where adaptation to the threats posed by change could take place: 'it is perhaps in his stiff-necked insistence on hard business facts, and unwillingness to appreciate, or perhaps pander to, Chinese mentality and custom, that the British trader in China fails, if he really does fail, in competition with his rivals'.[18] 'Stiff-necked' Britishness, then, was an identifiable problem. The climate engineered by British treaty port socialisation was increasingly seen as a hindrance to British trade. This is not to argue that conservatism in business practices was the problem, as has been argued for British firms in India, but that socially and culturally the treaty port *status quo*, like the colonial economy in India, served to limit the flexibility and activities of British firms.[19] Minimising the effects of that process and actively countering some aspects of it were proposed solutions to some of the problems facing British firms by 1928.

Increasingly, moreover, hegemonic popular and consumer nationalism was a major challenge for foreign firms. Where once the union jack flying over the company compound was a source of pride, it became more and more problematic for British businesses to be so identifiably foreign after 1925. There were serious anti-British boycotts in 1925-27, and British companies also found themselves affected by the repercussions of anti-Japanese boycott activity thereafter – if their plants or operations in China used Japanese raw materials, or if their ships transported Japanese goods. The power of the boycott fractured any common front among foreign powers in China beyond all hope of realignment. Moreover, after the boycott came the appeal to the nationalist wallet to buy *guohuo*, national goods, which became a key selling point in the advertising and propaganda of Chinese firms such as Nanyang Brothers. Cigarettes, matches and textiles all became patriotic purchases that the Chinese nationalist consumer might and did make. Western goods and fashions remained popular, but the question became: who was to make them or sell them in China? 'Female compatriots who wish to perform the practical labour of promoting national goods should proceed to Lao Jie Fu [a silk store] and buy more low-priced but beautiful Chinese silk', thereby killing 'two birds with one stone' ran a 1934 Shanghai radio advertising song.[20] With the advent of this mass consumer nationalism, British companies had to adapt.

As well as distancing themselves from the settler politics which made future May Thirtieth incidents latent, companies set about trying to distance themselves from the stiff-necked Britishness which attracted the attention of the boycott weapon. One way of doing so which made sound business sense anyway was to de-anglicise themselves, or to localise their operations and their operational identity in China: to recruit more Chinese, at higher levels, and to subsume their own identity within joint Sino-British subsidiaries. In this they were encouraged by British diplomats and trade representatives, who remained content to leave commercial matters to the energies of the private sector – unlike the Japanese – but who nonetheless urged British companies to adapt to fend for themselves better in a looming non-treaty China.

As settler die-hards grouped in the British Residents' Association, larger interests continued to seek representation through the China Association or instead built up closer direct links with the British diplomatic establishment. The British presence had never been cohesive and united, but different interest groups had managed to coexist before 1925. The survival of the transnationals and larger agency houses meant for the first time a policy of active hostility towards settler politics, as shown in chapter 4. The agency house John Swire & Sons exhibits the shift well.[21] Originally founded in about 1816, its driving force in the nineteenth century was John Samuel Swire, the 'Senior', who established the Shanghai subsidiary Butterfield & Swire in 1866 to handle purchases of tea and silk, and sales of cotton piece goods. Swire's soon became involved in shipping, notably establishing CNCo in 1872, which by the end of the century was the largest of the Yangzi shipping lines, and had also achieved a prominent position in the Chinese coastal trade. The company's operations remained fairly diverse, and included sugar refining in Hong Kong after 1884, a Hong Kong dockyard (1900) and insurance. The heavy presence in Hong Kong should not distract from the much greater profitability of Shanghai. Swire's, like other British companies, operated out of two main hubs in China: Hong Kong for the south, and Shanghai for central and northern China, but Shanghai remained the key to its operations. By the 1920s the firm was led by G. Warren Swire, a forceful, conservative personality, who was nevertheless not shy of facing radical change. The China subsidiary, Butterfield & Swire, was always tightly controlled by the partners in London (one of whom visited China each year), although the structure of the company required the right men to be working on the spot in China.

The company was quick to instruct its Shanghai managers to push for treaty port moderation in the later 1920s, for instance through the Joint Committee of the British Chamber of Commerce and China Association at Shanghai.[22] N. S. Brown was made Swire's Shanghai manager in 1929 in order to 'get on to the Council and try and get a real move on progressively', by acting as a conciliatory and restraining influence in its politics and society. A personable mixer who had joined the company in 1900 to 'better his position', this Glaswegian's networking skills became his 'very great asset'. The British Consul-general and the Legation felt he was 'overenthusiastic', but recognised that he was 'partly for business reasons no doubt, dead set on cultivating the Chinese who matter; and he has tackled his task in a thoroughgoing way – much to the disgust of the average "Shanghailander"'.[23] With diplomatic encouragement British companies like Swire's and BAT used their oligarchic control of the SMC to introduce Chinese representation on to the council against Shanghailander objections. This marked their public acceptance of the equal social status of Chinese leaders such as Yu Xiaqing, and also ensured closer and more frequent intercourse with them. Swire's kept a man on the SMC for most years down to 1941 (Brown, 1930–32; G. E. Mitchell, 1937-42), sharing responsibility at times with such useful Chinese connections as Yu, who sat on the SMC from 1929 to 1941 but who also sat on the Chinese municipality's mayor-appointed Municipal Council in 1927 and 1932-36, Liu Hongsheng (SMC, 1930–33) and Xu Xinliu (SMC, 1929-38).[24]

Warren Swire felt, in 1928, that 'We must try to get more in touch with the Chinese and with happenings behind the scenes'.[25] On his visit the following year he was planning, on the recommendation of Sir Frederick Whyte, to meet a formidable list of businessmen and politicians (but businessmen had priority) such as Chen Guangfu (K. P. Chen, Shanghai Commercial & Savings Bank), Xu Xinliu (National Commercial Bank), Li Ming (Bank of China), Song Ziwen, Kong Xiangxi and Wang Zhengting. The Chinese he met on that trip were all at pains to 'lay stress on personal private entertainment'. In view of the initial success of Sir Frederick Whyte's mission, Swire's also contemplated appointing their own 'diplomatic agent', and later delegated a compradore to work as an adviser at the National Government's Ministry of Finance.[26] Similarly, ICI in 1931 felt 'almost out of touch with influential Chinese', and therefore with Nanjing, and this was its 'chief weakness'. In tandem with a reorganisation in 1933 the company's new manager set out actively to 'cultivate' influential Chinese, and later appointed a suitable candidate as a director of the China company.[27] In 1929 Arnhold's Beijing manager asked the Governor of the Bank of England to use any influence 'it might possess in commercial circles ... to induce them to send out first-class representatives charged with a mission to establish closer personal relations with Chinese circles'.[28] This, in fact, was what Sir Frederick Whyte had already done. Other individuals such as N. S. Brown and Lampson had also contributed, and the open-minded diplomatic energy of the Keswick brothers at Jardine's, or ICI's Valentine St John Killery, sent out in 1933, was a good substitute for their youth.

Setting the example at the top was one matter, but it had to be followed through at lower levels in firms. Swire's set about an overhaul of their established practices with the aim of divorcing the company culture from complicity in the norms of the settler world. They needed new staff, and new Chinese staff too, to establish new personal relations within companies, and externally – including with its customers – reform the compradore system, and in a sense rethink their identity.

Attitudes and structures within British companies were in need of analysis and reform. Swire's and others were concerned about the characters of their men, managers or otherwise. In May 1928 Swire wrote to his Hong Kong and Shanghai managers about a letter he had received from Joseph Bailie, a professor at the Chinese Institute of Technical Training in Shanghai. Bailie:

> gave us what he called a 'message from some Chinese friends'. Although he said expressly that he was merely alluding to a general principle applicable to foreigners as a whole, this message was ... a lesson in manners and can be summarised in the following incident ... It sounds perhaps a little near home, but we are perfectly certain he did not have us in mind. Dr. Woo, the director or manager of Han Yang, wishing to arrange a charter, came into the office of a foreign firm and finding the shipping clerk out, sat down to read the paper. The shipping clerk returned in due course, rather made Dr. Woo feel by his general bearing that he was taking a liberty in reading the paper, sat down, put his feet on the desk, lit a cigar without any offer to Dr. Woo and then asked what he wanted. One must of course not forget that the foreign educationist in China has his own point of view and doubtless he exaggerates, but he is quite right to rub it in.[29]

Swire's were actively concerned in a debate about the culture of business in the treaty ports, and about the interaction of their (British) staff with the (Chinese) customers and subordinate staff. Two years later Swire stressed as requirements for the head of the China Navigation Company that the man:

> understands *and acts on* the present need for cultivating in and out of office and so educating Chinese ship-owners and businessmen. ... All this presupposes that the head of the Department finds it easy, if not congenial, to establish these personal relations ... [A. V. T. Dean] was too direct in his manner to please the Chinese ...[30]

Swire's were not alone in this: in 1929 E. J. Nathan, manager of the KMA in Tianjin, was anxious to have better-trained senior staff and also felt that bad labour relations at one mine were due to the manager there being 'temperamentally unsuited for handling delicate situations, being far too excitable and irascible'.[31] Other companies were anxious to get rid of such dead wood, as they always had been if individuals got in the way of business, but there was, however, a powerful political push to remove compromising personalities in the years after 1925.

Changing private attitudes among new staff and those who remained in China was difficult, if not impossible, but various moves were made, as chapter 4 showed, to provide more scope for Britons and Chinese to mix socially in treaty port public life, and little things helped shift company culture in the right direction, such as the decision of APC's house journal to discontinue a column poking fun at Chinese use of English.[32] Some of the commercial elite considered the problem of staff attitudes so intractable that it was only worth tackling in London, in particular among new recruits, and Joseph Bailie suggested to Swire's in his May 1928 letter that they replaced their 'staff as they become superannuated, by young men who know the Chinese language, customs and manners, and who go out determined to retrieve the good name of Britishers in the Far East'.[33] In fact economics dictated that the new generation of men was recruited to supervise an expansion in the number of Chinese employees, but new skills and sensitivities were required. In 1931 BAT's Cunliffe-Owen told Lampson that 'the future of such enterprises as his lay in the development of the Chinese element. He was accordingly now going to concentrate on getting fewer foreigners; but these foreigners were to be men of good calibre, and must all of them have a good working knowledge of Chinese.'[34] The KMA was starting to think along similar lines: it wanted to recruit tactful men who already had Chinese language ability, learning the language on the job was not good enough, and Swire's planned to send men to Nanjing for similar reasons.[35] These companies became concerned with getting better-educated men, graduates where possible, to join their operations. The standard of personnel recruited for China had historically been poor, and the stagnation of the early twentieth century had not spurred companies to think much about improving recruitment standards, but political changes made it vital by the end of the 1920s. What the British lacked, and what they were never going to establish, was an institution for training China hands like the Japanese Toa Dobun Shoin (East Asia Common Culture Academy) in Shanghai, more than half of whose graduates in 1929 had entered commerce. The pool of graduates trained in Chinese (and English) and an interdisciplinary curriculum, culminating in a field trip into the Chinese interior to collect research data, was an undoubted boon to Japanese activities in China.[36]

Getting better young men out to China was useful only if they were encouraged not to fall for the temptations of a colonial attitude when they got there. More attention to breaking social taboos was needed, for instance improving social relations with Chinese in routine business. The question of the 'entertaining' of Chinese clients, competitors, and worthies, vexed Swire's in the late 1920s. Foreign agents were told in 1925 that they should call on Chinese shippers monthly 'and not just leave it to their compradore as at present', but there was little progress at the start.[37] But such social cultivation had to become more personal, less ceremonial, and should involve the foreign staff and the Chinese more directly: 'when it is necessary to get in touch with some important Chinese for any purpose ... you will have to do so in your own houses ... a much better compliment than entertaining in a hotel'.[38] To this end the Shanghai manager's house was replaced in 1934 by a much grander building – 'the only gentleman's house in the place'[39] – reservations about the cost being overruled for pragmatic reasons. It is clear from memoirs and accounts of the end of the 1930s that staff of these companies interacted with many more Chinese on a social level than was the case in the 1920s, and that the *mores* engendered by settler society were being broken down. But the process also required closer relations between Britons and Chinese within companies.

## The compradore

When discussing the treatment of Dr Woo, Joseph Bailie went on to lay a large part of the blame for such attitudes on the structure of foreign companies' business: 'the crux of the situation is the present system of transacting business through Compradores … your hands are tied in your attempts to make the proper friendly gestures to the Chinese'. This point was also stressed by Chinese businessmen themselves, for example by Chen Guangfu in conversation with Warren Swire in 1929.[40] Logically, breaking down the barriers meant restructuring organisations.

Many British businessmen also felt that the compradore system needed replacing or modernising. Scandals and inefficiency provided sound reason, too: in 1927, for example, the Hongkong & Shanghai Bank's Beijing compradore absconded with around $1.4 million that had been paid in only as far as the compradoric 'bank within a bank'. Swire's themselves also had problematic episodes with a number of men which revealed the 'extent to which control had fallen into the hands of the compradore organisation'.[41] Bankruptcies and defalcations highlighted the essential problem of indirect control, and moreover Chinese customers often tended to identify the compradore more closely with his foreign company than was actually the case under the existing system. The compradoric layer also added to costs, and as British companies were as reliant on market flexibility in trade as in manufacturing, trading through compradore organisations denied them the opportunity to deal with customers directly and swiftly.[42] The developing trend in business after World War I was towards more direct contacts between buyers and sellers, which bypassed the commission of the agency houses like Swire's and of their compradores' organisations. Increasing competition from Chinese and foreign companies made for much more complex business which required strict delineations of business and control which the compradoric partnership failed to deliver – and there is some evidence that British competitors, such as some Japanese firms, were experimenting with non-compradore structures from the end of the nineteenth century onwards.[43] Improvements in relations with the Chinese business community also came at the expense of the compradores.

Swire's cost-conscious response from the late 1920s onwards was to attempt to set up a system of salaried 'Chinese managers', whose time and work would be fully committed to the firm and would be fully integrated into its structure. It was accompanied by a concerted drive to reclaim sensitive areas of business from compradoric control. Labour contracts had usually been farmed out through compradores and efforts were made, for financial reasons, to find the true levels of costs and investigate the savings possible through direct hire.[44] This was paralleled by moves to reassert total control over all aspects of Swire's shipping business, and accompanied moves elsewhere in the Swire organisation to cut out contractors and compradores, so as to become more responsive to the conditions and demands of Chinese passengers and customers. With the development of new ships in the early 1930s European pursers took over the duties of the compradores as they affected the first-class Chinese passengers.

Swire's were also conscious of how firms from other nations treated their staff – German businesses, for example, or American insurance companies, which worked through Chinese staff members integrated into their company structures. Often, such innovations were reduced in cynical British eyes to merely according 'face' to the Chinese involved, or extra financial incentives. But there were also attempts at Swire's to identify their compradores more closely with the company, for example by allowing them room in a section of the Shanghai private office suite. The following year J. K. Swire informed London that another British manager had decided 'to have his Compradore to sit in his room with him; he is a long way the best of the young school and the sort of man that it will pay to treat as a colleague'.[45] This seemingly rather petty gesture needs remarking. At one level it appears to be merely pandering to British assumptions about Chinese status self-consciousness, or 'face', but it also concerns the breaking down of a literal barrier, and of figurative boundaries between Chinese and Britons, in this case between colleagues in the same company. By accepting this new level of intimacy the manager was in effect arguing for a new common identity rooted in the company, and one that transcended nationality. Expatriate Britons in China tended to differ from settlers in their loyalty to the firm (encouraged by company socialisation), rather than to Britain in China. Such trends as these tended to reinforce that difference sharply, while drawing Chinese employees in as well. Swire's had a 'bad name among Chinese' even in 1934 because of 'defects in control and management' and low salary prospects.[46] Battling against that reputation prompted fundamental structural reform in the company.

Insurance was the area chosen by Swire's for introducing this managerial system in the late 1920s. Their business was under threat from foreign competition, whilst the compradores considered the work beneath them. Swire's also traditionally distrusted Chinese agents, feeling that they were likely to be corrupted by local elites and relatives.[47] To counter this a new, young Chinese insurance organisation was installed. It was also designed to handle the rapid growth of the potential of the industry in the 1920s, especially as town improvement schemes opened up more towns to commercially less hazardous business. Chinese clerks took over routine work and freed foreign staff to drum up and inspect new business.[48] Swire's also took other new measures to reform their traditional workings and save money, notably by awarding their agencies in smaller outports such as Zhenjiang or Weihaiwei to Chinese firms, instead of foreign ones. Similarly, by 1932 only the APC's agent in Zhenjiang was British.[49]

Replacing the compradore involved integrating his staff into the existing British structure whilst recruiting new men not tainted with old-fashioned ways. 'A buck Chinese over the whole lot/Insurance dept. to learn Chinese' were the options Warren Swire scribbled on a letter dealing with the future of the Chinese insurance organisation. There were 'obstructionists' among managers in China who were opposed to employing Chinese in formerly European posts.[50] Swire's man in Shantou declared in 1931 that, as he was old-fashioned, as his Chinese staff were old-fashioned, and as his customers were old-fashioned, he failed to see the need for change.[51] While segregationist thinking found the appointment of Chinese to previously European staffed positions difficult to accommodate, there were tremendous savings to be made from employing 'good-class Chinese' ('none are overpaid at present' was one understatement in 1930), especially as there were 'very few jobs of a routine nature which can not be done as well, if not better, by good Chinese or by women clerks'. And, unlike British women clerks, Chinese employees would not leave (or be forced to leave) their jobs on getting married. In early 1925 Swire's had talked enthusiastically of recruiting a 'definite class of 'B & S Chinese' ... and getting the reputation among educated Chinese of being *the* firm to get into'. And, as Swire's remarked in 1928, 'there is a limit beyond which it no longer pays to employ foreigners'.[52] Appointing Chinese as agents in the smaller treaty ports would allow British staff to be used where they could be most effective and where the lonely hazards of outport life, which could undermine their usefulness, could be avoided.

By 1930 the formation of a Chinese house staff replacing foreign staff at Swire's was in full swing, their loyalty assured, it was hoped, by good salaries. An attempt was made to apply to Chinese applicants the same class criteria that were applied to British staff: they were to 'be recruited in very much the same way as the foreign staff i.e. partly from the University, partly from the Public Schools and partly from the Grammar Schools'.[53] This shared background, and a common loyalty to the firm, would make it easier for Britons and Chinese, it was hoped, to get on together. And opportunities for interaction were increased in Shanghai, where they were expected to lunch together in the previously exclusive 'foreign tiffin room'. Westernised young Chinese, in a radical departure from the usual treaty port prejudices, were seen as offering the best hope. Although there were some exceptions – men like the Shantou manager – most Britons began to equate 'old-fashioned' with inefficiency and with old-fashioned corruption. This reform, begun in something of a panic, was strengthened, formalised and deepened in the 1930s, especially after a comprehensive survey of Chinese staff in 1934.[54] The issue had become central to Swire's development as an organisation in China. Localisation was a common feature in British firms facing decolonisation, or transition, for example in Malaya. But it required sustained commitment if it was to work, such as it received at Swire's.[55]

Localisation took place in other companies and paralleled changes in such British-dominated institutions as the CMC, the Salt Gabelle and the Shanghai Pilots' Association, albeit much more slowly.[56] BAT, for instance, could already boast the reasonably thorough integration of Chinese into much of the company's structure by the 1920s, and the company relied on Chinese in all parts of its business for its success, although industrial management remained the preserve of foreigners whilst Chinese were left as clerks, distributors and advertisers. But, as Sherman Cochran noted, with the anglicisation of BAT's management in the 1920s 'the entire organisation seems to have become even more dependent on Chinese than it had been under American executive leadership'. Localisation at BAT was a political response to Guomindang pressure. In late 1927 'the company temporarily stopped sending new American representatives to China and permanently appointed Chinese to fill many posts in the company's marketing system previously held by Westerners', though it still kept industrial management in Western hands.[57]

Companies faced what they considered to be a shortage of trained Chinese technical staff, a situation which partly resulted from restrictive practices – mostly, but not only, sins of omission – that precluded Chinese from employment in certain foreign dominated fields (the Shanghai pilot service, for example). Active foreign involvement in training and employing Chinese engineers was also lacking. This resulted in a shortage of young Chinese trained in practical fields along Western lines, a fact always alluded to by opponents of sinification. It was also an echo of the general situation within the Chinese technical and scientific professions. The geography (urban and coastal) and small number of establishments employing graduates prompted many to abandon science for other fields.[58] As a result of political pressure, and the efforts of industrial reformers such as Joseph Bailie, private companies and the public utilities in Shanghai began to accept Chinese apprentices and also to employ them after training.[59] Some foreign firms worked directly with an FBI/China Association scheme to train engineers, whilst Hong Kong University's engineering graduates began to be more widely accepted by British companies. As a result of this increase in trained Chinese engineers the KMA, for example, was able to replace many foreign staff after 1934.[60] Swire's closed down their Hong Kong sugar refinery in 1928 for a major restructuring and localisation of employment there, largely in a bid to cut costs, and in the 1930s they employed their first Chinese wireless operators, accountants and wharfingers. Chinese ships' officers had been used on the Upper Yangzi in times of trouble for pragmatic and insurance reasons. But by 1930 Chinese customers, who wanted the cheapest shipping rates for their goods, were also objecting to the cost of foreign officers.[61] The market was pushing British employers to train and recruit more Chinese, and to employ them in positions of greater responsibility, much more integrated into the company than had previously been the case. Such transformations certainly happen slowly, but, where economic and political dictates demanded it, old prejudices which had only too successfully blocked reform in the past began to be surmounted. Comments on new staff may show how low expectations of their new colleagues might be among Britons, but they also show how a company like Swire's was determined to change its recruitment practices and the position of Chinese in the firm: the assessments of such men often hinged crucially on their ability to deal with treaty port Britons.[62]

To implement and oversee reform of Chinese staff issues, Swire's set up a Department of Chinese Affairs (DOCA) in 1934.[63] The DOCA took over all recruitment of Chinese clerical staff and welfare provision. Holidays were introduced for the first time, and Chinese staff were allowed access to cheap credit in the form of small loans. The DOCA also became responsible for mediating labour disputes. Importantly it also took over and formalised the development of contacts with Chinese business and official personalities, recruiting Chinese advisers from outside the company to help. Unofficial personalities, too:

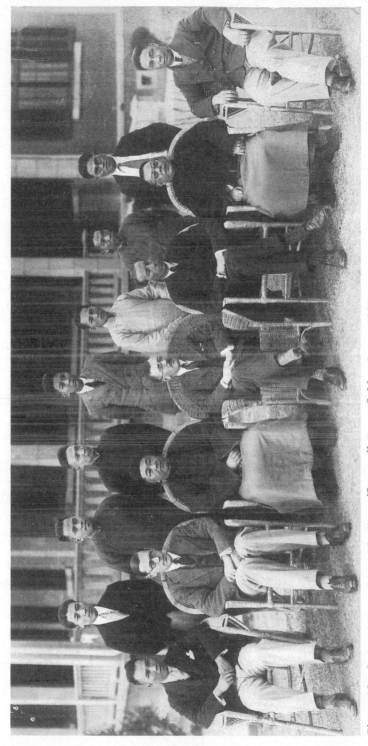

**Figure 10** Swires in transition: Nanjing office staff, Butterfield & Swire, 1933

DOCA's senior Britons went to represent the firm at Shanghai gangster weddings when asked to attend. The first adviser was British-educated T. K. Tseng, who had rowed for his college at Cambridge, and was later a government Vice-minister. Swire's had previously relied on an imperial fixer with Indian experience, Sir Frederick Whyte, but George Findlay Andrew, the first DOCA director, rather better fitted the bill. A missionary child, born in Guiyang, Andrew returned to China as a CIM missionary in 1908, serving in Gansu province. He acted as an informal British agent there in World War I, earning an OBE, then engaged in famine relief work in Gansu and elsewhere, building up excellent contacts with Chinese figures, until he joined Swire's. By institutionalising the formation and implementation of 'Chinese' issues in the firm Swire's strengthened their ability to cope with political and economic change, and developed a solid platform for the flexibility implicit in the appointment of a man like Andrew. Swire's had to engage in meaningful communication not only with their customers but also with their staff, Chinese officials and the other figures it was necessary to cultivate. DOCA's activities compounded other structural and behavioural reforms to enable Swire's to re-establish control over the company, and to help the company in the transition to the non-treaty world.

### Sino-British companies

In 1925 Warren Swire had described Swire's idea of Sino-British co-operation as 'to keep ourselves to ourselves ... but to work in friendly competition with Chinese concerns of standing'.[64] This generally meant market-sharing agreements. Events moved too far to allow this complacent approach to continue: cementing friendly relations led logically to Sino-British companies. The psychological repercussions of co-operation might still be felt to outweigh practical ones, but this approach was becoming anachronistic. The DOT's 1933 report bluntly stated for the first time that co-operation with Chinese businesses would be the surest way of being successful in China. By this it meant active collaboration, for which British companies would have to be better prepared than before.[65] Joint Sino-British enterprises were undertaken largely for political reasons, as an expression of goodwill, but also as a way of cementing the presence of British companies into the Chinese economy in a less obviously alien way. They were also undertaken to solve local and short-term problems. Co-operation was not entirely new, although treaty port *mores* were cynical about such exercises, and the drawing of diplomatic distinctions could make it legally awkward while extraterritoriality still existed. What changed in the 1930s was that sectors of the British economic presence actively and publicly set out (with full British official support) to quite openly establish joint projects and enterprises with leading Chinese and companies.

Co-operation had always been acceptable if the British enterprises involved felt they were on top, and some companies, especially BAT and ICI, had traditionally relied on mergers and co-operation to knock out the competition – or else for political reasons to prop it up.[66] Swire's and Jardine's were worried by the threat of the restriction of coastal and inland navigation rights to Chinese companies. Swire's felt the need to placate their competitors and pre-empt nationalistic policy decisions by the National government, and experimented by forming the Taikoo Chinese Navigation Company for their Upper Yangzi trade. The line was incorporated in 1930, after two years' deliberation, in the face of these threats and in the light of the continuing boycott of British trade at Wanxian after British gunboats had bombarded the town in 1926. In a memorandum prepared by the Shanghai CNCo manager the reasons for setting up the company were spelt out:

> A desire to try out Anglo-Chinese co-operation so as to have some idea before restrictive navigation legislation is enacted, of the best way to adapt ourselves to changed conditions not only above Ichang but elsewhere.
> – To dispel the distrust felt for the Four Companies' motives on the Upper River – without this there can be no progress or prosperity on the run.
> Identify ourselves more closely with Chinese shipping circles and thereby
> – Minimize popular prejudice against our steamers.[67]

That the company came to be run on the Upper Yangzi rather than, as originally planned, the Middle River shows the politically expedient nature of these plans and negotiations; they became linked more with Swire's political problems on the Upper River, and the structure of their carrying trade, than with any long-term goals.[68]

In the face of the expected growth, with probable government aid, of Chinese insurance companies, Swire's established, in co-operation with Chen Guangfu's Shanghai Commercial & Savings Bank, the Pao Foong Insurance Company.[69] In their various moves and discussions Swire's stole a march on other companies. Jardine's rejected jointly owned companies in 1928 as unfeasible, as 'the Chinese would at once want things done their own way', while Chinese management would lead to abuses, and in 1931 they seemed to their Hong Kong manager to be 'left behind owing to their illiberal and conservative attitude which they were adopting as contrasted with [Swire's]'.[70] But others moved on the issue as well. In May 1931 ICI felt that 'manufacture in China ... would greatly improve our position there' and structural co-operation with the Yong Li Soda Company seemed to be the answer, although a joint venture never materialised.[71] The same year the chairman of BAT told Lampson that 'he was now forming, as a sort of subsidiary enterprise, a Chinese tobacco company ... in case ... the position of foreign controlled companies should become too difficult'.[72] Although three out of the four Sino-foreign banks begun before 1932 had failed, the Chartered Bank of India Australia & China had informal, tentative talks with Chen Guangfu about a possible complementary link in 1930.[73] Swire's passed on to the Hongkong & Shanghai Bank a proposal, deemed to be 'fantastic', from their new Chinese friends for a Chinese Navigation Bank. Based in Hong Kong, the Hongkong & Shanghai Bank's approach was more conservative than that of the British companies in China. Its policy in the 1930s was to adapt itself and attempt 'to prove its continued value to the Government of China'.[74]

An important aspect of co-operation was the overt involvement of leading Chinese figures as directors of companies or as participants in bodies previously restricted to European members. This was an especial feature of Victor Sassoon's dramatic entry into the Shanghai business world in the 1920s. The International Investment Trust, set up in 1930, included many of the Chinese names on Warren Swire's 'hit list'. Sassoon's Shanghai Land Investment Company also counted Yu Xiaqing as a director. Sassoon's biggest investments were in property: in the long term he needed all the Chinese friends he could get.[75] Sassoon's move is singularly interesting, in that a British land interest – which by its very nature was a rooted interest – began acting like a local interest and building up local alliances. Compromises and agreements also had to be made with local authorities, and without reference to consuls and agreements. While the SMC continued its struggle over sovereignty in the external roads areas, the hived-off utility companies had to seek the co-operation of Chinese utility firms, and the agreement of the Chinese municipal authorities, to continue functioning in the districts. Business abandoned this political struggle.[76]

From early treaty port days onwards Chinese capital had played an important role in British activities in China; in the 1930s that alliance became more visible. Leading Chinese figures sat on company boards, Sino-British companies were established, and other mutually beneficial alliances with Chinese capital were explored. Some of these moves were indicative of panic among the British business community. Mostly they were evidence of a major shift in attitudes towards the Chinese as businessmen, and towards the nature of business in China. An aloof 'Britishness', and largely ceremonial personal relations with the Chinese, began to be replaced by a compromise relationship, based on the shared identification of key interests with specific individuals or interest groups. If the concept of 'British' interests in China had always been something of a misnomer, by the 1930s the reality of the interpenetration of Chinese and British interests was actually being made apparent. The era of the transplantation of British companies to the treaty port world was drawing to a close. All effective players in the China market would have to be transationals now.

How did such changes affect CNCo's treatment of Chinese passengers? As well as starting to integrate (or re-title) their staff, Swire's made moves to integrate their passengers. Jardine's were already doing so on some of their ships. In mid-1928 the Swire discussion centred largely on converting existing ship superstructures. London wrote in August that in the future 'there will be no question in China of foreign or Chinese first class accommodation and therefore we had better meet probable future market requirements now'.[77] The CNCo ships *Wuhu* and *Wusueh* were to be a new generation, with accommodation supposedly reflecting the shift in Swire's thinking by the end of the 1920s. An intermediate saloon was designed, and economising on the fittings was warned against, owing to the attention to such details expected by 'the growing numbers of Chinese who both demand and are willing to pay for comfort on the European Standard'. The first-class accommodation was to be managed by a foreign purser and his Chinese staff, and was not included in the compradore's contract. Chinese passengers wishing to travel saloon class would buy their tickets at the foreign agent's office.[78] The progress of such transformations was often convoluted, but in their drive to rethink their physical relationship with Chinese passengers Swire's and other companies were at the same time undermining the traditional treaty port system, and searching for new forms of business in post-treaty China.

### The China Printing & Finishing Company
The new, post-treaty port style of British enterprise developing in China in the 1930s is also represented by a newcomer to manufacturing in Shanghai. As in India, a further feature of the changing character of the British commercial presence was the growth in representation of British multinationals, and direct investment in manufacturing in China.[79] Firms entered to seek new markets, but also to defend existing ones. Cotton was a case in point. The collapse in Britain's cotton piece goods exports to China was staggering: exports had fallen from 587 million yards in 1913 to 69 million by 1930. The British share of imported cotton cloths fell from 55.3 per cent in 1902 to 13.2 per cent in 1930: Japan's share rose from 2.7 to 72.2 per cent.[80] Although Chinese production increased rapidly in this period, imports from Japan and

Japanese production in China itself were a bigger threat. Japanese mills there quadrupled their production of cloth between 1924 and 1936; Chinese mills tripled theirs, while British production rose by 5 per cent.[81] Despite the rise in indigenous production, the chief enemy came to be seen as Japan, a view reinforced by the global nature of Anglo-Japanese trade rivalry in the 1930s. There were eventually three British responses to this onslaught: the unsuccessful attempt by industry organisations to negotiate with the Japanese in 1934, lobbying with the British and dominion governments for protectionist policies, and the individual competitive strategies of individual firms.[82]

The Calico Printers' Association (CPA) in Manchester was no exception. In order to keep some presence in the China market in the face of competition from Chinese and Japanese production it bought, in 1923, a printing and finishing works at Bailianjing in Shanghai. There it printed Japanese-made cloths for the Chinese market via a wholly-owned subsidiary, the China Printing & Finishing Company. However, political boycotts against Japan hit the CPA hard. Japanese supplies became unreliable, and the firm was having to buy stocks too far ahead for comfort.[83] To 'exclude all taint of Japanese participation', and thereby evade boycott confiscations – which bedevilled other British firms – the CPA decided to construct a new spinning and weaving plant at Liujiazui, across the river from the Shanghai International Settlement. In fact the existing plant was never going to be a success on its own, and the advantages of integrated production and complete control over the manufacturing process also appealed to the CPA (although it was then an unusual step to take). It later even considered buying cotton direct from Chinese growers.[84] The CPA was buoyed by the Shanghai battle in 1932, which seemed to have postponed the threat of the rendition of the International Settlement for some time to come, although the plant was constructed outside the settlement, largely for commercial reasons. Market and political considerations were inescapably intertwined for the company.

Interested in the Japanese model of supervision of labour, though, the company imported a small cadre of British foremen to Pudong, who together with Russian supervisors, and some 2,000 workers, made up the work force. The firm eschewed the contract labour system – whereby labour hire was effectively contracted out to foremen – and rejected any thought of a compradore structure, recruiting its workers directly, although in practice bastard labour contracting practices could still develop unofficially.[85] The model for much of CPF's approach to production and sales in China was BAT, but reforming recruitment practices was not always simple. After a series of strikes, and in a bid to prevent 'external interference' with the mill, especially after it detected moves to establish a union presence, the company used a variety of approaches to improve its knowledge of activism among the work force, and to deal with activists. These approaches included direct talks with the local authorities to encourage the police to deal with any radical presence in the Pudong area, contact with Li Ming (another name from Warren Swire's list, who became a director), and also friendly (and secret) contact with Du Yuesheng, leader of the Shanghai Green gang (Qingbang), whose hold on labour in Pudong was too strong to evade.[86] The CPA did not establish a joint venture directly, although its Shanghai managing director took on a director-ship in a Chinese worsted yarn company to build up contacts, but it was forced, like Swire's, to develop close relations with a range of local figures – from gangsters to businessmen.

The new plant was up and running by late 1935. Raw cotton from north China was processed, and grey cloths were sent by barge up the Huangpu to the Bailianjing works for printing. This was a very modern-style relocation of production from the industrialised world to the industrialising, although it was unusual for the time for a British firm. The relocation was literal, as the CPA shipped out British personnel and machinery to China, machinery was sent to avoid having to buy from the Japanese. Plants in Scotland and Lancashire were being closed down; the CPA cut the number of its mills from eighty-five to eleven between 1899 and 1933, the great majority after 1921, and continued to close down inefficient units throughout the 1930s as new overseas ventures were planned: in India, Sumatra, Manila and Australia.[87] In terms of sales the company obviously touched 'only the fringe of the market', but it did well nonetheless. Printed cottons were sold to up-country wholesalers, as well through some sixty-five Chinese salesmen in the Shanghai area, and this was a keenly market-sensitive operation. The most successful innovation was the introduction of 'branded lines': developing brand loyalty directly with the Chinese public, using the 'Lun Chang' trademark. Extensive advertising in the Chinese press in the treaty ports and in the interior was aimed at spurring on customer recognition, and sales were very high.[88]

Owned by Manchester, and running as part of a growing global network established by the CPA, the Lunchang operation represented nonetheless a different kind of localisation. The key to success was acting efficiently, knowing the market and targeting it with modern sales techniques and manufacturing. Politically Lunchang took little note of treaty port politics. A bigger transnational like ICI, which operated throughout China, had kept out of public treaty port life until 1933 as a matter of policy, although the advantages of involvement eventually outweighed the disadvantages.[89] But both companies were party to what had become by the end of the 1930s the dismantling of effective settler power in the SMC in favour of expatriate interests. Britain in China in itself did not interest CPA, which sought instead to cut production costs, gain easy access to its market, and to do so from what it presumed was a stable base.

For businesses the transfer of responsibility in firms to Chinese, or the placing of companies in formal collaborations which limited British control, tinkered with some of the central tenets of Britishness. Swire's, for example, were keen to get their compradores to 'understand our scruples' and strongly believed that the reliability of their own business ethics was a strong advantage in trade in China.[90] This often stated belief in the attractiveness of British honesty to the Chinese was related to wider paternalist ideas about British policy and activities in China, and was a core communal myth. The danger of the new generation of businessmen's 'greater understanding of, and sympathy with the Chinese' was best articulated by a hostile H. G. W. Woodhead in 1932: 'In the past the British merchant has gained a reputation for integrity and scrupulousness. Is he, in future, to resort to wholesale bribery to secure 'justice' against defaulting creditors ... ?'[91] In fact the whole process of arranging Sino-British companies and closer 'co-operation' entailed the abandonment of bedrock tenets of previous British practice. The need to openly identify British interests with those of Chinese business and the National government was obviously incompatible with the traditional apartness and neutrality practised by the British. It was, indeed, much closer to the standard relationship between Chinese companies and their *de facto* local authorities. BAT's shedding of its foreignness in its competition with Nanyang Brothers in effect turned Sino-foreign rivalry in the cigarette industry into a competition over who was more Chinese.[92]

Business responses to nationalism were complex, but then so were the challenges it offered. The Qing company law of 1904, revised in 1914, was partly concerned with reclaiming economic sovereignty for the Chinese state. The Nanjing regime introduced a barrage of commercial legislation, and although most Chinese firms, for example, still refused to register under the 1929 Company Law, British firms were in a stickier position.[93] To refuse to adapt to developments in the legal framework of commerce in China could expose them to legal challenges from National government agencies; to blithely adapt might expose them by offering too much information to those same agencies. In response, while localising their business cultures in China, many British firms also began transferring their actual company registration to Hong Kong throughout the 1930s.[94]

There was, then, confusion about the type of market businesses ought to target. Should they follow up on their structural integration in and dependence on the China trade, and truly sinify their public face and priorities, or should they cling on to their Britishness and colonial trappings? Swire's vacillated over their Chinese passenger accommodation, for example, largely so as not to alienate foreign custom, which was less elastic: the nationalistic Chinese public might not patronise British companies, however much they tried to reach out, and the continued – although admittedly still modest – growth of Chinese competition throughout the 1930s partly endorses this view. Chinese customers did make patriotic purchases.[95] Jardine's and the Hongkong & Shanghai Bank had their headquarters in colonial Hong Kong and were initially less willing to compromise their British loyalties and character. Business dictated the necessity of localisation but continued distrust of the Chinese, and imperial dignity, suggested otherwise for some. Nevertheless Jardine's Tony Keswick, through the close links he established with Song Ziwen, came to epitomise the new-thinking younger British business leader in China.[96] Ambivalent reform also characterised the other sector that stood a good chance of surviving the transition to the post-treaty era: Protestant missions.

## Transforming British Protestant missions

Mission work was ever characterised by a certain level of ambivalence. Societies worried that any transfer of responsibility to Chinese Churches might encourage the development of fundamentalist movements closely allied to practices prevalent in Chinese folk religion, or else lead to compromises with elements of Chinese culture that were seen as antithetical to Christian belief. Individual missionaries hardly wanted to reform themselves out of their own jobs too speedily. But, like businesses, they had little choice as the century developed but to retreat from the certainties of the heyday of treaty port culture. Finance led the way here too. Mission work in China may be divided neatly into three stages before 1949: somewhat aggressive expansion down to 1900 and the Boxer events; a period of complacent calm in the aftermath of that crisis, down to about 1926; then rapid change after the crisis of the Nationalist revolution. The centrality of the Boxer experience to the mission enterprise has been noted in chapter 2; in general, however, the bloody settlement of the crisis made mission work safer, more settled and by the mid-1920s complacent, despite the range of problems mission work increasingly faced. The nationalist revolution was a less sanguine trauma, but caused nationwide upheaval in mission work. The rise of Chinese nationalism posed a latent threat to missions' freedom of action, and nationalistic anti-Christian campaigns, combined with shifting intellectual currents, seriously hampered efforts to gain wider social acceptance. By the late 1920s there was broad agreement along the spectrum of Protestant missions that to be able to stay on in China, and to be effective, a wholesale overhaul of mission practices, structures, personnel and thinking was necessary. Not least, missions had to denationalise themselves, separating themselves from treaty port society and, like businesses, more thoroughly integrate themselves into China.

The mid-1920s crisis brought a number of developments to a head: changing intellectual currents in China and in the West, an organised anti-Christian movement, and also the first appearance at the highest levels of government of Christian converts. Maugham's missionary caricatures in *On a Chinese Screen* painted a picture of bleak Victorian fundamentalism still prevalent in the China field in the 1920s. Maugham was not alone in his impressions, and younger Chinese intellectuals and students were themselves largely more interested in Western science, by whose standards the fundamentalist Protestantism which so characterised mission Christianity seemed obscurantist, while British treaty port writers like Reginald Johnston also attacked missions on similar grounds.[97] Some mission personnel were also conscious of the need for change. By 1929 E. R. Hughes, who had worked as an evangelical missionary for the LMS in Fujian since 1911, had come to the conclusion that the mission enterprise had made no effort to engage intellectually or sympathetically with Chinese culture and as a result its successes were shallow. Moreover, anti-missionary propaganda lambasted missions as hand in glove with imperialism, and Hughes concluded in one letter to a colleague that 'while in the ordinary sense of the term there is no truth in the charge, yet in the spirit and methods of our work I find something which approximates closely enough to spiritual imperialism'.[98] Hughes resigned to work for the Chinese YMCA in Shanghai on literary and research work, and was eventually to leave China for an academic career in Britain and the United States.

Anti-Christian thought was given a political articulation and structure throughout the politically contentious 1920s. An anti-Christian movement was launched by the Anti-Christian Student Federation and the Great Anti-religious Federation in response to the 1922 National Christian Conference and its tactlessly entitled report *The Christian Occupation of China* (1922). In 1924 the Educational Rights Recovery movement organised student strikes and attacks on mission schools and colleges, initially in response to the heavy-handed action of a British headmaster in Guangzhou who had refused his students permission to form a student union. The May Thirtieth movement and the Nationalist revolution exacerbated this activity. Students rebelled, and often so did Chinese staff. This poisoned relations but also revealed, in effect, severe structural problems in mission education, in relations between staff and students and between foreign heads and teachers and Chinese staff.[99] The experience of the best part of a decade of strife prompted many missionaries to conclude that relations with their converts, colleagues and organised Chinese Christianity had to be renegotiated.

Many individual missionaries were driven by the events of the Nationalist revolution to question their own assumptions, and much of this debate, for example in the pages of the *Chinese Recorder*, was articulated as a question of 'race' and of institutional and individual race relations. Ideas about the world-wide decline of 'white' supremacy were as prevalent in mission debate as in other fields. It was not a debate unique to China, and it must be viewed in the context of missionary reaction to political developments in India, and in the still wider context of the 1928 International Missionary Council meeting in Jerusalem. This body, which represented Protestant groups world-wide, laid stress that year on the necessity of the process of 'indigenisation' of Church and mission structures.[100] Support for the mission enterprise was also waning in some British circles as a result of the spread of liberal theological ideas and secular intellectual changes. Lack of support was also apparent from the funding difficulties many societies faced, a long-term problem only partly exacerbated by the world depression after 1929. CMS income, for example, reached a high point of £651,610 in 1920 but by 1934 had sunk to £391,676.[101] Cutbacks necessitated by this decline also encouraged speedier reform as missions, like British businesses, realised that Chinese employees were cheaper.

The market for souls was also in flux. It was apparent that mission work could no longer be targeted largely at the villages of China and the Chinese peasantry. This historical solution to the steadfast opposition of the Chinese bureaucratic elite was increasingly inadequate. The mission enterprise needed to reach an accommodation with the emerging political and economic elites at national and local levels and to accelerate and modernise the educational work it had begun in the early years of the century. For their part the new 'better-educated classes' were felt by some to show greater willingness and openness to Christian work, and Christianity achieved a greater prominence in republican Chinese political life than ever it had before. Most symbolic and beguiling, in missionary eyes, was the conversion of Chiang Kai-shek and the influence of the Song sisters and Kong Xiangxi. The sincerity of the gesture remains disputed, but David Yui of the YMCA officiated at Chiang's wedding, Wang Zhengting was briefly General Secretary of the YMCA, Kong Xiangxi had been a secretary, and so had an estimated 148 government officials. For the first time, Protestant missions appeared to have friends in high places.[102] The shortcomings of the mission sector threatened to make it a wasted opportunity.

Mission behaviour had certainly altered after 1900, and there had been a drawing back from the excesses which had served to antagonise rural communities in the build-up to the crisis. But mission societies indulged in a more fundamental fit of introspection in and after 1927. London deputations or secretaries from the LMS, the BMS and the Friends' Service Council (FSC) made investigative trips to China. The pages of mission publications in China such as the *Chinese Recorder* and the *Educational Review* were also forums for this introspection. Union organisations and *ad hoc* groups, such as representatives of the Christian Colleges and Universities in China, also met and discussed future plans. In 1927 the CIM held a series of meetings, both in London and among their displaced workers in China, which assessed the situation there and discussed future tactics. It was widely realised that on their return a different relationship with Chinese Christians and Chinese Churches would be required.[103] The BMS announced the need for 'fraternal' relations to replace 'paternal' ones.[104] The deputations came up with similar, unsurprising, conclusions, but most were in line with the Baptists' call for a new relationship.[105] Chapter 3 showed how far the mission world shared in the beliefs and practices of the settlers and sojourners they so often criticised: in their segregationist living patterns and relations with Chinese staff and colleagues, and often in their identification with the broader community of Britons in China, missionaries appeared to many observers, including many in their own ranks, to be identified too closely with Britain in China.

For a variety of reasons, then, missionary societies were faced with the fact that the tone and structure of their presence in China were no longer tenable as it had stood since the Boxer settlement. In response they accelerated the transfer of responsibilities to Chinese Churches and union (interdenominational) organisations, purged their personnel and recruited more Chinese into positions of administrative and executive responsibility throughout the various organisations attached to their missions, evangelical, educational and medical.

### Churches

'Indigenisation' was a major theme in mission and Chinese Christian debate long before 1925. The mission ideal had always been to foster self-governing, self-financing and self-propagating churches, although the actual attainment of the ideal was patchy. The 1922 China National Christian Conference (the first with a majority of Chinese delegates and a Chinese chairman) created a National Christian Council, which was intended to help Protestant missions work towards speedier sinification.[106] The meeting also set in motion the formation of a Church of Christ in China (Zhongguo jidujiaohui), an interdenominational body composed mainly of Presbyterian and Congregationalist Churches which held its first general assembly in 1927. The crisis of 1925–27 prompted many other groups to join or to contemplate joining, sometimes in great haste, or to accelerate such processes in their own churches. The Shanghai Council of the CIM, for example, announced the need for 'more speedy carrying out of the original policy of the Mission to establish self-supporting and self-propagating churches'. By 1931 the key aim of the CIM's forward movement was said to be the 'rapid transfer to Chinese leadership of the pastoral care and oversight of the Chinese Churches'.[107] For its part, the Anglican Church in China was formally recognised as an independent 'constituent member' of the Anglican communion in 1930, whilst at diocesan levels the direction of missionary labour and the handling of funds were transferred region by region to diocesan – that is, Chinese Church – boards.[108] Different approaches characterised the reforms of different missions. The LMS was more open to reform than the publicly more cautious WMMS, which was eager to lay stress on working together 'with no question of who is head and who is tail'.[109] Variations were also related to geographical factors, and to assimilation into treaty port society: Methodist conservative H. B. Rattenbury was based in the treaty port of Hankou, for instance. CMS missionaries in west China effectively stalled organisational changes which handed authority over to their Church in 1928, and in its South China Victoria diocese, based in Hong Kong, the devolution of authority to the Church in 1929 was actually reversed in 1935. The presence of British congregations in colonial Hong Kong had previously been used to justify the establishment of a segregated Chinese-only synod in 1913. It was claimed that British lay Anglicans would be unwilling to accept Chinese direction of Church affairs.[110]

The devolution of authority to Chinese Churches involved many thorny issues – the ownership of Church property, the control of mission funds and the ultimate control of the direction of mission efforts and the place of the mission in general. Sinification often meant the merging of Church and mission structures and the subordination of missionaries to the authority of the Chinese Church. Transferring mission property to the Chinese Church symbolised in concrete form the state of relations between Church and Mission, and the role of the mission councils in China began to be questioned by some Chinese Christians, who thought Christianity well enough established in China to propagate itself. These issues, and the nature of relations between Britons and Chinese within the Churches and missions, were influenced by perceptions of the Chinese character and abilities, and the expectations raised by missionary lifestyles. Such points involved questions of financial and doctrinal distrust. There was a grave danger, thought the CIM's London Council in 1929, that 'power may fall into the hands of unspiritual men, as the true spiritual leaders do not necessarily come to the front'. H. F. Wallace of the English Presbyterian Mission foresaw in 1927 'endless suspicions and slanders and faction feuds' resulting from the devolution of financial responsibility.[111] Some feared that their 'dramatic instinct' would sweep Chinese Christians into evangelistic excesses if there was no doctrinally consistent restraint from foreign supervisors.[112] Many of these reservations were, of course, part of the long-term debate about the process of conversion and the propagation of Christian Churches. Others were rooted in conservatism, and in the bitterness of mission personnel personally distressed by the speed and temper of change. Mabel Geller reported ambivalently that her Chinese colleagues 'have managed so splendidly on their own initiative that I simply do not count nowadays, and am very often not even asked to join in things. It is a very healthy state of affairs, ... but it seems very strange.'[113]

The development of Chinese control of interdenominational organisations was unstoppable. The Chinese element in the NCC was strengthened in 1927, and in the following year there was a reorganisation after which both missionary and Chinese delegates were to be elected by the Chinese Churches, thereby strengthening its Chinese character. Other bodies such as the Nurses' Association of China and the China Christian Education Association altered the balance of control towards their majority Chinese membership.[114] Some of this sinification was literally nominal. The *China Mission Year Book* became the *China Christian Year Book* in 1926, and the previous year the China Medical Missionary Association had become the China Medical Association. These changes were, nonetheless, symbolic, and did reveal shifts in emphasis from foreign mission to Chinese institution.

*Foreign staff*

Within individual societies there was widespread acknowledgement of the room for change. For a start, many missions weeded out those they felt had become unsuitable, or whose unsuitability came to be perceived as unhelpful, and those whom Chinese mission workers intimated, or stated, were no longer welcome. Missions responded to criticisms of their personnel by Chinese workers similar to those directed against British businesses. Miss Harrison, at the Lester Chinese Hospital in Shanghai, was sent home in 1929 by the LMS ostensibly on 'medical grounds' but really because of 'temperamental difficulties'. She was 'not fitted for the fine team-work, and the understanding of the hundred and one little things that show under the polite exterior of a Chinese staff', nor was Miss L. K. Rayner in Hong Kong. Dora Clarke, an LMS matron, who countermanded the orders of Chinese doctors, was eased out in 1930, as it was feared that her attitude towards the Chinese staff 'might easily provoke very serious consequences'.[115] The WMMS was keen to allow the return after 1927 only of those 'acceptable to the Chinese'. This excluded B. B. Chapman, with his 'perhaps unconsciously overbearing temperament', a Mr Helps, the Revd Lindsay, who was 'somewhat lacking in tact and sympathy and ... not a persona grata to the Chinese', and a Mr Scholes, 'who had given offence in one or two directions almost past bearing'.[116] The CIM also decided that the old, the unhealthy and those unable 'to adapt his or her mind to the new conditions' should not be allowed to return. They also sent individuals who had caused particular problems back to different districts.[117] This purging of personnel after 1927 was not a phenomenon unique to British organisations, as many North American missionaries did not return. Many others in all societies resigned from ill health or because of the trying experiences of the revolutionary years. In 1927 there were 8,250 Protestant missionaries of all nationalities allotted to missions in China, the following year 4,375. By 1930 the figure had reached only 6,346, and until 1936 it fluctuated below that figure.[118] In effect, over a quarter of foreign missionaries had departed, and moreover, as shown below, the face of the mission enterprise had been very much indigenised.

A proportion of these missionaries were replaced, and the infusion of new workers was an opportunity for missions to adapt to changes at a greater pace and with greater ease. The CIM took the opportunity to use the experienced workers to establish new missions while allocating existing missions to new workers, uninfluenced by past association or habits of leadership and authority, and theoretically more able to work liberally with the Chinese.[119] Missions were widely aware that their new workers should be prepared to work with the Chinese on different terms than formerly. This was accompanied by a desire for better-quality personnel. Lack of professionalism and of language skills, poor education and reliance on a surfeit of enthusiasm became a hindrance. This applied especially to nursing and medical staff, but also to evangelical workers. The China mission field might be identified with the aristocratic Cambridge Seven, who joined the CIM in 1884 trailing their sporting prowess at the university, but the class reality was very much less exclusive.[120] The Revd A. A. Taylor and his wife (LMS) were not allowed to return to China and were recommended for service elsewhere, 'where their lack of early cultural environment will not tell against them with the people whom they hope to influence'. Taylor was working-class, a former dock clerk who had left school at the age of fourteen and had returned to study only in preparation for missionary work. His colleagues suggested 'that he might get a lonely station in the South Seas' where his ability to 'do anything in the house with his hands ... would come in useful'.[121] In one sense the changes demanded by the situation served to reinforce an exclusive class identity for missions, although class was intertwined with issues of education. What the British presence needed in the mission field, as in the business field, was trained, talented individuals.

Like businesses, however, missions also saw the need to replace British personnel with Chinese in mission or mission support posts, especially in medical and educational areas. Social and intellectual changes were such that within the BMS it was thought that 'a third class of mission worker ... the Chinese worker with a foreign training' would have to be recognised.[122] This led to debates about the best way of getting and retaining Chinese workers, debates which were also common in British business circles. In the LMS it was pointed out that there was now no need for clerical missionaries, as so much work was being devolved into Chinese hands; this was especially true of nursery and primary schools, where more administrative and teaching work could be done by Chinese teachers.[123] Getting suitable staff for schools and hospitals would also mean having to pay them more than Chinese staff had been paid so far, paying them at the rates for comparable work outside the missions and, in some cases, almost on Western lines, and giving them 'a better status, more opportunity and more responsibility.'[124] In 1929 a Dr Hsia of the Central China District of the LMS insisted on taking a furlough and expected financial arrangements comparable to those enjoyed by foreign mission workers (in his case seven months' paid leave and return travel expenses to Britain), to the impotent consternation of the district council.[125]

> Life's not the same, no bit the same, and we must be aware
> In case we tread upon the corns of those who breathe hot air.
> 'May I do this,' 'Would you like that,' must be our attitude:
> 'Would $500 rise suffice to buy you better food?'

ran one piece of mission doggerel from late 1928.[126] Such requirements raised new financial problems for cash-strapped missions, but societies did begin to appoint more Chinese staff to mission educational and medical positions as well as to positions on joint organisations, and as colporteur supervisors, mission workers, ministers, deaconesses, evangelists and pastors.

There had been debate within mission circles about the direction and nature of mission education before 1927. A 1921–22 China Educational Commission recommended greater integration of schools with the Chinese national and provincial educational systems. Many schools were seriously disrupted by Chinese students, and sometimes staff, as a result of political disturbances, starting with the campaign for Educational Rights Recovery in 1924. By 1928, when mission schools and colleges began to reopen, it was realised that an 'entirely new situation' was facing mission educationalists in which 'the foreigner has no business in a position that could be occupied creditably by a Chinese associate'.[127] This was reinforced by the policies of the new regime. In 1928, as part of its consolidation of political control, the Nationalist government enacted educational legislation requiring the registration of all schools and higher education institutions.[128] To be registered it was necessary to have a Chinese Head and a predominantly Chinese board of governors or trustees. This aspect of registration was widely accepted, and carried out, by mission societies, it was considered a 'wise thing to do', and some schools had already devolved such authority.[129] Most were happy with the results, which in some cases seem to have improved relations with Chinese staff and restored discipline among rebellious students in ways no longer possible for foreign principals in an irrevocably politicised educational atmosphere. However, the continued mission presence in schools made for awkward relationships, especially as they affected missionaries who had previously worked in more leading roles, and new British recruits were preferred, such as a Mr Monro at Medhurst College, Shanghai, who had 'the right attitude towards the new regime of Chinese control in the college, and towards Chinese students [had] a feeling of intelligent sympathy'.[130] Changes in education law therefore saw missions devolve authority and responsibility for institutions which were integral to the recruitment of their converts and staff; this devolution meant that schools and colleges began to be more effectively transformed into institutions Chinese in character.

A further aspect of registration was the formal banning of religious education as part of the curriculum. This caused some resignations among more evangelical personnel as societies opted to secularise the formal curriculum and concentrate more broadly on Christian education. The China Inland Mission was not happy about registration, but the BMS Home Committee accepted it in 1931. The public displays of

Christianity widely demanded, even if only implicitly, by mission colleges and schools were a sensitive issue, and were also incompatible with the modernisation of mission education. At their graduation ceremony in 1928 the students of the West China Union University at Chengdu were each handed a Bible. Such displays, the students complained, lowered the value of the education they had received and gave the impression that they had to make a public profession of Christianity to obtain their degrees. Fearful of registration but also fearful of losing pupils the CIM in London stressed to opponents of the process in China the necessity of continuing to teach 'secular subjects to secure pupils'.[131] Here again economic imperatives operated to bolster reform.

Sinification in health work involved two basic processes; firstly, the provision of better-paid opportunities and more responsibilities for Chinese doctors; secondly, the devolution of control of medical missions to the Chinese Churches. Both processes were intimately tied up with a third, the improvement of the standard of medical work. Despite such obvious exceptions as the Peking Union Medical College the 1922 *Survey* of mission work had revealed an appalling overall picture of medical work. The situation in some hospitals – as regards standards of hygiene – often appalled doctors and new recruits fresh from Britain. It was also widely recognised that the prevailing general standards threatened the continuation of medical work, especially if the National government chose to register teaching hospitals and nursing schools, as it had educational establishments. Another threat lay in the inability of mission hospitals, as generally constituted and run, to appeal to wealthier Chinese patients, whose expectations of standards of cleanliness and comfort had greatly increased, in sickness as in health – as steamship companies also realised. Improvements were often aimed at wooing this class of patient, who would thereby be subsidising the more charitable aspects of hospital work and making up for an increasing shortfall in funds from abroad.[132]

The 1922 *Survey* identified the 'crux' of the problem as staff and urged an increase in foreign staff numbers to make up for the shortfall in Chinese doctors, who were also not impressed by mission standards – in their case, of pay and accommodation, and, traditionally, of status.[133] But recruiting extra foreign staff was no longer economically or politically affordable by the end of the decade, and Chinese doctors, even those trained by missions, were largely unwilling to work in mission hospitals. Some efforts were made to arrange foreign salaries for suitable candidates, or salaries which competed with the rates they would receive elsewhere in China.[134] It was not always possible, but more Chinese doctors were employed and at market rates. By 1932 the

EPM was planning to have Chinese workers appointed by 'a Chinese body' and 'orientated' towards the Chinese Church or the institution they worked for, rather than the mission. By sinifying the appointment procedure the mission also intended to suppress salary demands based on foreign rates by distancing itself from the process.[135] Patterns of responsibility, however, could be changed in hospitals where little else could be immediately reformed.

In a thorough report in 1928 the EPM condemned its existing hospitals and recommended a series of improvements, including organisational measures which would thoroughly anchor its hospitals into the communities they served by allowing the Chinese Churches and public, through guilds and chambers of commerce, to join in their management. The EPM undertook to build a new hospital in Shantou with local Chinese financial contributions and in agreement with the mayor. The level of sophistication and complexity of business required the appointment of a business manager. Traditionally most hospitals were administered by the foreign doctors themselves, but this was no longer sensible or possible. By 1932 the EPM was planning with a view to 'ultimate devolution' of the hospitals to the Chinese Church and a board of trustees, in line with a 1926 plan of the China Medical Association Missionary Division which also interested the LMS.[136] Doubts about 'practical problems of ethics and religion' in handing over control to a 'local heathen community' were raised by Rattenbury in Hankou.[137] However, where the CMS handed over control to a Chinese medical superintendent it was noted that the work flourished, and relations with the local community and authorities were very good.[138]

So the sinification of the mission presence in China was accompanied by, and characterised by, its modernisation, professionalisation and secularisation. British doctors and teachers often scoffed at the standards of their Chinese colleagues, but it is clear that the old mission order had obscured serious problems in mission hospitals and educational institutions, and in many ways a sinicised institution was a better one. Moreover, like businesses and municipal institutions, missions were no longer able to rely on the explicit protection of the structures of informal empire. As in those other spheres of the British presence they had to make significant compromises, with the *de jure* Chinese state, *de facto* local authorities, and those Chinese they were involved with, as institutions or as individuals. It involved a significant shift in their attitudes towards the Chinese. 'It had not been realised that in the Christian Church so many competent and responsible Chinese teachers were to be found,' recalled H. B. Rattenbury, lamely, in 1942. This realisation was such a shock because of the prevailing attitudes towards Chinese capabilities.[139] British Protestant missions were forced to attempt to transform themselves from 'foreign missions' to *Chinese* Christian Church and to compromise with modernising trends in Chinese society, in Chinese Christianity, in education and in medicine. They aimed to secure pupils, or patients, and therefore funds, and to secure themselves in China.

The proper sinification of personnel and institutional structures also required changes in physical and social structures. To attract sufficiently qualified Chinese professionals – indeed, even to retain those trained in mission hospitals and colleges – it was realised that the housing traditionally allotted to such Chinese staff was inadequate.[140] What was seen as discrimination by some Chinese professionals was seen by most Britons as part of the psychological necessity of recreating British homes, but these foreign-style buildings created problems as buildings. For some they symbolised the essential foreignness of the mission institutions and, perhaps, of their message. William Sewell was 'tempted to wonder if a few plaster houses put up by the Chinese themselves would not have been really better' than the 'magnificent buildings' of the West China Union University in Chengdu.[141] Foreign-style mission homes were accused of fostering social isolation and segregation, and prolonging racial divisions. Foreign-style buildings were conspicuous and often arrogantly and uncompromisingly foreign, and a smaller-scale fusion of the two increasingly became the aim of Church and educational architecture. The geography of building was also important. In 1928 the South China District Committee of the LMS decided to build a new residence in Kowloon rather than on Hong Kong island, in order to dissociate itself from secular colonial society by showing the Chinese that 'we are in earnest and desire to be placed in the place where we consider work is to be done'.[142]

Alterations of institutional and physical structures needed to be matched by changes in missionary lifestyles and especially social and business relationships. Critics such as E. R. Hughes felt that in the past these had militated against the opportunity for close and intimate relations.[143] Tea at meetings of the Senate of the West China Union University at Chengdu was, from 1927, 'served by one Chinese and one foreigner. Chinese tea and pastry are served, and one foreign cake.' In 1931 the All-China Conference on Religious Education delegates, for the first time, did not divide on racial lines and eat separately.[144] Such measures do seem to have reflected or encouraged changes in patterns of social behaviour at such institutions as colleges and hospitals. Social relations were never without problems raised by cultural differences, but greater efforts had to be made.

This informal equality in relations was accompanied and confirmed by a sinification of the language of mission work. Obviously, the translation of Christian texts and proselytisation were central to the mission enterprise, and had been since the first British missionary, Robert Morrison, published his pioneering Chinese dictionary (1815–23). But British missions functioned in English, and seemed to have made too few attempts to function in Chinese. Mission councils and institutions voted to provide Chinese language minutes of their meetings after 1927 – and Morrison's society, the LMS, also adopted regularised official Chinese names for its constituent bodies for the first time.[145] The 1921 Nurses' Association of China conference 'consisted almost exclusively of foreign nurses, and English was the only language spoken, except for half a day (of the week) when Chinese was spoken'. By 1930, with a majority of Chinese members, Mandarin was on a par with English.[146] Such was the sensitivity of this issue that at the 1929 NCC conference there were 'signs of revolt' by delegates 'at the apparent 'English language' domination of the report and findings, although the NCC was officially bilingual and Chinese texts of minutes were authoritative.[147]

Missionaries needed to redefine their relationship with their Chinese colleagues. The key elements of this relationship were their subordination to the Chinese Church, a new emphasis on racial equality (and thereby on 'colleagueship'[148]) and a de-emphasising of the essential foreignness of missions. The only way that could be done was to subordinate evangelisation to Chinese bodies and personnel. The new relationship raised practical difficulties. Indigenisation of control meant accelerating the employment of more Chinese in evangelical and pastoral positions. The CMS set up a new theological college for that reason in 1930, but Chinese evangelists were in short supply. Evangelical work was considered by the Chinese a socially demeaning occupation, and paid too little, whilst graduates were 'seriously out of touch with the kind of congregation to which they would be expected to minister'.[149] This was a corollary of the usual problem faced by the missions, a problem that was growing more acute. The Chinese doctors and nurses they trained, and the graduates of their universities and theological colleges, were more likely to take work in China's urban centres than work for little remuneration for the missions. Theologically dedicated Chinese graduates were also more likely to prefer educational positions or to seek work with union organisations such as the NCC or the Chinese YMCA.

Old ways persisted. No amount of subordination to the Chinese Church, or integration with Chinese colleagues, circumvented the need most Britons felt for the company of their fellow nationals and, more important, the preference they felt for working with their fellow nationals. Certainly they were never allowed to forget their foreignness. There were continued anti-foreign demonstrations or incidents in many places. At times of wider crisis, such as the general evacuation or the Nanjing incident, they were all British, and all foreign, together; and they were all, of course, still protected by extraterritoriality.

### Intellectual assessment of the Chinese market

The historical legacy of the opposition of the Chinese intelligentsia to Christianity was the focusing of missionary efforts on the countryside and the poor until the beginning of the twentieth century. This left the Churches unable to tap into the intellectual ferment in China's education represented by the May Fourth Movement (or to counter its hostility robustly) or into the new world of the Chinese bourgeoisie.[150] An appeal to the educated Chinese could be conducted only through Christian literature in Chinese, but previous efforts to produce Chinese books were considered too narrowly didactic and lacking an awareness of 'modern thinking and perplexities'. The Christian Literature Society (CLS) was felt to have failed to produce a literature 'in Chinese with proper Chinese cultural background' which would appeal to these groups. In 1931 it was even claimed 'that the imprint of the CLS is almost sufficient to kill the sale of a book'.[151] Transferring the management to a Chinese board was one suggestion for dealing with the similar problems of the Religious Tract Society, but content, not management, was the problem. Literary work required that closer investigation and understanding of Chinese culture and society which E. R. Hughes felt the mission body had historically neglected. He and others set out to remedy the situation by working with the Chinese YMCA to create acceptable Chinese works in a Chinese style. Karl Reichelt's mission to the Buddhists, which did much to alter previously hostile Western images of that religion, also set out to enlighten foreign missionaries. Having attended a series of lectures, William Sewell agreed with those who said, 'if only they had known of these things before they would never have been so destructive in their approach to Buddhism'.[152] As the next chapter will show, this turn towards seriously understanding the basic tenets of Chinese culture was part of a broader turn in Sino-British cultural relations, one which embraced Chinese philosophy, art, drama and even music.

Reaching an accommodation with indigenous customs and religion was also a prominent new theme, as it had been since the first Jesuit missions and the 'rites controversy'. Old-fashioned missionaries would still dismiss Confucianism as 'backward looking and uninspiring' and Buddhism as 'world-weary' or 'a terrible admixture of devil worship, priestcraft, and empty ritual', but more liberal individuals realised the essential need for a sinicised Christianity. A liberal like Hughes might make his own informal but symbolic personal pilgrimage to Qufu, birthplace of Confucius, in 1931, but the difficulties posed by the tenacity of local custom had to be faced rather more pragmatically.[153] Hostility to converts continuing to participate in customs central to Chinese cultural practice, which served at times to divorce Chinese Christians from their communities, had sometimes had disastrous results – the rural conflict which fuelled the Boxer events, for example.[154] W. H. Geller of the LMS suggested a special Christian service to be held on the Chinese festival of Qingming, 'giving thanks for Parents, Teachers, Heroes, Patriots and the like', to co-opt some of the strength of such customs. The 'mental attitudes' involved were considered to be of potentially 'great value'. More honestly it was admitted that abolishing the veneration of ancestors constituted 'an obstacle to people desiring to adopt the Christian faith'.[155] It also left missions open to the charge that they cut Chinese Christians off from Chinese national life and deracinated them. The need to make mission work more Chinese also pushed missions to consider how to make the Christianity they propagated less foreign.

In a similar way, BAT and Swire's started their advertising in China with European scenes and figures but soon came to realise that the best way to approach the Chinese market was through Chinese scenes and figures recognisable to Chinese customers.[156] In missions and in businesses there were those who failed to realise the value of sinified packaging of their products, and some who objected on principle. But as patriotic purchasing became an effective political weapon so the indigenisation of the foreign was a necessary part of the process. The contradictions in the concept of a national product have already been identified: most of the goods being advertised as patriotic purchases were in fact foreign products such as cigarettes or matches.[157] Equally problematic, then, was the issue of re-presenting mission activities as Chinese. Much of this reform of presentation grew out of the wider trends in mission thinking represented by the 1928 Jerusalem Meeting and the ongoing debate about indigenisation. In general, however, it represented another facet of the dismantling of the uncompromisingly Western characteristics of missions and their churches. It signalled a change in attitude from the contemptuous dismissal symbolised by The Christian Occupation of China to a greater understanding of the integrity of Chinese custom and culture.

The other great shift in mission work was dictated by the economic plight of the Chinese peasant, which led some societies to commit workers and funds to 'social' goals, such as the rural reconstruction experiments of James Yen at Dingxian, and the investigation surveys of John Lossing Buck (initially of the American Presbyterian Mission,

North) and his co-workers at Nanjing. This activity was accompanied by work with those caught up in China's industrial centres, such as that of Joseph Bailie (whose activities were to inspire Rewi Alley) and Dame Adelaide Anderson and others dealing with industrial conditions in Shanghai. Both these themes were debated over and over again in the *Chinese Recorder*, which devoted much space to the Social Gospel view, the importance of which also reflected the interest taken in it by Chinese organisations such as the Chinese YMCA and the NCC and, it was felt, by Chinese students in general. These experiments also brought missions into a closer relationship with the National government as it debated its own rural reconstruction programmes.[158]

The result of this sinification was that missionaries found themselves generally working with, rather than over, Chinese Christians – in union organisations, in churches and in mission institutions, and listening at last, rather than dictating, to them. The change was not easy for some to make, and Chinese were often portrayed as being unready for new responsibilities and insecure in their new posts. Nevertheless many missionaries found the new situation satisfying. Although mission societies, by continuing to exist, still in fact kept the financial structures and the nature of their mission intact, the character of the mission enterprise had been changed drastically by the middle of the 1930s. The old institutionalised paternalism was in terminal decline, and missionaries found themselves having to learn how 'to serve and not to rule' the Chinese Church.[159]

## Conclusion

Passports aside, in no other sense was the British presence in China more homogeneous than in the field of the attitudes and demands of treaty port culture, which danced to a settler tune, and which reached its fullest and most complacent state in the early republican period. If the pervasiveness of that culture made it difficult for later commentators to differentiate adequately the competing and disparate interests which actually operated under the flag in China, it is clear that the inter-war emergency the British faced saw missions and an important section of the British commercial presence break away and restate their separate identity. Staying on meant changing: contemporary Chinese observers saw little to differentiate the sectors of the British presence. A developing discourse of anti-imperialism tarred all sectors of the foreign presence with the same brush. During the most severe crises Chinese Christians demanded that their mission colleagues should distance themselves from 'imperialism'. But the greater shift was more oblique. The engine of change was the desire to continue operating in the new nationalist China, but there was a threat posed also to businesses by commercial competitors, and changing markets, and to missions by intellectual change in China and the West, and shrinking financial resources. And among these dynamic sectors of the British presence there was recognition that settler certainties were poisoning their operations, and their ability to respond flexibly to change.

Across the board in the British presence, the requisite for successful adaptation to nationalism was transformation of some sort into a hybrid Sino-foreign organisation. The essential flexibility and dynamism of operators on the China coast after 1842 was grounded on co-operation and collaboration with Chinese to take full advantage of the opportunities opened up by extraterritoriality and the treaty port system. Lulled though they were into complacency in the early years of the republic, this theme re-emerged as central to those acting in the changing environment in China. Settlers went through the motions, as chapter 4 showed, but their own power and existence was predicated on the maintenance of apartness, and on the restriction of Chinese – and any non-British access – to meaningful power in the institutions they dominated. And, as we have seen, while British diplomats encouraged businesses to adopt new policies, and collaborate with Chinese, their attitude to the settlers was hostile. For both the mission and the business sectors of the British presence, effective collaboration and the transfer of power or responsibility to Chinese was a more efficient use of personnel, and for missions it was also a refocusing of energies towards the true aims of the enterprise – planting self-propagating churches.

The political emergencies coincided with the entry of new types of firm and the growth into the China market, or the expansion of the work of new types of international organisation. Companies like ICI and CPA had little interest in maintaining the settler establishment, while the dictates of the market ensured that they set out from the start to operate as effectively as possible in an extremely competitive environment. Maximising their links with politicians and senior business figures made sound business sense, while integrating themselves into the Chinese scene as far as was possible through Chinese personnel or collaborators was a logical necessity. Companies like Swire's, operating in China since the late 1860s, set out to prevent themselves being pushed out of the Chinese market. To that end they started operating more as local players than as foreign companies, and, conversely, as transnationals in internal culture and character rather than solely British.

The importance of the culture of semi-colonialism to the Sino-

British imbroglio in the 1920s comes through clearly, in the strategies adopted by those sectors of Britain in China which were determined to stay on in China, and which stood a good chance of being able to do so. The placing of the compradore's desk in the Shanghai office, the dining patterns of conferencing Chinese and British mission workers, the facilities offered the Chinese wallet on the British steamship: these were all important areas in which the affected colonialism of the British presence was renegotiated. We have also seen how some treaty port elements resisted such changes, or were ambivalent about them. Despite some resistance, with encouragement from British diplomats, and prompted also by the market, institutions which benefited from informal empire effectively embarked on the decolonisation of their own structures, personnel and practices, and also of such intangibles as social relations and attitudes. When Oxford graduate M. W. Scott arrived in Hong Kong in 1934 to work for Swire's he was met at the quayside not by fellow Britons from the Butterfield & Swire office, nor by the sight of 'sinister' coolies at work, but by one of the newly trained, British-educated Chinese assistants, J. C. L. Wong. Scott's introduction to his new job came in a meeting as an equal with a Chinese colleague – who promptly took him out for a 'chop stick meal'.[160] The forging of a new relationship with a nationalistic post-colonial China did not simply stem from Foreign Office memoranda and treaty renegotiation. Chapter 4 laid stress on the activities of the British state as it set about dismantling settler power; for their part the firms and institutions set about creating a new culture of Sino-British interaction. The final aim was that young men and women setting out for China in the 1930s might be better educated and better prepared for dealing with China and Chinese. Most important, the culture into which they would be socialised would be less antagonistic towards China and the Chinese, less separated from them, and more integrated into the China they would be working in. In one clear sense, such British institutions had started to decolonialise themselves.

## Notes

1  *The Economist*, 4 May 1996, 81; Osterhammel, 'Imperialism in Transition', 284.
2  B. R. Tomlinson, 'Colonial Firms and the Decline of Colonialism in Eastern India 1914–47', *Modern Asian Studies*, 15 (1981), 455–86.
3  Claude Markovits, *Indian Business and Nationalist Politics, 1931–1939: The Indigenous Capitalist Class and the Rise of the Congress Party* (Cambridge, 1985), 62–3.
4  S. E. Stockwell, 'Political Strategies of British Business during Decolonisation: The Case of the Gold Coast/Ghana, 1945–57', *Journal of Imperial and Commonwealth History*, 23 (1995), 277–300; Nicholas J. White, *Business, Government, and the End of Empire: Malaya, 1942–1957* (Kuala Lumpur, 1996).
5  Geoffrey Jones, *British Multinational Banking* (Oxford, 1993), 391.

6 ST – 13, p. 35; SP, JSS III 2/10, BSS to JSL, 24 April 1931; *NCH*, 30 June 1928, 564, 30 June 1928, 564.
7 SP, JSS III 2/7, JSL to BSS, 15 June 1928, BSS to JSL, 10 August 1928 and encs.
8 SP, JSS III 2/7, BSS to JSL, 3 August 1928.
9 SP, JSS III 2/9, BSS to JSL, 10 January 1930.
10 R. P. T. Davenport-Hines, 'The British Engineers' Association and Markets in China, 1900–1930', in R. P. T. Davenport-Hines, ed., *Markets and Bagmen: Studies in the History of Marketing and British Industrial Performance, 1830–1939* (Aldershot, 1986), 102–30.
11 DOT, *Report of the British Economic Mission to the Far East, 1930–31* (London, 1931), 10, 55–6; W. J. Reader, *Imperial Chemical Industries: A History*, I, *The Forerunners, 1870–1926* (London, 1970), 341; Sherman Cochran, *Big Business in China: Sino-foreign Rivalry in the Cigarette Industry, 1890–1930* (Cambridge MA, 1980); Patrick Brodie, *Crescent over Cathay: China and I.C.I., 1898–1956* (Hong Kong, 1990), 97–8, 106–9; Thomas, 'Foreign Office and the Business Lobby', 331.
12 Mizoguchi Toshiyuki, 'The Changing Pattern of Sino-Japanese Trade, 1884–1937', in Duus, Myers and Peattie, eds, *Japanese Informal Empire in China*, 10–30.
13 Feuerwerker, *Foreign Establishment in China*, 17; W. C. Kirby, *Germany and Republican China* (Stanford CA, 1984), 24.
14 Brodie, *Crescent*, 76–87; Cochran, *Big Business, passim*; Zhang Zhongli, 'The Development of Chinese National Capital in the 1920s', in Tim Wright, ed., *The Chinese Economy in the Early Twentieth Century* (Basingstoke, 1992), 44–57.
15 James Reardon-Anderson, *The Study of Change: Chemistry in China, 1840–1949* (Cambridge, 1991), 279; Robert A. Kapp, 'Chunking as a Center of Warlord Power, 1926–1937', in M. Elvin and G. W. Skinner, eds, *The Chinese City between Two Worlds* (Stanford CA, 1974), 150–2.
16 DOT, 1931 33, 27.
17 Parks M. Coble, *The Shanghai Capitalists and the Nanking Government, 1927–37* (Cambridge MA, 1986), 13–18; David Faure, 'The Chinese Bourgeoisie Reconsidered: Business Structure, Political Status and the Emergence of Social Class', unpublished paper (1997).
18 PRO, FO 228/4280/39 67x, Lampson to Sir E. F. Crowe (DOT), 20 October 1930.
19 Tomlinson, 'British Business in India', 107.
20 C. F. Remer, *A Study of Chinese Boycotts, with Special Reference to their Economic Effectiveness* (Taibei edition, 1966), 118–36, 218–31; Cochran, *Big Business*; Virgil Kit-yiu Ho, 'The Limits of Hatred. Popular Attitudes towards the West in Republican Canton', *East Asian History*, 2 (1991), 87–104; Carlton Benson, '"Consumers are also Soldiers": Subversive Songs from Nanjing road during the New Life Movement', paper presented at the seminar on 'Inventing Nanjing Road: Consumer Culture in Shanghai, 1864–1949', Cornell University, July 1995, 13–45, citation from 32.
21 This paragraph is based on Sheila Marriner and Francis E. Hyde, *The Senior: John Samuel Swire, 1825–98: Management in Far Eastern Shipping Trades* (Liverpool, 1967).
22 SP, JSS II 2/7, BSS to JSL, 9 March 1928, and *ibid.*, 25 May 1928.
23 SA, Misc APP 1, N. S. Brown to JSL, 22 August 1900; PRO, FO 228/4273/24 63, Minute by A. F. Aveling on Shanghai S/O, 30 October 1930; FO 228/4283/6 69b, Shanghai No. 18, 3 February 1930.
24 *Xiandai Shanghai dashiji, 1919–49* (Chronology of Contemporary Shanghai, 1919–49) (Shanghai, 1996), 1064–8; Henriot, *Shanghai*, 52–4, 58–62.
25 SP, JSS II 2/7, JSL to BSS/HK, 23 September 1928.
26 SP, ADD 15, H. W. Robertson to G. W. Swire, 11 January 1929; G. W. Swire, letter extract, 15 February 1929.
27 Imperial Chemical Industries, London, Papers relating to ICI (China), 1927–31 (hereafter ICI), ICHO/REP/0486, 'The Possibilities of Chemical Manufacture in China and the Prospects of ICI Participation Therein', I, General considerations' J. W. Gibb, May 1931; Brodie, *Crescent*, 187–8.

28  BOE, OV104/27, 'Interview with Major A. Barker' with the Governor (Montagu Norman), 3 June 1929.
29  SP, JSS II 2/7, JSL to BS Hong Kong (hereafter BSHK) and BSS, 11 May 1928.
30  SP, ADD 15, G. W. Swire to J. K. Swire, 2 May 1930.
31  Bodleian Library, Oxford, E. J. Nathan Papers (hereafter Nathan papers), E. J. Nathan to P. C. Young 15, 24 July 1929.
32  *The Pipeline*, 18 March 1931, 99.
33  SP, JSS II 2/7, JSL to BSHK and BSS, 11 May 1928.
34  Lampson Diaries, 27 March 1931.
35  Nathan papers, E. J. Nathan to P. C. Young, 24 July 1929; SP, ADD 15, J. K. Swire to N. S. Brown, 19 March 1930, 16 June 1930, and enc.
36  Reynolds, 'Training Young China Hands', in Duus, Myers and Peattie, eds, *Japanese Informal Empire in China*, 210–71.
37  SP, ADD 15, J. K. Swire to JSL, 5 June 1925.
38  SP, JSS II 2/7, JSL to BSS, 13 April 1928; JSS II 2/6, JSL to BSS, 16 December 1927.
39  SA, Misc. architectural letters, G. W. Swire, 22 March 1929.
40  SP, JSS II 2/7, JSL to BS HK and BSS, 11 May 1928; ADD 15, G. W. Swire to J. K. Swire, 8 February 1929.
41  King, *History*, III, 352; SA, Misc 96/9, C. C. Roberts, 'Chinese Staff Report', 31 March 1934.
42  Jerry L. S. Wang, 'The Profitability of Anglo-Chinese Trade, 1861–1913', *Business History*, 35 (1993), 43–4, 65.
43  Peter Duus, introduction to 'Trade and Investment', in Duus, Myers and Peattie, *Japanese Informal Empire in China*, 8.
44  SP, JSS III 2/7, JSL to BSS/HK, 27 April 1928; JSS XI 1/6, Alfred Holt & Co. to JSL, 5 April 1928 and encs.
45  SP, ADD 15, G. W. Swire to C. C. Scott, 31 January 1929, J. K. Swire to G. W. Swire, 10 May 1930.
46  SA, Misc 96/9, C. C. Roberts, 'Chinese Staff Report', 31 March 1934.
47  ST – 16, p. 25.
48  SP, JSS II 2/10, BSS to JSL, 2 October 1931; JSS II 2/9, BSHK to JSL, 5 September 1930.
49  SP, JSS III 2/8, JSL to BSS, 9 August 1929; *Directory of China and Japan*, 1932.
50  SP, JSS II 2/7, marginal notation on BSS to JSL, 2 March 1928; on obstructionists see ADD 15, G. W. Swire to JSL, [February] 1929.
51  SP, JSS I 3/6, C. C. Scott to JSS, 19 June 1931.
52  SP, ADD 15, J. K. Swire to JSL, 20 May 1930, and 5 June 1925.
53  SP, ADD 15, J. K. Swire to JSL, 3 March 1930.
54  SA, Misc 96/9, C. C. Roberts, 'Chinese Staff Report', 31 March 1934.
55  White, *Business, Government and the End of Empire*, 243–9.
56  George Philip, *The Log of the Shanghai Pilot Service, 1831–1932* (Shanghai, 1932), 185, VI.
57  Cochran, *Big Business*, 22–40, 134, 165, 193, 213.
58  SP, JSS XI 1/6, H. W. Robertson to Alfred Holt & Co., 9 October 1928; Philip, *Log of the Shanghai Pilot Service*, 185, VI; Reardon-Anderson, *Study of Change*, 177–85.
59  Porter, *Industrial Reformers*, 98–121; SP, ADD 15, G. W. Swire to JSL, 17 May 1929.
60  Tim Wright, *Coal Mining in China's Economy and Society, 1895–1937* (Cambridge, 1984), 131.
61  SP, ADD 19, BSHK to JSL, 17 July 1928; ST – 13, p. 37; SP, JSS II 2/10, BSS to JSL, 9 October 1931; JSS III 2/9, BSS to JSL, 2 May 1930.
62  See the comments on two young engineers in SP, JSS II 2/7, JSL to BSS, 10 February 1928; JSS II 2/8, BSS to JSL, enc. BSHK to Alfred Holt & Co., 25 January 1929; ADD 15, G. W. Swire to JSS, 11 January 1929.
63  This paragraph is based on T. J. Lindsay, 'Organisation and Development of the Chinese Staff to 1941', and chapters 7–9 of Lindsay, 'No Mountains: Life in China and work in Taikoo (Butterfield & Swire) from March 1935 to February 1949', unpublished Ms.; biographical materials on G. F. Andrew, both in SA.
64  SP, ADD 15, JSL to BSS and Hongkong, 1 May 1925.

65 DOT, *1933*, 11.
66 Wright, *Coal Mining*, 128–31; Brodie, *Crescent*, 80; Cochran, *Big Business*, 78–81.
67 On Wanxian see Chapman, *Chinese Revolution*, 112–13; PRO, FO 228/4273/15 63, Memo by A. F. George, 'Proposed Anglo-Chinese Shipping Concern', 9 April 1930; the four companies were CNCo, Jardine's Indo-China Steam Navigation Company, the China Merchants and the Japanese Nippon Kissen Kaisha. FO 228/4273/15 63, 'On proposed Anglo-Chinese S.S. Co.', 7 February 1930.
68 Lampson Diaries, 11 October 1928.
69 SP, JSS II 2/9, BSS to JSL, 11 June 1930; JSS II 2/10, BSS to JSL, 25 July 1930, BSS to JSL, 27 February 1931, BSS to JSL, 8 May 1931.
70 SP, JSS III 2/7, BSS to JSL, 14 September 1928. Lampson Diaries, 21 February 1931.
71 ICI ICHO/REP/0486, 'The Possibilities of Chemical Manufacture in China'; Brodie, *Crescent*, 87–91.
72 Lampson Diaries, 27 March 1931. On the difficulties raised by the National government's economic and tariff policies for ICI see Reardon-Anderson, *Study of Change*, 278–85.
73 Grover Clark, *Economic Rivalries in China* (New Haven CT, 1932), 76–7; Thomas, *Vanished China*, 156–63.
74 HSB, LOH I 103.248 66/181, A. B. Lowson to V. N. Grayburn, 28 October 1930, enc., Brown to Lowson, 21 October 1930; King, *History*, III, 362.
75 Zhang and Chen, *Shasun jituan zai jiu Zhongguo*, 103–6; *Finance and Commerce*, 3 January 1934, back cover; *Finance and Commerce*, 10 January 1934, front cover.
76 Jones, *Shanghai and Tientsin*, 33.
77 SP, JSS III 2/7, JSL to BSS, 21 September 1928.
78 SP, JSS III 2/11, BSS to JSL, 24 April 1931; JSS III 2/9, BSS to JSL, 18 April 1930.
79 Tomlinson, 'British Business in India', 100–4.
80 Henry Clay, *Report on the Position of the English Cotton Industry* (n.l., 1931), 42; Kang Chao, *The Development of Cotton Textile Production in China* (Cambridge MA, 1977), 97.
81 Peter Duus, 'Zaikabo: Japanese Cotton Mills in China, 1895–1937', in Duus, Myers and Peattie, eds, *Japanese Informal Empire in China*, 88.
82 A. J. Robertson, 'Lancashire and the Rise of Japan, 1910–1937', *Business History*, 32 (1990), 87–105; Clemens Wurm, *Business, Politics and International Relations: Steel, Cotton and International Cartels in British Politics, 1924–1939* (Cambridge, 1993).
83 Manchester City Library and Archives, M75, Papers of the Calico Printers' Association (hereafter CPA), Minute Book 14, 1 December 1931, 7 March 1932.
84 CPA Minute Book 18, 30 April 1935, 10 September 1935.
85 CPA Minute Book 14, 19 April 1932; Steve Smith, 'Workers and Supervisors: St Petersburg 1906–1917 and Shanghai 1895–1927', *Past and Present*, 139 (1993), 155–73; Jean Chesneaux, *The Chinese Labour Movement, 1919–1927* (Stanford CA, 1968), 57–64.
86 CPA Correspondence, 18, Hargreaves to Lee, 9, 28 March 1937; Alain Roux, *Le Shanghai ouvrier des années trente: coolies, gangsters et syndicalistes* (Paris, 1993), 148.
87 CPA Minute Book 14, 23 August 1932; Minute Book 15, 31 March 1933; Minute Book 23, 4 October 1938; Geoffrey Turnbull, *A History of the Calico Printing Industry of Great Britain* (Altrincham, 1951), 248–9.
88 CPA Minute Book 20, 11 August 1936; Correspondence, 18, Hargreaves to Lee, 8 April 1937.
89 Brodie, *Crescent*, 186.
90 SP, JSS II 2/7, JSL to BSS and Hong Kong, 11 May 1928 (and encs); JSS III 2/7, BSS to JSL, 21 December 1928 and encs.
91 H. G. W. Woodhead, *The Yangtsze and its Problems* (Shanghai, 1931), 147.
92 See also the analysis of merchant co-operation in Sichuan with the Chongqing warlord, Liu Xiang, in Kapp, 'Chunking as a Center of Warlord Power', 158–9; Cochran, *Big Business* , 218.

93 William C. Kirby, 'China Unincorporated: Company Law and Business Enterprise in Twentieth Century China', *Journal of Asian Studies*, 54 (1995), 43–63.

94 Bickers, 'Colony's Shifting Position in the British Informal Empire', 54.

95 William D. Wray, 'Japan's Big-Three Service Enterprises in China, 1896–1936', in Duus, Myers and Peattie, eds, *Japanese Informal Empire in China*, 54–6.

96 SP, ADD 16, J. S. Scott to G. W. Swire, 10 December 1932.

97 As 'Lin Shao Yang' in *A Chinese Appeal to Christendom concerning Christian Missions* (London, 1911) and under his own name in *Letters to a Missionary* (London, 1918).

98 LMS China Fukien, Box 15, E. R. Hughes to F. H. Hawkins, 8 February 1929. For a scholarly examination of the theme see Brian Stanley, *The Bible and the Flag: Protestant Missions and British Imperialism in the Nineteenth and Twentieth Centuries* (Leicester, 1990).

99 *CCYB 1925*, 51–60, 269; *CCYB 1926*, 225–6. On the anti-Christian movements see Ka-che Yip, *Religion, Nationalism and Chinese Students: The Anti-Christian Movement of 1922–27* (Bellingham WA, 1980), and Jessie Gregory Lutz, *Chinese Politics and Christian Missions: The Anti-Christian Movements of 1920–28* (Notre Dame IN, 1988).

100 *CCYB 1929*, 252–3.

101 Gordon Hewitt, *The Problems of Success: A History of the Church Missionary Society, 1910–1942*, I (London, 1971), 481, 485.

102 LMS NC Box 28, W. F. Dawson to F. H. Hawkins, 22 January 1931; Shirley Garrett, 'The Chambers of Commerce and the YMCA', in Elvin and Skinner, eds, *Chinese City between Two Worlds*, 237.

103 *China's Millions*, August 1927, 128; December 1927, 180, 189; June 1928, 94; SOAS Library, Ms. 380302/2, Mann papers, Ebenezer Mann, 'News Letters from China, 1926–1938' September 1927, 520–1.

104 Regents Park College, Oxford, Angus Library, Baptist Missionary Society Archives (hereafter BMSA), *BMS Annual Report … 1929*, 14.

105 See *Report by Mr. F. H. Hawkins on his Visit to China as special Deputation from the Directors* (London, 1928) and W. Parker Gray and C. E. Wilson [BMS], *Report of a Visit to China, 1929*, both in SOAS, Council of British Missionary Societies papers (hereafter CBMS) E/T/China 15, Mission reports, and the file on the Quakers' 'China Deputation, 1929–30', FSC CH/10.

106 F. Rawlinson, ed., *The Chinese Church as Revealed in the National Christian Conference … 1922* (Shanghai, 1922), 30–40; Latourette, *History of Christian Missions*, 796–98.

107 CIM, London Council Minutes, Vol. 15, 1 February 1928; *China's Millions*, July 1931, 120.

108 Hewitt, *Problems of Success*, II, 219, 225, 280, 286.

109 WMMSA Hupeh fiche 387, H. B. Rattenbury to C. W. Andrews, 23 December 1927, Andrews to Rattenbury, 24 January 1928; Hupeh fiche 388, Andrews to Rattenbury, 14 February 1928.

110 Hewitt, *Problems of Success*, I, 286, 224–6.

111 CIM, London Council Minutes, Vol. 16, 2 January 1929; EPMA Lingtung Swatow box 44, H. F. Wallace to Maclagan, 30 June 1927.

112 EPMA Hakka Box 28, 'Wukingfu Girls' School Report for 1931'; South Fukien Box 19, H. M. Moncrief to Maclagan, 11 September 1928.

113 LMS CC Box 44, Geller to F. H. Hawkins, 22 July 1927.

114 *CCYB 1928*, 72; *1929*, 225; Hewitt, *Problems of Success*, II, 215; *Nurses' Association of China: Report of Conference 1928* (Shanghai, 1928), 18; *Educational Review*, April 1928, 220, October 1931, 517.

115 LMS CC Box 43, J. L. H. Paterson to F. H. Hawkins, 30 November 1929; SC Box 25, L. K. Rayner to F. H. Hawkins, 6 March 1928, 18 June 1928; CC Box 46, T. C. Brown to F. H. Hawkins, 1 May 1930, CC Box 48, J. L. H. Paterson to F. H. Hawkins, 22 May 1930.

116 WMMSA, Hunan Correspondence fiche 212, W. W. Gibson to C. W. Andrews, 19

December 1927; Hupeh Correspondence fiche 388, H. B. Rattenbury to C. W. Andrews, 27 February 1928; Hupeh Correspondence, fiche 399, H. B. Rattenbury to C. W. Andrews, 17 September 1929; SC Correspondence, fiche 576, C. W. Andrews to Edgar Dewstoe, 27 March 1928; Hupeh Correspondence fiche 389, H. B. Rattenbury to C. W. Andrews, 28 March 1928.

117 CIM, London Council Minutes, 9 May, 14 November 1928.

118 A. J. Austin, *Saving China: Canadian Missionaries in the Middle Kingdom, 1888–1959* (Toronto, 1986), 219–20; *CCYB 1928*, 114–15; C. L. Boynton and C. D. Boynton, eds, *1936 Handbook of the Christian Movement in China under Protestant Auspices* (Shanghai, 1936), ix.

119 Leslie T. Lyall, *A Passion for the Impossible: The China Inland Mission, 1865–1965* (London, 1965), 100–2; *China's Millions*, 15 March 1929.

120 Dr and Mrs Hudson Taylor, *Hudson Taylor and the China Inland Mission* (London, 1920), 381.

121 LMS CC Box 44, Mabel L. Geller to F. H. Hawkins, 6 December 1929, W. I. Coxon to F. H. Hawkins, 10 December 1929; LMS Candidates Papers, Box 32. In fact to Geller's horror he was sent to India, where the 'need for cultured gentlemen' was even greater, although in 1930 his service with the LMS ended; Norman Goodall, *A History of the London Missionary Society, 1895–1945* (London, 1954), 620.

122 BMSA China Sub-committee Minutes, Vol. 10, 20 July 1928.

123 E. H. Clayton, 'The Place of the Foreigner in Secondary Schools', *Educational Review*, January 1928, 41; LMS China Fukien Box 16, L. G. Philips to F. H. Hawkins, 13 July 1931, enc. 'Minutes of Fukien District Committee, July 1931'.

124 WMMSA, *Visitation of the Work of the Wesleyan Methodist Missionary Society in China, 1920. Report of the Deputation*, [London, 1920], 33.

125 LMS CC Box 42, T. Cocker Brown to F. H. Hawkins, 30 November 1929.

126 LMS NC Box 26, encl. in Thomas Biggin to F. H. Hawkins, 28 October 1928.

127 J. G. Lutz, *China and the Christian Colleges, 1850–1950* (Ithaca NY, 1971), 232–70; E. W. Wallace, 'The Outlook for Christian Education in China', *IRM*, 17 (January 1928), 211; *Educational Review*, January 1928, 6.

128 Lutz, *China and the Christian Colleges*, 255–70.

129 Earl Herbert Cressy, 'Christian Education in 1928', *CCYB 1928*, 270–2; A. L. Warnshuis, 'Changes in Missionary Policies and Methods in China', *IRM*, 17 (April 1928), 312–14; WMMSA SC fiche 204, S. K. Laird, Report, 21 January 1930.

130 LMS CC Box 43, Catherine M. Robertson to F. H. Hawkins, 29 May 1928.

131 CIM, London Council Minutes, Vol. 16, 2 January 1929, 10 December 1930; Williamson, *British Baptists*, 136; SOAS PP MS 16/3, W. G. Sewell, journal letter, 10 July 1928.

132 *The Christian Occupation of China* (Shanghai, 1922), 429–41; EPMA Lingtung Swatow box 38, E. H. Scott, 'First Impressions of the Swatow Hospitals', 17 February 1931; EPMA Lingtung Swatow box 34, H. R. Worth, 'Swatow Women's Hospital Annual Report, 1929'.

133 *Christian Occupation of China*, 429; Harold Balme, *China and Modern Medicine: A Study of Medical Missionary Development* (London, 1921), 201–2; BMSA CH/12, C. H. Wilson, 'China Reports', 16 April 1929.

134 LMS CC Box 11, H. M. Byles, 'Decennial Report, 1930'; EPMA South Fukien Box 12, Maclagan to H. J. P. Anderson, 25 July 1930.

135 EPMA Fukien, South Box 12, 'Inter-council Conference, 8–12 February 1932'.

136 EPMA Lingtung Swatow Box 34, 'Inter-council Conference on Mission Work, 17–20 November, 1928'; Box 38, Campbell Gibson to Maclagan, 17 November 1931; Box 43b, E. H. Scott letter, 9 October 1930; Fukien, South Box 12, 'Inter-council Conference, February 1932'; LMS CC Box 44, 'Minutes of the Central China District Council, January–February 1928'.

137 WMMSA Hupeh fiche 388, Rattenbury to C. W. Andrews, 14 February 1928.

138 Hewitt, *Problems of Success*, II, 260.

139 H. B. Rattenbury, *Understanding China* (London, 1942), 63. See also Karen Minden, 'The Multiplication of Ourselves: Canadian Medical Missionaries in West China',

in Ruth Hayhoe and Marianne Bastid, eds, *China's Education and the Industrialised World* (Armonk NY, 1987), 139–57.

140 CBMS E/T/China 15, Mission reports, Box 361, Parker Gray and Wilson, *Baptist Mission Society: Report of a Visit to China 1929.*

141 SOAS Sewell papers, PP MS 16/3, W. G. Sewell, journal letter, 5 May 1928.

142 LMS SC Box 25, C. Dixon Cousins to F. H. Hawkins, 25 July 1928.

143 LMS China Fukien Box 15, E. A. Preston to F. H. Hawkins, 5 January 1929, enc. Hughes to Preston, 19 December 1928.

144 FSC CH/5/4, W. G. Sewell, journal letter 4 May 1927; R. Rees, 'All-China Conference on Religious Education', *Educational Review*, October 1931, 377–8.

145 LMS CC Box 42, 'Report of the 19th Annual Meeting of the China Council of the LMS for the Year 1929', 7, in T. Cocker Brown to F. H. Hawkins, 17 April 1929.

146 LMS CC Reports Box 11, Miss Sharpe, 'Annual Report, 1930'.

147 BMSA CH/12, C. E. Wilson, 'China Reports', 20 May 1929; *National Christian Council of China Biennial Report*, 1929–31 (Shanghai, 1931), 129.

148 WMMSA SC fiche 590, A. H. Bray to C. W. Andrews, 11 October 1929.

149 Hewitt, *Problems of Success*, II, 219–20, 281.

150 WMMSA Synod Minutes 1928, fiche 196, John Foster, 'Haigh College Report, Year 1928'; LMS NC Reports Box 10, J. D. Liddell, 'Report for 1928'.

151 WMMSA Hupeh fiche 391, C. W. Andrews to H. B. Rattenbury, 4 January 1929; Hupeh fiche 400, H. B. Rattenbury to A. W. Hooker, 11 February 1930; LMS SC Box 26, A. L. Warnshuis to F. H. Hawkins, 19 June 1931; LMS CC Box 44, C. G. Sparham to F. H. Hawkins, 17 October 1928, enc. David Z. T. Yui [YMCA] to C. G. Sparham, 8 October 1928.

152 WMMSA Hupeh fiche 398, G. A. Clayton to A. W. Hooker, 22 February 1930; LMS CC Reports Box 11, E. R. Hughes, 'Annual Report, 1931–32'; Holmes Welch, *The Buddhist Revival in China* (Cambridge MA, 1968), 238–53; FSC CH5/4, W. G. Sewell, journal letter, 3 September 1927.

153 LMS CC Reports Box 11, 'Report on the Work of F. G. Onley during 1930'; SOAS PP MS 49, Scott papers, Box 3, file 22, F. J. Griffith, 'The Mission to the Mongols, 15 September 1929'; LMS CC Reports Box 11, E. R. Hughes, 'Annual Report, 1931–32'.

154 Roger R. Thompson, 'Twilight of the Gods in the Chinese Countryside: Christians, Confucians, and the Modernising State, 1861–1911', in Daniel H. Bays, ed., *Christianity in China: From the Eighteenth Century to the Present* (Stanford CA, 1996), 53–72.

155 LMS CC Reports Box 11, Geller, 'Decennial report, 1930'; CC Box 46, 'Minutes of the Standing Committee of China Council of the LMS, Hankow, 18, 19, 24 May 1931', in T. Cocker Brown to F. H. Hawkins, 28 May 1931; WMMSA Hupeh fiche 405, H. B. Rattenbury to W. A. Grist, 11 February 1931, enc., *Veneration of Ancestors* ... , 1.

156 Cochran, *Big Business*, 35–8; SP, JSS V 1/2a, JSL to BSHK (Taikoo Sugar Refinery), 26 July 1929.

157 Wen-hsin Yeh, 'Shanghai Modernity: Commerce and Culture in a Republican City', *China Quarterly*, 150 (1997), 389–93.

158 LMS CC Reports Box 11, T. Cocker Brown, Decennial Report 1930; Charles. W. Hayford, *To the People: James Yen and Village China* (New York, 1990); James C. Thomson, Jr, *While China faced West: American Reformers in Nationalist China, 1928–1937* (Cambridge MA, 1969); Porter, *Industrial Reformers*, 98–129.

159 LMS CC Box 43, NCDN, 20 September 1928, 'Present Opportunities for Missionaries in China', enc. in C. G. Sparham to F. H. Hawkins, 21 September 1928.

160 SOAS PP MS 49, Scott papers, Box 1, folder 5, M. W. Scott, letter to parents, 11 February 1934.

# CHAPTER SIX

# After colonialism

Britain in China changed. The cumulative effect of the victory of the diplomats, and the manifold changes in the structures of treaty port life and business, and the even greater changes in the dreams of settlement Shanghailanders and others had hitherto nursed, was the decolonisation of the British presences in China outside Hong Kong. British diplomats surrendered the treaty tools through which they had exercised influence or hampered the freedom of action of the Chinese state. They reduced the geographical scope and powers stemming from the self-aggrandising policies and practices of Britain in China, while nudging its inhabitants to reform, or mend, their private relations with Chinese. After 1927, in short, the British state began reasserting its control over its subjects in China, and transformed the character of the presence operating there under British protection from a mock Raj to a more orthodox, smaller expatriate presence. By the 1930s, for the first time since the end of the East India Company's monopoly in 1834, the state was largely dictating what constituted Sino-British relations. The foundations of the settler presence were fatally and deliberately undermined. At the same time, those sectors of the British presence which were not solely reliant on the treaty system for their continued operations in China set about distancing themselves from it, and drawing up their own compromises with the Chinese state, with the Chinese market and with Chinese popular nationalism.

This study endorses the view of historians who have warned against too simplistic a notion of the power of the treaty system to serve as a tool of foreign interests – for example, those who have argued that the key to successful commercial operations in China was market sensitivity, not treaty power. Quite obviously, China remained a sovereign independent state, and the projection of foreign power into Chinese society was even more limited than the admittedly already limited reach of the Chinese state. Quite obviously, also, for all their noises

[ 219 ]

otherwise, the British communities in China were co-operative Sino-British ventures. Visions of modern Chinese history which solely see the country assaulted and browbeaten by aggressive foreign imperialism serve nationalistic myth-making rather than an understanding of China's tangled relations with the world. But it is also clear that the British-protected establishment that developed under the treaty umbrella served to distort these economic and political realities; not least amongst the British-protected subjects who operated in China, and who themselves developed a semi-autonomous, private enterprise imperialism. The mental world of the treaty system, for Britons, and for Chinese affected by it, was a different, parallel world to that mapped out in the treaties and protected by the diplomats.

The experience of China is in that sense a story of informal imperialism's flexibility, and also its limits. British relations with China (outside the cultural sphere) were mostly set in China itself, and exhibited a broad repertoire of forms: war, treaty, and the military actions and demonstrations which came somewhere in between, as well as the colony, leased territories, concessions and settlements, and, beyond those, extraterritoriality and inland navigation rights. Beyond that too, there was the mind of the settler: bored, lonely salesmen in provincial cities, enterprising real estate developers on treaty port fringes, and the others – jacks of all colonialist trades like J. O. P. Bland – who demonstrated in their actions and attitudes a commitment to a broader British enterprise, empire, and to Britain in China. This repertoire facilitated the operation under the British flag in China, in the treaty ports and beyond, of a wide range of interests and groups. But they operated too, and for too long, beyond the effective reach of the British state. Sino-British relations before the 1930s were hamstrung by a semi-autonomous colonialism which the British state tolerated, but which it was to find reasserting control over somewhat awkward. The breadth and flexibility of informal imperialism were overridden by the dictates of settler interests, and the practices and assumptions that served to protect and to replicate the settler world.

Accounts of the projection of British power into China puzzle over its apparent lack of relative success. Even after dismissing as unhistorical the notion that there was ever a 'grand colonial design', we are still left pondering why China actually remained so relatively untouched, at least until the onset of Japanese expansionism in 1931. The resilience, ultimately, of the Chinese state, and of Chinese society, seems the likeliest explanation for the lack of progress that kept Britons in particular bound to their Bunds. Another explanation argues that the compradore system and the collaborative nature of 'British' enterprise in China served as a buffer – indeed, the treaty ports themselves may be seen as the compradore system writ large. When Warren Swire and his fellow directors complained in the mid to late 1920s that the compradoric structure of their business served to hinder their direct contact with Chinese society and the economy, they add evidence to this analysis. But the picture has another side, as this volume has shown. The British enterprise in China was dominated by settler interests – and the point of the settler enterprise was the Bund itself, not the projection of power farther into China. Britons stayed bound to it because they had property interests there, built manufacturing plants (after 1895), invested in municipal utilities, or worked for treaty port administrations and services. The mental realm of Britain in China of course extended far beyond the formal treaty ports and the informal nodes of the treaty system: settler justifications of the *status quo* centred partly on Shanghai, Tianjin or Hankou acting as 'gateways to China'. But when settlers bleated about the 'Foreign Office school of thought', and the lack of mettle of their representatives in the 1930s, they were condemning lack of support for their own local enterprises. They wanted no forward policy: they had come far enough.

The lack of notable forward progress should also cause us to think about China's basic unimportance to Britain. As long as the treaty system and most-favoured-nation status ensured fair access for British trade, while minor adjustments could be made by diplomats, or grander ones by armed force, China did not tax the energies of the British state. The crisis stemming from the British discovery of the joy of tea in the eighteenth century had led via Macartney to the Opium Wars. But the best part of a century's trade had hardly had an impact on the British economy. Dreams of the China market in the twentieth century did not justify battering away for greater concessions while the scale of British interests was so small, and while they were in long-term decline: the China market for British exports declined overall by 50 per cent from 1871–75 to 1934–38. The comparative lack of economic development was compounded by structural economic changes in Britain's role in the world economy. In particular British trade with the empire greatly increased in importance at the expense of the areas of informal influence such as Latin America and China.[1] Strategic worries prompted the diplomats to demand Weihaiwei in 1898, but they did very little with it – and there was hardly much to it in the first place. They supported the extensions of Kowloon into the New Territories, and of the Shanghai International Settlement and the Tianjin British concession, but hardly as steps on a longer road. Diplomats and statesmen worried about imperial prestige, imperial balances of power, and about Chinese nationalism setting an example of Asian liberation for India or South-east Asia, but they hardly worried overmuch about the China market. And the pretensions of British settlers were tolerated until they became intolerable, and threatened, after May Thirtieth, to queer the China pitch for other British interests.

Nationalistic myth-making can hardly be dismissed; it was fuelled by the impact of Britain in China – the daily indignities of the exercise of foreign power as well as May Thirtieth incidents – as much as by the Japanese assault. Together with the actions of other powers, the British presence served to signify how China was wronged, and to stimulate Chinese nationalism.[2] To take one prominent example, the discriminatory policies practised before 1928 against Chinese in regard to most of the public gardens built by the SMC became a hugely symbolic and resonant icon of colonial racism and imperialist wrong in Shanghai. In the distorted version of the regulations, widely believed but demonstrably untrue, British settlers were accused of erecting an insulting sign reading 'Chinese and dogs not admitted'. As a result, the sign story has become a familiar ingredient in the narratives of nationalistic awakening to be found in Chinese memoirs and histories.[3] Writing in one of many rebuttals of the story, this one issued by settler propagandists in Tianjin who presumably felt tarred by the same brush, Reginald Johnston noted in 1927 that 'it is the kind of slander which takes a lot of killing, and survives even the most authoritative denials'.[4] Indeed, the story continues to live. And Chinese were barred from the parks, by British settlers acting as if they were living as colonists, setting out markers for colonisers' segregation from a subject people. British diplomats set out to disabuse them of this notion after 1927.

Theorists of the imperialism of decolonisation would point out that one interpretation of what happened in China after 1927 was that it was a reconfiguration of British activity, led by the British state and transnational business enterprises, which benefited specific forms of enterprise at the expense of the redundant agency house firms and the old treaty port establishment.[5] In their redefinition of British interests the diplomats turned to boost those sectors which could flexibly adapt to modern nationalism, but which were also more closely connected with the metropole. There is some truth in this picture, the more so because it actually highlights the fact that the interests operating with greatest success in China, and which dominated British policy there until the transformation, were not metropolitan but peripheral settler interests. This survey argues strongly, then, for the irrelevance to China of much of the saga of finance capitalism mapped out by recent revisionism, and other works have reinforced this conclusion when focusing on later periods.[6] The diplomatic reshaping of Sino-British relations in the years before the Pacific War was led by diplomatic imperatives which were concerned with British commercial concerns but also with strategic interests and questions of imperial prestige – it was not prompted by commercial opinion and the China lobbies. And it was designed to deny settler dreams, not to expedite expatriate ambitions.

This book has also been centrally concerned with those settler dreams, and has examined how a colonial culture was developed, maintained and replicated, a process whose singularity is highlighted – and very much more clearly exhibited – by the fact that China was not a colony. The mechanisms familiar from studies of colonial societies in South-east Asia and East Africa were used to protect the British settler community that developed on the China coast. Many of these practices were also rooted in metropolitan attitudes to class, which were partly raced – and, as we have also seen, class distinction and perceptions in old forms and new guises also underpinned the settler establishment. Many of these practices were actually more important in the China context than in formal colonies, as settlers lacked the absolute certainties of formal colonialism – and laws, for example, abetting segregation, or forbidding marriage with indigenous men or women. They also lacked, in the treaty system, an assured, unassailable future. The stridency of the treaty port propagandists, and the rigidity of the practices which preserved British identity from dilution or deterioration, stemmed from the fundamental insecurity of the position of the improvised settlements in China.

Stridency and rigidity also stemmed from the great lie on which Britain in China was founded: the lie that British interests could be at all easily separately isolated and identified as such. Disentangling the share ownership of foreign enterprises, for example, has been shown to make the notion of identifying interests by their nominal nationality questionable; if firms were British-managed, and structured so that control was British, then so they were deemed. Even a company like Swire's effectively admitted in the early 1930s that it lacked control over many aspects of its business: outside its core central administration the real Britishness of Swire's operations remains to be proven. The bulk of the revenue of the SMC, and presumably much investment in it, was provided by the Chinese inhabitants of the International Settlement; the majority of the residents of the settlement were Chinese, and so were the majority of SMC employees. The fictions the treaty system ran on occluded the fact that its beneficiaries were mostly Chinese, who supplied capital, and labour, and who consumed the tangible and intangible advantages offered, from technology transfer, legal frameworks for trade, even forms of political asylum. In the grey zones of multiple imperialisms opened up by the treaty system and most-favoured-nation conventions, and in the networks of informal and formal collaboration between Chinese and the many types of British subject who made up the treaty world, the articulation and preservation of nationality and identity, and the guarding of boundaries, became central features of the settler experience.

Settlers were often driven by their local interests and loyalties to oppose British China policy, but they had to balance antagonism with a need to demonstrate loyalty and utility to the British empire. By the twentieth century the British state was hardly interested in protecting transnational enterprise in China with ships, troops and treaties, and so Britain in China had to demonstrate the Britishness of its enterprise, and did so through practices – stretching from celebrating Empire Day, through sex and marriage taboos, to returning to fight in the World Wars – which preserved that identity. The articulation of settler identity was at all times a matter of balance, and of careful renegotiation in the light of the changing priorities of the British state. Moreover, unlike the Japanese, the British had no forward policy in China, and it was not at all convenient for them to encourage Chinese to take British-protected status, as happened with Amoy Chinese who registered as Taiwanese residents to benefit from extraterritoriality as Japanese *sekimin* ('registered people') in 1898.[7] Sekimin were used to push Japanese interests forward in China, but British diplomats took care, in the twentieth century in particular, to try and divest Eurasians of British nationality, and to deny, or limit, the extension of British nationality to Chinese firms or individuals. British Indians, Parsis in particular, played a prominent role in the early development of Hong Kong and Shanghai, but they were never used as sub-imperialist agents.

There is a strain in the literature on colonial cultures which fails to engage with the reality of the culture of the coloniser, caricaturing its inhabitants, and portraying them, not least, as conscious colonisers, or agents of empire. But this approach distorts the relationship between the periphery and the origins of empire's recruits in the metropole. They arrived in China from all over the British Isles as individual recruits, or through extended family networks, or were hired through press advertisements. There were no regulations through which the British state regulated or encouraged this influx and its development in China. Certainly elsewhere in the empire Britons were offered incentives to emigrate, and to colonise. Japanese schemes encouraged settlement in Manchuria, for example – some 322,000 went between 1932 and 1945 – but there were no such schemes to staff the Chinese Raj.[8] Although British and British-protected subjects took advantage of international treaties, and of locally mediated agreements such as Shanghai or Tianjin land regulations, to construct their new lives and communities, this study would argue for a closer look at the individ-

ual decisions which made it a fundamentally normal aspect of imperial Britain for Britons to leave their home in city or shire to seek a new
life far away. The disjuncture between empire told and empire lived
could be as vast for the coloniser as it was for the colonised.[9]

Modern Britons lived in an empire world, in a world opened up
through empire to temporary or permanent migration. The society of
the coloniser was composed of ordinary Britons, part of the massive
flow of emigrants and sojourners who left the British Isles in the nineteenth and twentieth centuries. These ordinary men and ordinary
women made sense of their surroundings, and made new lives for
themselves, by re-creating the domestic and familiar in foreign contexts and by adopting new attitudes, vocabularies and forms of social
interaction from the imperial repertoire, from India and from South-
east Asia. They mostly remained British, and subjects of the British
empire, but, as Arthur Ransome argued in 1927 of settlers from Britain
in China's capital city 'their primary allegiance is to Shanghai'.[10] On
the periphery these Britons took on new identities, taking advantage,
as individuals of many nationalities did, of the opportunities wittingly
and unwittingly offered by colonialism. 'Ideal pre-fabricated collaborators' (in Ronald Robinson's words) as long as it suited British policy,
they became the 'low-white danger' (in Sir John Pratt's words) when
their usefulness had expired. Moreover the banality of the communities they created, and the practices which maintained them in China,
lies in sharp contrast to the nationalistic anti-imperialism their enterprise gave birth to. The dull, dreary, philistine world of the Briton in
China serves as a miserable culprit for the painted evils of imperialism
and the 'century of national humiliation' it allegedly gave rise to.

This settler culture was located equally in the metropole and on the
periphery, in British society and in treaty port society, on the literal
London stage and on the metaphorical China stage. Late nineteenth
and early twentieth-century Britons grew up in an imperial culture,
and if China was so heavily represented in the heart of the empire, then
how much more integral to the identity and mentality of ordinary
Britons were the sites of formal empire. The index of interest in China
waxed and waned with events there, peaking in 1900, in 1911, in
1925–28 and again in the 1930s, when publishers sought out new
books, or reprinted old ones, and topical villains drew in theatre
crowds and moviegoers. Old stereotypes persisted (and persist), and
new ones settled down beside them, but between the end of World War
I and the Sino-Japanese War, and because of the Nationalist revolution,
a paradigmatic shift in attitudes to China and to Chinese took place in
British culture. The changes, as shown below, continued to be fed by
the changing political situation in East Asia, and are also fed back to

reinforce those very changes. As Britons grew to have a healthier regard for Chinese culture they developed a healthier regard for contemporary China. Britain in China was always intertwined with the world of China in Britain, and the empire of fact was always connected with the empire of mind.

The undoing of the China problem was also partly the work of a disparate group of individually motivated Britons and Americans. They were pragmatists, not idealists, men such as missionary-turned-academic E. R. Hughes, and Swire's (1929–35) Shanghai manager N. S. Brown, who looked at the often rancid state of relations between Chinese and Britons at the height of the crisis of the late 1920s and worked to alter British behaviour and understanding, and to bring Chinese and Britons together. Interest groups certainly had some impact then, but not the formal representative organisations – the China Association or the British Residents' Association. These sectoral lobbies were heard, and were recognised as part of the structure of representation of British interests, but they had little tangible impact. The BRA's strength encouraged the shelving of treaty reform in 1931, but the Japanese invasion of Manchuria was by far the greater catalyst, however settler memories have represented events. In Malaya, Nicholas White has argued, individual power brokers had more impact on policy than institutionalised business interests.[11] Similarly, in China, the greater long-term impact came from looser networks of concerned individuals with some access to diplomats who mostly networked amongst themselves, and with Chinese figures, to restore relations which seemed irreparably ruptured by end of the Nationalist revolution. E. R. Hughes's trajectory took him from orthodox missionary work in Fujian, via attempts to contribute to Sino-foreign interaction on the periphery, to intellectual and other efforts to bring them together in and from the metropole. He became, as I shall show below, one of a group of individuals who worked with, or had worked in, China or were merely interested in it, and who set out to raise British awareness of events in China, and to garner support for China in the face of the Japanese invasions. Just as the impact of individual efforts at empire's birth has been underestimated in the search for focused pressure groups clamouring for sectoral interests, so too their activities at the close of the Chinese Raj have been under-reported.

These conclusions are reinforced by two short surveys of later periods: the years after 1938, one year after the onset of the Sino-Japanese War, and after 1948, one year before the establishment of the PRC. They show how the settler communities and settler certainties continued to unfold in the face and in the aftermath of war, and also how broader shifts in metropolitan British cultural relations with China continued to underpin that change. They also point to the steady shift of balance in the British presence back, for the first time since the 1860s and the rise of Shanghai, to Hong Kong. This reconfiguration of the way British firms, in particular, dealt with the China market was more than a mere function of the communist victory in 1949 or the years of uncertainty during the 1946–49 civil war.[12] It began before the Pacific War, and resolved, at least until the reopening of China after 1978, the question of the rivalry between the cities of Hong Kong and Shanghai. It certainly resolved the tension between informal and formal empire.

## After 1938

Our Briton travelling out to a job in China in the late 1930s, say in 1938, saw it in a different light. Political and cultural changes – in the culture of colonialism, and in British cultural relations with China – primed new recruits in different ways, and the looming question of war with Japan also sharply focused British minds. In 1932 treaty port public opinion, and the settler propagandists, were largely supportive of Japanese activity in Manchuria, and especially in Shanghai. In settler minds the 'concert' of the 'powers' was still functioning to teach China a lesson; like Sir Meyrick Hewlett, they were still spanking the recalcitrant Chinese. By 1938 most settlers realised what others feared in 1931, that Japan's actions were also aimed at sweeping out other foreign interests. Incidents such as the aerial machine-gunning of British ambassador Sir Hughe Knatchbull-Hugessen's car in August 1937, and Japanese attacks on Western naval vessels in December 1937, were seen as deliberate messages.[13] Indeed, support for Japan became an expression of support for an enemy of the British empire, sole remaining protector of British interests in China.

Earlier recruits were taught to see nothing in Chinese political life but hopeless corruption, and fractured provincialism, which could be resolved only under foreign tutelage. In 1938 they would mostly have had no doubt that the Chiang Kai-shek regime was the legitimate government of China – unless their politics were left-leaning, and perhaps influenced by a growing body of information on the activities of the CCP.[14] In the first decade of its existence, responding both to its own ideological underpinnings, but also to the mass cultural nationalism that was increasingly hegemonic in China, the Nanjing government had reasserted China's sovereign status and independence. This process certainly saw no simple roll-back of foreign power, and the Guomindang's anti-imperialism was somewhat ambivalent, as the growing threat of Japan caused it to be wary of alienating other poten-

[ 227 ]

tial supporters. But, even so, the achievements of the administration were significant. Despite the developing civil war with the Chinese Communist Party, and despite Japanese aggression in north China, the regime was largely seen internationally as the legitimate government of China, and the 'unequal treaties', as they were now almost uncritically known, were in the process of revision. In the mind abroad, if not on the ground at home, the Republic of China had at last achieved legitimacy; more important, so had China's nationalism. The Pacific War years would later see an unprecedented and unsurprising barrage of pro-Chinese publications and activity in Britain, mostly geared to supporting the allied regime of Chiang Kai-shek. But there also developed a counter-argument as the war dragged on, fed by reports of the corruption, literal and seemingly moral, of the Chongqing government, that turned to the CCP in particular as offering the best hope for the nation-building and national salvation aims of Chinese popular nationalism. A residual ambivalence on the part of British diplomats about the Guomindang's fitness to represent that nationalism was partly behind the ease with which Britain recognised the PRC in 1949.[15] Nationalism was the force to be reckoned with, not any single party or leader.

There was a also clear sense that Chinese nationalism had been victorious in its propaganda battle with the treaty port establishment to assert its legitimacy as a force in Western eyes. In one sense the old missionary discourse on the 'uplift' of China was partly transmuted, as it became more accepted that Chinese nationalism might and ought to uplift China itself. Bland, Gilbert and the rest were shouted down by the English-language publicists of the new regime, and by its foreign friends. They were still read, and many of the volumes discussed in chapter 2 would still be read, but new voices came to dominate in the 1930s. Some of their older colleagues sang different tunes. H. G. W. Woodhead began the 1930s in solid opposition to the Guomindang regime, and to British diplomatic surrenders of settler interests. He was accused by the authorities of being paid by Japanese interests to put their case, and his publications were barred from the Chinese mails. By the late 1930s his monthly journal *Oriental Affairs* was accused by Japanese interests of being a Chinese-funded vehicle for attacks on them.[16] J. O. P. Bland never recovered his sense of humour, and spent the 1930s fighting a puzzled rearguard action over the authenticity of the key source used in *China under the Empress Dowager*.[17]

While events overtook the established voices the confidence of the propagandists also ebbed. And although the process of treaty and treaty port reform had been dampened by the Manchurian crisis (1931), the

Shanghai incident (1932) and the slow years of Sino-Japanese conflict afterwards, the heart had already been ripped out of Britain in China. A new recruit to the British establishment would still find British-run or dominated municipal councils in Shanghai and Tianjin, and on a smaller scale at Xiamen. The SMC still recruited Britons and despite increased levels of Chinese recruitment the upper echelons of the administration were mostly still British. The public and private institutions that characterised the settler world mostly still existed, but the parks were mixed, Chinese sat on the council, the courts had been returned and National government and Guomindang organs contested the remaining sovereignty of the foreign authorities. After 1932 the SMC also lost effective sovereignty to the Japanese military in the north and east of the International Settlement. After the battle for Shanghai in 1937 these areas were lost for good. British ships still sailed China's inland waters under the shadow of the China station's gunboats, and British troops were still stationed in Shanghai and Tianjin, but this was the normality not of Britain in China's heyday but of the conflict to come.

Britain in China was still recruiting. Britons came out to work for expatriate companies moving into the China market, or for companies already there. Clearly, as the previous chapter showed, the culture of business was changing, and the culture of colonialism too. Our new recruit would probably still keep amongst his own fellow nationals, trying to recreate the familiar to deal with the loneliness and disorientation of expatriation, and led too by the need to find his feet in new employment. But in business, and in the social life of business, the employee of the later 1930s would find himself interacting with more Chinese than his older colleagues would have done, and he would probably be better educated than them, and less instinctively hostile to the new world he found himself in. China also now attracted women and men actively interested in the country, rather than in changing it, or joining Britain in China: Osbert Sitwell, Harold Acton, and William Empson were just some of those who lived in Beijing in the late 1930s. Arthur Waley, the influence of whose own translations and studies was profound, noted this 'great turning point' in Sino-British relations in a wartime essay when discussing Britons who had gone 'not to convert, trade, rule or fight but simply to make friends and learn'.[18]

Shanghai policeman Maurice Tinkler's career partly illustrates some of the changes, and the changing threats to the established British position. Effectively forced into resigning in early 1930, under the harsher post-May Thirtieth reforming regime, Tinkler initially sought a new life in the United States, but returned to Shanghai in late 1933. After a series of low-status jobs he became head of security at the new CPA mill in Shanghai in 1935. Tinkler's treatment of Chinese women workers was part cause of a violent strike which broke out at the plant in May 1939. Coming at a time of increased tension between the Japanese and the British in China, which had led to the stand-off at Tianjin, the strike provided a useful opportunity for ratcheting up anti-British agitation in the city. Hi-jacked by the Japanese-sponsored Daminhui (Great People's Society), despite efforts by striking workers to keep the conflict non-political, the stoppage lasted until late November, when the CPA was forced to pay a hefty sum as a labour guarantee to get its employees back to work. Tinkler himself had been killed by Japanese marines on 5 June, and was buried with pomp and ceremony in a demonstration of sombre solidarity.[19] In London and China British diplomats were shocked and angry at the incident, and protested vigorously to the Japanese. In private they adopted another tone. 'It is a pity so many of our disputes with the Japs are over such very vile bodies,' wrote one retired British consul.[20] So ended Tinkler's dreams. Too late for the old treaty port good times – when 'the foreigner did very little work ... made money easily and spent it easily' – his was a life warped by the colonialism of Britain in China, and by its class, sex and race taboos.[21] He was also one of the first victims of the British war with Japan.

If Britain in China had been changed, where it had not been abolished, China in Britain was also very different. The number of Chinese students had increased markedly. The perception of, and reception of, Chinese culture in the West had also begun a fundamental shift – and again this was further highlighted by the assault of Japanese militarism. The scares about Limehouse of the 1910s and 1920s subsided. Shilling shockers and *exposés* continued to appear, but even Thomas Burke satirised the impact of his own books in a work for children in 1935 (*Billy and Beryl in Chinatown*). Chinese officials and others set about a new kind of cultural diplomacy. British diplomats throughout the nineteenth century had made an issue of Chinese referring to them with the term *Yi*, roughly translated as 'barbarian'. Turning this long-standing grievance around, cinema portrayals of Chinese as uncivilised became the target of the ire of the National government and Chinese abroad. Films of the 1930s set in China drew protests because they concentrated salaciously on aspects of contemporary China that the National government did not wish to see emphasised, such as warlordism in *Shanghai Express* (1932), or dealt with rural poverty – such as *The Good Earth* (1937). Nanjing used its consuls abroad to protest against the distribution of offensive films, while the Chinese consul-general in Los Angeles attempted to intervene before films were shot. 'It is carrying matters rather far to insist that every Chinese appearing on the silver screen must be portrayed with angelic qualities,' protested *Oriental Affairs* in response to an effective official boycott of Paramount movies in late 1936 because of complaints about *The General Died at Dawn*. However, this combination of censorship, fear of losing markets and Nanjing's offers of help in film production in return for a veto over content were the main factors in a pronounced shift towards the angelic.[22] In the 1930s the biggest new impacts on British minds, however, came from young Chinese student and intellectual sojourners in Britain, and from Chinese art.

The Chinese Exhibition at the Royal Academy, Burlington House, London, from 28 November 1935 to 7 March 1936 was the single most important Asian cultural event of the inter-war period in Britain – indeed, internationally – receiving some 420,000 visits (the second most popular winter exhibition of the Academy up to that date). Organised by a committee of experts and collectors led by Sir Percival David, the exhibition drew in some 3,000 pieces from thirty-five countries, including Japan and the United States, but the core of the collection was provided by the Chinese government, which sent some 900 pieces from the Palace Museum collection (which were shipped to Britain by the Royal Navy). The express aim of the Chinese authorities was cultural diplomacy, and the desire to 'make the West appreciate the beauty of Chinese art'.[23] The direct political importance of the exhibition was not lost on British observers, or in fact on the Japanese: the Palace Museum items were in storage in Shanghai to protect them from Japanese actions in north China. The impact was as cultural as political. British visitors saw a wide and integrated selection of ceramics, paintings, sculptures and frescoes, designed to impress upon the observer the richness of Chinese culture, and the 'creative power and inner genius of the Chinese'. But they also learnt, through the wide range of publications and the lecture programme that accompanied the exhibition, of its accessibility to a Western audience.[24] The obvious political conclusion to be drawn was that this was a rich culture, different and geographically distant, but closer to the Western mind than might be thought, one indeed to be subsumed within a broader category of civilisation.

This latter point was reinforced implicitly by the broader turn towards engagement with Chinese culture encouraged by the popularity of writers in English like Lin Yutang and Xiao Qian (Hsiao Ch'ien), and by explicitly pro-Chinese publications such as *China: Body and Soul* (1938), a collection of short essays on Chinese culture and Japanese aggression, but mostly dealing with cultural matters, edited by former missionary E. R. Hughes.

Lin Yutang's *My Country and my People* (1936) was published in the month before the Burlington House exhibition ended. Lin was the son of a Chinese Protestant pastor, and had abandoned seminary training himself, to edit the *China Critic* in Shanghai. An idiosyncratic survey of Chinese life, literature and character, with swipes at 'old China hands', Rodney Gilbert, Woodhead and Arthur H. Smith, *My Country and my People* proved immensely popular. Pearl Buck contributed the introduction, but the success was Lin's, a result of the combination of humour and down-to-earth metaphysics which was designed to make accessible the 'bases' and life of China, and to decry the 'constant, unintelligent elaboration of the Chinaman as a stage fiction' in the works of the treaty port British. The book capped off a bout of British public sinophilia, and in its opening caricature of the 'old China hand' – with a nod to Ransome – dug another nail into the settler coffin.[25] It certainly replaced Smith, or Dyer Ball, as the logical handbook for those going to the country, and Lin followed up this success with *The Importance of Living* (1938) and other works. Xiao Qian spent the years 1939–44 in Britain and his writings and anthologies in English argued for a thorough re-examination of British attitudes towards China and the Chinese. Xiao hoped to 'surprise' his readers into a 'deeper understanding of China'. 'Do you enjoy being distorted?' he asked at the beginning of his corrective to picturesque, missionary and 'Hollywood' distortions, *China: But not Cathay* (1942).[26]

If 1936 had seen significant interest in China in Britain, events after July 1937 showed British and Chinese activists attempting to build on it to garner support in the face of China's crisis. Hughes's volume, published to raise funds for Chinese victims of the conflict, was intended to bring to the reader 'a sense of China as a fact: something, that is, which a man can see in relation to himself, homely, rational, of the nature of flesh and blood, but also of the spiritual order'.[27] The rational was provided by Sir Arthur Salter, a former National government adviser, writing on 'China's new unity', and excerpts from a 1937 League of Nations report on Japanese narcotics activities in occupied China, together with an attack on Japan's 'fascist militarism' by Harold Laski. This was balanced with pieces from Roger Fry and Laurence Binyon on Chinese architecture and painting, Arthur Waley on the Daoist philosopher Zhuangzi, Innes Herdan on Li Bai, and sketches by Hughes and the historian Eileen Power. The rehabilitation of Chinese culture, and of China itself, in the British imagination was moving into the mainstream. Britons, then, were getting a very different view of China in Britain by the end of the 1930s, one mediated by prominent cultural and political figures, many of whom were not directly concerned in their work with China.

But the shift in British attitudes was not just fed by the discovery of the glories of Chinese culture or philosophy. The hegemonic grip of the treaty port propagandists was broken. Lin Yutang waged war against Gilbert and Woodhead; Tang Liangli battled against residual public racism in the English-language *People's Tribune*; E. R. Hughes published a history, *The Invasion of China by the Western World* ('They brought guns, opium, and Bibles, and to sober peace-loving citizens there was no distinction between the three: they were all equally obnoxious and deleterious'[28]); but the most notably influential work was missionary child Pearl Buck's novel *The Good Earth* (1931).[29] Buck made ordinary Chinese people, peasants, real for the first time to the mass Western public. Although her story was written before the Japanese invasions, it could hardly fail to strike deep chords – especially when the news coming out of China after 7 July 1937 laid deep stress on the impact of the invasion on ordinary people, and photography and newsreel film made the scale of the conflict and the unfolding human disaster plain to see. The film of *The Good Earth*, released in 1937 (and produced with National government assistance) can hardly have failed to deepen this impression. Although the battle for Shanghai (August–November 1937) was a severe blow to the Nanjing government, it was played out in easy view of the world's press, and various incidents took place in the International Settlement itself. Notable amongst them – not least because it was immediately fictionalised in an international best-seller – was the bombing of the Cathay Hotel and New World department store which killed some 1,750 people, including twenty-six foreigners, among them Frank Rawlinson, prominent missionary journalist and editor of the *Chinese Recorder*.[30] The informal extraterritoriality which spared foreigners from China's domestic upheavals had ended. Buck's influence was also indicative of the way that the dominant discourse on China in the West was increasingly coming from the United States, and its citizens, rather than from observers of other nations.

Much of this change in attitudes came to a head in the organised agitation in support of China which mushroomed after the outbreak of the war. The most actively political campaigning organisation that developed was the China Campaign Committee, which held its first public rally at the end of September 1937.[31] Formed by a loose coalition of Chinese in Britain, self-described friends of China and left-wing groupings, the committee developed a network of local committees which used a full, imaginative activist repertoire to raise public awareness in Britain about the war in China. It raised money for medical aid, aided the despatch of medical personnel to China, and tried to persuade people to boycott Japanese goods. Demonstrations, exhibitions, publications and lecture tours (including one by Xiao Qian) all drove home the same pro-China message, although it also acted to raise awareness specifically about the CCP. The committee's left-wing flavour (it was mostly staffed by Communist Party members) suited the tenor of the times, which was also heavily influenced by the publication of Edgar Snow's *Red Star over China* by the Left Book Club in October 1937.

The foreign presence in China itself was changing in other ways. Crucially, the dominance of British social practices, and even British English, was being sharply undermined by the growing US presence in China, but also in Shanghai, for example, by the more tangible cosmopolitanism that developed in the city through the 1930s with the influx of Russian refugees from the Japanese occupation of Manchuria, and Jewish refugees from central Europe, but especially as Western-educated Chinese returned to China. Shanghai's developing modernity and commercial culture was specifically not a British modernity, but much more American in character, and fed by Hollywood as much as by 'Americanised' returned students. At the diplomatic level British relations with the Nanjing regime were good – although only the British Leith-Ross mission to reform the Chinese currency in 1935–36 had any significant impact[32] – but the regime was promiscuous in its friendships, building close links with the USSR and Germany, and notably, as conflict with Japan loomed, with the United States.

W. H. Auden and Christopher Isherwood's travelogue *Journey to a War* (1939) indicated how far China was joining a mainstream, and how far events in China were no longer treated as if occurring in a willow-pattern never-never land inhabited by comic opera soldiers. It was partly because there was developing a sense of a global fight against fascism that tied China's struggle against Japan to republican Spain's battle against Franco and his allies. But Auden and Isherwood also twisted the knife into the treaty port world. Their much anthologised description of a Shanghai where the 'tired and lustful businessman will find everything to gratify his desires' bolstered the image of the cosmopolitan city of sin that so undid settler assertions of the wholesomeness of their little world. And in his sonnet 'Hong Kong' ('Here in the East the bankers have erected/A worthy temple to the comic muse') Auden brought a first-class mind quietly to bear on Stella Benson's 'tenth-rate' men.[33]

## After 1948

And if our traveller had gone out to work in China in 1948 he or she would have found an almost total eclipse of the British presence. This was partly a function of the war, as the China theatre was mostly a US-dominated field, despite British efforts to hang on in, and partly a function of civil war, and the economic, political and social crisis that had developed in China. The British, from very early on in the build-up to the Pacific War, had reined themselves back in from Britain in China to Hong Kong, and during the war itself regaining Hong Kong was the main plank of British China policy. But the collapse of the British empire in East and South-east Asia from December 1941 to February 1942 was also a signal disaster for British relations with China, coming as it did after the policy of appeasement to Japan, which had seen the closure of the Burma road from July to October 1940.[34] Questions of imperial prestige had long motivated British diplomats and politicians, as well as individual Britons in colonial situations. The impact of the collapse of British empire in Asia on the Chiang Kai-shek regime showed that they were right to worry about it.

The response to this shaky start was robust and pragmatic. For a start the diplomats started planning for the abrogation of extraterritoriality and related issues. And through a variety of overt and covert operations British diplomats, soldiers, spies, and women and men somewhere in between the latter categories, attempted to keep other British options open in China. The ambiguities of the China war, its porous front lines, and the multiplicity of forces and interests involved, combined with corruption to make it a fertile field for buccaneering.[35] Operation 'Remorse', for example, initiated by the British covert action Special Operations Executive (SOE) in July 1944, raised substantial funds in Nationalist currency (£77 million by December 1945) using businessmen in khaki to play the Chinese black market. Walter Fletcher of the rubber firm Hecht Levis & Kahn set up networks of distributors and buyers of Indian rupees, watches, diamonds, cigarette paper and medicines – anything, in fact, that would sell. The aim was to buy influence, safety and food for prisoners, to smooth the British path back into Hong Kong by suborning provincial governments and, in Fletcher's words, 'to keep the British foot in the China door'. American drugs may have been what Chinese customers wanted to buy, he mused at one point, but 'I do not see why we should assist American trade.' 'Remorse' instead 'fostered British trade'.[36] The British Army Aid Group set up in somewhat freelance style by Australian Lindsay Ride, a Hong Kong physiology professor, worked to establish and maintain communications links with occupied Hong Kong, encouraging prisoners to escape, and striving to make sure that British forces were in position to take advantage of the peace and reclaim the colony.[37] SMP figures found openings in SOE and in SIS. Communications were opened up with the Chinese Communist Party in Yenan. Michael Lindsay, who had gone to Peking University in 1937 ostensibly to introduce the Oxbridge tutorial system by way of an educational experiment, had begun supplying *matériel* to the Chinese communists. Lindsay later fled the city at Pearl Habor to spend the war years, with his wife Li Hsiao Li, as a radio adviser for the CCP in their Jin-Cha-Ji base, and then in their wartime capital Yan'an.[38] Lindsay's cousin Tom was deputy to Findlay Andrew, Swire's fixer of issues Chinese, who worked for SOE during the conflict. Britain in China fought an unorthodox war and kept it largely in the family. In the midst of battle, and after a shattering defeat which alienated their new ally, China, the British worked hard to keep all their options open, but the only fixed point became Hong Kong.[39] The treaty ports and the advantages of informal empire were certainly sacrificed for the maintenance of British imperial prestige through the restitution of the Hong Kong colony, but they were being sacrificed anyway before the war began.

Settler options had closed; and the war had depopulated Britain in China. British refugees from the Japanese-occupied zones or war zones, or those fearing the extension of Japanese control to the International Settlement at Shanghai, or the British concessions at Xiamen or Tianjin, had left for Hong Kong, and home, or new homes in the dominions after 1937. But for many others there was a clear sense that if they were to leave they would be losing all they had. Abandoning Shanghai meant abandoning jobs, property, savings, superannuation and pensions. Also, as former customs official Owen Gander remarked in his diary in April 1942, those still in Shanghai at the end of the war stood a better chance of regaining their old positions. Being dismissed on 17 December 1941 in his twenty-seventh year of service had somewhat puzzled Gander, who could see no reason 'why the position of foreigners in the service should have been affected by the political situation'.[40] For most British residents in China, outside Hong Kong, the onset of the Pacific War was an anti-climax. Although some Britons were arrested swiftly by the Japanese, and despite most senior municipal or business administrators resigning, or being asked to resign, most British residents in Shanghai, for example, were allowed to carry on with their private activities for another fourteen months, until the majority of them were interned.[41] These 6,000 Britons were thus the single largest concentration of British subjects living their lives under enemy occupation outside the Channel Islands. The British Residents' Association became a community support agency. Shanghailanders worked, shopped, stole, got married, died and fantasised about escape.[42] They worried about their futures, suffered the intense boredom of war and were faced with the tricky indignities of the Japanese occupation, and the indignities of the shortages and restrictions of wartime Shanghai. The Japanese authorities ordered them to wear armbands, and requisitioned their cars (if they had them) and often their homes. After his vehicle was confiscated in March 1942 Harry Arnhold found himself taking a bus to his office, standing 'amongst coolies reeking of garlic, carrying baskets of fish'; the journey was an ordeal. SMC health official J. Chadderton and his wife found themselves having to learn how to cook.[43] Community symbols were removed, the statues of eminent Britons on the Bund pulled down, and the Shanghai Volunteer Corps was abolished with sensitive decorum by the now Japanese-dominated SMC. Most Britons were interned by March 1943. Conditions were far better than in similar camps in Hong Kong, or the occupied colonial possessions, but the humiliations rankled. 'My coolie ate better food,' noted gasworks superintendent William Henry in his diary.[44]

Just as they were being interned in February and March 1943 the British and US governments signed the treaties which abolished extraterritoriality and the treaty port system. With the peace in 1945 came the business of sorting out the legal details of the return of the settlements to Chinese control. Trickier still, in some ways, was the business of sorting out the human details. SMC employees were anxious to return to their jobs, only their jobs no longer existed.[45] Former SMP Deputy Commissioner H. D. M. Robertson, the highest-ranking interned officer, wrote from camp to the incoming British consul-general listing the 264 British policemen ready to get back on to the Shanghai beat.[46] The new Guomindang administration of the city was not going to employ them; it was not even going to pay their pensions. The manoeuvres of the 1920s and 1930s to protect the employees of the settlement bore little fruit.

Liquidation commissions were established in Beijing, Tianjin, Xiamen and Shanghai to deal with the unfinished business of the old administrations. Shanghai's commission was not established until October 1946, and included Shell manager T. S. Powell, who had sat on the SMC from April 1939 until late 1941. Shanghai mayor Wu Guochen praised the SMC in his opening address to the commission as a 'model of municipal governments' – which was not quite the same as a model settlement – but there were no funds, and certainly no sterling funds, for the new municipality to fulfil the contracted obligations of the SMC regarding municipal bonds, the emergency loan from the Hongkong & Shanghai Bank in 1940, or the pension and superannuation claims of former employees. Hyperinflation, food crises and political struggles in the city focused Chinese minds elsewhere than on the debts of the dead past.[47]

Events overtook the slow-moving commission, and in 1950, with no possibility of a settlement after the retreat of the Guomindang, the British government made *ex gratia* payments of about £1.5 million to former British employees of the municipal councils, and committed itself to pension payments of some £70,000 a year. With this action it demonstrated a sense of responsibility towards the treaty port legacy which it had previously made efforts to evade, and effectively recognised a moral debt to the personnel of the SMC. The Foreign Office had also liaised with the Colonial and War Offices in 1945–46 to find employment for these men and women.[48] Members of the SMP who requested work went to Germany, or to former Italian colonies under British military administration, while a few found temporary employment in the Hong Kong police. On the whole, however, colonial administrations did not want them: there was no place in the administrative ranks of the formal empire for the redundant employees of freelance imperialism. Those serving in Libya or Somalia must have felt that their internment had never ended.

Businesses restarted, attempting to regain properties which had been appropriated by the Japanese military, or by Japanese firms, and which had often been appropriated in turn by the victorious Nationalists. Companies had to deal with labour disturbances, and with the pressing social problems of a country in turmoil. They also had to learn how to do business within a post-treaty framework that had been only sketchily worked out. Swire's and other companies had to face the loss of inland navigation rights, and to contemplate rebuilding not only businesses shattered by war but ones also deeply threatened by the peace. There were still over 4,500 Britons in Shanghai, for example, in 1948, working in many of the areas that had kept settlers employed before the conflict, or coming out to join British companies. But stepping off the boat into a job was not the simple operation it had once been. Foreign arrivals needed a visa issued by a Chinese consulate, and ten days after arrival had to apply for a registration certificate, which when issued needed to be carried at all times. In the treaty era immigration procedures were fairly lax, although a passport had been a requirement for travel outside the concessions; in post-treaty China the foreigner was placed in a specific, regulated position in relation to the Chinese state. The very fact of registration with the Chinese authorities was heavily symbolic: treaty foreigners had previously registered only with their own officials.[49]

The Americanisation of Shanghai's urban culture in particular was intensified and consolidated by the arrival of US military and relief personnel, and military and relief dollars and goods. SOE's bid to keep the British commercial foot in the China door was swamped by the US cultural and economic presence. The best imaginative account of this change in the culture of the city was provided in a 1984 novel by the son of the former manager of CPA's Lunchang cotton mill. J. G. Ballard's *Empire of the Sun* takes narrative short cuts with the occupation history of the city, but stands out as an impressionistic portrayal of the changing mentality of commercial Shanghai, notably in the young central character's relationship with American mass popular culture. The US presence began to serve as a focus for campaigns, led by students, against the Guomindang, notably a movement protesting at the rape of a Beijing student, Shen Chong, by US military personnel in Beijing in late 1946. The eponymous hero of Zhang Leping's popular *San Mao* cartoon strip was regularly booted into the gutter by passing US Navy personnel.[50]

Those with land or business interests which could not be transferred had little choice but to make a go of a new dispensation that saw little point in the British. But other British interests had been shifting the nominal base of their operations to Hong Kong since before the war, as the historical relationship between the cities of Hong Kong and Shanghai shifted back in Hong Kong's favour for the first time since the 1860s. This process was accelerated in the post-war era. As the British trade mission to China in late 1946 noted, 'now that there are no longer any foreign concessions left in Shanghai, [Hong Kong] is the nearest place to the main centres of population and of trade in China where there is a system of law and administration on Western lines with political, economic and financial stability'.[51] Foreign companies, the trade mission reported, were already moving to the colony from the mainland. New company registrations in Hong Kong between 1946 and 1949 totalled 953. Many were China companies which switched registration under emergency regulations, including some of the most familiar and politically prominent treaty port names: Liddel Brothers, the Moller companies, Calder Marshall, G. E. Marden, Sir Victor Sassoon's Cathay Hotels, and even the Shanghai Club.[52] They transferred from fear of instability, expropriation, war and civil war, and had been doing so since 1937, but also from fear of Chinese law and its application or abuse. After years of defending extraterritoriality in China by claiming that without adequate legal structures they could not be expected to throw themselves on the mercy of Chinese courts, British traders viewed with apprehension the legislative efforts of the National government. The Qing commercial code of 1904, the National government's 1929 Commercial Code and the redrawn code of 1946 were drawn up as tools of economic nationalism, and also as attempts to encourage Chinese economic development. They served, as William C. Kirby has indicated, to facilitate the extension of the reach of the state.[53] Registration in Hong Kong tied many of these firms more closely to the colony; the revolution meant that 'Shanghai ... transferred itself bodily there'.[54]

Although the establishment of the People's Republic of China on 1

October 1949 took place before the country was fully controlled by the CCP armies, it marked the formal opening of a new chapter in Sino-foreign relations. Committed to economic nationalism and anti-imperialism, tempered by a swing in external relations towards the USSR and the Eastern bloc, the new regime was certainly hostile towards autonomous Western activities. With the onset of the Korean War in particular, it grew hostile to any non-communist foreign presence. The government effectively froze Western firms out of China, as it turned to the communist bloc for trade relations and developmental expertise. Swift formal British recognition of the change of government on 6 January 1950 brought few tangible gains for traders. Within five years taxation policies and labour questions had been used to force most British enterprises to extricate themselves from their activities in China.[55] They were not forced out – indeed, personnel found themselves trapped for years awaiting exit permits – but they were not made to feel welcome. Missionaries in particular began to find themselves the target of concentrated antagonistic pressure from the new regime, which saw them as agents of imperialism and encouraged the development of new Protestant interdenominational organisations which severed their links with mission bodies. The CIM decided to pull out in December 1950.[56]

Some settlers had fled China while they could. Among the 1,220 refugees evacuated from Shanghai on the SS *General Gordon* in September 1949 were 221 Britons – the symbolism of their leaving on a ship named for a key figure of the bellicose settler past seemingly not noted. Many settler names resurfaced in Hong Kong; they were present at the SVC centenary dinner in April 1954 together with many old Macanese and Chinese comrades from the different militia companies. A detailed plan of the founding SVC victory, the 1854 battle of Muddy Flat, was inserted into the programme, a small consolation of past glory in retreat and defeat.[57] Others went farther afield. Noel Kent, whose grandfather, G. L. Skinner, had arrived in Shanghai in the 1860s, spent the war years in the Royal Indian Air Force but returned to resume his position with Algar & Co. in 1946. Kent left Shanghai in 1949; like many settlers, he hardly knew Britain and instead moved to a world which in its attitudes seemed in many ways to replicate the one he had been forced to leave: South Africa. 'We were Overseas Britons,' noted Arch Carey, who had lived in China since the age of ten, 'with no place to go.' He chose the United States.[58] Others never left China. Mansel Hay Thorburn, father of young John who had died while trying to 'make good' in 1931, remained in China after his son's death, dying, a widower, at the age of sixty-nine in a Shanghai apartment in November 1954.[59] Thorburn, quite clearly, and for whatever reasons, felt that he had nowhere else to go. Rewi Alley, former Shanghai fire-man and industrial safety officer of the SMC, latterly an organiser of the Chinese Industrial Co-operatives, stayed on as a 'Peace Worker', one of a number of sympathisers to do so. The diplomats excluded them from their lists of remaining British subjects: their politics seem to have deracinated them.[60] The reality of the 'Britishness' behind the passport started to vex the diplomats. Many of the Britons staying on were the White Russian or Chinese wives of British men, widowed, divorced or just abandoned. In June 1951 the figures for Shanghai British subjects – excluding foreign spouses – were broken down into[61]:

| | | |
|---|---|---|
| A. | Britons | 597 |
| B. | Eurasians with UK roots (born in British territory, or maintaining 'strong links' through marriage or contact) | 21 |
| C. | Eurasians without strong British roots | 248 |
| D. | British-registered persons | 21 |

Categories B and C were reckoned to include about 140 'Hong Kong Portuguese' who were British by 'technicality only'. Their interests were restricted, it was claimed, to China, Hong Kong and Macao. 'Many would discard their British nationality,' asserted the Shanghai Consul-general 'without any qualms whatsoever if it suited them to do so. This was demonstrated clearly,' he continued pointedly, 'in 1941–42.' Prejudices about Eurasians remained, stiffened by claims about wartime experiences. The bulk of the remaining Eurasians had a British parent, or grandparents, and a 'strong sentimental attachment' to their nationality. Only a hard core of about forty would stay on in Shanghai regardless of changes, but the Eurasian sector of Britain in China was becoming a major part of its legacy in the aftermath of 1949. As Table 5 shows, the decline in the numbers of British subjects remaining in China was rapid. 'I have no power to order anybody to stay or to go,' noted Consul-general S. L. Burdett in a speech to one of the BRA's last annual meetings, held at the Country Club on 29 November 1950, but the diplomats clearly wanted all non-essential personnel to leave.[62] 'Spy' trials and the execution of foreign nationals in Beijing in August 1951, trials of Canadian nuns for allegedly killing orphans in Canton, or of other missionaries for supposedly scalding infants to death in Nanjing, deeply worried officials. The position of the missionary presence became extremely uncomfortable.[63] Still, in Shanghai the remaining Britons lived 'very comfortably', if stressfully: by 1953 some had been forced to wait two years for their exit visas.[64] In November 1950 there were still sixty-two British children attending a British School, although the community had lost its hospital, and the Bubbling Well cemetery had been requisitioned by the city authorities

– who were later to obliterate all but the names from the tombstone inscriptions when they relocated the graves. In post-treaty China even the foreign dead were to be shaken up. Empire Day was celebrated at the Shanghai Club in May 1951, and the Consul-general held King's Birthday celebrations but gave only a 'prudent speech'. The clubs in fact began to close, or to be closed down, or requisitioned by the authorities. The Shanghai Club became an International Seamen's Club in 1956.[65] The race track became a parade ground and People's Park, and the race club building the Shanghai public library. The symbolism of the remaking of new Shanghai effectively countered the inherent symbolism of the settler monuments and buildings.

**Table 5** Number of British subjects in China at specific dates, 1950–51

| Consular district | February 1950 | 26 January 1951 | 1 October 1951 | 31 December 1951 |
|---|---|---|---|---|
| Canton | | 67 | 15 | |
| Chongqing | | 231 | 65 | |
| Hankou | | 243 | 35 | |
| Kunming | | 26 | 5 | |
| Nanjing | | 44 | 14 | |
| Peking | | 70 | 34 | |
| Qingdao | | 60 | 20 | |
| Shanghai | 1,850 | 1,311 | 697 | |
| Tianjin | | 175 | 107 | |
| Xiamen | | 57 | 5 | |
| Total | | 2,284 | 997 | 903 |

*Sources* PRO, FO 371/83499, Shanghai No. 178, 22 February 1950; FO 371/92336 Peking No. 217, 26 January 1951; FO 371/92334, FC 1582/27, FO minute, 25 August 1951. (The numbers have been revised on this document to include 1 October and 31 December 1951.)

Burdett's 1950 speech is interesting. As a consular official who had first arrived in China in 1920, Burdett, like many of the Shanghai settlers, had seen the city occupied by a revolutionary force before, in 1927. He commented on the difference, noting in particular that the community was much less divided than it had been before, and that 'Life is more simple and the atmosphere far more friendly than in 1927'. Still, a drunken assault on a Chinese by a young British banker was a much more serious issue than it had been in the 1920s. The diplomats tracked their imprisoned charges, locked up for black market offences, smuggling or alleged spying. Some certainly deserved it, but even murderers and thieves caused diplomatic frets. Two British

Jehovah's Witnesses, however, still operating in Shanghai in September 1955 prompted only wry bemusement.[66]

Even when the exit permit was issued, leaving was not easy: when Swire's Tianjin manager left in July 1951 customs officials 'turned out every article of his luggage on to the (dirty) floor, took off his shoes and socks, and tore out the lining of all his suits'.[67] About forty exit permits a month were issued in Shanghai in mid-1951, and British diplomats worried, as ever, that 'business leaders' were too 'bound up in their own local difficulties' to be aware of how the Korean War in particular threatened them. Jardine's still had some sixty-four adult employees and their families, while an estimated 500 Britons were still in Shanghai who worked 'outside the main firms'. These were men like R. Martin, still in Shanghai in June 1954 and described as 'a typical "Shanghailander", who has held various jobs in this city where he is likely to remain so long as he can earn a living'.[68] Earning a living became problematic, and in the aftermath of the Korean War the pace of disengagement accelerated. British firms pulled out of the city, surrendering their local assets against liabilities: Swire's in December 1954, the Hongkong & Shanghai Bank and the department store company Whiteway Laidlaw in April 1955. ICI, CPA and G. E. Marden all applied to hand over their interests in early 1956. Such settlements in Shanghai usually included company assets in other towns and cities. When Patons & Baldwins left in 1957 only Shell was left, under Chinese managers, until it closed down its Shanghai office in 1966.[69]

Most of these firms did not leave China, of course; they withdrew to the rock of Hong Kong, where British diplomats puffed up the threat of an assault on the 'Berlin of the East' to make the colony a key Cold War issue in East Asia.[70] Firms and individuals certainly lost out, but the enforced reorientation of British interests solely towards Hong Kong was hardly at variance with British policy after 1927. And it was much tidier to have them holed up in Hong Kong. Hong Kong was a formal colony, and British authority over its own nationals was unchallenged there. They were subject to British law, and they could act out their colonial pretensions on a colonial stage. Many of the precious partners in the treaty port enterprise also made their way to the colony: Chinese, Eurasian, Indian and British enterprises, together with transnational groups, fled back to the Hong Kong, from where, in one sense, such interests had moved to Shanghai in the 1850s and 1860s. Hong Kong's post-war economic success was heavily indebted to the Shanghai infusion.[71] When the first British ambassador to China, Lord Macartney, made his embassy in 1792–94, he had carried instructions which amongst other things ordered him to request a 'small tract of ground or a detached island' as a depot for the British China trade.[72]

That British ambition had been met five times over with the establishment of the first treaty ports and Hong Kong in 1842, and had proved midwife to Britain in China and the illegitimate settler establishment which developed in the interstices of empire. With the effective closing of the PRC to non-communist states after 1949, and the slow nudging out of all Western interests, the British position in China was reduced to that first requested by Macartney at the Qianlong emperor's summer palace in 1793: one 'detached island' depot, Hong Kong.

## *Notes*

1 Cain and Hopkins, *British Imperialism*, ii, 36–9 (figure from 39).
2 John Fitzgerald, *Awakening China: Politics, Culture, and Class in the Nationalist Revolution* (Stanford CA, 1996).
3 Bickers and Wasserstrom, 'Shanghai's "Chinese and Dogs not Admitted" sign'.
4 *A Mischievous Slander*, Tientsin British Committee of Information, Memorandum 19 (Tianjin, 1927).
5 Osterhammel, 'Imperialism in Transition'.
6 The revisionist account is Cain and Hopkins's *British Imperialism*; a recent critique is David Clayton, *Imperialism Revisited: Political and Economic Relations between Britain and China, 1950–54* (Basingstoke, 1997).
7 Barbara J. Brooks, 'Japanese Colonial Citizenship in Treaty Port China: The Location of Koreans and Taiwanese in the Imperial Order' paper presented to the conference on 'Foreign Communities in East Asia in the nineteenth and twentieth centuries', Lyon, March 1997.
8 Young, *Japan's Total Empire*, 307–411, figure from 328.
9 Thomas, *Colonialism's Culture*, 167–8.
10 Ransome, *Chinese Puzzle*, 28.
11 White, *Business, Government and the end of empire*, 268.
12 Catherine Schenk, 'Commercial rivalry between Shanghai and Hong Kong during the collapse of the Nationalist Regime in China, 1945–1949', *International History Review* 20 (1998), 68–98.
13 Lee, *Britain and the Sino-Japanese War*, 89–95.
14 Such as Edgar Snow, *Red Star over China* (London, 1937); Agnes Smedley, *China's Red Army Marches* (New York, 1934, London, 1936); Harold Isaacs, *The Tragedy of the Chinese Revolution* (London, 1938).
15 Nancy Bernkopf Tucker, *Patterns in the Dust: Chinese-American relations and the recognition controversy, 1949–1950* (New York, 1983), 20–7.
16 SMP IO 9121/1, 'Reports on various local foreign and Chinese periodicals, 12 February 1935.
17 Trevor-Roper, *Hermit of Peking*, 225–64.
18 Arthur Waley, 'A Debt to China', reprinted in Hsiao Ch'ien (Xiao Qian) ed., *A Harp with a Thousand Strings: A Chinese Anthology in Six Parts* (London, 1944), 342.
19 PRO, FO 371/24662, F1011/31/19, Sir Arthur Clark Kerr to Roert Howe, 6 December 1939, enclosing Shanghai No. 390, 27 Nov. 1939; SMA Q 199-1-1, China Printing and Finishing Company records, minutes of directors, 20 December 1939; Barnett, *Economic Shanghai*, 65–7.
20 PRO, FO 371/23458, F5525/528/10, A. D. Blackburn to J. F. Brenan, 7 June 1939.
21 IWM, Tinkler papers, Tinkler to Edith 16 December 1925.
22 *Oriental Affairs*, December 1936, 269–70; Dorothy Jones, *The Portrayal of China and India on the American Screen, 1896–1955: the evolution of Chinese and Indian Themes, Locales, and Characters as Portrayed on the American Screen* (Cambridge,

MA, 1955), 4, 38–9.

23 Chinese Organising Committee, quoted in Warren I. Cohen, *East Asian Art and American Culture: A Study in International Relations* (New York, 1992), 123; *NCH*, 10 April 1935, 57; for Foreign Office documents on the exhibition see the file L198/198/405 in PRO, FO 370/470.

24 Laurence Binyon, 'Introduction' to *The Chinese Exhibition: A Commemorative Catalogue of the International Exhibition of Chinese Art, Royal Academy of Arts, November 1935 – March 1936* (London, 1936), viii; R. L. Hobson, 'The Chinese Exhibition at Burlington House', *Apollo* 22, No. 132 (December 1935), 311–12.

25 Lin Yutang, *The Importance of Living* (London, 1938), 360–8; *My Country and My People*, revised edition (London, 1939), 6–11 (quotation from 11).

26 SOAS administrative archives, Jiang Yi personnel file; Xiao Qian, *Traveller without a Map* (London, 1990), 72–121; Hsiao Ch'ien (Xiao Qian), ed., *Harp with a thousand strings*, xiii; *China: But Not Cathay* (London, 1942), 1.

27 E. R. Hughes, 'Editor's Preface', in Hughes, ed., *China: Body and Soul* (London, 1938), 7.

28 E. R. Hughes, *The Invasion of China by the Western World* (London, 1937), 19.

29 Michael H. Hunt, 'Pearl Buck: Popular Expert on China, 1931–1949', *Modern China*, 3 (1977), 33–64.

30 Vicki Baum, *Nanking Road* (London, 1939), also published as *Hotel Shanghai*.

31 This paragraph is based on Arthur Clegg, *Aid China, 1937–1949: A Memoir of a Forgotten Campaign* (Beijing, 1989), and Xiao Qian, *Traveller without a map*, 84–8.

32 Endicott, *Diplomacy and Enterprise*, 102–49.

33 W. H. Auden and Christopher Isherwood, *Journey to a War* (London, 1939), 237–8.

34 Christopher Thorne, *Allies of a Kind: the United States, Britain and the War against Japan, 1941–45* (London, 1978); Chan, 'Abrogation of British Extraterritoriality in China', 260–64.

35 Chan, 'Abrogation of British Extraterritoriality in China', 257–91; Lloyd E. Eastman, 'Facets of an ambivalent relationship: smuggling, puppets and atrocities during the war, 1937–45', in Akira Iriye, ed., *The Chinese and the Japanese: Essays in Political and Cultural Interactions* (Princeton NJ, 1980), 275–303; Aldrich, 'Britain's Secret Intelligence Service in Asia'.

36 PRO, HS 1/291, 'B/B.3' to 'D/Fin', 26 June 1944. Information on Remorse comes from the following SOE files: HS 1/170, 172, 291, 292, and 293, especially 'History of Mickleham and Remorse', 2 January 1946, HS 1/292.

37 Edwin Ride, *BAAG, Hong Kong Resistance, 1942–1945* (Hong Kong, 1981).

38 Michael Lindsay, *The Unknown War: North China 1937–1945* (London, 1975); on British intelligence activities see NARA RG 38, Records of the Office of the Chief of Naval Operations, Office of Naval Intelligence, China-Malay desk, Box 1, Naval Attache Chunking, 'Some Notes on Foreign Diplomatic Representatives in Chunking', 27 August 1947, and RG 226, Records of the Office of Strategic Services, Box 496, folder 1573, 'British Intelligence in China', Military Attache, Chunking, 26 January 1945; on Michael Lindsay and Li Hsiao Li see the research in progress of Susan Lawrence, to whom I am indebted for copies of these files.

39 James T. H. Tang, 'From Empire Defence to Imperial retreat: Britain's China Policy and the Decolonisation of Hong Kong', *Modern Asian Studies* 28 (1994), 317–37.

40 IWM 86/44/1, Owen Gander Diary, 17 December 1941, 25 April 1942.

41 On the SMC see: FO 371/46191, F2717/63/10, J. W. Allan, 'Report on the Shanghai Municipal Council', 20 Sept. 1942.

42 The dangers and ambiguities of this cohabitation are examined in Bernard Wasserstein, *Secret War in Shanghai, Treachery, Subversion and Collaboration in the Second World War* (London, 1998), and Robert Bickers, 'Settlers and Diplomats: the end of British hegemony in the International Settlement, 1937–45', paper prepared for the conference 'Wartime Shanghai, 1937–45', Lyon, October 1997; Hugh Collar, *Captive in Shanghai: A Story of Internment in World War Two* (Hong Kong, 1990).

43 Hoover Institution Archives, Stanford, H. E. Arnhold mss, 'Shanghai 1941–45'.

44 IWM, 86/87/1, W. Henry diary, 4 June 1944.

45  PRO, FO 371/46192, F9711/63/10, General Carlo de Wiart to Cabinet Office, 6 November 1945.
46  PRO, FO 671/563, H. D. M. Robertson to British Consul-general, 13 September, 1946.
47  PRO, FO 671/565, Shanghai Liquidation Commission files, Minutes of the First meeting, 29 November 1946; Marie-Claire Bergère, '"The Other China": Shanghai from 1919 to 1949' in Christopher Howe, ed., *Shanghai: Revolution and Development in an Asian Metropolis* (Cambridge, 1981), 26–30. See also Tianjin dang'an guan and Nankai daxue fenxiao dang'anxi, comp., *Tianjin zujie dang'an xuanbian* (*Selected records of the Tianjin concessions* (Tianjin, 1992), 538–69.
48  See the files F44/10 in PRO, FO 371/53588-53592.
49  The figures are from SMA Q 1-18-310 p. 24; Dorothy Gould, *Do's and Don'ts for Foreigners coming to Shanghai today* (Shanghai, 1947).
50  Jeffrey N. Wasserstrom, *Student Protests in Twentieth Century China: the View from Shanghai* (Stanford CA, 1991), 39–42; Suzanne Pepper, *Civil war in China: the political struggle, 1945–1949* (Berkeley CA, 1978), 52–8; Zhang Leping, 'San Mao liuliangji' (San Mao's wanderings) (1947–48) in *Zhang Leping huaji* (Collected drawings of Zhang Leping) (Shanghai, 1984), 61–112.
51  *Report of the United Kingdom Trade Mission to China October to December 1946* (London, 1948), 151.
52  Special Announcements, 9 August 1946, 23 August 1946, 29 November 1946, *The Ordinances of Hong Kong 1946* (Hong Kong, 1946); Registrar of the Supreme Court, *Annual reports*, 1946–1949.
53  William C. Kirby, 'China Unincorporated: Company Law and Business Enterprise in Twentieth Century China', *The Journal of Asian Studies* 54 (1995), 43–63.
54  W. H. Ingrams, *Hong Kong* (London, 1952), 244.
55  Hooper, *China Stands Up*; Thomas N. Thompson, *China's Nationalisation of Foreign Firms: The Politics of Hostage Capitalism, 1949–57* (Baltimore MD, 1979); Wenguang Shao, *China, Britain and businessmen: political and commercial relations, 1949–57* (Basingstoke, 1991).
56  PRO, FO 371/92334, J. R. Sinton to British Consul General, Shanghai, 20 December 1950; Hooper, *China stands up*, 109–34; see also George Hood, *Neither bang nor whimper: the end of a missionary era in China* (Singapore, 1991).
57  *The Times*, 28 September 1949, 4; *Shanghai Volunteer Corps: Centenary Dinner held at the Royal Hong Kong Yacht Club on Friday, 2nd April 1954* (Hong Kong, 1954).
58  Arch Carey, *The War Years at Shanghai, 1941–45–48* (New York, 1967), 291.
59  Scottish Record Office SC70/1/1350, 739–42, Death certificate; Inventory, Mansel Hay Thorburn.
60  Brady, 'West meets East', 114–20.
61  PRO, FO 371/92336, Shanghai No. 277, 2 June 1951.
62  PRO, FO 371/92259, FC1611/3, Shanghai No. 483, 6 December 1950 enclosing 'Minutes of the Fifteenth Annual Meeting of the British Residents' Association of China', 29 November 1950; FO 371/92334, Foreign Office No. 757, 11 May 1951.
63  See the files and incidents reported in PRO, 371/92331-2; Hooper, *China Stands Up*, 115–34.
64  PRO, FO 371/105315, Humphrey Trevelyan to W. D. Allen, 1 December 1953; FO 371/105317, F. W. H. London to J. S. H. Shattock, 17 August 1953. For a popular account of this period see Noel Barber, *The Fall of Shanghai: The Communist takeover in 1949* (London, 1979).
65  PRO, FO 671/581, 'Foreign cemeteries in China'; Shanghai No. 249, 28 May 1951, FO 371/92259; *Huangpu quzhi* (Huangpu gazetteer), 561.
66  PRO, FO 371/92259, FC1611/3, Shanghai No. 483, 6 December 1950 enclosing 'Minutes of the Fifteenth Annual Meeting of the British Residents' Association of China', 29 November 1950; FO 371/92335, FC1583/7, Foreign Office minute 13 April 1951; FO 371/114997, 'Shanghai Fortnightly summary', 20 September 1955.
67  PRO, FO 371/92332, Tianjin Consul-general to Peking, 12 July 1951.
68  PRO, FO 371/92334, Shanghai No. 204, 21 June 1951; FO 676/487, Shanghai No. 205, 25 June 1954.

69  PRO, FO 371/114997, Shanghai Fortnightly Summary; FO 371/120866, 'Events in Shanghai'; Thompson, *China's Nationalisation of Foreign Firms*, 57, 60; Nien Cheng, *Life and Death in Shanghai* (London, 1986), 5.
70  Louis, 'Hong Kong: the Critical Phase'.
71  Bickers, 'The Colony's shifting position in the British informal empire in China', in Brown and Foot, eds, *Hong Kong's Transitions*, 33–61; Siu-lin Wong, *Emigrant Entrepreneurs: Shanghai Industrialists in Hong Kong* (Hong Kong, 1988).
72  H. B. Morse *Chronicles of the East India Company Trading to China* (Oxford, 1926), ii, 237.

# SELECT BIBLIOGRAPHY

## Primary sources

### Bank of England archives

ADM 16      Misc. Papers Charles Addis
G 1\206     Governors' papers, E. R. Peacock
OV 104\1    China
OV 104\66   China Consortium

### Bodleian Library, Oxford

Lionel Curtis papers
Edward Jonah Nathan papers
Bodleian MSS Eng. misc. d.1223–2: Sir Edmund Backhouse memoirs, 'Deca-
dence Mandchoue' and 'The Dead Past'.

### British Library, Manuscripts Department

Stella Benson papers
Lord Chamberlain's Department, papers and plays
Macmillan archive, letters of Stella Benson and Bertram Lenox Simpson
Sydney Schiff papers, Stella Benson's letters to Stephen Hudson

### Cambridge University Library

Add Ms. 6762–6802, Diaries of Stella Benson, 1902–33

### Friends' House Library, London

Friends Service Council, China Sub-committee Minutes
Friends Service Council, Missionary Correspondence

### Hongkong & Shanghai Banking Corporation Group Archives, HSBC Holdings, London

SHG II 551              Peking Letter Book 1924–31
S16.1                  Personalities and Narratives
LOH I 103.243–250      Semi-official Letters from Shanghai 1928–31
LOH I 103.351          Semi-official Letters to Shanghai

### Hoover Institution Library and Archives

H. E. Arnhold Ms., 'Shanghai 1941–45'

### Imperial Chemical Industries, London

Papers relating to ICI (China)

## SELECT BIBLIOGRAPHY

*Imperial War Museum, London*
F. W. Bunter papers
Charles H. Drage papers
Owen D. Gander diary
T. J. N. Hilken papers
E. V. Lees papers
J. E. March memoir
Mr Moneypenny memoir, 'Ningpo more far'
J. M. Philips papers
W. F. Scott papers
H. C. Simms papers
R. M. Tinkler papers

*India Office Library and Records, London*
Jack Bazalgette collection, Letters 1926–28

*Manchester City Library and Archives*
M75, Papers of the Calico Printers' Association

*Middle East Centre, St Antony's College, Oxford*
Killearn papers, Diaries of Sir Miles Lampson, 1926–33

*National Maritime Museum, Greenwich*
H. T. Baillie Grohman papers
Sir Louis H. K. Hamilton papers

*National Archives and Records Administration, Washington DC*
RG 59      Inspection of Foreign Service Posts
RG 84      Shanghai Consulate-general Post Files
RG 84      Tientsin Consulate-general Post Files
RG 263     Shanghai Municipal Police Special Branch Files

*Public Record Office, Kew*
BT 59      Department of Overseas Trade, Overseas Development Council
BT 60      Department of Overseas Trade, Correspondence and Papers
FO 228     Embassy and Consular Archives China, Correspondence Series 1
FO 369     General Correspondence, Consular
FO 371     Foreign Office General Correspondence, Political
FO 372     Foreign Office General Correspondence, Treaty
FO 395     Foreign Office: News Department, general correspondence
FO 670     Embassy and Consular Archives China, Ningpo
FO 671     Embassy and Consular Archives China, Shanghai Correspondence
FO 676     Embassy and Consular Archives China, Correspondence Series 2
FO 800     Private Collections, Ministers and Officials, various
FO 917     Embassy and Consular Archives China, Shanghai Supreme Court,
           Probate records

HO 45      Home Office, registered papers
HS 1       Special Operations Executive: Far East: Registered Files
MEPO 2     Metropolitan Police, Office of the Commissioner, correspondence
           and papers
MEPO 3     Metropolitan Police, Office of the Commissioner, correspondence
           and papers, special series
WO 106     Directorate of Military Operations and Intelligence
WO 191     Peacetime Operations, Shanghai Defence Force War Diary
WO 208     Directorate of Military Intelligence

*Regents Park College, Oxford, Angus Library*
Baptist Missionary Society archives

*School of Oriental and African Studies Library, London*
Council for World Mission: archives and library of the London Missionary
   Society
Council of British Missionary Societies papers
John Swire & Sons, papers
Revd and Mrs E. J. Mann papers
Sir Frederick Maze papers
Methodist Church Overseas Division: Methodist Missionary Society Archives
   and Women's Work Collection
Papers of Sir A. G. N. Ogden
Overseas Missionary Fellowship: China Inland Mission papers
Presbyterian Church of England Foreign Missions Committee and Women's
   Missionary Association archives
W. Sheldon Ridge papers
Royal Institute of International Affairs: Far East Department papers
Papers of the Scott family and the North China and Shantung Mission: Revd P.
   M. Scott; Revd F. J. Griffith, M. W. Scott.
William G. Sewell papers

*Shanghai Academy of Social Sciences*
Chinese Business History Resource Centre, Liu Rongsheng archives

*Shanghai Municipal Archives*
China Printing & Finishing Company records
Shanghai Municipal Council, Secretariat files, 1919–30
Shanghai Municipal Police, Personnel files, Administration files

*Shell Archive Centre, London*
GHS/3c/3 Summaries of Minutes of Board meetings, 1922-1949

*John Swire & Sons, London*
Transcripts of interviews with ex-Swire employees undertaken by Christopher
   Cook and used in his book *The Lion and the Dragon*. These have been

quoted anonymously, by request of the archivist, but are numbered consecutively in surname alphabetical order of interviewee, followed by the page of transcript, e.g. ST [Swire Transcripts] – 6, p. 5.
Ships' Plans
Misc. – Personal Memoirs, T. J. Lindsay, 'No Mountains: Life in China and Work in Taikoo (Butterfield & Swire) from March 1935 to February 1949', unpublished memoir
Misc. 121 'China inter-war Political Letters 1925–1938'
Misc. 122/I, 'Wartime SMC Letters'
JS&S staff papers

*Theatre Museum, London*
Production files
British Theatre Association Library

*Thomas Fisher Rare Book Library, University of Toronto*
J. O. P. Bland collection

*United Reformed Church, London*
Papers relating to the English Presbyterian Mission

*Papers in private hands*
Noel Kent, letter book and papers
Maurice Lister, unpublished 'Memoirs'

*Interviews (on condition of anonymity)*
F.G.W., interview, 13 September 1996
F.P., interview, 13 March 1996

## Published works

Unless otherwise stated, all publications are London.
Acton, Harold, *Memoirs of An Aesthete*, 1948.
Airlie, Shiona, *Thistle and Bamboo: The Life and Times of Sir James Stewart Lockhart*, Hong Kong, 1989.
Aldrich, Richard J., 'Britain's Secret Intelligence Service in Asia during the Second World War', *Modern Asian Studies*, 32 (1998), 179–217.
*All about Shanghai and Environs: A Standard Guide Book*, Shanghai, c.1934.
Allman, N. F., *Shanghai Lawyer*, New York, 1943.
Alloula, Malek, *The Colonial Harem*, Minneapolis MN, 1986.
Anderson, Benedict, *Imagined Communities: Reflections on the Origin and Spread of Nationalism*, revised edition, 1991.
Anderson, Perry, 'A Belated Encounter', *London Review of Books*, 20:15, 30 July 1998, 20:16, 20 August 1998.
Appleton, William W., *A Cycle of Cathay: The Chinese Vogue in England during the Seventeenth and Eighteenth Centuries*, New York, 1951.

Arnold, David, 'European Orphans and Vagrants in India in the Nineteenth Century', *Journal of Imperial and Commonwealth History*, 7 (1979), 104–27.

Atkins, Martyn, *Informal Empire in Crisis: British Diplomacy and the Chinese Customs Succession, 1927–1929*, Ithaca NY, 1995.

Atwell, Pamela, *British Mandarins and Chinese Reformers: The British Administration of Weihaiwei (1898–1930) and the Territory's Return to Chinese Rule*, Hong Kong, 1985.

Auden, W. H., and Christopher Isherwood, *Journey to a War*, 1939.

Austin, A. J., *Saving China: Canadian Missionaries in the Middle Kingdom, 1888–1959*, Toronto, 1986.

Balhatchet, Kenneth R., *Race, Sex and Class under the Raj: Imperial Attitudes and Policies and their Critics, 1793–1905*, 1980.

Ball, J. Dyer, revised by E. T. C. Werner, *Things Chinese; or, Notes Connected with China*, Shanghai, 1925.

Balme, Harold, *China and Modern Medicine: A Study in Medical Missionary Development*, 1921.

Barber, Noel, *The Fall of Shanghai: The Communist Take-over in 1949*, 1979.

Barlow, Tani E., ed., *Formations of Colonial Modernity in East Asia*, Durham NC, 1997.

Barnett, Robert W., *Economic Shanghai: Hostage to Politics, 1937–1941*, New York, 1941.

Barrett, T. H., *Singular Listlessness: A Short History of Chinese Books and British Scholars*, 1989.

Bayly, C. A., 'Returning the British to South Asian History: The Limits of Colonial Hegemony', *South Asia*, 17 (1994), 1–25.

Bayly, C. A., *Empire and Information: Intelligence Gathering and Social Communication in India, 1780–1870*, Cambridge, 1996.

Benson, Carlton, '"Consumers are also Soldiers": Subversive Songs from Nanjing Road during the New Life Movement', paper presented at the seminar on 'Inventing Nanjing Road: Consumer Culture in Shanghai, 1864–1949', Cornell University, July 1995.

Bergère, Marie-Claire, '"The Other China": Shanghai from 1919 to 1949', in Christopher Howe, ed., *Shanghai: Revolution and Development in an Asian Metropolis*, Cambridge, 1981.

Berridge, Virginia, 'East End Opium Dens and Narcotic Use in Britain', *London Journal*, 4 (1978), 3–28.

Best, Antony, *Britain, Japan and Pearl Harbor: Avoiding War in East Asia, 1936–41*,1995.

Betta, Chiara, 'Silas Aaron Hardoon (1851–1931): Marginality and Adaptation in Shanghai', School of Oriental and African Studies Ph.D. thesis, 1997.

Bickers, Robert, 'History, Legend, and Treaty Port Ideology, 1925–1931', in Robert Bickers, ed., *Ritual and Diplomacy: The Macartney Mission to China, 1792–1794*, 1993.

Bickers, Robert, 'New Light on Lao She, London, and the London Missionary Society, 1921–1929', *Modern Chinese Literature*, 8 (1994), 21–39.

Bickers, Robert, '"Coolie work": Sir Reginald Johnston at the School of Oriental Studies, 1931–1937', *Journal of the Royal Asiatic Society*, Series III, 5 (1995), 385–401.

Bickers, Robert, 'Death of a Young Shanghailander: The Thorburn Case and the Defence of the British Treaty Ports in China in 1931', *Modern Asian Studies*, 30 (1996), 271–300.

Bickers, Robert, 'The Colony's Shifting Position in the British Informal Empire in China', in Judith M. Brown and Rosemary Foot, eds, *Hong Kong's Transitions, 1842–1997* (1997).

Bickers, Robert, 'Settlers and Diplomats: The End of British Hegemony in the International Settlement, 1937–45', paper prepared for the conference 'Wartime Shanghai, 1937–45', Lyon, October 1997.

Bickers, Robert, 'Shanghailanders: The Formation and Identity of the British Settler Community in Shanghai, 1842–1937', *Past and Present*, 159 (1998), 161–211.

Bickers, Robert, and Jeffrey N. Wasserstrom, 'Shanghai's "Chinese and Dogs not Admitted" Sign: History, Legend and Contemporary Symbol', *China Quarterly*, 142 (1995), 444–66.

Bland, J. O. P., *China: The Pity of It*, 1932.

Blofeld, John, 'Sino-British Cultural Relations', *China Society Occasional Papers*, c. 1946.

Blofeld, John, *City of Lingering Splendour: A Frank Account of Old Peking's Exotic Pleasures*, 1961.

Bloom, Clive, 'West is East: Nayland Smith's Sinophobia and Sax Rohmer's Bank Balance', in C. Bloom, ed., *Twentieth Century Suspense: The Thriller Comes of Age*, 1990.

Bodley, R V C, *Indiscreet Travels East*, 1934.

Bowie, C. J., 'Great Britain and the Use of Force in China, 1919 to 1931', University of Oxford D.Phil. thesis, 1983.

Boynton, C. L., and C. D. Boynton, eds, *1936 Handbook of the Christian Movement in China under Protestant Auspices*, Shanghai, 1936.

Brady, Anne-Marie, 'West meets East: Rewi Alley and Changing Attitudes towards Homosexuality in China', *East Asian History*, 9 (1995), 97–120.

Briney, R. E., ed., C. Van Ash and E. S. Rohmer, *Master of Villainy: A Biography of Sax Rohmer*, Bowling Green OH, 1972.

*British Empire Exhibition 1924 Official Catalogue*, 1924.

*British Empire Exhibition 1924 Official Guide*, 1924.

Brodie, Patrick, *Crescent over Cathay: China and I.C.I., 1898–1956*, Hong Kong, 1990.

Brooks, Barbara J., 'Japanese Colonial Citizenship in Treaty Port China: The Location of Koreans and Taiwanese in the Imperial Order', paper presented to the conference on 'Foreign Communities in East Asia in the Nineteenth and Twentieth Centuries', Lyon, March 1997.

Brownfoot, J., 'Sisters under the skin: Imperialism and the Emancipation of Women in Malaya, c. 1891–1941', in J. A. Mangan, ed., *Making Imperial Mentalities: Socialisation and British Imperialism*, Manchester, 1990.

Bruner, Katherine F., John K. Fairbank and Richard J. Smith, eds, *Entering China's Service: Robert Hart's Journals, 1854–1863*, Cambridge MA, 1986.

Buck, David, 'Appraising the Revival of Historical Studies in China', *China Quarterly*, 105 (1986) 131–42.

Burgess, Alan, *The Small Woman*, 1957.

Butcher, John G., *The British in Malaya, 1880–1941: The Social History of a European Community in Colonial South-east Asia*, Kuala Lumpur, 1979.

Byrne, Eugene, *The Dismissal of Sir Francis Aglen as Inspector of the Chinese Maritime Customs Service, 1927*, Leeds, 1995.

Cain, P. J., and A. G. Hopkins, *British Imperialism* (two volumes), 1993.

*Calendar of the District of Northern China (E.C.)*, Shanghai, 1937.

Callaway, Helen, *Gender, Culture and Empire: European Women in Colonial Nigeria*, Basingstoke, 1987.

Carey, Arch, *The War Years at Shanghai, 1941–45–48*, New York, 1967.

Carroll, John M., 'Colonialism and Collaboration: Chinese Subjects and the Making of British Hong Kong', *China Information*, 12 (1997), 12–35.

Castle, Kathryn, *Britannia's Children: Reading Colonialism through Children's Books and Magazines*, Manchester, 1996.

*The Celestial Empire*, Shanghai.

*Central China Post*, Hankou.

Ch'en, Jerome, *China and the West: Society and Culture, 1815–1937*, 1979.

Chan, K. C., 'The Abrogation of British Extraterritoriality in China, 1942–43: A Study in Anglo-American–Chinese Relations', *Modern Asian Studies*, 11 (1977), 257–91.

Chao, Kang, *The Development of Cotton Textile Production in China*, Cambridge MA, 1977.

Chao, Thomas Ming-Heng, *The Foreign Press in China*, Shanghai, 1931.

Chapman, H. Owen, *The Chinese Revolution, 1926–27*, 1928.

Chesneaux, Jean, *The Chinese Labour Movement, 1919–1927*, Stanford CA, 1968.

Chesterton, Ada E., *Young China and New Japan*, 1933.

*The China Critic*, Shanghai.

*The China Express and Telegraph*.

*China in Chaos*, Shanghai, 1927.

*China Mission Year Book*, (after 1925 *The China Christian Year Book*), Shanghai.

*China Year Book*, Tianjin and Shanghai.

*China's Millions*, London.

*The Chinese Exhibition: A Commemorative Catalogue of the International Exhibition of Chinese Art, Royal Academy of Arts, November 1935 - March 1936*, 1936.

Chinese Maritime Customs, *Chinese Maritime Customs IV. Service Series No.1. Service List*, Shanghai, 1925–38.

Chinese Maritime Customs, *Documents Illustrative of the Origin, Development, and Activities of the Chinese Customs Service* (seven volumes), Shanghai, 1939.

*The Chinese Recorder*, Shanghai.

*The Christian Occupation of China*, Shanghai, 1922.

Clark, Grover, *Economic Rivalries in China*, New Haven CT, 1932.

Clay, Henry, *Report on the Position of the English Cotton Industry*, 1931.

Clayton, David, *Imperialism Revisited: Political and Economic Relations between Britain and China, 1950–54*, Basingstoke, 1997.

Clegg, Arthur, *Aid China, 1937–1949: A Memoir of a Forgotten Campaign*, Beijing, 1989.

Clifford, Nicholas R., *Retreat from China: British Policy in the Far East, 1937–1941*, 1967.

Clifford, Nicholas R., *Spoilt Children of Empire: Westerners in Shanghai and the Chinese Revolution of the 1920s*, Hanover NH, 1991.

Coates, Austin, *China Races*, Hong Kong, 1983.

Coates, P. D., *The China Consuls: British Consular Officers, 1843–1943*, Hong Kong, 1988.

Coble, Parks M., *The Shanghai Capitalists and the Nanking Government, 1927–37*, Cambridge MA, 1986.

Cochran, Sherman, *Big Business in China: Sino-foreign Rivalry in the Cigarette Industry, 1890–1930*, Cambridge MA, 1980.

Cohen, Paul A., *Discovering History in China: American Historical Writing on the Recent Chinese Past*, New York, 1984.

Cohen, Paul A., 'The Contested Past: The Boxers as History and Myth', *Journal of Asian Studies*, 51 (1992), 82–113.

Cohen, Paul A., *History in Three Keys: The Boxers as Event, Experience, and Myth*, New York, 1997.

Cohen, Warren I., *The Chinese Connection: Roger S. Greene, Thomas L. Lamont, George E. Sokolsky and American-East Asian Relations*, New York, 1978.

Cohen, Warren I., *East Asian Art and American Culture: A Study in International Relations*, New York, 1992.

Collar, Hugh, *Captive in Shanghai: A Story of Internment in World War Two*, Hong Kong, 1990.

Connor, Alison W., 'Lawyers and the Legal Profession during the Republican Period', in Kathryn Bernhardt and Philip C. C. Huang, eds, *Civil Law in Qing and Republican China*, Stanford CA, 1994.

Cook, C., 'The Hongkong and Shanghai Banking Corporation in Lombard St', in F. H. H. King, ed., *Eastern Banking: Essays in the History of the Hongkong and Shanghai Banking Corporation*, 1983.

Cook, C., *The Lion and Dragon: British Voices from the China Coast*, 1985.

Crow, Carl, *Handbook for China (including Hong Kong)*, fourth edition, Shanghai, 1926.

Crow, Carl, *Foreign Devils in the Flowery Kingdom*, New York, 1940.

Darwent, Revd C. E., *Shanghai: A Handbook for Travellers and Residents*, Shanghai, 1912.

Darwin, John, 'Imperialism and the Victorians: The Dynamics of Territorial Expansion', *English Historical Review*, 112 (1997), 614–42.

Davenport-Hines, R. P. T., 'The British Engineers' Association and Markets in China, 1900–1930', in R. P. T. Davenport-Hines, ed., *Markets and Bagmen: Studies in the History of Marketing and British Industrial Performance, 1830–1939*, Aldershot, 1986.

Davenport-Hines, R. T. P., and Geoffrey Jones, 'British Business in Asia since 1860', in R. T. P. Davenport-Hines and Geoffrey Jones, eds, *British Business in Asia since 1860*, Cambridge, 1989.

Davidson-Houston, J.V., *Yellow Creek: The Story of Shanghai*, 1962.

Davin, Delia, 'Imperialism and the Diffusion of Liberal Thought: British Influences on Chinese Education', in Ruth Hayhoe and Marianne Bastid, eds, *China's Education and the Industrialised World: Studies in Cultural Transfer*, New York, 1987.

Davis, C. Noel, *A History of the Shanghai Paper Hunt Club, 1863–1930*, Shanghai, 1930.

Dawson, Raymond, *The Chinese Chameleon: An Analysis of European Conceptions of Chinese Civilization*, 1967.

Dayer, Roberta, *Bankers and Diplomats in China, 1917 to 1925: The Anglo-American Relationship*, 1981.

Dayer, Roberta, *Finance and Empire: Sir Charles Addis, 1861–1945*, Basingstoke, 1988.

Department of Overseas Trade, *Report of the British Economic Mission to the Far East, 1930–31*, 1931.

Department of Overseas Trade, *Trade and Economic Conditions in China, 1931–33*, 1933.

Department of Overseas Trade, *China: Notes on some Aspects of Life in China for the Information of Business Visitors*, 1934.

Dobson, Richard, *China Cycle*, 1946.

Drage, Charles, *General of Fortune: The Story of One-arm Sutton*, 1963.

Drage, Charles, *Taikoo*, 1970.

Duus, Peter, introduction to 'Trade and Investment', in Peter Duus, Ramon H. Myers and Mark R. Peattie, eds, *The Japanese Informal Empire in China, 1895–1937*, Princeton NJ, 1989.

Duus, Peter, 'Zaikabo: Japanese Cotton Mills in China, 1895–1937', in Peter Duus, Ramon H. Myers and Mark R. Peattie, eds, *The Japanese Informal Empire in China, 1895–1937*, Princeton NJ, 1989.

Duus, Peter, Ramon H. Myers and Mark R. Peattie, eds, *The Japanese Informal Empire in China, 1895–1937*, Princeton NJ, 1989.

*Eastern Engineering* (supplement to *The China Express and Telegraph*).

Eastman, Lloyd E., 'Facets of an Ambiguous Relationship: Smuggling, Puppets, and Atrocities during the War, 1937–1945', in Akira Iriye, ed., *The Chinese and the Japanese: Essays in Political and Cultural Interactions*, Princeton NJ, 1980.

Elvin, Mark, 'The Administration of Shanghai, 1905-1914', in Mark Elvin and G. William Skinner, eds, *The Chinese City between Two Worlds*, Stanford CA, 1974.

Endicott, S. L., *Diplomacy and Enterprise: British China Policy, 1933–37*, Manchester, 1975.

*Educational Review*, Shanghai.

Esherick, Joseph W., *The Origins of the Boxer Uprising*, Berkeley CA, 1987.

Fairbank, J. K., *Trade and Diplomacy on the China Coast: The Opening of the Treaty Ports, 1842–1854*, Stanford edition, Stanford CA, 1969.

Fairbank, J. K., *Chinabound: A Fifty Year Memoir*, New York, 1982.

Fairbank, J. K., M. H. Coolidge and R. J. Smith, *H. B. Morse: Customs Commissioner and Historian of China*, Lexington KY, 1995.

*Far Eastern Review*, Shanghai.

Faure, David, *China and Capitalism: Business Enterprise in Modern China*, Hong Kong, 1994.

Faure, David, 'The Chinese Bourgeoisie Reconsidered: Business Structure, Political Status and the Emergence of Social Class', unpublished paper, 1997.

Feetham, Richard, *Report of the Hon. Mr Justice Feetham, CMG, to the Shanghai Municipal Council* (three volumes), Shanghai, 1931.

Fei Chengkang, *Zhongguo zujie shi* (History of Concessions in China), Shanghai, 1991.

Feuerwerker, Albert, 'China's History in Marxian Dress', in Feuerwerker, ed., *History in Communist China*, Cambridge MA, 1968.

Feuerwerker, Albert, *The Foreign Establishment in China in the Early Twentieth Century*, Michigan Papers in Chinese Studies 29, Ann Arbor MI, 1976.

*Finance and Commerce*, Shanghai.

Fishel, W. R., *The End of Extraterritoriality in China*, Berkeley CA, 1952.

Fitkin, Gretchen Mae, *The Great River: The Story of a Voyage on the Yangtze Kiang*, Shanghai, 1922.

Fitzgerald, C. P., *Why China? Recollections of China, 1923–1950*, Melbourne, 1985.

Fitzgerald, John, *Awakening China: Politics, Culture, and Class in the Nationalist Revolution*, Stanford CA, 1996.

Fogel, Joshua A., *The Literature of Travel in the Japanese Rediscovery of China, 1862-1945*, Stanford CA, 1996.

Fogel, Joshua A. ,'Shanghai-Japan: The Japanese Residents' Association of Shanghai', paper prepared for the conference 'Wartime Shanghai, 1937–45', Lyon, October 1997.

Foster, John, *Chinese Realities*, 1928.

Fung, Chung-p'ing, *The British Government's China Policy, 1945–1950*, Keele, 1994.

Fung, E. S. K., *The Diplomacy of Imperial Retreat: Britain's South China Policy, 1924–31*, Hong Kong, 1991.

Fussell, Paul, *Abroad: British Literary Travelling between the Wars*, Oxford, 1980.

Garrett, Shirley, 'The Chambers of Commerce and the YMCA', in Mark Elvin and G. William Skinner, eds, *The Chinese City between Two Worlds*, Stanford CA, 1974.

Gayn, Mark J., *Journey from the East*, New York, 1944.

Gilbert, Rodney, *What's Wrong with China*, 1926.

Giles, H. A., *Chaos in China*, Cambridge, 1924.

*A Glimpse of China: A Handbook of Information for the Resident and Visitor*, Nanjing, 1934.

Gompertz, G. H., *China in Turmoil: Eye witness, 1924–1948*, 1967.

Goodall, Norman, *A History of the London Missionary Society, 1895–1945*, 1954.

Gould, Dorothy, *Do's and Don'ts for Foreigners coming to Shanghai Today*, Shanghai, 1947.

Grant, Joy, *Stella Benson: A Biography*, 1987.

Gratton, F. M., *The History of Freemasonry in Shanghai and Northern China*, revised by R. S. Ivy, Tianjin, 1913.

Green, O. M., *Discovering China*, 1938.

Green, O. M., *The Foreigner in China*, 1943.

Gull, E. M., *Facets of the China Question*, 1931.

Gull, E. M., *British Economic Interests in the Far East*, 1943.

Haffner, Christopher, *The Craft in the East*, Hong Kong, 1977.

Haffner, Christopher, *Amoy: The Port and the Lodge: The Corinthian Lodge of Amoy No. 1806 E.C.*, Hong Kong, 1978.

Haggie, Paul, *Britannia at Bay: The Defence of the British Empire against Japan, 1931–1941*, Oxford, 1981.

Hankow, British Municipal Council, *Annual Report of the Hankow Municipal Council, 1926*.

Hannaford, Ivan, *Race: The History of an Idea in the West*, Washington DC, 1996.

Harrop, Phyllis, *Hong Kong Incident*, 1943.

Hayford, C. W., 'Arthur H. Smith and his China Book', in S. W. Barnett and J. K. Fairbank, eds, *Christianity in China: Early Protestant Missionary Writings*, Cambridge MA, 1985.

Hayford, C. W., *To the People: James Yen and Village China*, New York, 1990.

Henriot, Christian, *Shanghai, 1927–1937: Municipal Power, Locality and Modernization*, Berkeley CA, 1993.

Henriot, Christian, 'Cities and Urban Society in China in the Nineteenth and Twentieth Centuries: A Review Essay in Western Literature', in *Jindai Zhongguo shi yanjiu tongxun (Newsletter of Modern Chinese History)* 21 (1996), 151–75.

Henriot, Christian, *Belles de Shanghai: prostitution et sexualité en Chine aux XIXᵉ–XXᵉ siècles*, Paris, 1997.

Hevia, James L., 'Leaving a Brand on China: Missionary Discourse in the Wake of the Boxer Movement', *Modern China*, 18 (1992), 304–32.

Hevia, James L., *Cherishing Men from Afar: Qing Guest Ritual and the Macartney Embassy of 1793*, Durham NC, 1995.

Hewitt, Gordon, *The Problems of Success: A History of the Church Missionary Society, 1910–1942*, I, 1971.

Hewlett, Sir Meyrick, *Forty Years in China*, 1943.

*The History of Freemasonry in Northern China, 1913–38*, Shanghai, 1938.

Ho, Virgil Kit-yiu, 'The Limits of Hatred: Popular Attitudes towards the West in Republican Canton', *East Asian History*, 2 (1991), 87–104.

Hobart, Alice Tisdale, *Within the Walls of Nanking*, 1928.

Hodgkin, Henry, *China in the Family of Nations*, second edition, 1928.

Hoe, Susannah, *The Private Life of Old Hong Kong: Western Women in the British Colony, 1841–1941*, Hong Kong, 1991.

Holmes, Colin, 'The Chinese Connection', in Geoffrey Alderman and Colin Holmes, eds, *Outsiders and Outcasts: Essays in Honour of William J. Fish-*

*man*, 1993.

*Hong Kong Administrative Reports for the Year 1932*, Hong Kong, 1933.

Hong Kong, Registrar of the Supreme Court, *Annual Reports*, 1946–49.

Honig, Emily, *Sisters and Strangers: Women in the Shanghai Cotton Mills, 1919–1949*, Stanford CA, 1986.

Hood, George, *Neither Bang nor Whimper: The End of a Missionary Era in China*, Singapore, 1991.

Hooper, Beverley, *China Stands Up: Ending the Western Presence, 1948–50*, Sydney, 1986.

Hu Shih and Lin Yu-tang, eds, *China's own Critics: A Selection of Essays*, Peking, 1931.

Hughes, E. R., *The Invasion of China by the Western World*, Oxford 1937.

Hughes, E. R., ed., *China: Body and Soul*, 1938.

Hunt, Michael H., 'Pearl Buck – Popular Expert on China, 1931–1949', *Modern China*, 3 (1977), 33–64.

Hunt, Michael H., *The Making of a Special Relationship: The United States and China to 1914*, New York, 1983.

Hunter, Jane, *The Gospel of Gentility: American Women Missionaries in Turn-of-the-Century China*, New Haven CT, 1984.

Huskey, James, 'Americans in Shanghai: Community Formation and Response to Revolution, 1919–1928', University of North Carolina Ph.D. thesis, 1985.

Hutchins, F. G., *The Illusion of Permanence: British Imperialism in India*, Princeton NJ, 1967.

Ingrams, W. H., *Hong Kong*, 1952.

*International Review of Missions*.

Iriye, Akira, *After Imperialism: The Search for a New Order in the Far East, 1921–1931*, Cambridge MA, 1965.

Iriye, Akira, *Across the Pacific: An Inner History of American–East Asian Relations*, New York, 1967.

Isaacs, Harold, *Scratches on our Minds: American Images of China and India*, New York, 1958.

Jackson, Innes, *China only Yesterday*, 1938.

Johnston, Reginald Fleming ('Lin Shao Yang'), *A Chinese Appeal to Christendom concerning Christian Missions*, 1911.

Johnston, Reginald Fleming, *Letters to a Missionary*, 1918.

Johnston, Tess, and Deke Erh, *Near to Heaven : Western Architecture in China's old Summer Resorts*, Hong Kong, 1994.

Johnstone, William Crane, *The Shanghai Problem*, Stanford CA, 1937.

Jones, Dorothy, *The Portrayal of China and India on the American Screen, 1896–1955: The Evolution of Chinese and Indian Themes, Locales, and Characters as portrayed on the American Screen*, Cambridge MA, 1955.

Jones, F. C., *Shanghai and Tientsin, with Special Reference to Foreign Interests*, 1940.

*The Jubilee of Shanghai, 1843–1893*, Shanghai, 1893.

Kapp, Robert A., 'Chunking as a Center of Warlord Power, 1926–1937', in M. Elvin and G. W. Skinner, eds, *The Chinese City between Two Worlds*, Stanford CA, 1974.

Kennedy, Dane, *Islands of White: Settler Society and Culture in Kenya and Southern Rhodesia, 1890–1939*, Durham NC, 1987.

Kennedy, Dane, *The Magic Mountains: Hill Stations and the British Raj*, Berkeley CA, 1996.

Killam, G. D., *Africa in English Fiction 1874–1939*, Ibadan, 1968.

King, C., 'The First Trip East – P&O via Suez', in F. H. H. King, ed., *Eastern Banking: Essays in the History of the Hongkong and Shanghai Banking Corporation*, 1983.

King, F. H. H., ed., *Eastern Banking: Essays in the History of the Hongkong and Shanghai Banking Corporation*, 1983.

King, F. H. H., *The History of the Hongkong and Shanghai Banking Corporation*, III, *The Hongkong Bank between the Wars and the Bank Interned, 1919–1945: Return from Grandeur*, Cambridge, 1988.

Kirby, William C., *Germany and Republican China*, Stanford CA, 1984.

Kirby, William C., 'China Unincorporated: Company Law and Business Enterprise in Twentieth Century China', *Journal of Asian Studies*, 54 (1995), 43–63.

Kirby, William C., 'The Internationalization of China: Foreign Relations at Home and Abroad in the Republican Era', *China Quarterly*, 150 (1997), 433–58.

Kohn, Marek, *Dope Girls: The Birth of the British Drug Underground*, 1992.

Koo, Wellington, *Memoirs* (two volumes), New York, 1948.

Kreissler, Françoise, *L'Action culturelle allemande en chine: de la fin du XiX$^e$ siècle à la Seconde Guerre Mondiale*, Paris, 1989.

Lane, M., *Edgar Wallace: The Biography of a Phenomenon*, revised edition, 1964.

Lang, Matheson, *Mr Wu Looks Back: Thoughts and Memories*, 1941.

Lanning, George, and S. Couling, *The History of Shanghai*, I, Shanghai, 1921.

Latourette, K. S., *A History of Christian Missions in China*, 1929.

Latourette, K. S., 'Chinese Historical Studies during the Past Nine Years', *American Historical Review*, 35 (1930) 778–97.

Lavin, Deborah, *From Empire to International Commonwealth: A Biography of Lionel Curtis*, Oxford, 1995.

Le Fernbach, R. R., *A Child's Primer of Things Chinese*, Tianjin, 1923.

Lee, B. A., *Britain and the Sino-Japanese War, 1937–1939: A Study in the Dilemmas of British Decline*, Stanford CA, 1973.

Lee, Sophia, 'The Foreign Ministry's Cultural Agenda for China: The Boxer Indemnity', in Peter Duus, Ramon H. Myers and Mark R. Peattie, eds, *The Japanese Informal Empire in China, 1895–1937*, Princeton NJ, 1989.

Levy, Daniel S., *Two-gun Cohen: A Biography*, New York, 1997.

Lin Yutang, *My County and my People*, 1936.

Lin Yutang, *The Importance of Living*, 1938.

Lindsay, Michael, *The Unknown War: North China, 1937–1945*, 1975.

Logan, John, *China: Old and New*, Hong Kong, 1982.

Louis, Wm. Roger, *British Strategy in the Far East, 1919–1939*, Oxford, 1971.

Louis, Wm. Roger, 'Hong Kong: The Critical Phase, 1945–49', *American His-*

*torical Review*, 102 (1997), 1052–84.

Lutz, Jessie Gregory, *China and the Christian Colleges, 1850–1950*, Ithaca NY, 1971.

Lutz, Jessie Gregory, *Chinese Politics and Christian Missions: The Anti-Christian Movements of 1920–28*, Notre Dame IN, 1988.

Lyall, Leslie T., *A Passion for the Impossible: The China Inland Mission 1865–1965*, 1965.

MacKenzie, John M., 'On Scotland and the Empire', *International History Review*, 15 (1993), 714–39.

MacKenzie, John M., 'Heroic Myths of Empire', in John M. MacKenzie, ed., *Popular Imperialism and the Military, 1850–1950*, Manchester, 1992.

MacKenzie, John M., *Propaganda and Empire: The Manipulation of British Public Opinion, 1880–1960*, Manchester, 1984.

MacKenzie, John M., *Orientalism: History, Theory and the Arts*, Manchester, 1996.

Mackerras, Colin, *Western Images of China*, Hong Kong, 1989.

Mangan, J. A., *The Games Ethic and Imperialism: Aspects of the Diffusion of an Ideal*, Harmondsworth, 1986.

Markovits, Claude, *Indian Business and Nationalist Politics 1931–1939: The Indigenous Capitalist Class and the Rise of the Congress Party*, Cambridge, 1985.

Markovits, Claude, 'Indian Communities in China, c. 1842–1949', paper presented to the conference on 'Foreign Communities in East Asia in the Nineteenth and Twentieth Centuries', Lyon, March 1997.

Marriner, Sheila, and Francis E. Hyde, *The Senior: John Samuel Swire, 1825–98: Management in Far Eastern Shipping Trades*, Liverpool, 1967.

Marshall, P. J., 'The Whites of British India, 1780–1830: A Failed Colonial Society', *International History Review*, 12 (1990), 26–44.

Marshall, P. J., 'Imperial Britain', *Journal of Imperial and Commonwealth History*, 23 (1995), 379–94.

Martin Wilbur, C., and Juie Lien-ying How, eds, *Missionaries of Revolution: Soviet Advisers and Nationalist China, 1920–1927*, Cambridge MA, 1989.

Martin Wilbur, C., *The Nationalist Revolution in China, 1923–28*, Cambridge, 1983.

Martin, Brian G., '"The Pact with the Devil": The Relationship between the Green Gang and the Shanghai French Concession Authorities, 1925–1935', in Frederic Wakeman Jr and Wen-hsin Yeh, eds, *Shanghai Sojourners*, Berkeley CA, 1992.

Martin, Brian G., *The Shanghai Green Gang: Politics and Organised Crime, 1919–37*, Berkeley CA, 1996.

Maugham, W. Somerset, *On a Chinese Screen*, 1922.

Maugham, W. Somerset, *The Painted Veil*, Harmondsworth, 1952 (1925).

Maugham, W. Somerset, *Collected Plays*, III, 1952.

Mayers, F. M., N. B. Dennys and C. King, *The Treaty Ports of China and Japan*, Hong Kong, 1867.

McAleer, Joseph, *Popular Reading and Publishing in Britain*, Oxford, 1992.

Melman, Billie, *Women and the Popular Imagination in the Twenties: Flap-*

*pers and Nymphs*, 1988.
Metcalf, Thomas R., *Ideologies of the Raj*, Cambridge, 1995.
Meyer, Maisie J., 'The Sephardi Jewish Community of Shanghai, 1845–1939: The Question of Identity', London School of Economics Ph.D. thesis, 1994.
Minden, Karen, 'The Multiplication of Ourselves: Canadian Medical Missionaries in West China', in Ruth Hayhoe and Marianne Bastid, eds, *China's Education and the Industrialised World*, Armonk NY, 1987.
Miners, Norman J., 'From Nationalist Confrontation to Regional Collaboration: China–Hong Kong–Britain, 1926–41', in Ming K. Chan, ed., *Precarious Balance: Hong Kong between China and Britain, 1842–1992*, Armonk NY, 1994.
Ming, Hanneke, 'Barracks Concubinage in the Indies, 1887–1920', *Indonesia*, 35 (1983), 65–93.
Mitchell, Timothy, *Colonising Egypt*, Cambridge, 1988.
Moore, W. J., *Shanghai Century, or, 'Tungsha Flat to Soochow Creek'*, Ilfracombe, 1966.
Morse, H. B., *Chronicles of the East India Company Trading to China*, II, Oxford, 1926.
Munn, Christopher, 'Anglo-China: Chinese People and British Rule in Hong Kong, 1841–1870', University of Toronto Ph.D. thesis, 1998.
Murphey, Rhoads, *The Outsiders: The Western Experience in India and China*, Ann Arbor MI, 1977.
Nakagane Katsuji, 'Manchukuo and Economic Development', in Peter Duus, Ramon H. Myers and Mark R. Peattie, eds, *The Japanese Informal Empire in China, 1895–1937*, Princeton NJ, 1989.
*North China Daily News*, Shanghai.
*North China Herald*, Shanghai.
*North China Star*, Tianjin.
*Nurses' Association of China: Report of Conference, 1928*, Shanghai, 1928.
O'Malley, Sir Owen, *The Phantom Caravan*, 1954.
*The Ordinances of Hong Kong, 1946*, Hong Kong, 1946.
*Oriental Affairs*, Shanghai.
Osterhammel, Jürgen, 'Imperialism in Transition: British Business and the Chinese Authorities, 1931–37', *China Quarterly*, 98 (1984), 260–86.
Osterhammel, Jürgen, 'Semi-colonialism and Informal Empire in Twentieth Century China: Towards a Framework of Analysis', in W. J. Mommsen and Jürgen Osterhammel, eds, *Imperialism and After: Continuities and Discontinuities*, 1986.
Osterhammel, Jürgen, 'British Business in China, 1860s–1950s', in R. T. P. Davenport-Hines and Geoffrey Jones, eds, *British Business in Asia since 1860*, Cambridge, 1989.
Osterhammel, Jürgen, 'Britain and China, 1842–1914', in Andrew Porter, ed., *The Oxford History of the British Empire*, III, *The Nineteenth Century* (Oxford, 1999).
Osterhammel, Jürgen, 'China', in Judith M. Brown and Wm. Roger Louis, eds, *The Oxford History of the British Empire*, IV, *The Twentieth Century* (Oxford, 1999).

Peattie, Mark R., 'Japanese Attitudes toward Colonialism', in Ramon H. Myers and Mark R. Peattie, eds, *The Japanese Colonial Empire, 1895–1945*, Princeton NJ, 1984.

Peattie, Mark R., 'Japanese Treaty Port Settlements in China, 1895–1937', in Peter Duus, Ramon H. Myers and Mark R. Peattie eds, *The Japanese Informal Empire in China, 1895–1937*, Princeton NJ, 1989.

*Peking and Tientsin Times*, Tianjin.

Pelcovits, Nathan A., *Old China Hands and the Foreign Office*, New York, 1948.

Pemble, John, *The Mediterranean Passion: Victorians and Edwardians in the South*, Oxford, 1988.

Pennell, W. F. V., *A Lifetime with the Chinese*, Hong Kong, 1974.

Pepper, Suzanne, *Civil War in China: The Political Struggle, 1945–1949*, Berkeley CA, 1978.

*The People's Tribune*, Shanghai.

Peters, E. W., *Shanghai Policeman*, 1937.

Philip, George, *The Log of the Shanghai Pilot Service, 1831–1932*, Shanghai, 1932.

*The Pipeline.*

Platt, D. C. M., *The Cinderella Service: British Consuls since 1825*, 1971.

Porter, Robin, *Industrial Reformers in Republican China*, Armonk NY, 1994.

Pott, F. L. Hawks, *A Short History of Shanghai, being an Account of the Growth and Development of the International Settlement*, Shanghai, 1928.

Power, Brian, *Ford of Heaven*, 1984.

Pratt, Sir John T., *War and Politics in China*, 1943.

Purcell, Victor, *The Memoirs of a Malayan Official*, 1965.

Radtke, Robert W., 'The British Commercial Community in Shanghai and British Policy in China, 1925–1931', University of Oxford D.Phil. thesis, 1991.

Ransome, A., *The Chinese Puzzle*, 1927.

Rasmussen, A. H., *China Trader*, 1954.

Rasmussen, O. D., *Tientsin: An Illustrated Outline History*, Tianjin, 1925.

Rattenbury, H. B., *Understanding China*, 1942.

Rawlinson, F., ed., *The Chinese Church as Revealed in the National Christian Conference ... 1922*, Shanghai, 1922.

Rawlinson, J. L., *Rawlinson, The Recorder and China's Revolution: A Topical Biography of Frank Joseph Rawlinson*, Notre Dame IN, 1990.

Rawski, Thomas, *Economic Growth in Prewar China*, Berkeley CA, 1989.

Reader, W. J., *Imperial Chemical Industries: A History*, I, *The Forerunners, 1870–1926*, 1970.

Reardon-Anderson, James, *The Study of Change: Chemistry in China, 1840–1949*, Cambridge, 1991.

Rees, Ronald, *Life in China, 1922–1947* [Harrow, 1971].

Remer, C. F., *A Study of Chinese Boycotts, with Special Reference to their Economic Effectiveness*, Baltimore MD, 1933 (Taibei edition, 1966).

Remer, C. F., *Foreign Investments in China*, New York, 1933.

Renford, R. K., *The Non-official British in India to 1920*, Delhi, 1987.

*Report of the Advisory Committee together with other Documents respecting the China Indemnity*, 1926.

*Report of the United Kingdom Trade Mission to China, October to December 1946*, 1948.

Reynolds, Douglas R., 'Training Young China Hands: Toa Dobun Shoin and its Precursors, 1886–1945', in Peter Duus, Ramon H. Myers and Mark R. Peattie eds, *The Japanese Informal Empire in China, 1895–1937*, Princeton NJ, 1989.

Ride, Edwin, *BAAG: Hong Kong Resistance, 1942–1945*, Hong Kong, 1981.

Rigby, R. W., *The May 30 Movement: Events and Themes*, Canberra, 1980.

Ristaino, Marcia R., 'Port of Last Resort: The Diaspora Communities of Shanghai', forthcoming.

Robertson, A. J., 'Lancashire and the Rise of Japan, 1910–1937', *Business History*, 32 (1990) 87–105.

Robinson, Ronald, 'Non-European Foundations of European Imperialism: Sketch for a Theory of Collaboration', in R. Owen and B. Sutcliffe, eds, *Studies in the Theory of Imperialism*, Harlow, 1972.

Roux, Alain, *Le Shanghai ouvrier des années trente: coolies, gangsters et syndicalistes*, Paris, 1993.

Russell, A. K., *Liberal Landslide: The General Election of 1906*, Newton Abbot, 1973.

Schenk, Catherine, 'Commercial Rivalry between Shanghai and Hong Kong during the Collapse of the Nationalist Regime in China, 1945–1949', *International History Review*, 20 (1998), 68–98.

Scully, Eileen P., 'Taking the Low Road to Sino-American Relations: "Open Door" Expansionists and the Two China Markets', *Journal of American History*, 82 (1995), 62–83.

Segalen, Victor, *René Leys*, translated by J. A. Underwood, 1990.

Seton, Rosemary, '"Open Doors for Female Labourers": Women Candidates of the London Missionary Society, 1875–1914', in Robert Bickers and Rosemary Seton, eds, *Missionary Encounters: Sources and Issues*, 1996.

Sewell, W. G., *Land and Life of China*, 1933.

*Shanghai Commercial and Shopping Pocket Guide*, Shanghai, c. 1935.

*Shanghai Evening Post and Mercury*, Shanghai, Chongqing and New York.

Shanghai Municipal Council, *Annual Reports*, 1863–1943.

Shanghai Municipal Council, *Municipal Gazette*, 1908–43.

Shanghai shi Huangpu quzhi bianji weiyuanhui, ed., *Huangpu quzhi* (Huangpu District Gazetteer), Shanghai, 1996.

Shao, Wenguang, *China, Britain and Businessmen: Political and Commercial Relations, 1949–57*, Basingstoke, 1991.

Sherry, Norman, *The Life of Graham Greene*, I: *1904–1939*, 1989.

Shiel, M. P., 'About Myself', in A. R. Morse, *The Works of M. P. Shiel: A Study in Bibliography*, Los Angeles, 1948, 5–7.

Sims, W. S., *The Story of Union Lodge No. 1951, E.C., Tientsin, North China*, Tianjin, 1931.

Sitwell, Osbert, *Escape with Me! An Oriental Sketchbook*, 1939.

Smith, Arthur H., *Chinese Characteristics*, Shanghai, 1890.

Smith, C. A. Middleton, *The British in China and the Far Eastern Trade*, 1920.

Smith, J. N., *China's Hour*, 1930.

Soothill, W. E., *China and the West: A Sketch of their Intercourse*, 1925.

Soothill, W. E., *China and England*, 1928.

Spence, Jonathan D., *The China Helpers: Western Advisers in China, 1620–1960*, 1969.

Stanley, Brian, *The Bible and the Flag: Protestant Missions and British Imperialism in the Nineteenth and Twentieth Centuries*, Leicester, 1990.

Stephens, Thomas B., *Order and Discipline in China: The Shanghai Mixed Court, 1911–27*, Seattle WA, 1992.

Stockwell, S. E., 'Political Strategies of British Business during Decolonisation: The Case of the Gold Coast/Ghana, 1945–57', *Journal of Imperial and Commonwealth History*, 23 (1995), 277–300.

Stoler, Ann, 'Rethinking Colonial Categories: European Communities in Sumatra and the Boundaries of Rule', *Comparative Studies in Society and History*, 31 (1989), 134–61.

Stoler, Ann, 'Making Empire Respectable: The Politics of Race and Sexual Morality in Twentieth Century Colonial Cultures', in Jan Breman, ed., *Imperial Monkey Business: Racial Supremacy in Social Darwinist Theory and Colonial Practice*, Amsterdam, 1990.

Stoler, Ann Laura, *Race and the Education of Desire: Foucault's History of Sexuality and the Colonial Order of Things*, Durham NC, 1995.

Strachey, Lytton, *Characters and Commentaries*, 1933.

Strahan, Lachlan, '"The Luck of a Chinaman": Images of the Chinese in Popular Australian Sayings', *East Asian History*, 3 (1992).

Strahan, Lachlan, *Australia's China: Changing Perceptions from the 1930s to the 1990s*, Cambridge, 1996.

Sun Wên [Sun Yatsen], *Kidnapped in London*, Bristol, 1897.

Tanaka, Stefan, *Japan's Orient: Rendering Pasts into History*, Berkeley CA, 1993.

Tang, James T. H., *Britain's Encounter with Revolutionary China, 1949–1954*, New York, 1992.

Tang, James T. H., 'From Empire Defence to Imperial Retreat: Britain's China Policy and the Decolonisation of Hong Kong', *Modern Asian Studies*, 28 (1994), 317–37.

Taylor, P. M., *The Projection of Britain: British Overseas Publicity and Propaganda, 1919–1939*, Cambridge, 1981.

Teichman, Sir Eric, *Affairs of China*, 1938.

Thomas, Nicholas, *Colonialism's Culture: Anthropology, Travel and Government*, Oxford, 1994.

Thomas, Pauline Y. N., 'The Foreign Office and the Business Lobby: British Official and Commercial Attitudes to Treaty Revision in China, 1925–30', London School of Economics Ph.D. thesis, 1981.

Thomas, W. H. Evans, *Vanished China: Far Eastern Banking Memories*, 1956.

Thompson, Roger R., 'Twilight of the Gods in the Chinese Countryside: Christians, Confucians, and the Modernising State, 1861–1911', in Daniel H. Bays, ed., *Christianity in China: From the Eighteenth Century to the Present*,

Stanford CA, 1996.

Thompson, Thomas N., *China's Nationalisation of Foreign Firms: The Politics of Hostage Capitalism, 1949–57*, Baltimore MD, 1979.

Thomson Jr, James C., *While China faced West: American Reformers in Nationalist China, 1928–1937*, Cambridge MA, 1969.

Thorne, Christopher, *The Limits of Foreign Policy: The West, the League, and the Far Eastern Crisis of 1931–1933*, 1972.

Thorne, Christopher, *Allies of a Kind: The United States, Britain and the War against Japan, 1941–45*, 1978.

Tianjin dang'an guan and Nankai daxue fenxiao dang'anxi, comp., *Tianjin zujie dang'an xuanbian* (Selected records of the Tianjin concessions), Tianjin, 1992.

Tientsin, British Municipal Council, *Handbook of Municipal Regulations*, Tianjin, n.d. [c. 1923].

Tomlinson, B. R., 'Colonial Firms and the Decline of Colonialism in Eastern India, 1914–47', *Modern Asian Studies*, 15 (1981), 455–86.

Tomlinson, B. R., 'The Contraction of England: National Decline and the Loss of Empire', *Journal of Imperial and Commonwealth History*, 10 (1982), 58–72.

Tomlinson, B. R., 'British Business in India, 1860–1970', in R. T. P. Davenport-Hines and Geoffrey Jones, eds, *British Business in Asia since 1860*, Cambridge, 1989.

Toshiyuki, Mizoguchi, 'The Changing Pattern of Sino-Japanese Trade, 1884–1937', in Peter Duus, Ramon H. Myers and Mark R. Peattie, eds, *The Japanese Informal Empire in China, 1895–1937*, Princeton NJ, 1989.

Trevor-Roper, H., *Hermit of Peking: The Hidden Life of Sir Edmund Backhouse*, Penguin edition, Harmondsworth, 1978.

Tucker, Nancy Bernkopf, *Patterns in the Dust: Chinese–American Relations and the Recognition Controversy, 1949–1950*, New York, 1983.

Turnbull, Geoffrey, *A History of the Calico Printing Industry of Great Britain*, Altrincham, 1951.

Tyau, M. C. T. Z., *London through Chinese Eyes, or, My Seven and a Half Years in London*, 1920.

Wakeman Jr, Frederic, *Policing Shanghai, 1927–1937*, Berkeley CA, 1995.

Wakeman Jr, Frederic, *The Shanghai Badlands: Wartime Terrorism and Urban Crime, 1937–1941*, Cambridge, 1996.

Waldron, Arthur, *From War to Nationalism: China's Turning Point, 1924–1925*, Cambridge, 1995.

Wang Zhicheng, *Shanghai E'qiao shi* (History of the Russian Émigré Community in Shanghai), Shanghai, 1993.

Wang, Jerry L. S. 'The Profitability of Anglo-Chinese Trade, 1861–1913', *Business History*, 35 (1993), 39–65.

War Office, *Notes on Shanghai*, 1928.

Wasserstein, Bernard, *Secret War in Shanghai: Treachery, Subversion and Collaboration in the Second World War*, 1998.

Wasserstrom, Jeffrey N., *Student Protests in Twentieth Century China: The View from Shanghai*, Stanford CA, 1991.

Weale, Putnam, *Manchu and Muscovite*, 1904.

Weale, Putnam, *Indiscreet Letters from Peking*, 1907

Weale, Putnam, *Why China sees Red*, New York, 1926.

Welch, Holmes, *The Buddhist Revival in China*, Cambridge MA, 1968.

White, Nicholas J., *Business, Government, and the End of Empire: Malaya, 1942–1957*, Kuala Lumpur, 1996.

Whyte, Sir Frederick, *China and Foreign Powers: An Historical Review of their Relations*, second and revised edition, 1928.

Wilbur, C. Martin, *The Nationalist Revolution in China, 1923–28*, Cambridge, 1983.

Wildenthal, Lora, 'Race, Gender, and Citizenship in the German Colonial Empire', in Frederick Cooper and Ann Laura Stoler, eds, *Tensions of Empire: Colonial Cultures in a Bourgeois World*, Berkeley CA, 1997.

Wilhelm, Richard, *The Soul of China*, 1928.

Wilkinson, E. S., *Shanghai Country Walks*, second and revised edition, Shanghai, 1934.

Williamson, H. R., *British Baptists in China, 1845–1952*, 1957.

Wong, J. Y., *The Origins of an Heroic Image: Sun Yatsen in London, 1896–1897*, Hong Kong, 1986.

Wong, J. Y. *Deadly Dreams: Opium, Imperialism and the Arrow War (1856–60) in China*, Cambridge, 1998.

Wong Siu-lin, *Emigrant Entrepreneurs. Shanghai Industrialists in Hong Kong*, Hong Kong, 1988

Woodhead, H. G. W., *The Yangtsze and its Problems*, Shanghai, 1931.

Woodhead, H. G. W., *A Visit to Manchukuo*, Shanghai, 1932.

Woodhead, H. G. W., *A Journalist in China*, 1934.

Woodhead, H. G. W., *My Experiences in the Japanese Occupation of Shanghai*, 1943.

Woodhead, H. G. W., ed., *China Year Book*, 1912–39, Tianjin and Shanghai.

Wray, William D., 'Japan's Big Three Service Enterprises in China, 1896–1936', in Peter Duus, Ramon H. Myers, and Mark R. Peattie, eds, *The Japanese Informal Empire in China, 1895–1937*, Princeton NJ, 1989.

Wright, Arnold, ed., *Twentieth Century Impressions of Hong Kong, Shanghai and other Treaty Ports of China*, 1908.

Wright, Tim, *Coal Mining in China's Economy and Society, 1895–1937*, Cambridge, 1984.

Wright, Tim, 'Shanghai Imperialists versus Rickshaw Racketeers: The Defeat of the 1934 Rickshaw Reforms', *Modern China*, 17 (1991), 76–111.

Wright, Tim, '"The Spiritual Heritage of Chinese Capitalism": Recent Trends in the Historiography of Chinese Enterprise Management', in Jonathan Unger, ed., *Using the Past to serve the Present: Historiography and Politics in Contemporary China*, Armonk NY, 1993.

Wu, William F., *The Yellow Peril: Chinese Americans in American Fiction, 1850–1940*, Hamden CT, 1982.

*Xiandai Shanghai dashiji, 1919–49* (Chronology of Contemporary Shanghai, 1919–49), Shanghai, 1996.

Xiao Qian (Hsiao Ch'ien), *China: But not Cathay*, 1942.

Xiao Qian (Hsiao Ch'ien), ed., *A Harp with a Thousand Strings: A Chinese Anthology in Six Parts*, 1944.

Xiao Qian, *Traveller without a Map*, 1990.

Yan Fusun, *Shanghai suyu dacidian* (Dictionary of Shanghai Colloquialisms), Shanghai, 1924 (Facsimile edition, Tokyo, 1971).

Yeh, Wen-hsin, 'Shanghai Modernity: Commerce and Culture in a Republican City', *China Quarterly*, 150 (1997), 375–94.

Yip, Ka-che, *Religion, Nationalism and Chinese Students: The Anti-Christian Movement of 1922–27*, Bellingham WA, 1980.

Young, L. K., *British Policy in China, 1895–1902*, Oxford, 1970.

Young, Louise, *Japan's Total Empire: Manchuria and the Culture of Wartime Imperialism*, Berkeley CA, 1998.

Zhang Zhongli, 'The Development of Chinese National Capital in the 1920s', in Tim Wright, ed., *The Chinese Economy in the Early Twentieth Century*, Basingstoke, 1992.

Zhang Zhongli, ed., *Dongnan yanhai chengshi yu Zhongguo jindaihua* (The History of the South-east Coastal cities and China's Modernisation), Shanghai, 1996.

Zhang Zhongli and Chen Cengnian, *Shasun jituan zai jiu Zhongguo* (The Sassoon Group in Old China), Beijing, 1985.

Zou Yiren, *Jiu Shanghai renkou bianqian de yanjiu* (Research into Population Change in old Shanghai), Shanghai, 1980.

# INDEX

Note: page numbers in *italic* indicate illustrations; 'n.' after a page reference indicates a note number on that page.